Rethinking Documentary

Rethinking Documentary
New Perspectives,
New Practices

Edited by Thomas Austin and Wilma de Jong

Open University Press

Open University Press
McGraw-Hill Education
McGraw-Hill House
Shoppenhangers Road
Maidenhead
Berkshire
England
SL6 2QL

email: enquiries@openup.co.uk
world wide web: www.openup.co.uk

and Two Penn Plaza, New York, NY 10121—2289, USA

First published 2008

A catalogue record of this book is available from the British Library

ISBN-13: 978-0-33-5221912(pb)   978-0-33-5221929(hb)
ISBN-10: 0335221912(pb)   0335221920(hb)

Typeset by Kerrypress, Luton, Bedfordshire
Printed in the UK by Ashford Colour Press Ltd., Gosport, Hampshire

The **McGraw·Hill** Companies

Contents

Notes on Contributors

Thomas Austin is Senior Lecturer in Media and Film at the University of Sussex. He is the author of *Hollywood, Hype and Audiences: Selling and Watching Popular Film in the 1990s* (2002) and *Watching the World: Screen Documentary and Audiences* (2007).

Paul Basu is senior Lecturer in Anthropology at the University of Sussex. Prior to converting to anthropology, he worked in film and television production, and he continues to be an active visual anthropologist and exhibition designer. His publications include *Exhibition Experiments* (co-edited with Sharon Macdonald, 2007) and *Highland Homecomings: Genealogy and Heritage Tourism in the Scottish Diaspora* (2007).

Danny Birchall is the web manager at the Institute of Contemporary Arts and writes a column on online cinema for *Sight & Sound* magazine.

Ishmahil Blagrove, Jr is a senior producer/director of Rice N Peas Films, an independent production company he founded in 1999. He is also the editor of the company's monthly online magazine, ricenpeas.com. He has directed several films including: *Acholi Wedding* (2007), *A Homecoming for Jobs in Africa* (2006), *Death of a Matriarch* (2006), *Man Dem Nor Glady'O* (2006), *Hasta Siempre* (2005), *Bang! Bang! In Da Manor* (2004), and *Roaring Lion* (2002).

Michael Chanan is a documentary filmmaker, writer and Professor of Film and Video at Roehampton University, London. In the 1970s, he made films on contemporary music for BBC2, and in the 1980s on Latin America for Channel Four. He is the author of books on film, the social history of music, and the media. His latest film is *Detroit: Ruin of a City* (with George Steinmetz, 2005) and his book *The Politics of Documentary* was published in 2007.

John Corner is Professor in the School of Politics and Communication Studies at the University of Liverpool. He has written extensively on media history, institutions and forms. Recent work includes the co-edited collections *Media and the Restyling of Politics* (2003), *New Challenges for Documentary* (second edition, 2005) and *Public Issue Television* (with Peter Goddard and Kay Richardson, 2007). He is currently researching aspects of media-political relations and documentary aesthetics.

Nick Couldry is Professor of Media and Communications at Goldsmiths, University of London. He is the author or editor of seven books including *Listening Beyond the Echoes: Media, Ethics and Agency in an Uncertain World* (2006), *Media Consumption and Public Engagement: Beyond the Presumption of Attention* (with Sonia Livingstone and Tim Markham, 2007) and *Media Rituals: A Critical Approach* (2003).

Wilma de Jong is a Lecturer in Media and Film at the University of Sussex. As an independent film producer/maker, she owned a film company for 14 years and produced prize-winning films on social/cultural/political subjects. She is the co-editor of *Global Activism, Global Media* (2005), and is currently preparing a research project on contemporary documentary production processes, and a book on creativity and innovation in documentary production.

Jon Dovey is Professor of Screen Media at the University of the West of England. He was a film-maker and video artist before becoming an academic. He is the editor of *Fractal Dreams, New Media in Social Context* (1996), the author of *Freakshows: First Person Media and Factual TV* (2000) and co-author of *New Media: A Critical Introduction* (2002). His most recent book is the co-authored *Game Cultures* (2006).

Marilyn Gaunt has made over 50 films for British television since 1968. Her film *Kelly and Her Sisters* won BAFTA, RTS, Grierson and Broadcast Awards in 2002. *Living on the Edge* won a Silver Globe at the Hamburg Mediafest, and in 2004 *Lin and Ralph: A Love Story* was nominated for a Grierson Award for best documentary on a contemporary issue.

Craig Hight is Senior Lecturer in Screen and Media Studies at the University of Waikato, New Zealand. He has co-written, with Jane Roscoe, *Faking It: Mock-documentary and the Subversion of Factuality* (2001), and is currently writing a book on television mockumentary series.

Annette Hill is Professor of Media at the University of Westminster. She is the author of *Reality TV: Audiences and Popular Factual Television* (2005), and *Restyling Factual TV: The Reception of News, Documentary and Reality Genres* (2007). Her previous books include *Shocking Entertainment* (1997), and *TV Living: Television, Audiences and Everyday Life* (with David Gauntlett, 1999).

Su Holmes is Reader in Television at the University of East Anglia. She is the author of *British TV and Film Culture in the 1950s: Coming to a TV Near You!* (2005) and co-editor of *Understanding Reality Television* (2004), *Framing Celebrity: New Directions in Celebrity Culture* (2006) and *A Reader in Stardom and Celebrity* (2006).

Deborah Jermyn is Senior Lecturer in Film and TV at Roehampton University, London. She is the author of *Crime Watching: Investigating Real Crime TV* (2006) and co-editor of *Understanding Reality TV* (2004) and has published widely on the representations of women in contemporary popular television.

Alexandra Juhasz is Professor of Media Studies at Pitzer College, California. She produced the feature film *The Watermelon Woman*, as well as many educational documentaries on feminist issues such as teenage sexuality, AIDS, and sex education. She is the author of *AIDS TV: Identity, Community and Alternative Video* (1996) and co-editor of *F Is for Phony: Fake Documentary and Truth's Undoing* (2006). She has recently completed her first 'book' on the web, *Media Praxis: A Radical Web-Site Integrating Theory, Practice and Politics.*

Erik Knudsen is a filmmaker and Professor of Film Practice at the University of Salford, Manchester. He is also Head of the Editing Department at the Escuela

Internacional de Cine y Televisión in Cuba. His films include: *Heart of Gold* (2006), *Sea of Madness* (2006), *Brannigan's March* (2004), *Bed of Flowers* (2001), *Signs of Life* (1999), *Reunion* (1995), and *One Day Tafo* (1991).

Jo Littler is Senior Lecturer in Media and Cultural Studies at Middlesex University, London. She is the author of *Radical Consumption? Shopping for Change in Contemporary Culture* (forthcoming, 2008), editor of the 'Celebrity' issue of *Mediactive* (2003), and co-editor, with Roshi Naidoo, of *The Politics of Heritage: The Legacies of 'Race'* (2005).

Bill Nichols has lectured widely and published over 100 articles. Among his several books, *Representing Reality* (1991) provided the first rigorous examination of documentary film form while *Introduction to Documentary* (2001) continues to serve as the most widely-used textbook in the field. He is the Director of the Graduate Program in Cinema at San Francisco State University.

Silke Panse's post-doctoral research explores the tensions between subjectivity and objectivity in different conceptual and material contexts. Her essay "The Bullets confirm the story told by the potato": object subjectivity and materials without motives in CSI' is published in the anthology *Reading CSI*. She has written on documentary as painting in *Third Text*, and organized the conference 'Werner Herzog's cinema: between the visionary and the documentary'. She is a Visiting Lecturer at Chelsea College of Art and Design and the University College for the Creative Arts, Canterbury.

Michael Renov is Professor of Critical Studies and Associate Dean of the USC School of Cinematic Arts. He is the author or editor of several books on documentary including *The Subject of Documentary* (2004), *Theorizing Documentary* (1993), and *Collecting Visible Evidence* (1999). One of three editors of the Visible Evidence book series for the University of Minnesota Press, he has juried documentary competitions at Sundance, Silverdocs, It's All True (Brazil), and the Buenos Aires International Independent Film Festival.

Jerry Rothwell is a documentary film-maker with a track record of people-based films on themes of mental health, art and education. Since 2005, he has focused on directing documentary features, including *Deep Water* (co-directed with Louise Osmond), about Donald Crowhurst's ill-fated voyage in the 1968 round-the-world yacht race. His current project *Heavy Load* is about a group of people with learning disabilities who form a punk band.

Sue Thornham is Professor of Media and Film at the University of Sussex. She is the author of *Passionate Detachments* (1997), *Feminism and Cultural Studies* (2001), and *Women, Feminism and Media* (2007), co-author of *Television Drama: Theories and Identities* (2004), and editor of *Media Studies: A Reader* (1996 and 1999), and *Feminist Film Theory: A Reader* (1999).

Ana Vicente joined London-based sales agency Taskovski Films in 2005 as festival co-ordinator, and was responsible for TV sales of their art-house line-up, including the documentary *Czech Dream*. She moved to EastWest Film Distribution's London office in 2006 to manage the promotion and selection of films for festivals and international sales.

Paul Ward is a Senior Lecturer in the School of Media at the Arts Institute at Bournemouth, where he teaches animation theory and history. He is the author of *Documentary: The Margins of Reality* (2005) and numerous articles on documentary and animation-related topics.

Mike Wayne works at Brunel University and convenes the MA in Documentary Practice there. He is the author of *Marxism and Media Studies: Key Concepts and Contemporary Trends* (2003) and editor of *Understanding Film: Marxist Perspectives* (2005).

Patricia R. Zimmermann is Professor of Cinema, Photography and Media Arts at Ithaca College in Ithaca, New York. She is the author of *Reel Families: A Social History of Amateur Film* (1995) and *States of Emergency: Documentaries, Wars, Democracies* (2000), and co-editor with Karen Ishizuka of *Mining the Home Movie: Excavations in Histories and Memories* (2007). She is also co-director of the Finger Lakes Environmental Film Festival.

Acknowledgements

We are indebted to the contributors to this book who, with lots of enthusiasm but often with a lot less time, still managed to deliver somewhere near the deadlines. Thank you all, you were a pleasure to work with. Special thanks to Chris Cudmore and Jack Fray at Open University Press for your support, and to Mike Stones for the cover design(s). We appreciate your patience and noticed the slight smiles on your faces when your first proposals for the cover were rejected. We got there in the end. More special thanks to Michael Lawrence for your tireless and cheerful editing, and to Tony Cokes for your images.

This book is dedicated to our partners and children, who might have appreciated a less absent look in our eyes every now and then. To Tony and Romany, Charlotte and Noah, with love.

The Introduction includes revised versions of some passages from Thomas Austin (2007) *Watching the World: Screen Documentary and Audiences*, Manchester University Press. Chapter 2 is a revised version, in English, of Bill Nichols, 'Evidence: Fragen nach dem Beweis', in Michael Cuntz (ed) (2006) Die Listen der Evidenz, DuMont Press. Chapter 5 includes revised versions of some passages from Silke Panse's entry on Winfried and Barbara Junge in Ian Aitken (ed) (2005) *The Encyclopaedia of the Documentary Film*, Routledge. Chapter 20 includes revised versions of some passages from Jon Dovey, 'It's only a game show: *Big Brother* and the theatre of spontaneity', in Ernest Mathijs and Janet Jones (eds) (2004), *Big Brother International: Format, Critics and Publics*, Wallflower Press.

Introduction

Rethinking documentary

Thomas Austin and Wilma de Jong

The early years of the twenty-first century have witnessed significant and ongoing changes in the technological, commercial, aesthetic, political, and social dimensions of documentaries produced for, and viewed on, a range of differently configured screens. They include, among others, the spread of new digital production and editing equipment; the increasing 'intimization' (van Zoonen 1991: 217) of content facilitated by this; the continued proliferation of television formats; a so-called 'boom' in theatrical features; and the phenomenon of DIY footage posted on websites like YouTube and Google Video. These sometimes dizzyingly rapid developments call for a rethinking of notions of documentary, in terms of both presumed object/s of study, and key theories and methods of inquiry. Accordingly, this book puts ideas and constructions of documentary under some critical pressure. It assesses their assumptions, relevance and limitations, their disputed borders and rhetorical Others, and, where necessary, proposes new tools and arguments with which to examine a complex and shifting terrain.

Drawing together original contributions from scholars and practitioners, employing a variety of critical approaches from film studies, media and cultural studies, and anthropology, and encompassing both national and trans-national perspectives, this collection investigates some of the manifold practices and objects that might be grouped under the expansive and contested concept of screen documentary in the present moment. Crucially, such a project needs to look backwards as well as forwards, to inquire into past understandings of, and interventions in, documentary, as well as those happening now. So the chapters gathered here consider some recent changes while taking care not to ignore key continuities, precedents and precursors in the rush to engage with the new. In the process, they often draw on earlier debates in documentary theory, practice, and politics, but when necessary inflect them in new ways. For instance, how might one retain a workable notion of documentary when the mode has become dispersed across an ever-widening cultural landscape, across different platforms and formats? What aesthetic tendencies and possibilities have been hitherto neglected by scholars and/or practitioners? What new critical models might be needed to engage with the diversity of documentary in the current decade, and what prior analyses might be retained or redeployed? What further insights might be gained when existing concepts of documentary are themselves interrogated via this process, rather than simply asserted or imposed on new objects?

Even as the spaces occupied by documentary extend, the accompanying diversification and hybridization of the field throw into question some of the foundational claims made for it. These include the already much-debated issues of indexicality, evidentiality and trust, along with a series of cultural and moral distinctions which tend to elevate documentary as a truth-telling discourse, standing more or less beyond, but always needing to be defended from, the temptations and contaminations of fiction and 'mere' entertainment. Critical thinking has vigorously scrutinized both these sets of claims already, but will need to do so again, in the light of the diffusion of documentary across new media platforms and an intensified interpenetration between fictional and non-fictional modes. In these contexts, what, if anything, makes documentary distinct or necessary as a means of mediating and engaging with the world? Are popular cultures moving towards a 'postdocumentary' moment, as some scholars have suggested?[1] Contributors give differing answers to these and other pressing questions. In the process, they confront the persistence of some other 'old' issues in new settings, most notably those of power, the politics of representation, and ethics. How should long-standing debates on gender, ethnicity, and class be brought to bear on this arena? And how might perennial queries over the efficacy of documentary, as a spur to critical awareness (of the self and others) or a self-serving exercise in smug epistephilia and voyeurism, be revisited and reconsidered?

Defining screen documentary has never been a simple task. Many viewers (including, if they are honest, students and scholars of the form) have probably on occasions had a sense of documentary that is comparable to Justice Potter Stewart's much-cited remark about pornography, 'I don't know what it is, but I know it when I see it' (Williams 1989: 5). While this has probably always been the case, in many different contexts and moments, it is perhaps even truer at the present time, given the rapid and continuing proliferation of delivery systems, textual hybrids and mutual borrowings across the wide field of documentary and its porous neighbouring territories. These range from fiction film and television, to 'mockumentaries', to 'reality television' (itself describing a spectrum from light entertainment to more 'serious' formats) to art practice, to journalism, to DIY web culture. So how best to approach the thorny question of definition?

Bill Nichols' familiar characterization of screen documentary as grounded in the promise of delivering 'views of the world' (1991: ix) is flexible and suggestive enough to be worth retaining. But by itself it cannot (and is not intended to) arbitrate on disputed cases at the margins of the mode. John Corner has suggested that 'the term *documentary* is always much safer when used as an adjective rather than a noun'. He writes, 'To ask "is this a documentary project" is more useful than to ask "is this film a documentary?" with its inflection toward firm definitional criteria and the sense of something being more object than practice.' As Corner notes, despite its relative commercial fragility, cinema documentary 'still has the strong contrast with its dominant Other – feature film – against which it can be simply defined as "nonfiction".' On the other hand, non-fiction on (British) television 'describes half the schedule and so the question of generic identifiers becomes immediately more troublesome' (2002: 258).

Ultimately, in the case of cinema, television, and, increasingly, the internet, individual viewers will have their own preconceptions and expectations of material labelled 'documentary' (either by themselves or by others), and these may or may not accord with more established definitions. However, such understandings – and associated ideas of what should be excluded from the category – will always be socially shaped by a host of factors, which may include advertising hype, and trade and journalistic discourses about documentary, in addition to the textual logics of any screened material.

Paul Arthur (2005: 20) gives a summary of some factors shaping the slippery notion of (film) documentary when he writes: 'Some theorists assert that doc [*sic*] itself is a genre, although a more sensible approach would describe it as a mode of production, a network of funding, filming, postproduction and exhibition tendencies common to work normally indexed as "documentary".'[2] Crucially, however, Arthur omits commonly proposed or deployed audience assumptions, orientations and viewing strategies from his list. As Dai Vaughan has argued, in a passage on documentary film which also has relevance to the mode's appearances on other viewing platforms: 'What makes a film "documentary" is the way we look at it; and the history of documentary has been the succession of strategies by which film-makers have tried to make viewers look at films this way.' Vaughan continues: 'To see a film as documentary is to see its meaning as pertinent to the events and objects which passed before the camera; to see it, in a word, as signifying what it appears to record' (1999: 84–5). Of course, as Vaughan is aware, such a response can never be entirely 'guaranteed' on the part of any viewer, even allowing for the significant discursive interventions made via marketing, scheduling, reviewing and scholarship in demarcating a territory called 'documentary'. Such decisions may inform, but do not automatically predetermine, viewers' responses. Thus, ambiguously marked material may on occasions still be watched and made use of by audiences as a 'documentary experience'.[3] Border disputes and viewer expectations of, and disposi-tions towards, documentary and its neighbours are considered indirectly in several of the following essays, and are raised in more detail in Annette Hill's chapter on television audiences below.[4]

One of the most celebrated developments in Anglophone screen documentary in recent years has been the so-called 'boom' in theatrical and DVD sectors of the US and UK markets.[5] In addition to relatively big earners like *Fahrenheit 9/11* (US, 2004), *March of the Penguins* (US, 2005), *Bowling for Columbine* (US, 2002), and *An Inconvenient Truth* (US, 2006),[6] less spectacular successes also gained more exposure than might have been expected. For example, *Cesky Sen/Czech Dream* (Czech Republic, 2004), a provocative hoax film involving the launch of a non-existent hypermarket, secured small but significant distribution deals in 12 countries, a record for a documentary from Eastern Europe. Moreover, the total number of documentaries gaining theatrical release in the US climbed significantly, from an average of 15 in the late 1990s to around 40 in 2003 and 50 in 2004. As Arthur notes, this figure accounted for 'roughly ten percent of total film releases but more than one-fourth of the rosters for smaller, non-studio distributors' (2005: 18).[7]

With distributors facing rising marketing costs in the cinema sector, post-theatrical markets such as DVD have become increasingly important. Much as in the case of many arthouse and 'independent' fiction films, cinema is being treated as a loss leader prior to DVD release. Pat Aufderheide (2005: 26) notes that:

> Sales of documentaries on DVD tripled between 2001 and 2004 ... to nearly $4 million in the US. Online purchases ... have boosted DVD figures, while smaller scale web campaigns and viral marketing via email have encouraged the 'house party' trend of group viewings, particularly for political documentaries.

There are some suggestions that the 'boom' may have peaked,[8] and it is still too early to say what its lasting consequences may be. However, it is certain that more people than previously have been watching documentaries in cinemas and on DVD, in the US and the UK at least. Nevertheless, it is important to keep a sense of perspective. While some documentaries have crossed over to the multiplex sector, the majority remain very much a niche taste, and deliver a fraction of the revenues earned by successful fiction films. In addition, moves to champion theatrical documentaries (or the remediation of documentaries on the web, of which more below) should not obscure the long-standing and still vital role played by television as the major exhibition window and source of funding in many countries. However, much like the cinema sector, contexts of production, distribution and exhibition for television documentaries have been undergoing important changes in recent years. As Simon Cottle (2004: 82) has pointed out: 'New technologies of production and delivery, heightened competitiveness, industrial centralization, fragmenting audiences and internationalizing markets have all dramatically impacted on the "production ecology".' Cottle is discussing the environment for natural history programmes, but there are few if any television markets that remain untouched by these trends.[9] Moreover, the dominance of formatted reality shows in the schedules has polarized opinion (and is explored further in Part III of this book). Nick Fraser, series editor of the BBC's 'Storyville' documentary strand, comments: 'Documentaries look good in festivals and play well in cinemas. But their true begetter is television, a fickle medium currently besotted with fictionalised versions of the real. Will television come forward and assure the future of documentaries?' (Fraser 2007: 38).

Meanwhile, significant shifts are also occurring online. Relatively cheap digital technology has widened access to the means of production for a multitude of filmmakers, activists, wannabes, and commercial operators across the world,[10] and the internet's international reach has made it an outlet with the potential to find audiences without relying on traditional channels of distribution and exhibition. However, breaking through the clutter to capture viewers, and monetizing the process successfully can remain problematic. Moreover, some would argue that the internet falls short of the alternative public sphere that it once promised. How might the particular (technological, aesthetic, political and commercial) capabilities and constraints of the internet play a part in shaping online documentaries and non-fiction? And how might conventions established prior to the diffusion of the internet persist in online materials?

Part I of this book, 'Critical perspectives on documentary forms and concepts', begins with John Corner's analysis of the emergence of a field of Anglo-American 'documentary studies' since the mid-1970s. Corner pays particular attention to three key debates, on definition, aesthetics, and cognition. In doing so, he locates persistent intellectual divisions between studies of cinema and television (a distinction which he, and this book as a whole, both recognize and work across), and identifies issues for future research. One of the influential commentaries discussed by Corner is Bill Nichols' (1976) consideration of the ideological implications of an unproblematized claim to realism made in certain documentaries. In his essay here Nichols returns to questions of ideology, via an exploration of how documentaries deploy 'evidence' which, paradoxically, is implicitly located beyond discourse, yet can only ever be rendered *as* evidence 'within a discursive or interpretive frame'. Nichols argues that this observation should not lead to a suspicion of such rhetorical frameworks as always dissembling, however. Moreover, that documentary 'sets out to move us' should not result in its critical dismissal, since its visual rhetoric 'can contest the status quo as readily as it can confirm it'.[11] Michael Renov's chapter similarly extends an ongoing inquiry, in this case his interrogation of autobiography and documentary. Drawing on examples from the 1970s to the present, and from avant-garde film to Michael Moore to 'domestic ethnography', he shows how 'private truths [and] inner realities have come to be the business of documentary as much as public proclamations'. Renov suggests that this foregrounding of filmmakers' subjectivity is not entirely new, but is rather an overlooked tradition in documentary. And he argues against 'the charge that autobiographical works evade or elide politics'.

An interest in subjectivity also informs Thomas Austin's chapter on Werner Herzog's *Grizzly Man*. Austin investigates the 'double authorship' of the film, whose protagonist and originator of much of its footage was already dead when the film was assembled and promoted under the name of Herzog as auteur. He also considers the formal and ethical dimensions of *Grizzly Man*'s representation of death, and the conflicting attitudes towards the natural world relayed in the film. Further interfaces between aesthetics and ethics are addressed in Silke Panse's analysis of *The Children of Golzow*, a series of 20 films about schoolchildren growing up in East Germany and adjusting to life in a capitalist state after unification. Panse contrasts the presentation of change in the Golzow films with the class determinism of Michael Apted's British television series *7-Up*. She also compares the films' 'sympathetically distanced' commentary and interviewing style with documentaries that use the 'alienated labour' of interviewees to assert the 'moral superiority of the viewer'. Interview methods are also raised by Mike Wayne in his discussion of the twin influences of positivist and interpretive/qualitative paradigms on documentary as a mode of generating knowledge. Wayne turns to the critical theory of the Frankfurt School in his exploration of how documentary might be capable of integrating these two approaches, along with the aesthetic and the political. This, he argues, gives documentary the potential to produce 'emancipated cognition and feeling' in its viewers.

In his chapter on ethnographic film, Paul Basu looks for innovations beyond the established canon of Jean Rouch et al. His analysis of BBC television/Discovery

Channel's *The Tribe* suggests that 'the series reproduces the very exoticist stereotypes that anthropologists have, for generations, striven to problematize'. By contrast, he argues, the films of Kim Longinotto explore gender relations in settings that have typically engaged anthropologists, while refusing some conventions of the discipline. Basu also examines media installations which employ video screens to 'extend the "work" of the artist-ethnographer to their audiences'. Erik Knudsen's essay explores the potential of documentary to move beyond 'the dominant paradigm exemplified by elements such as cause and effect, conflict and resolution, and psychologically explicable situations'. He writes:

> Dreams, imagination and intuition can and should be as much a part of documentary as factual observations can and should be a part of fiction. ... Documentary needs to find ways in which it can move the viewer in such a way as to also address their spiritual and transcendental reality.

The final piece in this section is by Michael Chanan, who considers various dimensions of the 'invisible' in documentary, from overlooked people and issues, to events occurring off-camera, to social relations and historical processes that cannot easily be rendered visible. Chanan ends by pointing to the potential of documentary to move 'beyond the representation of the way things appear, to become a metaphor for what is going on behind and beyond the image, which the camera is unable to record'.

Part II of the collection brings together the perspectives of scholars and practitioners to focus on issues of production in a range of institutional and cultural settings, and different critical contexts. Wilma de Jong draws on detailed research into the development and production of *Deep Water* (UK, 2006), tracing the agendas and inputs of various agents in the process, from small, independent producers to co-funders Pathé, Channel Four, and the UK Film Council, the latter an investor with more experience of the fiction film market. De Jong finds that 'tensions appeared which could be seen as frictions between different communities of practice' working from either fiction or documentary backgrounds. Turning to issues of ethics and responsibility, Jerry Rothwell notes the unprecedented scale of footage being recorded by people beyond the documentary profession. This shift 'opens up different kinds of relationships between filmmakers and subjects', often demanding a shared responsibility for 'the consequences of the film-making that go beyond the film itself'. Rothwell argues that:

> the ground rules for a 'joint exploration' model are an honesty about likely outcomes, about the context in which material will be used, and an accountability for the film's impact on the subject, all qualities which filmmakers are often criticized for lacking.

'From eight-man crew to one-woman band', Marilyn Gaunt's overview of her career to date in British television documentary, traces key shifts in working practices and technology, along with commissioning and management strategies. One growing problem she notes is the difficulty in persuading people to appear in documentaries if the film-maker no longer has editorial control over the final cut. In an interview with Wilma de Jong and Thomas Austin, producer John Smithson talks about his experience of fashioning documentaries for television and (more recently) cinema, and the enduring appeal of 'seeing the real'. Also interviewed by De Jong, Ralph Lee, Commissioning Editor for History at Channel Four, talks of the UK broadcaster's quest for innovation, audiences' expectations, and his belief that 'History is always most interesting where it's speaking to the present.'

Moving beyond the mainstream, in his chapter on the independent production company Rice N Peas, Ishmahil Blagrove, Jr critiques the stereotyping of black Britons on television, and traces the rationale behind films like *Bang Bang! In Da Manor* and *Hasta Siempre*. He discusses how Rice N Peas uses diverse methods to promote and screen its films, from cinemas to DVD pirates to the internet, and concludes: 'No longer dependent upon commissioning budgets, studio equipment, or even a crew, a budding documentary filmmaker may now produce a high end, broadcast-quality product with little more than a camera, a computer, and a good idea.' Sue Thornham's interview with the Chinese feminist, academic, and film-maker Ai Xiaoming is a reminder of the urgency that documentary retains as a political intervention in a climate of oppression. Ai talks about the political and practical difficulties that she has encountered, and her intention to make films as 'a form of rescue', retrieving the stories of ordinary people, often women, who have been excluded from authorized media representations of the 'new China'.

Part III explores 'Borders, neighbours and disputed territories' on the edges of the wide and always permeable terrain of screen documentary. Mutual borrowings between documentary and fictional modes are of course hardly new. But the particular instances, and consequences, of recent interpenetrations between documentary and its Others demand further attention. Paul Ward turns to the contested ground of drama-documentary to consider the ethical implications of dramatization, evidentiality, and performance in re-enactments of the fatal flight of United 93 on September 11, 2001. He asks, how do such films, and the speculative documentary *Death of a President*, both demand and contribute to 'a profoundly ethical debate about the representability and performativity of certain traumatic events'? Craig Hight's chapter addresses some of the ways in which 'mockumentary' 'engages with documentary's rhetorical address to its audience', changing its 'call to action into a *call to play*'. He explores how cross-platform mockumentaries exploit digital and online opportunities to offer their audiences 'multiple forms of play with the institutional forms and discourses of the fact–fiction continuum'. Annette Hill draws on empirical audience research – very much an under-used methodology in documentary studies – to consider how television viewers conceive of different types of documentary, and the mode's relation to neighbouring areas such as current affairs, 'reality television', and light entertainment. She argues that, 'The way viewers understand the relationship between different modes of representation within documentary, and more generally across factual television, highlights the degree to which documentary is changing.'

The last three chapters in the Part III all address the phenomenon of 'reality television' in ways that avoid simplistic knee-jerk responses, whether optimistic or pessimistic. They all focus on British instances of successful international formats from what is now a significant genre in many cultures and markets. Su Holmes and

Deborah Jermyn investigate ambivalences, tensions and contradictions around issues of class and gender in *Wife Swap*. They consider how the show '*stages* reality to play out questions that ultimately affect everyday life', arguing that:

> [It] lends itself to oppositional and ambivalent readings, offering up the promise of a thoughtful and provocative insight into contemporary gender roles and class identities in the context of what appears to be a cynical and deliberately incendiary manipulation of its participants.

Jon Dovey examines how the observational traditions of documentary are redeployed in 'reality television game shows' such as *Big Brother*, which are best understood as simulations rather like computer models or psychology experiments. He argues that such shows (unintentionally) contribute to issue-based talk in the public sphere, as documentaries have claimed to do. In the process, Dovey also links the development of *Big Brother* to the 'fakery' scandals of the late 1990s, and disagrees with Nick Fraser, quoted above, about the causes of 'traditional' documentaries' decline on television. Nick Couldry and Jo Littler analyse another 'reality game', *The Apprentice*, tracing how it works to naturalize norms of 'chaotic capitalism' and neo-liberal business practice, including the validation of aggressive and charismatic power, the devaluation of cooperation, and the championing of competitive individualism. Couldry and Littler argue that *The Apprentice*'s claims to realism and truthfulness function to deflect necessary political and ethical scrutiny of its core proposals: '[T]hose claims and those norms should ... be opened up to debate in a way that the ambiguous documentary/ game status of reality TV *precisely prevents*.'

The final section in the book addresses documentaries in the context of intensifying digitalization and multimedia convergence. Ana Vicente explores current developments in distribution and viewing platforms, from websites to video on demand, in both online and television manifestations. She concludes:

> The future of documentary distribution is now more promising than ever. New technologies have opened new avenues for documentary production and delivery to audiences ... while viewers are more actively searching for the content they wish to view on a growing multiplicity of platforms.

Danny Birchall considers a range of online materials to ask, 'what distinguishes documentary online from documentary made for other channels' and 'whether the internet has any distinct, useful or unique characteristics that offer documentary anything more than another means of distribution'. His answer attends to constructions of community online, political and campaigning films, the trend in 'dirty reality' including war and executions, and the intimacy and seriality of video blogging.

Part IV finishes with two analyses of the politics of documentary in some of its digital manifestations. Patricia Zimmermann investigates the new media ecologies of oppositional documentary in a time of 'war and empire'. She traces how digital technologies and live multimedia events have been used to construct new public domains in 'transitional zones and provisional places', thus requiring a re-conceptualization of documentary 'from a single analog film ... to a diversity of forms and content, indicating a plurality of strategies, interfaces, and public intersections'.

In the process, Zimmermann argues, 'the binary oppositions between commercial and non-profit, between amateur and professional, between performance and documentary, have dissolved in exciting, problematic and confusing ways'. Finally, Alexandra Juhasz moves from hope to frustration in her indictment of documentaries housed on YouTube. Juhasz's initial optimism about the accessibility and multivocality of the site as a potentially democratic media forum is tempered by her growing dissatisfaction with the banality and fragmentation of much that she finds there, even when searching under the heading of 'queer documentary'. It is, she argues, the lack of an engagement with theory, history or politics in so much of YouTube's material, and its inability to unite its users via any sense of collectivity, that causes the site to default on its radical promise. These two chapters bring an end to the book, but not to the debate about documentaries in the digital era, which, like others raised in these pages, will hopefully be taken up and continued by readers, scholars and practitioners, all variously invested in documentaries of the past, present and future.

Notes

1 See Corner (2002: 257). He makes this suggestion in relation to British television, where documentary elements have increasingly been combined with components from fictional, light entertainment and popular factual formats to produce a wide range of textual hybrids.

2 As Arthur notes, it is also possible to locate generic types with 'family resemblances' – such as musical or natural history material – within the category of documentary.

3 For more on this debate, see 'The aesthetics of ambiguity', in Vaughan (1999: 54–83); also Winston (1995: 252–8) and Ward (2005: 28–30).

4 See further discussion of audiences' expectations of, and uses derived from, documentary in Hill (2007) and Austin (2007).

5 For a more detailed consideration of reasons for the 'boom', including possible links to the 'reality television' phenomenon, see Austin (2007: 12–33). For some pointers to recent developments in continental Europe, see Ana Vicente's chapter in this volume.

6 These films' worldwide grosses (unadjusted for inflation) were: *Fahrenheit 9/11* $222m, *March of the Penguins* $127m, *Bowling for Columbine* $58m, and *An Inconvenient Truth* $49m (Bowen 2007). Thanks to Ana Vicente for this reference.

7 Arthur's figures exclude Imax releases and non-commercial venues.

8 For recent assessments, see Bowen (2007) and Gant (2007). See also some comments from distributors quoted in Austin (2007), Chapter 1.

9 For a brief consideration of multi-channel television in the UK, in terms of the new opportunities and new ghettoes it offers for documentary, see Austin (2007: 21–6).

10 One of the most celebrated examples of this trend is Jonathan Caouette's autobiographical *Tarnation* (US, 2003), reportedly made for just $218. This excludes several important costs, however, including an estimated $500,000

in clearance fees paid for rights to music and screen extracts, and the further costs of marketing and releasing the film in cinemas and on DVD.

11 See also Alexandra Juhasz's defence of 'realist feminist' documentary (1994), which offers an important counter to feminist film theory's anti-realist tendencies in the 1970s and beyond.

PART 1

Critical Perspectives on Documentary Forms and Concepts

Multiple screens, multiple voices. The 'exhibitionary context' of Kutlug Ataman's *Küba*, installed in a derelict sorting office, New Oxford Street, London. © Artangel.

1 Documentary Studies
Dimensions of transition and continuity

John Corner

In the past 30 years there has been a huge growth in the study and critical analysis of documentary and an increase, too, in the variety and conceptual ambition of ways of thinking about it. Until the 1990s, this can be seen as the steady development of recognition, within film and media studies, of the social and cultural importance of the documentary project and of the intellectual interest which attention to its history and forms offers. From the mid-1990s, this development has been accelerated, first of all, by the phenomenon of 'reality television', selectively drawing on documentary precedents, and then by the emergence (especially in the United States) of 'feature documentary' success in the cinema. Although the first of these shifts was widely seen as indicating the displacement and even the 'death' of documentary and the second as a possible 'renaissance' of it, to put the situation like this is to be unduly simplistic.

For some, 'reality television' brought a welcome freshness and increased openness to the business of documentary representation. It is also clear that a number of the most successful 'feature documentaries' draw selectively on the structures and aesthetics of reality shows (*Fahrenheit 9/11*, *Touching the Void*, *Capturing the Friedmans* and *Super Size Me*, for instance, all having their different linkages), while not being simply reducible to this model.

So the rethinking of documentary has partly occurred as a result of dynamics within the intellectual sphere, including an increasing focus on the conditions of 'representational' truth and an extension of aesthetic and discursive inquiry well beyond conventionally fictional forms (as seen, for instance, in the growth of critical work on biography, travel writing and historiography). But it has also been driven by the nature of changes in non-fiction practice itself, taking the object of study in some new directions, including a more central positioning within media culture and popular culture, and making the presence of 'documentary' on the research agenda and university syllabus less marginal than before.

In this chapter, I want to chart some of the lines of connection, tension and disjunction that hold the developing field of scholarship and criticism together, if sometimes only loosely. This is not a literature review of documentary studies and my citations will mostly be indicative, intended to recognize major contributions and characteristic approaches, and those only selectively.

I want to start by outlining the situation as it seemed to me in 1976, when I first started to teach documentary in a degree programme and to search for work that could inform my approach. From this account of a particular moment, I then want to move through some of the principal conceptual themes and concerns that have worked to shape the field since, a shaping that has involved relationships both of transformation and continuity.

The moment of the mid-1970s: refining the terms of analysis

The moment of the mid-1970s provides a productive point of departure for my account for reasons stronger than their autobiographical significance. The period between 1971 and 1976 saw the publication of major formative work in the development of documentary as an area of academic inquiry. In the United States, Lewis Jacobs, Roy Levin, Alan Rosenthal, Richard Barsam and Eric Barnouw all published books about documentary in the four years from 1971, providing a lasting basis of scholarship.[1] In Britain, Jim Hillier and Alan Lovell's volume *Studies in Documentary* (Hillier and Lovell 1972) gave critical emphasis to the importance of the documentary idea in British cinema. However, against this background I am particularly interested in two commentaries published in 1976 that quite radically departed from previous work in the way they posed documentary as an object of study. There were precedents, for sure, but I want to argue that these publications represented important shifts in thinking, directing us towards an agenda that is still active. One of the texts was British, Dai Vaughan's *Television Documentary Usage* a 36-page pamphlet published by the BFI in its successful 'Television Monograph Series' (Vaughan 1976). The other was from North America, Bill Nichols' article 'Documentary Theory and Practice', published in *Screen* (Nichols 1976). Although very different in intellectual tenor, both had a common interest in pursuing questions of documentary's textuality, including its grammar of representation, a good deal further than most previous work had attempted to do.

However, before giving these two contributions some close attention, I want to go back four years earlier to Hillier and Lovell's *Studies in Documentary*, published in Secker and Warburg's 'Cinema One' series. This was the first volume to engage exclusively with British documentary and one of the first published anywhere to treat documentary as worthy of close textual study. Its publication combined with the concurrent impact of Jacobs', Barsam's and then Barnouw's defining historical accounts of an international cinematic form (in the last two cases, that of 'Non-Fiction Film') to give the whole area greater academic visibility.

The book is divided into three main sections, each concerned with what is called (perhaps a little misleadingly) an 'epoch' of documentary. The first is on the documentary film movement of the 1930s and centres on critical exposition around the ideas and practice of John Grierson; the second focuses on Humphrey Jennings; and the third on the 'Free Cinema' movement of the 1950s, including the work of Lindsay Anderson and Karel Reisz. In retrospect, this might seem an odd structure – with 'documentary' effectively appearing to stop with the waning of the 'Free Cinema' movement at the end of the 1950s, notwithstanding the subsequent impact of the ideas of this movement on a broader range of cinema and television. Television's developments, particularly the huge shifts and achievements of the 1960s (for instance, in observational work, drama-documentary and 'current affairs' formats) are almost completely out of the frame of reference. In part, this can be explained by the remit of the book within a 'cinema' series of short studies, but its effect upon the placing of 'documentary' as a practice is undoubtedly distorting, making the whole account 'historical' in perspective and tone without an explicit argument for it being so.

Despite this sense of documentary as essentially an achievement of the cinema of the past (documentary as, by implication, 'over'), the book achieved its goal of making British documentary work more widely appreciated as part of the broader aim of gaining greater critical respect for British cinema. It is its second section, on Humphrey Jennings, that begins significantly to open up a closer analysis of formal structures. This section (written by Jim Hillier) is by far the longest of the three and its explorations, stimulated by Jennings' aesthetic originality, close in on localized detail and on rhetorical organization in ways that are suggestive for the critical scrutiny of documentary more generally. For instance, a lengthy discussion of *Fires Were Started* includes two double-page shot sequences to illustrate sustained passages of close analysis that are far removed from the kind of brisk thematic and formal summaries found in the broader, 'film history' surveys. It shows critical examination focusing in on documentary's fascinating and powerful modes of textual management in ways that would quite quickly be taken further.

Vaughan's (1976) text stands out against the established background immediately. First of all, in sharp contrast to *Studies in Documentary*, it is, as its title declares, a book entirely concerned with documentary as a television form, noting on a preliminary page that 'almost all serious documentary is now produced for television', a comment that, at the time, was not necessarily true outside of Britain, certainly not in the United States, and might now need some review in respect of Britain itself. Nevertheless, Vaughan's emphasis represented a significant extension and revision of the established cinema-based agenda for serious discussion of documentary. Again in contrast to *Studies*, it is a book about documentary 'now' not documentary 'then', documentary is something vigorously happening, not an object of retrospective assessment. A third distinguishing characteristic is the intensive focus placed on documentary texts as 'artisan' constructions of meaning, relatively independent of attention to the specific social topics that they address. With his wide experience as a film editor, one might have expected Vaughan to adopt the approach and language of those 'how to' manuals which had already appeared on both sides of the Atlantic. However, although he drew deeply on his experience in the editing room, Vaughan's originality lay in the conceptual energy he brought to bear on close exploration of the 'syntax' of documentary in the context of the pressing questions of ontology and epistemology which non-fiction representation posed.

Looking back on the book after an interval of over 30 years, I think the way in which it is structured by a positive sense of the possibilities of 'verité' is even more apparent than at the time (the chapter on 'verité' is by far the longest). For Vaughan, the absorption into television of the influences of observational filmmaking and modes of cine-verité, together with the availability of the new lightweight cameras and sync-sound, offers exciting potential for a 're-definition' of the entire documentary enterprise. Specifically, it offers the possibility, wholly positive for him if problematic for others, of relating strongly to *individual* rather than *general* truth and of thereby getting deeper, specific and more sustained connections with particular realities. In this way, he thought, documentary might move away from what he terms the 'mannerism' of conventional styles (to a degree inherited from the 1930s), with their 'appeal to predictability', their 'reliance on cliché', their constant trading on expectations.

Deploying a language occasionally at risk of losing its clarity to its theoretical ambition, Vaughan uses the idea of the 'putative event' (the event as it might have been without the camera's presence) against that of the 'pro-filmic' (what was actually before the camera) to work across a number of examples of contemporary observational practice. However briefly, he is also keen to position the audience within his framework of analysis. How do they accord status to what they see unfold? What kind of interpretative work is encouraged through watching the observational documentary diegesis develop (its apparently self-contained spaces, times and conditions of action)? What responsibility should viewers have for working out their *own* meanings from what they see and hear rather than (as in the modes of 'mannerism') depending upon strong guidance from the filmmaker? His commitment to the 'opening up' that observational formats offer is reflected in his final anxieties about the subversion of their capacities to document that a re-introduction of commentary and captions is likely to bring.

Vaughan's zealous championing of the documentary's new possibilities for productive ambiguity, for registering with a fresh energy the density, complexity and contradictions of actuality, is undertaken in full recognition of the paradoxes and indeed 'absurdity' that all documentary aspirations involve. It is by no means an exercise in the naïve or the unquestioningly naturalistic, as some defences of observationalism have risked becoming. It relentlessly pursues a set of questions about the grammar of television documentary practice, many of which have become more relevant rather than less with the debates about 'reality television' that were only to start 20 years later. To many of us teaching documentary at the time, Vaughan's spirited analytic push into television's symbolic densities was one to be followed, even when his allegiance to observational modes did not entirely convince.

Nichols' (1976) article shares with Vaughan's a new level of commitment to close, conceptually informed, analysis. While with Vaughan it is the excitement of working as an editor within new forms of observational practice that provides the stimulus, with Nichols the initial framing is political, the challenging of *documentary as ideology* in a context of neglect. 'The ideological smokescreen thrown up by documentary apologists, many of them ostensibly leftist' is put forward as one of the reasons for this neglect (1976: 34). Documentary is a category of 'illusionism' in pressing need of critique, an area of practice where the idea of the 'screen as window' is at its most pervasive. The article sees its task as 'confronting the challenge of realism' thus presented. In this respect, it has to be read within the context of the wider questioning of 'realism' that was a dominant strand of film studies at the time, often working with a sense of irremediable deficit and a search for 'alternatives'.[2]

Given the advantages of hindsight, it is hard not to identify a measure of vangardist foreclosure in these opening pages, documentary seen first and foremost as the candidate for some overdue downsizing. In fact, what follows (to be variously developed in Nichols' subsequent writings) is a highly original, subtle and suggestive account not only of documentary *limitations* but of documentary *possibilities*.

Taking as his main corpus of examples the work of the US radical film group 'Newsreel' (including films made by them and films they distributed), Nichols works his way through a tight typological scheme for studying documentary as a textual system. Within this scheme, influenced by various concurrent writings on 'film as system' (including work in the journal *Screen*), documentary is seen to be grounded in the logics of exposition. These logics involve various forms of address, direct and indirect, sync and non-sync, a complex (indeed, dual) idea of diegesis relating both to narrative and to expositional development, and strategies of sequence construction and linking. The 'Newsreel' films raise, for Nichols, acute problems regarding the promoting of the sound track to a position of dominance, particularly through commentary. 'Newsreel' seeks to use commentary to further enforce the relationship between film and reality, precisely the kind of transparent relationship that Nichols regards as central to the 'ideology of documentary'. 'Characters' also often have speaking parts in the films, typically as interviewees, and Nichols is alert to the way in which they may be used (in a manner resembling the deployment of commentary) to provide a mode of rhetorical management for the images, one that is frequently suspect in its claims-making. Here, following a line that would be developed in his later writing, he notes the variety of ways in which participant speech can be combined with deployment of images, including images of the participants themselves. He observes how the films of the 'Newsreel' group rarely undercut visually the statements of their interviewees, unlike some of the radical work of documentarists like Emile De Antonio.

Nichols' reflections are guided by his attention to the deficits in a particular body of 'left' independent cinema, whereas Vaughan is primarily concerned with an increasingly popular strand of television. Yet their suspicion of modes of discursive management, particularly that of image by direct-address speech, are interesting to compare and suggest that for Nichols, with his commitment to the 'expository' idea, the distortive potential of speech has to be challenged within the context of its recognized indispensability, whereas Vaughan's 'observational' emphasis places speech other than 'overheard' speech as secondary at best. Of course, Nichols' framework is explicitly political, whereas Vaughan's is only implicitly and partially politicized. Both are concerned with the preservation (or indeed, introduction) of a strong vein of complexity into the screened representation, connecting Nichols' discussion to the project of 'experimental cinema' at a number of points and Vaughan's to what are perceived as the inherent ambiguities and incoherences of ongoing reality itself. Finally, both raise questions about the positions taken up by the audience. Nichols' final subhead is 'The Viewer's Place in the Exposition'. Here, he clinches his sense of the deficiencies within the 'Newsreel' approach, a weakness common to many political filmmakers, 'a tendency to ease aside the distinction between the argument (the textual system) and the referent (the real conditions)' (1976: 47). Allied to this unproblematized realism, he notes how there is an assumption of unified and coherent subject positions, positions from which viewers seek out knowledge from a film and integrate it within consciousness. Nichols questions this assumption and, in a way that links with broader shifts underway in literary and cultural theory, looks towards less unified forms of invocation and towards methods that introduce a 'disturbance' of viewing subjectivities. Again, Vaughan's own concern with *not resolving* documentary referentiality into something entirely precise and 'contained' provides an interesting comparison, if one from a very different starting point.

Nichols' article came near the beginning of his writings on documentary, which were to become, internationally, the most significant body of scholarship on documentary we have, with a major impact both on teaching and research. Already, some of the key themes to be elaborated and revised in the later work are established. These include the interest in typological thinking that would quite soon (Nichols 1983) lead him to articulate a schema of documentary form (initially, fourfold – direct-address/ expository, verité/observational, interactive and self-reflexive) which, in its various revisions, has been subject to discussion ever since.[3]

In their contrasting framings of television and of independent cinema and in their shared concern with the micro-process of documentary in relation to its larger ambitions, both pieces provided inspiration. The division between those who focus on film and those who focus on television continues to be a significant factor in documentary scholarship, of course, raising important issues of institutionality as well as of cultural practice, even allowing for the growing number of researchers and critics engaging with both.

'Ideology', however, is no longer the confident, pivotal term it was within the film and media studies of the 1970s. Problems of sustaining a coherent theorization that could be applied in analysis, together with broader shifts in the political framing of cultural practice, have been factors here. Nevertheless, questions of power, knowledge and subjectivity remain on the agenda of documentary studies, and I shall suggest below that a more general 'rethinking' needs to achieve further development here. The reduction in scale of the 'ideological question' seems to me to have brought advantages, insofar as a more comprehensive appreciation of documentary history and practice, not emphatically tied to notions of deception and a framing attitude of suspicion, has produced a productively more complex and aesthetically expansive sense of the object of study. Documentary achievements and the continuing strengths of documentary production become more recognizable and open to inquiry within this frame, without the whole perspective thereby shifting from unqualified critique to unqualified affirmation.

I want now to consider some important themes in the subsequent development of inquiry and debate by using three headings: Definitions, Aesthetics and Cognition. These are inter-related, sometimes a little messily, but they give my discussion focal points by which to gather together a clearer sense of the broader pattern.

Debating documentary: three areas of dispute

Definitions

For some writers on documentary, the question of definition has been central, with failure to find an adequately tight set of generic criteria confirming their view that the documentary enterprise is fundamentally suspect. However, for many others, 'loose' definitions have been acceptable, with documentary seen to intersect across the junction points of a number of media modes and to be in the process of steady, continuous change. It is clear that a certain level of stability is required for documentary to be an adequate label for identifying films and television programmes as of a 'similar kind', but this level is one that can admit more contingency and variation, indeed a measure of contradiction, than scholars in search of an isolable generic system are often able to accept.

Exploring questions of definition, a number of points of reference emerge, variously guiding or blocking the conduct of dispute. There are attempts to stabilize documentary around matters of form, matters of subject and matters of purpose. Not everyone would agree with the use of these particular terms but my aim here is merely to differentiate broadly between types of definitional argument, not to prescribe a particular analytic vocabulary.

Proceeding by primary reference to *form* immediately runs into the problem of the very wide range of forms that documentary has employed, with little direct linkage between, say, many of the classic films of the 1930s, television documentary journalism, and the range of observational styles now in use. Stylistic connections *do* run across this vast body of work, it is true, but often only in partial and interrupted ways. Writers who have decided that the classic Griersonian style, strongly led by commentary, is 'core' documentary (either affirming the model or subjecting it to critique) have to ignore the considerable amount of international work that departs radically from this broad recipe. Those who, more recently, have taken varieties of observationalism to be 'core' (quite often, again, a 'core' to be challenged) have had to ignore not only much of the 'classic' work but also a whole rich tradition of television practice which extensively uses presenter address and interviews. Since the history of documentary does show such a variety of forms, including modes of dramatization in which actuality footage and sound are minimized and even excluded altogether, a formal stance on the definitional question does not get us very far. However, it is not surprising that formally-based models of documentary have regularly been employed (if sometimes only with caution) by academics, since trying to advance generic understanding by reference primarily to formal criteria is an established and often productive analytic route in other areas of literary, art and film scholarship.

Subject matter may seem an even more unlikely point of primary reference given the numerous topics and subjects which documentaries have addressed, yet it is clear that topic has a degree of definitional sensitivity within documentary studies if not always within the broader spheres of documentary production and documentary viewing. 'Serious' topics and, particularly, 'social problem' topics, have acquired core status here, quite understandably given the strong tradition both in the cinema documentary and in the varieties of television documentary of engaging with issues of national, and sometimes international, public (civic) significance. Documentaries with other kinds of content, including work on the arts, leisure activities, wildlife and on geographical themes (until the recent emphases on environmental degradation and climate change) have not been excluded but they have been put on the periphery so far as critical attention is concerned. Yet any attempt to tighten up a sense of documentary, whether with descriptive or prescriptive intent, by the criterion of subject/topic is likely to provide a stiff challenge. This is so even though the established precedent of work engaging with serious social issues will continue to act for many as an implicit but strong marker of 'documentary value'.

A third option is to emphasize documentary *purposes*. What is documentary work *trying to do* with its variously produced and designed portrayals of parts of the real historical world? Here, a key fault-line in debate can be discerned. For documentaries designed primarily to give pleasure, or to entertain, have routinely been seen to depart from 'documentary values', whatever the apparent connections with these values at the level of forms and even of broad content. This has been most obvious in the debate about 'reality television', where it has precisely been the idea of the purposes and then the consequences of the television industry's production of 'commodity diversions' that has been questioned against the commitment to public knowledge and to critical scrutiny perceived to be central to the documentary project. If we interpret 'purposes' broadly, they can be seen as a factor in production *method* (particularly the time spent on research and the working protocols for relating to, and 'using', participants) and also in *mode of address* and *tone*. 'Purposes' become an over-determining influence on 'treatment', producing potentially very different kinds of programme using the same broad formal repertoire and perhaps engaging with similar subject matter.

However, to try to secure a definitional argument around purposes would be unwise. First of all, they have been very different in specific character, even within a category description that emphasizes seriousness and knowledge (what Nichols (1991) has famously called the 'sobriety' of documentary as a discourse). They have ranged from forms of promotion and propaganda (a category always available to offset against 'documentary' as discussion of Moore's *Fahrenheit 9/11* has recently shown) to the many forms of journalistic inquiry and through to radical and sometimes reflexive explorations.[4]

Nevertheless, in many disputes about what is and what is not a documentary, or what is low in 'documentary values', it is likely that matters of purpose as they extend to treatment (and therefore connect finally with questions of form and subject) will be primary points of reference, even if not openly admitted to be such.

Aesthetics

Although I have given it separate consideration here, the study of documentary *aesthetics*, of the forms and techniques of imaginative creativity and the pleasures and satisfactions these generate, has not surprisingly been strongly framed by an interest in *cognition*, in how documentaries construct and project knowledge and the likely interpretation and use of this by viewers. As I noted above, within the early work of Bill Nichols there was a preoccupation with the structures and mechanisms of ideology, the concept itself providing a primary reason and context for documentary study. However, I also noted how a sense of the discursive fascination of documentary, together with the allure of its quest for 'the real' (theoretically suspect though this quest might be) often emerged in analysis too. Documentary presents more difficulty than fictional cinema in eliciting critical 'appreciation', recognition of its crafting as *positive creativity*. First of all, documentary is self-declaredly in the 'knowledge business' in a way that most feature filmmaking is not, whatever its thematic engagement with 'issues'. This relates it much more directly to the knowledge systems rather than the art-systems of society and places it more centrally as an object of epistemological and socio-political critique. Second, documentary is widely seen to lack the symbolic richness of narrative cinema both in its visual design and its textual organization. Cutting through to its devices of illusion and perhaps deception poses an analytic challenge certainly, but one that does not require the kind of imaginative engagement and textual sympathy that fictional works elicit as a preliminary stage even in critical analysis that moves on to identify deficits and limitations.

It would be hard to quarrel with the general judgement that documentary discourse is, on the whole, lower in imaginative and symbolic complexity than screen fiction. Certain types of drama-documentary and the more self-consciously 'styled' documentaries (one might, with some caution, speak of 'art documentary') would be at the higher end of a range, with many routine, competent exercises in documentary observation and reportage at the lower end. This has produced a situation in which scholarly attention from the perspectives of arts-grounded criticism has found it routinely more interesting to consider some kinds of documentary rather than others. The works chosen for attention have often provided 'deep' or 'rich' accounts for explication, textual enigmas to be taken up and perhaps contradictions to be pursued across what can be seen as their multiple levels and phases of aesthetic design (see Corner 2000). 'Documentary studies' has thus often involved study only of *certain forms* of documentary, with the US dominance of the international field still giving cinema the edge over television and with much reportage still relatively ignored, although this situation is quite rapidly changing.[5]

Within documentary production itself, there has, of course, been a much-remarked tension between an emphasis on producing that which is pleasing, documentary as a creative artefact, and producing knowledge, documentary as a 'message', perhaps an urgent one, about the real world. Some tensions of this kind are apparent in the 1930s British movement, for example in the comments of Grierson.[6] Although it is easy to observe that these two dynamics of practice are not essentially contradictory, recognition of potentially divergent priorities simply follows from looking at the history of work both in film and television.

We can perhaps distinguish two broad modes of the 'aesthetic' taken up as analytic themes in documentary study. Pursuit of both has benefited from the continuing connection with scholarship on fictional cinema and television. First of all, there is the long-standing concern with the *pictorial creativity* of documentary, the organization of its visual design and the 'offer of seeing' it variously makes to audiences, sometimes supported by music and often working in combination with modes of speech. Pictorialism is a continuing component of documentary practice, subject to further development and emphasis in recent work, although it has taken on a different and, one might argue, reduced form in observational accounts (where there is a flattening out towards naturalistic continuities) and in kinds of documentary journalism (where the tendency is towards a primarily illustrative function, often strongly literalist in support of commentary and presenter speech).

Second, there is an emphasis on the satisfactions offered by various modes of *narrative*, documentary as story-telling, including the investigative and revelatory dynamics often at work, as well as the distinctive forms of narrative structure employed in observational accounts and the direct alignment with fictional models produced in full dramatization.

Among international scholars, Michael Renov (see, for instance, Renov 1993 and 2004) has made a major contribution to the study of documentary as involving a specific *poetics*, and as requiring critical appreciation for its imaginative and often positive appeal to viewing subjectivities. By giving attention to the ways in which documentary can enhance our sense of the world and in the process contribute to the enrichment of film and television as creative arts, he has provided some counter to the risk of documentary being 'reduced' entirely to its cognitive functions, defining as these undoubtedly are.

Further work on documentary audiences offers among its possibilities that of exploring more thoroughly the specific kinds of relationship between form, content and viewing satisfaction which many documentaries offer (Hill (2007) is a major survey in this direction and Austin (2005) offers an illuminating case-study). It is likely that development of our understanding of documentary as an aesthetic practice will feature significantly in any serious 'rethinking' of approaches and evaluations (for one suggestive approach, see Cowie (1999) and for a range of critical writing on 'classic' texts, see Corner (1996) and Grant and Sloniowksi (1998)).

Cognition

Questions of knowledge generation, quality and uses have always been central to the study of documentary, whatever the different emphases and approaches to inquiry (Nichols (1991) is the defining account with Winston (1995, 2000) providing strong, historically-grounded studies with close attention to production contexts). If it is useful to see documentary positioned culturally somewhere between 'news' and 'drama' (to take reference points within the television system), then just as aesthetics makes strong connections with drama, so cognition highlights the relationship with forms of journalism.

A long-standing issue in documentary analysis has been the kinds of truth-claim that documentaries make and the frequent overstatement or over-projection of these claims, producing a consequent requirement to challenge them. Of course, not all documentaries desire to present their accounts as unproblematic (some have drawn attention to their own uncertainties of status) but the majority have worked variously to offer representations that can be taken in 'good faith' as a resource for understanding the world. Some of the films of the 1930s British Documentary Movement went further than this. They were, in many respects, self-conscious exercises in 'propaganda', intended to persuade as much as inform and organized to achieve this end by the deployment of a strong rhetorical design.

Documentary journalism has worked with protocols of 'truth' of a different sort from the 1930s and wartime films. However, in seeking validation through the rationalist and evidential discourses of journalism, marked by its tones of cool, professional inquiry and appraisal but increasingly subject to critical interrogation as to its real disinterestedness and integrity of construction, its claims have sometimes became equally suspect, if not more so than those of openly rhetorical filmmaking.

To some commentators (we can refer back to Vaughan here), observationalism seemed to eschew prepositional claims of any kind in favour of models of 'directness' or a responsibility for attributing significance largely transferred from the makers to the audience. However, the simplicity of purpose and authorial ingenuousness apparently at work in the observational mode have provided recent documentary scholarship with its primary critical focus. This is particularly so if many of the forms of 'reality television' are seen to draw and adapt significantly from work in this mode.

Taking a schematic view, the agenda of inquiry concerning documentary's cognitive profile (an agenda extending to connect with questions of intent and of aesthetics too) can be seen to involve two different, if related, planes of visual representation, regularly confused in debate and even in analysis.

The first plane is the plane of the *origination of the image*. Here, questions are raised, as they are in respect of photography, about the particular social ontology of the image and the conditions of its production. Long-standing questions of authenticity, concerning the possibilities of manipulation and trickery in the management of what is seen (and heard), have been joined more recently by anxieties about the deployment of digital reworking and even complete manufacture. Questions about origination are usually either about what actually was in front of the camera and/or about how the methods of filming (e.g. angles, framing, composition, lighting, filters) imported cultural value to its representation in the image. To use rather simplistic terms, how far was the image 'captured' and how far was it 'constructed'?

The second plane is the plane of the *organization of the image*. Here, the focus is on the editing together of different shots to provide various kinds of narrative and expositional continuity and then the combination of these shots with speech, including commentary, and sounds, including music. The epistemological and affective identity of a sequence of organized images and sounds is that of a *discourse* (an authored account, a descriptive version) rather than a *representation* as such, even though it is grounded in a sequence of representations.

Arguments about the adequacy to the truth of documentaries at the level of the origination of the image need to be differentiated from those about adequacy at the level of organization, but frequently they are not. For instance, it is quite possible for a documentary to assemble a wholly questionable account of, say, student poverty, from shot sequences, each one of which has a strong degree of integrity as location footage with minimal directorial intervention. It is also possible for a documentary to have a high degree of integrity and truth value as an account of the same topic while containing some sequences in which the precise relationships of the apparent to the real, the local truth-conditions of the image, are open to serious doubt.

The stronger recognition of the play-off between matters of origination and of organization might help to refine our critical engagement with documentary. The dominance of the 'reality television' issue in recent discussion of documentary internationally has sometimes encouraged the view that observational forms constitute the core of documentary practice and the core of its claims-making too. Such a position has undoubtedly served to misrepresent the full diversity of documentary portrayal, leading to a critical approach which proceeds as if what I have called factors relating to the origination of the image were all that needed attention.

Another, contrasting, focus for recent discussion has been the idea of 'performance', the kinds of self-conscious display of artefactual properties that can be a factor both of directorial and participant activity. Forms of 'reality television', particularly those involving tightly formatted situations such as *Big Brother*, have presented us with modes of observation in which high degrees of self-consciousness and openly performative display to camera (both in speech and action) are routine. This has generated new lines of relationship with viewers, perhaps thereby eliciting new levels of empathy and complicity with screened behaviour. Certainly, such a clearly 'knowing' relationship between action and camera sets up different relations between screened events and viewers from that variously established through the modulations of documentary naturalism.

Some writers (Bruzzi (2006) is a notable example) have suggested that a significant and welcome cognitive shift has occurred, freeing up viewing relations from the illusory grip of the established observational mode and perhaps even ushering in the possibility of a new 'politics of documentary form'. Once again, only with imaginative kinds of audience research on the changing forms of the factual across a range of work are we likely to see just how far new, more self-aware and more sceptical viewing relations have actually been encouraged.[7] For it seems clear that many of the new 'reality shows', as much as they offer open performance to a camera whose presence is acknowledged, have also often traded heavily on the promise of the directness and 'rawness' of their depictions as modes of 'captured reality'. Elements of reflexivity and the recognition of artifice have thus gone along with what can be seen as claims of transparency of a more traditional sort (Jerslev (2005) gives a shrewd analysis of contemporary documentary 'performance', at points taking issue with Bruzzi). Audience research might also be able to assess the extent to which the frameworks employed by viewers in watching kinds of reality show (variously leading to positive engagement, dislike or outright critical rejection) are extended into the viewing of the broader range of documentary accounts (producing, for instance, increased interest in viewing or a deepened cynicism about the whole project of documentary portrayal). Many scholars would welcome a heightened public scepticism about all of televisual representation but most would also want to sustain conditions in which documentaries could still play their part in the construction and circulation of public knowledge, conditions in which documentaries could 'still count'. Documentary can be an idea around which scholarship gathers in scepticism but it can also be an idea around which scholarship offers a critical defence, contributing to terms of development.

Of course, a whole range of documentary output, including the various reportorial modes, has only a secondary connection at best with the problems of what attempting to be a fly on a wall brings to filmmaking and to the intensive and pivotal relationships between filmmakers, participant behaviours and viewer perceptions that observationalism introduces. Although reality formats have modified the representational economy of documentary television in ways that have required address by most of those working within it, the different strands continue to require attention in their own specific terms of production, discursive organization, 'claim on the real' and social impact. Precisely how documentaries attempt to give us access to the world and to offer explicit and implicit propositions and judgements about it is still a rich and under-developed topic.[8] Research which not only pays attention to the cognitive profile of the different constituents of documentary representation but to the variety of 'knowledge-systems' which documentaries can employ, encouraging (and blocking) different ways of knowing and different kinds of knowledge, including emotional knowledge, is likely to be a rewarding line of further inquiry.

'Documentary': revision and development in an international field

The expansion of research and teaching interest in documentary shows both points of change and lines of continuity when judged against my marker of the mid-1970s. The sense of documentary as a broad area of practice under pressure from a changing media economy and from elements of the new audio-visual culture has certainly been a factor in this expansion, giving added significance to a deeper engagement with documentary history as well as with contemporary work.

With simplification, some key dimensions of the overall pattern can be summarized:

1. There has been a quite decisive shift away from locating the study of documentary confidently within the critique of ideology. The inescapably 'cognitive' character of documentary, and its function within the political economy of public knowledge, have been placed within more subtle but also often politically more uncertain contexts of inquiry, ones in which contingent, empirical questions concerning conditions of production and reception become more relevant than was once allowed for. Along with this stronger 'sociology of documentary', an affirmation of documentary achievement and the continuing possibilities for its enabling of political and social development have more frequently been expressed alongside, and sometimes in combination with, perspectives of critique. A renewed focus on documentary ethics (relating primarily to production but with implications for conditions of distribution and viewing too) can be seen to have 'replaced' in part a more directly political framing. However, the

requirement to locate film and television output within researched settings of political, economic and cultural power needs to be a feature of any new phase of scholarship in the area, whatever the diversity of approaches and emphases this might entail.

2. A richer and denser sense of documentary aesthetics has emerged, enhancing our sense of the interplay between documentary representation and subjectivity (including the social subjectivities of national, ethnic and gender identity) and usefully complicating the engagement with documentary knowledge and documentary knowing. The stronger recognition of creative achievement, not only in the past but in concurrent work, that has followed this has linked a little more closely the spheres of scholarship and of media production, including production training, in ways holding further potential for dialogue and mutual influence.

3. It is much harder now to place an exclusive emphasis on cinema when studying documentary, particularly in countries where an indigenous documentary cinema is marginal, if it exists at all. In many countries, including Britain, documentary television is an area of significant cultural work with a long and diverse history. Those approaches to documentary which engage with broadcasting primarily through the debate around 'reality television' are working with a framework likely to be severely skewed in its understanding of documentary's scope, values and continuing potential.

4. 'Documentary' as a category of practice continues to change within the terms of the wider economic and cultural shifts. The intensified non-professional circulation of images of the 'real' brought about by web applications is a specific example of the reconfiguration of contexts, while the use of the web as a medium for professional documentary applications, both in support of film and broadcast material and independently, is developing rapidly. Across these changes, a degree of continuity with previous practice will be maintained but there are indications that a more radical process of 'generic dispersal' is at work across the whole area of the 'non-fictional' than has occurred at previous stages of development.[9] Even allowing for the historical resistance of the area to defining criteria, the use of documentary-style portrayals as forms of entertainment has significantly complicated our sense of what the term can now be used to signify. The newer deployments of actuality materials for purposes primarily of diversion have created changed conditions for constructing serious documentary accounts for a popular audience, combining with broader transitions both in the use value and the exchange value of representations of reality. The recent successes of documentary in the cinema partly show the application of strategies that try to take account of these conditions in order to keep recognizable 'documentary spaces' open.

A field of documentary studies that attempts to connect with the widest range of international practice both on film and television, including that within journalism and current affairs, will certainly be a more comprehensive field of inquiry than has existed hitherto. Study of documentary needs to be criticism, sociology and history (seeing emerging forms within the context of their lineage). Scholarship will never 'resolve' the issue of definitions and borderlines, these will actually become more uncertain and 'thin' as audio-visual culture becomes more inter-generically fluid. Suspicion of the uses to which some documentaries are put and the kinds of trust they elicit will rightly be a prominent element of academic engagement. However, a refined awareness of the aesthetic and cognitive complexity of the documentary process should accompany this. And so should an emphasis on the continuing value and *necessity* of many of the kinds of media practices that have been categorized under this rich but problematic heading.

Notes

1   In sequence, the relevant volumes are Levin (1971); Jacobs (1971); Rosenthal (1972); Barnouw (1974); and Barsam (1974).

2   The critique of 'realism' as an aesthetic of political limitation, denying spectator's critical engagement with the world, has been a major point of theoretical address in film studies from the 1970s onwards. Although focused on fictional cinema, it variously impacts upon the (at this point marginal) attention given to documentary. Various alternatives, drawing on avant-garde practice, are recommended but there is also increasingly a developing defence of 'realist' work and its politics. See, for instance, Lovell (1980) and Juhasz (1994).

3   Nichols (1991) becomes, of course, the major point of reference for the growth of documentary studies during the 1990s, collecting together and developing further the ideas put forward in the earlier essays.

4   Among the recent commentaries on documentary and notions of propaganda see, for instance, Kelton Rhoads (2004).

5   Conference programmes provide a good opportunity to assess the pattern of interests. As I noted earlier, the arrival of 'reality television' gave television a new prominence, if mostly with a negative inflection. More research on documentary journalism and other documentary applications is now being pursued although the arrival of a dedicated journal for the field with the title *Studies in Documentary Film* suggests the residual power of older perspectives.

6   Hardy (1979) shows variations in Grierson's own emphasis here, documenting his obvious fascination with matters of innovative film form and aesthetics alongside a sometimes rather brusque commitment to 'sociological' purposes. Grierson strategically veered around on the question of just how important 'form' was in relation to 'content', a quite understandable variation in someone attempting to gain support from a variety of people whose interests in 'documentary' were grounded in different priorities.

7   Once again, Hill (2007) makes some important headway. Together with my colleague Kay Richardson, I tried to explore the difference between types of cognitive engagement with documentary material by using the terms 'transparent' and 'mediated' to describe levels of viewer awareness of the constructed character of documentary as an intervening variable in relating to and assessing what was 'shown'. See Richardson and Corner (1986).

8   For a much-cited account of the way that political engagement with a documentary can be explored, see Gaines (1999) and for a recent study of the use of participant memory as a documentary knowledge source, see MacDonald (2006).

9   I have suggested elsewhere that documentary is now to some extent a practice taking place in a 'post-documentary culture', one in which the social and aesthetic co-ordinates that provided it with an adequate if loose generic identity have shifted. See Corner (2000, 2004).

2 The Question of Evidence, the Power of Rhetoric and Documentary Film

Bill Nichols

All discourses, including documentary film, seek to externalize evidence – to place it referentially outside the domain of the discourse itself which then gestures to its location there, beyond and before interpretation. Reference to this external location then names and renders visible what awaited nomination. Evidence refers back to a fact, object, or situation – something two or more people agree upon, something verifiable and concrete – but facts and events only acquire the distinctive status of evidence within a discursive or interpretive frame. Evidence, then, is that part of discourse, be it rational-philosophic, poetic-narrative, or rhetorical, charged with a double existence: it is both part of the discursive chain and gives the vivid impression of also being external to it. In other words, facts become evidence when they are taken up in a discourse; and that discourse gains the force to compel belief through its capacity to refer evidence to a domain outside itself.

The recent and compelling documentary, *An Injury to One* (US, 2002), about the history of Butte, Montana, as a mining town and the murder there of a Wobbly (Industrial Workers of the World) organizer, Frank Little, in 1917, demonstrates vividly how facts convert to evidence and how their evidential status is contingent on the discourse to which they attach. At one point, director Travis Wilkerson recounts the story of a large flock of geese that land on the enormous lake that fills the open pit mine that still dominates the town. The lake is extremely toxic, loaded with copper, cadmium, zinc, nickel, lead, arsenic and sulfates; it has a ph of 2.5, 'roughly comparable to battery acid', Wilkerson tells us in his intense but flatly spoken commentary. A storm takes the geese by surprise and they land on the lake. In the morning, 342 geese are dead. They are blistered with lesions, their esophagi and trachea corroded, and their livers bloated with toxic quantities of heavy metals. Wilkerson recounts that representatives for ARCO, the company that now owns the mine, assured the townspeople that the water was actually safe; the geese died 'because of something they ate', not from exposure to the lake water. Wilkerson concludes this section of his stunning film with an observation:

> As the geese help to demonstrate, history, in this case, cannot be so easily expurgated [as the company's original name: Anaconda]. In an act reminis-

cent of a mass suicide, the geese hurled themselves into the open wound in the heart of the town. Perhaps using the only manner they knew, these creatures were trying to tell us something because it seemed to have escaped our notice. They were directing us to the scene of a crime.

The facts do not, as Wilkerson's sardonic tone suggests, speak for themselves: they must be seen, and heard, and thence interpreted, an act that fissures into multiple directions depending on the purposes and goals of the interpreter. ARCO interprets the death of 342 geese as a case of a bad dietary choice; Wilkerson interprets it as a 'mass suicide' meant to be understood as the silent testimony of witnesses to a crime. The event, however, can only be seen as accidental death, testimony or anything else within the interpretive frame provided for it. Cast back by discourse into the external world, facts take up a place outside discourse and are made to do so in a way that allows their reincarnation as evidence to overlay perfectly the fact to which it corresponds.

The indexical quality of the photographic image is ideally suited to this purpose. A perfect tautology appears to come into being between fact, object or event, on the one hand, and evidence, on the other, so that reference to a piece of evidence marries signified and referent in a single stroke. As the story of the geese suggests, the fact or event does not come into being as evidence; this status accrues later, when it is recruited to a discourse: 'bad food', 'mass suicide', and so on for the geese, for example – these labels become affixed to that which simply was. And they seem to stick because of an indexical bond between image and referent, that which exists outside the discursive chain.

Sometimes facts speak but in ways not intended by the speaker or filmmaker. The viewer, too, may convert fact to evidence, sometimes in ways that run against the grain of their initial recruitment. For example, in *Tongues Untied* (US, 1989), Marlon Riggs' powerful documentary about being black and gay in America, he cross-cuts between a protest march in Selma, Alabama, in the 1960s and a gay pride parade in New York City in the 1980s. For Riggs, the parallel is evidence of a continuous lineage of protest and struggle for civil liberties and individual rights. But there is a tremendous difference in the two pieces of footage if we examine them not as part of Rigg's stunning visual testament but as visible evidence of two distinct historical moments.

In the Selma march, what is most striking is the rich diversity of the marchers themselves: younger and older African-Americans, younger and older whites, male and female, primarily but not entirely well-dressed, religious leaders and lay people, all marching to confront a racist society with their visible, demonstrable protest. The two most prominent banners read, 'We March with Selma' and 'We Shall Overcome'. The Gay Pride march footage features a contingent of young black men, with two bare-chested black males carrying a banner that reads, 'Black Men Loving Black Men Is A Revolutionary Act'. The goal of mobilizing a broad, inclusive range of people to confront racism and champion civil rights has yielded to the proclamation of difference, the affirmation of an identity and politics that seeks to embrace the like-minded and gain the public recognition of others. The spectrum of ages, classes and races incorporated into and patently visible in the Selma march has disappeared.

Belonging and activism are now predicated on a specific combination of race, gender and sexual orientation. The male and female, mostly younger but occasionally older on-lookers, along with a number of primarily white police officers lining the route of the gay pride parade, are a far more diverse group than the marchers themselves. The unity of purpose of an earlier time has yielded to the identity politics of a later one, or so an interpreter could argue just as forcefully as Riggs can argue for a line of continuity.

Careful consideration of this act of converting fact to evidence occurs in R. G. Collingwood's *The Idea of History*, written in 1946, and dedicated to the idea of history as a scientific undertaking. During an extended discursion of 'historical evidence', Collingwood debunks the view that history amounts to citing the testimony of credible authorities whose remarks can be cut and pasted together to provide the requisite history. This outdated method relies on facts drawn from earlier, authoritative accounts – and whose status as evidence can go unquestioned for that reason – that now form the backbone of a new narrative. By contrast, Collingwood argues that good history writing requires making inferences that are always based on questions directed towards a careful examination of the facts themselves. They can only come to serve as valid evidence when freshly taken up in the author's own interpretative discourse. The historian must pose questions that infer what really happened rather than adopt the views of others. Wilkerson's comment about the geese, 'Perhaps using the only manner they knew, these creatures were trying to tell us something because it seemed to have escaped our notice', becomes a standing assumption of critical inquiry: facts and events exist, but their conversion into evidence depends on the analytic powers of the interpreter, be he historian or filmmaker.

But in the middle of this call for a methodologically rigorous history, Collingwood suddenly takes a surprising turn. A sub-heading entitled, 'Who Killed John Doe?' announces the detour. Contrary to the strictly expository style of all the previous sections, Collingwood now adopts a semi-fictional voice. The section begins, 'When John Doe was found, early one Sunday morning, lying across his desk with a dagger through his back, no one expected that the question of who did it would be settled by means of testimony.' Here is a case where Collingwood can demonstrate the necessity of inferential analysis that, when done properly, will lead to a clear-cut solution.

Using Collingwood's own dicta that 'everything in the world is potential evidence for any subject whatever' (1946: 280), and that we should focus not on the content of statements but on the fact that they are made (1946: 275) – in other words, that our analysis must not accept what others represent the case to be but must ask, 'What light is thrown on the subject in which I am interested by the fact that this person made this statement?' – we can ask, Why does Collingwood tell this who-done-it story in the middle of his disquisition on history? Clearly, it serves as an example, if not allegory, for good historical investigation. It serves Collingwood's goal of giving the impression that history writing can become a science, capable of determining what really happened in an unambiguous manner through an independent examination of the facts and testimony. Inferences lead to knowledge and knowledge leads to the one and only logical solution: the rector did it. Ambiguity is dispelled thanks to the hard, inferential work of the historian laboring in the vineyards of the local, empirically verifiable event. Not all rectors should now be suspected of murder, nor should all murders be attributed to rectors, but in this concrete case, with these facts and statements and with this set of questions to transform facts and statements into evidence, the rector's guilt can be cleanly determined.

By presenting a Sherlock Holmes-like murder mystery Collingwood can arrive at a specific solution to a concrete question. The solution lacks generalizing power: it tells us nothing about the behavior of rectors, or the causes of murder, in general. His example offers a definite conclusion, based on asking questions whose answers generate evidence: a footprint in the wet soil of the lawn becomes admitted as evidence as soon as we ask a question such as, 'Who might have crossed the lawn that fateful night but only after the rain fell?'

Though instructive, Collingwood's choice of a murder mystery as metaphor reduces his method to factual determinations that cannot account for historical complexity. He neglects to add to his assertion 'everything in the world is potential evidence for any subject whatever' *and for a wide range of interpretations*. The murder mystery involves facts, questions, evidence and interpretation of a different order from those involved when we ask what brought about the transformation of communism into totalitarianism, why capitalism undergoes cycles of growth and recession, why genocide occurred in Rwanda in the 1990s, or what influence populism has had on American politics. Questions such as these propel us into a realm rather remote from the indisputable evidence, clear-cut verification procedures and singular conclusions that Collingwood naturalizes as the common stuff of history through his exemplary fiction.

Collingwood, in fact, builds his conception of proper historiography on the Aristotelian notion of 'inartistic proofs', evidence, that is, that exists outside, or can readily be made to appear to reside outside, the discursive chain. Examples include laws, witnesses, contracts, oaths, and confessions obtained by torture (a practice reserved, in Aristotle's time, for slaves since citizens would give their own testimony artistically, that is, with benefit of the rhetorical arts). This is the evidence that can most easily be 'thrown out' of the discourse as fact in order to be reeled back in as evidence. Science, like murder mysteries, works with objective facts; the form a precise account of them takes is of minor consequence. Form, for Collingwood, is little more than a question of style; the proof is in facts that serve as evidence. Careful interpretation leads us down a straight and narrow path to the truth, not into a labyrinth of competing interests and interpretations whose relative merits may be decided more by power, or at least rhetoric, than by logic.

Although seemingly the most irrefutable of evidence, inartistic proofs were of minor concern to Aristotle. The 'artistic proofs' that were the heart and soul of rhetorical discourse concerned him much more. Though frequently necessary, inartistic proofs still have to be incorporated into a discourse where they would become convincing. Alone, the inartistic proofs might be necessary but hardly sufficient. Only when such proofs took on their second life as evidence inside a body of signification

– discourse – did it become possible for a convincing argument to emerge. *How* inartistic proofs become incorporated into the discourse thus matters more than *what* these proofs reveal in and of themselves.

What concerned Aristotle, Cicero and Quintillian, among others, were the artistic proofs that strove to guarantee the ethical credibility of a speaker, the emotional response of an audience, and the convincingness of an argument (including the convincingness of inferences or interpretations drawn from inartistic proofs). These are questions regarding rhetorical not philosophic or logical discourse. The protocols of philosophy, or, today, science, eschew such discourse. Rhetoric or persuasive speech mires us in deception; it lacks a moral compass; it leads to ideology rather than knowledge. Or so it seemed to Plato and so it seemed to Roland Barthes, when, in 1964, he wrote his seminal essay, 'The Rhetoric of the Image'.

Barthes' essay, which, for me, marks the beginning of the end for an understanding of the crucial role of rhetoric in contemporary culture (except as handmaiden to ideology), asks questions about the meaning of an image, in this case, an advertisement for Panzani pasta sauce in the form of a photograph of a shopping net filled with fresh vegetables and Panzani products, their labels clearly legible. Like Collingwood, Barthes is moved to question authority, to refuse to accept the advertisement at its word. Barthes asks of the image, as Collingwood did of his suspects, How does it disguise what it says as something natural and obvious?

Like Collingwood's who-done-it, the mystery of meaning is once again carried to one and only one conclusion. The image represents ideology. It does so because it sets out to naturalize Panzani and to hide its production as a commodity. Products – most importantly, a can of pasta sauce – are equated in the image with the fresh, wholesome bounty of the farm. A perfect tautology exists: fresh vegetables are Panzani; Panzani is fresh vegetables, nothing more or less. This naturalizing gesture is, for Barthes, the fundamental move of ideology. Or as he puts it:

> To the general ideology, that is, correspond signifiers of connotation which are specified according to the chosen substance [sound, image, gesture and so on, BN]. These signifiers will be called *connotators* and the set of connotators a rhetoric, rhetoric thus appearing as the signifying aspect of ideology.
>
> (1977: 49)

In this early essay by Barthes, little has changed since the days of Plato. Later, Barthes will side with Aristotle and the capacity of text and image to please more than distract, to subvert as well as serve ideology, but the suspicion cast upon an advertising image that is allowed to stand for all images points to an anti-ocular tendency in a large swathe of 1970s French theory. Although the later Barthes departs from it, he does not return to the question of ideology that he initially posed. With an anxious gaze, compounded by the mourning for the loss of his mother that revolves so clearly around the photographic in *Camera Lucida*, Barthes places himself in the company of Lacan, Althusser, Foucault, Debord, Bataille, Baudrillard, and film theorists such as Christian Metz, Jean-Louis Baudry, Jean-Louis Comolli, Jean-Pierre Oudart, and others.[1] Like the alluring appearance of Zambinella in Balzac's novella, *Sarrasine*, the image deceives and seduces, often with an artful innocence that necessitates suspicion and close analysis. The power of rhetoric to move an audience by establishing a credible, compelling, and convincing case of any kind, on any subject, for any purpose becomes reduced to the power of rhetoric to put ideology into practice.

The linkage of the visual with the ideological through the Lacanian imaginary fueled much of this distrust of the visual. Since ideology serves a hegemonic function by persuading individuals that their own best interests and even their fundamental sense of identity are tied up with the status quo and an image of themselves that always arrives from elsewhere, it is but a small step to understand ideology as a rhetorical procedure antithetical to knowledge. Outside ideology, and outside the guile of rhetoric, knowledge in the form of science or critical theory awaits. Such knowledge does not reside in the image, however, but in an analytic discourse for which the image serves as evidence of an ideological operation.

This line of thought returns us to Plato's attack on rhetoric as a corrupting form of flattery, or deception. Plato terms the proper cultivation of the body 'gymnastics' and its corrupt form *kosmētikē,* or cosmetics, those flattering applications of ornament that render appearances false. In an attempt to preserve the centrality of rhetoric as discourse measured by its effects without dismissing it as sheer deception, Quintillian differentiates between the use of cosmetics such as color, ornament, gesture and emotion for venal and noble purposes. His negative example involves slave dealers who use cosmetics to increase the value of those whom they sell by giving them a flattering appearance. Such an appearance renders the slave over-valued and any subsequent transaction dishonest.

This contrasts, for Quintillian, with the art of the noble orator who does not regard speech itself as a slave whose worth can be distorted, but, instead, sees speech as an instrument for the expression of views strongly believed and compellingly conveyed.[2]

> In place of the cosmetic body Quintillian puts a political body ... As the place of political relations, the body escapes from the moral disdain of metaphysics ... The body — image, passion, pleasure, effect, and affect — gains legitimacy in politics and in rhetoric too ... By all these shifts Quintillian succeeds in justifying the definition of rhetoric as wisdom ... To ensure the victory of justice, eloquence is thus within its rights to apply itself not only to instructing the soul but also to moving the body.
>
> (Lichtenstein 1993: 88–9)

Rhetoric, in other words, may sometimes be deceptive but it is also the only means we have as social actors, or citizens, for conveying our beliefs, perspectives, and convictions persuasively. Barthes, however, makes the indexical image innocent, like the body of the slave. Those who would exploit this image or body for gain apply the cosmetics of rhetorical connotations, i.e., ideology. Ideology robs the image, the slave or speech of innocence. But what if slaves, or images, have something to say about all this? What if they always bear meanings already? What if cosmetics, or a rhetoric of persuasion, does not only deceive but also shocks, disturbs, provokes or defamiliarizes, displaying the old in a new, revelatory manner? In this case, the rhetoric of the image is not necessarily complicit with an already dominant ideology. Instead it belongs to a struggle for domination in which the meaning and effect of an image or film cannot be determined in advance as simply and always ideological.

Barthes identified the seductions of the slave dealer, and rightly so, in an advertisement for pasta sauce. His analysis, though, was less a critique of advertising, something he scarcely commented on at all, than the deceptive practice of the image itself. Although he would later call denotation 'the last of the connotations' (1974: 9), at this point, he identifies an evidentiary tautology in the denotative level of the image. The photograph of a tomato or a red pepper confirms the 'having been there-ness' of such vegetables, before the camera, and that they now arrive before us. The connotative level of the image works its deceptive magic on this fact by establishing an identity between garden produce and a canned pasta sauce. The evidence is thrown back, outside the discursive maneuvers of connotation, to nature, to the fact of the prior existence of these vegetables that now equal, thanks to a rhetoric of deception, a can of sauce.

The result is to overlay the indexical quality of the image with rhetorical signification that achieves an ideology effect. It is an insidious effect because the evidence of pre-existing facts (tomatoes, peppers, onions, and so on) allows the claim of identity between produce and product to profit from the indexical properties of the image. The connotative advertising message 'plunges into the story of the denoted scene as though into a lustral bath of innocence' (1977: 51).

Critical theory, up to this point, has sided more with Plato than with Aristotle. It has cast suspicion upon rhetoric as a deceptive practice and held out for the type of conclusive truth that Collingwood called for, even if it does so in the name of Marx rather than historiography or in a spirit that challenges conclusiveness but still holds vision and the image suspect. Barthes' 'The Rhetoric of the Image' can be seen as the nail in the coffin of visual culture, consigning it to perpetual suspicion about the deceptive practices and ideological effects of a proliferating image culture. How can we escape this thicket? How can we develop a critical perspective that will understand the function of images and rhetoric as politically polysemous and ideologically polymorphous? For they are so, are they not? Do rhetoric and images always sell us a bill of goods?

We should remember that Barthes' attention in this early period was drawn to advertising images, Hollywood epics, journalistic photographs, and liberal humanism at its most wishful – in the 'Great Family of Man' exhibit. His writing, like Collingwood's, stole up on these facts to identify them as evidence of misdeeds (ideological or criminal) from a place apart. There remained, for Barthes and almost all the other cultural theorists an outside to rhetoric and ideology from which their own writing originated. Call it scientific knowledge or philosophy, Marxism or deconstruction, it preserved a sanctuary that false appearances could not touch. Can we abandon such a sanctuary and yet retain a sense of critical engagement in which speech acts that are designed performatively to have an effect, to convince and to move, can begin as the rhetorical move of one but become the political movement of many?

Barthes' use of a denotative level of uncoded meaning, for example, becomes like the body of the slave in ancient Greece, which the slave dealer, 'dresses up' in order to deceive via the connotations of an ignoble 'cosmetics'. But what if the metaphor is wrong? What if the body of the slave, or a photographic image, or any other image, is already coded as soon as it enters into any system of communication or exchange? What if any persuasive analysis of such bodies and images takes place *within* an ideological arena rather than outside it? Meaning will emerge from a situated, contested interpretative act rather than be the definitive result of a process of questions and inferences or an unmasking of deception.

In asking these questions I am proposing that rhetoric is indispensable, indeed integral, to any form of persuasive, embodied speech and that it is precisely because rhetoric is measured by its effects that it holds great importance for the body politic. I am also assuming that documentary film is itself a form of embodied speech, a speech that arrives as the voice and gestures of the film's body.[3] The 'voice of documentary', as I have called it elsewhere, refers to a given film's situated, embodied expression as it is conveyed by spoken words and silences, intertitles, music, composition, editing, tone or perspective with a primary emphasis on the effect of this symbolic form of action on the viewer.[4] This differentiates voice from style: style directs our attention from the film to the filmmaker; voice directs our attention to the fact of being addressed. Voice functions within an ideological, affective arena in which meaning is up for grabs rather than subject to final determination.

The voice with which an image or film speaks is capable, of course, of innumerable effects – many of which may well be ideological but not necessarily ideological in the sense of reinforcing the status quo. Speech and images may embody counter-ideologies designed to subvert or reject the status quo.[5] To reexamine the tradition of 'downcast eyes' and suspicion about the rhetoric of the image as ideology invites an investigation of, among other things, representational film practice where speaking on behalf of counter-ideologies is frequently the *raison d'être* of the work in the first place. Documentary filmmaking, with its strong ties to a tradition of liberal ameliorations and radical transformations of social practices is one such practice. The body of the film, and the filmmaker, with its expressive mix of passion and knowledge, set out to move us. Such movement can contest the status quo as readily as it can confirm it; such movement is the constitutive domain in which power and pleasure combine to achieve political effect.

Remember Collingwood's advocacy of an approach in which evidence is what appears in response to a question. From this perspective, a fact can become evidence despite itself, despite reticence or a lack of any intention of serving as evidence. (Symptoms consistently possess such a quality.) Like Sam Marlowe's portrait in *The Trouble with Harry* (US, 1955), an object, an image, say, can suddenly turn into evidence once we pose a question. Such questions do not arise from the image or the fact, object or event for which it stands, but from what we ask of it. Barthes' own questions had this quality about them, but Barthes seemed content to locate a meaning and effect *in* the image as if his interrogation exposed what the image itself sought to conceal through its cosmetic application of a 'lustral bath of innocence' to a consumer product. When we recognize that evidence emerges as a response to the questions we pose, we are in a position to recognize the ambiguity of that evidence: with a different question, different evidence may have emerged from the same facts, objects or images.

The image, like a footprint in the grass or a stain on a coat, has the ability to offer evidence of more than one thing, within more than one ideological frame, with more than one rhetorical and political effect, depending on what we ask of it. The radically different interpretations, resulting from sharply distinct questions, of the Rodney King footage are a vivid example. Rhetorically, these questions retroactively fabricated quite different 'lustral baths of innocence', as it were, for Mr. King or for his assailants. That is to say, opposing perspectives and different questions led to radically disparate interpretations by the prosecution and the defense at the two trials of the police officers accused of beating Mr. King.[6] The voice of documentary is largely given over, as a rhetorical utterance designed to move us, to shaping and focusing the polysemous quality of sound and image. Innocence, and other qualities, emerge after the fact, as that which a rhetorical voice desires to confer on what will be identified as evidence.

Despite the certainty rhetorical utterances wish to confer, images retain a fundamental ambiguity that who-done-it mysteries, advertising, and other forms of reductionism ignore. Barthes' later writing embraces such a view, although he never went back to revise his earlier writing about the image and its ideological effect. For every social issue, divergent positions emerge, with overlapping forms of evidence used as answers to different rhetorical questions. No denotative plane of certainty underpins these differences. The voice and gestures of the orator or the film's body seek to move us in relation to those social issues and conflicts that do not lend themselves to scientific determination and unanimous agreement.

Style, form, and voice are the heart and soul of persuasive engagement, and persuasive engagement is at the core of political discourses and social practices, whatever their ideological consequences. We inhabit an arena that remains fully within the shadow of ideology. There is no exit, only the constant effort to pose questions, present evidence, and make arguments that advance upon what has come before. Leaving certitude behind moves us into an arena of radical doubt that cannot be dispelled so much as deferred, suspended and, ultimately, embraced as part and parcel of an advance, a movement, whose direction and velocity remain open to all the vicissitudes of history.

Notes

1   The best treatment of a distrust of the visual as a hallmark of twentieth-century critical theory is by Martin Jay (1993). This trend also characterizes a great deal of Cultural Studies and makes introductory texts to this field such as Merzoff or Cartwright strongly cast as cautionary tales about the seductive, ideological power of mass media and cultural practices in a consumer society.

2   This discussion of Quintillian's correction of Plato's apparent condemnation of rhetoric draws heavily on Jacqueline Lichtenstein's discussion (1993: 86–8).

3   I take this phrase, 'films body' from Vivian Sobchack (1992). She writes,

> [The film] visibly acts visually and, therefore, expresses and embodies intentionality in existence and at work in a world. The film is not,

therefore, merely an object for perception and expression; it is also the subject of perception and expression ... More to the point would be a discussion that focuses on cinematic technology's function of materially embodying perception and expression as a situated, finite, centered and decentering *lived-body* that, through its commutation of perception and expression, is able to accomplish the signification of vision as significant.

(1992: 167)

4   I first discuss 'voice' in Nichols (1983), and modify some of that discussion in Nichols (1991).
5   See Göran Therborn (1980) for a lucid discussion of the various forms of ideology that are operative in any given social formation. Therborn's treatment of ideology dissolves the Althusserian notion of ideology-in-general, akin to the 'general ideology' adopted by Barthes in 'The Rhetoric of the Image', into its component parts in a given historical moment. A general ideology that constitutes the subject may remain operative but concrete class ideologies and counter-ideologies are the common sites of political struggle, unless redesigning the subject is our sole and exclusive goal.
6   See 'The Trials and Tribulations of Rodney King', in Nichols (1994) for a full discussion of the Rodney King footage and its use in the trials of the police officers charged with beating Mr. King.

3 First-person Films

Some theses on self-inscription

Michael Renov

Most critical commentators and even casual viewers would agree that it's an exciting time for documentary – measured in terms of popular attention, institutional legitimacy or scholarly output – and for those of us interested in the documentary project. By 'documentary project', I refer here not to the single-minded, formal or rhetorical orthodoxy of the sort associated with the Griersonians of the 1930s or the direct cinema devotees of the 1960s so much as a broad-based, loosely-knit community of interest worldwide that supports and sustains documentary *culture*.

Now culture, according to the late Raymond Williams, is one of the two or three most complicated words in the English language (1983: 87). Developing from its earliest usages as a noun of process (the tending of something, crops or animals), the word began to refer to more abstract processes by the mid-nineteenth century, eventually entailing both material production and signifying practices. Williams writes of the word's rich etymological sources, to the Latin noun, *culter* – ploughshare, that which tills the earth and prepares the way for seeding – and thus to a kind of husbandry as well as to the verb *colere* and its various meanings – to cultivate, protect, and honor with worship. Williams' discussion supports my own expanded sense of documentary culture in the present moment, referring as it does to a set of practices both material and symbolic and to a diverse cast of characters whose husbandry, protection, and honoring of the documentary project have facilitated its reinvention.

But my concern here is for autobiography, a domain which has produced and sustained a culture of its own with roots in literature, painting, and performance. Filmic autobiography remains little discussed in the academy to date although that situation is beginning to change.[1] My own twenty-year-long fascination for autobiography may have something to do with the paradoxes and contradictions that arise when the worlds (indeed, the *cultures*) of documentary film and literary autobiography collide. Let me explain. When I have spoken about the ideas contained in my book, *The Subject of Documentary*, I have at times been challenged by those who see the films of which I write as self-absorbed, overly emotionalized, and brimming with the platitudes of 1990s identity politics. These works are found to be either too straightforward (too on-the-nose and insufficiently ironic) or, perhaps more damning for documentary scholars, not straightforward enough (too far removed from the earnest truth claims and activisms of the committed documentary).

I doubt that the latter expectation (not serious or political enough) attaches to these films' literary counterparts that appear to bear no such 'burden of representation' and, besides, have a pedigree that stretches back as far as Augustine in the late fifth century. It would take a very long digression to account for the weight of that expectation of political seriousness, the ways that documentary came into its inheritance as 'sober discourse'. (That digression would want to address the role of state support – in the Soviet Union, the UK and elsewhere – in the early decades of documentary's emergence or its centrality to oppositional political movements in Europe and the US in the 1930s or in Latin America in the 1960s.) I will want to return to this question, the charge that autobiographical works evade or elide politics, for I think, in answering that charge, we'll discover some of the grounds for first-person filmmaking's cogency and contemporaneity.

For now, I would like to offer my first thesis on filmic self-inscription for it has to do with the larger relations between autobiographical practices as discussed in the critical literature and the documentary project. It may help to explain why at least some documentary scholars have been slow to accept the autobiographical impulse within the tradition of non-fiction. I would put it this way: *the very idea of autobiography challenges the VERY IDEA of documentary*. Documentary studies is animated (or perhaps bedeviled) by debates regarding the potential for film, through recourse to 'facts' and the logical disposition of arguments, to produce something like 'verifiable knowledge'. Some see this as the epistemological glory of documentary discourse. Non-fiction film, understood in this way (as the arrangement of facts and arguments in filmic form), can turn for institutional support to standards of journalistic reportage, legal disputation, and historiography. Documentary is thus deemed capable of 'delivering the goods', furnishing 'visible evidence', producing knowledge and this capability is taken seriously.

Those who study autobiography – and here we are more likely to encounter literary critics than philosophers or historians – seem less attached to the factual, having long noted the constructed and incomplete character of all self-depiction. Most literary scholars have taken to heart the insights of the late sixteenth-century essayist, Michel de Montaigne, who embraced arbitrariness and indeterminacy in his writing of the *Book of the Self*. Despite his attention over many years and three volumes to topics ranging from friendship to cannibalism or the verses of Virgil, Montaigne's most consistent aims were the testing of his self-conception and the examination of a life lived. Montaigne remained skeptical about knowledge as a totalizable goal:

> I take the first subject that chance offers. They are all equally good to me. And I never plan to develop them completely. For I do not see the whole of anything; nor do those who promise to show it to us …Each particle, each occupation, of a man betrays him and reveals him just as well as any other.
> (1948: 219–20)

Though deeply resistant to globalizing epistemologies of the sort to be developed by René Descartes in the next century, Montaigne never shrank from self-knowledge ('No man ever treated a subject he knew and understood better than I do the subject

I have undertaken; ... in this I am the most learned man alive' (1948: 611)). Yet he avers the contingency and mutability of truth produced in the telling of the self:

> I do not portray being: I portray passing ... My history needs to be adapted to the moment. I may presently change, not only by chance, but also by intention. This is a record of various and changeable occurrences, and of irresolute and, when it so befalls, contradictory ideas: whether I am different myself, or whether I take hold of my subjects in different circumstances and aspects. So, all in all, I may indeed contradict myself now and then; but truth, as Demades said, I do not contradict.
>
> (1948: 611)

Given such Montaignian precepts, it would be fair to say that the sources and philosophical underpinnings of the culture of autobiography are far removed from those of the documentary mainstream which I have characterized (in a chapter of *The Subject of Autobiography* entitled 'Documentary disavowals and the digital') as aggressively modernist, devoted to suasion and certainty.

An understanding of the relations between documentary film and the culture of autobiography requires taking a deeper look at matters historical and technological. For, as regards autobiography, big changes occur after photography. The indexicality of the camera arts bears with it a far greater claim on the real than that associated with a Montaignian essay or a Rembrandt self-portrait. If, as Jerome Bruner (1993: 55) has written, 'autobiography is life construction through "text" construction', the building blocks of a filmic life construction can be not words (rich with connotation) or brushstrokes but indexical signs bearing the stamp of the real. The documentary tradition has long traded in that currency of the real, using it to build and sustain arguments or induce agency. But autobiography, even when constructed of indexical parts, remains an agnostic in the house of certainty.

Does it make sense, then, to think of autobiography as (or in relation to) non-fiction? The answer for me is a resounding yes although the character of that relationship is complex. One of my first efforts to speak publicly about filmic autobiography was entitled 'Fictions of the self in the non-fiction film', a title which I hoped would capture the founding paradox at issue. In my teaching, I have discovered that autobiography offers insight into the general epistemological condition of documentary. What hope have we of producing verifiable or factual accounts if films made on topics of which the maker holds special or even exclusive knowledge, namely, the self, are riddled with equivocation and uncertainty? Put another way, the 'truths' that autobiography offers are often those of the interior rather than of the exterior. I am tempted to call them psychological truths but that only betrays a preference for one kind of psychology (the psychoanalytic model) over another (the behaviorist model, ascendant in the 1950s, on which the truth-seeking of direct cinema is based).

In any case, it seems to me that autobiographical works can breed a kind of healthy skepticism regarding all documentary truth claims. Especially since the 1970s, documentary films have depended on interviews to advance their arguments and reinforce their historical armatures. But the partial and contingent character of self-knowledge so often and so self-consciously on display in autobiographical works cannot help but undermine our confidence in the stories people tell about themselves. So, in my view, if the *very idea* of autobiography challenges the *very idea* of documentary, there is a theoretical and pedagogical value that accrues from that friction.

By way of illustration, consider animator Faith Hubley's *My Universe Inside Out* (US, 1996), a whimsical and highly elliptical account of the artist's 72 years that is short on facts but rich in the evocation of childhood memory, sensory experience, and the quotidian pleasures of family life. It is an autobiographical work that activates both meanings of the corpus – the body of the artist (albeit abstractly rendered) as well as the body of work – for Hubley's film is alive with extracts from the scores of films made by her alone or in tandem with her late husband John Hubley. There is little doubt that the film is a work of autobiography judging by its retrospection, insistent use of the first person pronoun, the unleashing of private imagery that soars alongside the artist's spoken commentary, and the revelation of the end credits that warrants the voice, writing, drawing, and even the cello-playing on the track as the artist's own – a tour-de-force of self-inscription.

The very title, *My Universe Inside Out*, restates the paradox autobiography poses in the face of documentary truth claims. In offering to show us the universe, Hubley would seem to align herself with science or with documentary activism whose aim is comparable, to 'show us life'.[2] But what does the universe look like from the inside out and what does it mean to qualify the universe with the personal possessive pronoun 'my'? It is an interiorized, equivocal and fragmented, one-of-a-kind universe that we are given and in this Hubley's piece is prototypically autobiographical. But in what sense is the film also a documentary? Hubley plays fast and loose with the 'facts', tantalizing more than edifying the audience, offering visual correlatives for elusive interior states rather than demonstrative proofs. If the creative treatment of actuality (the Griersonian thumbnail definition) was meant to authorize the rearrangement of elements of the world given to the eye, that is, if 'actuality' is understood as equivalent to 'exteriority', then this film and much of the autobiographical oeuvre fails the test. But that would also mean that many of the most enduring documentary achievements of the past two decades – the personal and performative works since Marlon Riggs's *Tongues Untied* (US, 1989) that have so enlivened documentary culture – fall outside the pale. Private truths, inner realities have come to be the business of documentary as much as public proclamations. It makes more sense to rewrite this first thesis: *the VERY IDEA of autobiography reinvents the VERY IDEA of documentary*.

Thesis number two is a historical point. *Filmic autobiography is nothing new.* People have been making self-portraits on film and video for some time. But, once again, I need to reintroduce some notion of the received limits of documentary culture in order to make a necessary point. That's because autobiography is a tried and true form in the realm of the avant-garde rather than the non-fiction film. In his classic essay, 'Autobiography in avant-garde film', P. Adams Sitney makes the argument that 'what makes autobiography one of the most vital developments in the cinema of the late Sixties and early Seventies is that the very making of an autobiography constitutes a reflection on the nature of cinema' (1978: 202). The filmmakers Sitney writes about are some of the key figures of the North American Avant-garde – Hollis Frampton, Jerome Hill, Stan Brakhage, and James Broughton. In films as diverse as Frampton's *nostalgia*, Hill's *Film Portrait*, and Brakhage's *Scenes from Under Childhood*, the authority of chronology as well as the ontological status of the image is repeatedly called into question in ways that are medium-specific. Film has the power to stop and even reverse time's inexorable passage, providing a powerful tool for the obsessive investigation of the past, autobiography's stock-in-trade.

In *nostalgia* (US, 1971), a film Sitney calls 'the performative autobiography *par excellence*', a series of photographic images said to have been made by Frampton are given to our view. The film turns on a familiar autobiographical trope – the discovery of the artist's vocation – for Frampton's métier, prior to cinema, was photography. What we witness is the exhaustion and literal combustion of the old art form in favor of the new. As each image in turn begins to burn and turn to ash on what we see is a hot plate placed inches from the camera lens, we are taken out of our spectatorial comfort zone; these photographic images are shown to occupy a flat, two-dimensional picture plane rather than an illusionistic, three-dimensional space of the sort familiar from most cinematic experiences. The discomfort increases as we come to realize that the voice-over commentary accompanying each image is literally out-of-sync with it; what we hear describes the image to come rather than the one we see. Now this 'disjunctive synchronicity' as Sitney calls it is well suited to the autobiographical enterprise given its penchant for placing time out of joint in the service of intensive self-scrutiny. But in cinema such meta-critical escapades are rarely to be found outside the precincts of the avant-garde. Few if any scholars of the documentary film tradition in the 1970s thought to claim *nostalgia* or other autobiographical films like it for non-fiction, in part because the film so blatantly problematizes film's capacity to deliver the past as a narrative of continuity and historical understanding.

A parallel development in the realm of video art deserves mention in this context as well. Developing through the 1970s, conceptual artists, painters and sculptors such as Nam June Paik, Bruce Nauman, Vito Acconci, Richard Serra, Lynda Benglis, and Peter Campus began to experiment with the still-new video apparatus, seeing it as a way to push long-standing artistic preoccupations in new directions. Coming out of the art world of the 1960s, one such preoccupation was with the artist's own body (think 'body art', the Happening, the Living Theater). In 1976, art critic Rosalind Krauss went so far as to opine that 'most of the work produced over the very short span of video art's existence has used the human body as its central instrument' (1976, 1986: 179–80). It was Krauss's belief that narcissism could be generalized as *the* condition of the whole of artists' video. This position might have made sense to audiences schooled in the various video experiments of these first-generation artists, experiments that utilized video tools (the camera, mixer, the playback loop) as adjuncts of the human sensorium. Marshall McLuhan hyperbolized that television was an extension of the central nervous system, but it was video artists who demonstrated the medium's capabilities to write *through* the body, to write *as* the body. As I have argued in 'The Electronic Essay' chapter of *The Subject of Documentary*:

Durable, lightweight, mobile, producing instantaneous results, the video apparatus supplies a dual capability well suited to the [autobiographical] project: it is both screen and mirror, providing the technological grounds for the surveillance of the palpable world, as well as a reflective surface on which to register the self. It is an instrument through which the twin axes of essayistic practice (the looking out and the looking in, the Montaignean 'measure of sight' and 'measure of things') find apt expression.

(2004: 186)

Clearly, then, audio-visual autobiographical efforts are nothing new, but, until the 1990s, these practices tended to fall outside the consensual limits of documentary. The distinctions once drawn among avant-garde filmmakers, video artists, and documentarians seem less and less meaningful today. This may be about the 'convergence' we hear about so much in the media arts and industries or it may just mean that filmic avant-gardism and video art have been so fully absorbed into commercial culture (or annexed by the art world) that little turf remains. Post-1990s documentary culture has, to some degree, inherited and been transformed by the other two traditions.

Thesis three: *Filmic autobiography comes in many forms.* By this I mean to suggest, as I think is already clear, that autobiography (in literature and painting as in film and video) is a protean form, many-headed, given to variation. In my writing, I have described a range of autobiographical *modalities*, diverse approaches to the writing of the self through sound and image. In this matter of modalities, it is the graphological dimension that comes into play, the ways in which self-inscription is constituted through its concrete and distinctive signifying practices. Here I have in mind the essay film, the electronic essay, the diary film, the video confession, the epistolary mode, domestic ethnography, the personal Web page, and the blog. In each instance, varying possibilities for the expression of subjectivity and the telling of life stories arise. Those variances depend, in some measure, on the medium of choice as well as the discursive conditions that prevail. In *The Subject of Documentary,* I argue, for example, for the specificity of the confessional mode, an autobiographical type to be sure but one that unfolds always within a power relationship in which an authoritative interlocutor requires and judges, punishes and reconciles the speech act. I argue for video as having occupied a privileged place in the construction of late twentieth-century confessional culture. I have already spoken of the essayistic legacy of Montaigne. As discourse, the essay embroils the subject in history; self-enunciation and referential object are equally at issue. A self is activated as it measures itself in and against the world it surveys. But allow me a few special words about an autobiographical modality of less familiar coinage, the domestic ethnography.

Domestic ethnography is a mode of autobiographical practice that couples self-interrogation with ethnography's concern for the documentation of the lives of others, in particular, family members who serve as a mirror or foil for the self. Due to kinship ties, subject and object are bound up in one another. The result is self-portraiture refracted through a familial Other. As I argue in the book:

The notion of domestic ethnography has become an increasingly useful classificatory term for a documentary film type that has proliferated. In an era of great genealogical curiosity such as our own, shared DNA becomes a powerful incitation to documentary practice. Festivals and student screenings abound with films about aging or eccentric family members whose lives provide, if only implicitly, insight into the maker's own psyche or corporeal self.

(2004: 216)

But to say that this autobiographical mode is an increasingly common one is not to diminish its importance or appeal. Domestic ethnographies tend to be highly charged investigations brimming with a curious brand of epistephilia, a brew of affection, resentment, even self-loathing. Jonathan Caouette's *Tarnation*, among the most gripping – and unsettling – films I have seen in recent years, is a case in point.

In *Tarnation*, Caouette weaves a complex tale of family dysfunction and shared pathology. Having grown up in Texas in and out of foster homes, intermittently abused and without a father, his young mother, Renee Leblanc, a one-time beauty queen damaged by electro-convulsive therapy and heavy doses of lithium, Caouette, now in his early thirties, shows himself to be a compulsive and lifelong self-documenter. Initially cobbling the piece together on iMovie from countless hours of home videos, family photographs, his own short films, and photo-booth snapshots, Caouette is driven to find himself in the sounds and images of his past. Yet his self-portrait pivots on the figure of his mother, the other of his deepest, most inscrutable and defining relationship.

In a moment of present-tense epiphany near the end of the film, Jonathan speaks directly to his video camera. It is a vivid and gut-wrenching soliloquy, equal parts confession and domestic ethnography, the filmmaker struggling to understand his bond to a woman now so badly damaged and needy. I can think of no other work that so clearly expresses the *necessity* of the domestic ethnographic gesture. Why can't Caouette, well-launched in his reinvention of himself as a budding young New York artist living with his boyfriend and dog, shed his obsessive attention to his mother? Holed up in his bathroom and at point blank range to his camera, Jonathan says of his mother, she is 'always with me ... she's in my hair and behind my eyes.' The choice of Renee as subject is a (literally) inescapable one.

In *Tarnation* as in other instances of domestic ethnography, family life is shown to be the most fundamental crucible of psychosexual identity. Domestic ethnography offers up the maker and his subject locked in a family embrace. The tone of the work, as in *Tarnation*, can swing wildly from the comic, to the Gothic, to the elegiac; given the reciprocity, even consubstantiality, between subject and object, that volatility arises as a feature of the always ambivalent construction of self-knowledge enacted.

It's important to understand this thesis claim – autobiography comes in many forms – as a statement about formal or structural variation as much as about the plurality of autobiographical modalities (the confessional mode, domestic ethnography, the essayistic, etc.). Autobiography is typically depicted as life story-telling and, as such, might appear to be a predictably narrative form bound by the irreversibility of birth and aging toward death. As it happens, narrational stability of this sort turns out to be rare except in the instance of diaristic works bound to the flow of everyday life. The excursus, the epiphany, the flashback are not exceptional so much as emblematic of the temporality which memory work invites. Many cinematic works of autobiography offer a reflection or meditation on a life lived and thus approach their subject through a succession of sallies (as Montaigne characterized these textual moves), providing multiple even conflicting ideas about the self.

This has been true for literary autobiography as well. In *Minima Moralia: Reflections from Damaged Life*, a book that couples self-scrutiny with philosophical discourse, Theodor Adorno argued that:

> the value of thought is measured by its distance from the continuity of the familiar ... knowledge comes to us through a network of prejudices, opinions, innervations, self-corrections, presuppositions and exaggerations, in short through the dense, firmly-founded but by no means uniformly transparent medium of experience.
>
> (1978: 80)

Adorno's notions of the 'by no means uniformly transparent medium of experience' reinforces my own observation that the canny filmic autobiographer's approach to a life lived is often opaque, circuitous, in pieces. Think of a work such as Su Friedrich's *Sink or Swim* (US, 1990) in which the filmmaker's reconstruction of her relationship with her estranged father is offered through a succession of fragments, each beginning with a one-word chapter heading framed against black leader, twenty-six of them, one for each letter of the alphabet displayed in reverse order, beginning with 'z' for 'zygote' and the artist's conception. The film's textual coherence is uneven despite the fact that its narrative continuity (that is, the consistency of the autobiographical tale it tells) remains generally intact and this is so by virtue of its concatenation of several semiotic registers. While the first or 'zygote' chapter properly launches the film's autobiographical trajectory and the fragments that follow narrate a selective but continuous chronology of the artist's life, the sense of linearity is undermined by the thematic discontinuities among the chapters and chapter titles (ranging from 'temptation' and 'seduction' to 'pedagogy' and 'kinship') and by the frequently oblique character of the sound/image relations. Something of a dream logic prevails. Yet, in spite of its vagaries and relative opacity (or, perhaps, because of it), *Sink or Swim* enforces its autobiographical agenda. One senses that a very personal, indeed identity-forming, tale of family relations has been rendered in a form that evokes the tangled web of relationships and conflicting emotional valences.[3]

In turning to a more recent example of formal or structural eccentricity in the autobiographical film, it may be worthwhile recalling the debates surrounding the narrativity of documentary films in general. While nonfiction films tend to retain a strongly narrative character – that is, they often depend upon a chronology to enforce suspense as in the 'crisis structure' invented by direct cinema practitioners or to ground an argument (recall the controversies created by Michael Moore's departure from a strict chronology in *Roger and Me* (US, 1989) which his critics claimed unfairly impugned Ronald Reagan) – this isn't always the case. Brian Winston has argued that, for documentary, non-narrative 'works better in the head than on the screen' (1995: 113–19) yet Basil Wright's *Song of Ceylon* (UK, 1935), one of the more aesthetically satisfying of the Grierson-produced films, assumes a serial structure, its four parts displaying rhythms and themes disjunctive among their parts. Dziga Vertov's *Man with a Movie Camera* (Soviet Union, 1929), surely one of the most ambitious and influential of all documentary films, displays great formal and structural complexity.[4] As has been argued in recent books by Paul Arthur and Jeffrey Skoller, experimentalism of various sorts has maintained a consistent hold on the documentary imagination. Recalling Bruner's general description of the autobiographical project ('life construction through text construction') helps to explain the special attention given the form or structuration of filmic autobiography as a subset of documentary discourse.

In Jay Rosenblatt's *Phantom Limb* (US, 2005), an instance of filmic autobiography doubling as a work of mourning, anomalous structure is shown to be intrinsic to the film's logic. My brief account of it here will do scant service to its depth or complexity. Organized in 12 titled chapters that mimic the 12-step recovery programs endemic to our culture, *Phantom Limb* is filmmaker Rosenblatt's meditation on the death of his younger brother four decades earlier and on the guilt and suffering that have haunted family members since. As a work of mourning, it is produced decades after the fact, a clue to the deferred or dislocated temporality that death and mourning can engender. Using text – short, declarative sentences that provide a framework of past events – interspersed with home movies and archival footage, the film navigates a path between personal testimony and clinical description. The 12 chapter headings or steps (separation, collapse, sorrow, denial, confusion, shock, rage, advice, longing, depression, communication, return) narrate a hypothetical process rather than a story form; the extent to which this process reflects the filmmaker's own experience of mourning or recovery can only be inferred. The form though serial describes what might be considered a recursive narrative arc, one that loops back (as return), offering less resolution than absolution. Absolution, if achieved, results from the film's function as a more or less effective work of mourning familiar from the psychoanalytic literature. As a meditative vehicle (of the sort described by Stephen Tyler in his discussion of 'postmodern ethnography'), it may also function as an evocation of mourning and absolution for others (1986: 122–40).

My final thesis is: *the autobiographical embraces and is inflected by the political.* By this I don't mean to say that autobiography and politics are always or inevitably linked. But I do take exception to the claim that autobiography is, by definition, self-absorbed and solipsistic, outside of agency, incapable of encompassing or elucidating the social field. Montaigne's pronouncement on the essayist's double axis – the measure of sight (*how* one sees) always in tandem with the measure of things (*what* one sees) – puts us on the right track. Self-construction is only with great effort possible outside of social relations; as the site of our mobile, multiple, and often conflicting identities, it is shot through with politics.

In the early 1980s, Michel Foucault wrote that in the face of institutional and state violence and of massive ideological pressures, the central question of our time remained 'Who are we?' (1984: 420). Foucault claimed that in previous epochs, the struggle against domination and exploitation had taken center stage. Now, for an increasing number of people, the fight was against subjection, against the submission of subjectivity. According to Foucault, this circumstance called for a rigorous and historicizing interrogation of power as exerted and experienced. Subjectivity – that multilayered construction of selfhood imagined, performed, and assigned – was proposed as the current site of struggle that mattered most. The assertion of 'who we are', particularly for a citizenry massively separated from the engines of representation – the advertising, news, and entertainment industries – is a vital expression of agency. We are not only what we do in a world of images; we are also what we show ourselves to be. I would therefore argue that Jonathan Caouette's struggles for self-definition, his sorting through of identities that include southern, queer, child prodigy, abuse survivor, foster child, and mama's boy, is an act of survival rather than an aesthetic choice. *Tarnation*, like so many other works of its ilk, enacts a politics of the body (the guts, the bowels, the balls) rather than of the mind. But it is a vital politics nonetheless.

But that is the general case that I believe can be made for the political efficacy of autobiographical works. It is an argument for an 'identity politics' increasingly prevalent in the decades since the dissolution of movement or class-based political struggle. But it is also true that documentary works that are principally devoted to historical and ideological analysis (rather than identity politics) can also display a substantive autobiographical dimension. Think, for instance, of the essayistic works of Michael Moore, the man whose films have produced bigger box office than all other documentary films combined. Moore's *Roger and Me*, *Bowling for Columbine* (US, 2002), and *Fahrenheit 9/11* (US, 2004) are nothing if not the testing grounds of the filmmaker's subjectivity and political judgment. The deeply polarized reaction to these films, especially in the United States, is really a reaction to the man; the two are indissoluble. Such is the legacy of essayism. 'We go hand in hand and at the same pace, my book and I,' wrote Montaigne. 'In other cases one may commend or blame the work apart from the workman: not so here; he who touches the one, touches the other' (1948: 611–12). It is not just Moore's insistent return to Flint and his working-class roots or the ubiquity of Moore himself within the frame that accounts for the oeuvre's autobiographical flavor. His cinema is, above all else, a cinema of 'personal voice', an approach to filmmaking through which the most disparate source material can be linked and stabilized by the writing and voicing of the maker. In this sense, critics missed the point when they lambasted Moore for implying that a Reagan visit to Flint occurred before rather than after the election in *Roger and Me*. In a Michael Moore film, the visuals are always used to support the polemic which is, in turn, an extension of Moore's experience and political insight. He is an essayist, a political essayist, in a national culture that expects political *journalism* and of a particular sort (i.e., geared to information gathering, image-driven reportage, and balanced coverage). No wonder the strongest moments in a Michael Moore film depend more on sound than image: think only of his representation of the toppling of the Twin Towers in *Fahrenheit 9/11*. Film turns to radio. Memory and association rush in to fill the gaps left by the black screen. As always, it is the voice – primary agent of Moore's subjectivity – that supervenes and restores order.

Something similar could be said for the work of Cameroonian filmmaker Jean-Marie Teno. Since the early 1980s, Teno has produced a series of films that examine African, and especially Cameroonian, post-colonial experience, the dreams and deceptions, the ironies and the idiosyncracies, but always filtered through a personal lens, a personal voice. Again, it is the writing and the voice that set the tone. As Teno begins his most ambitious film to date, *Afrique: Je te plumerai* (1992), we are shown Yaoude, the capital city of the Cameroon. And, as we are introduced to the complexities and challenges of living in a land decades removed from French rule but still unfree, we are also told something of Teno's own youth and experience, offered anecdotes that make concrete the general. The film mixes satiric, comic, and musical elements, employs reconstruction, interview, and archival footage to produce a historically aware, nuanced yet didactic account of Cameroonian life. It is again the voice that threads its way through the film, the voice of the filmmaker, that underscores the ways that subjectivity, the 'I' of the writing self, can lead the way, personalize the subject matter and soften up the audience for greater receptivity. Teno's stated reasons for making the film are inarguably political: 'I sought the relationship of cause and effect between the unbearable past, with its colonial violence, and the present. I sought the reason why a land with well-structured traditional societies changed into an incompetent state.' But it is the personal and self-reflective dimension of *Afrique: Je te plumerai* that focalizes and contextualizes those political aims in a universalizing experiential framework.

By way of conclusion, I will reprise my tentative theses: (1) the *very idea* of autobiography reinvents the *very idea* of documentary; (2) filmic autobiography is nothing new; (3) filmic autobiography comes in many forms; and (4) the autobiographical embraces and is inflected by the political. I have posited these points in the spirit of exploration of the still little-known and have sought to persuade through recourse to examples drawn from quite disparate sources – animation, recent art-house fare, box office bonanzas, and Third Cinema. And yet I have only scratched the surface of a phenomenon that resists totalizing accounts and taxonomies. If I have preferred to speak at times of the autobiographical rather than of autobiography it is because the adjectival usage allows for the messiness and slippage endemic to the subject. I am convinced that our topic is one whose importance will only be enhanced in the years ahead. As I say at the close of *The Subject of Documentary*'s introductory chapter: 'The time has certainly arrived ... for a reassessment, for the open acknowledgement that the subject *in* documentary has, to a surprising degree, become the subject *of* documentary' (2004: xxiv).

Notes

1   Here I'm thinking of the series of conferences and screenings entitled 'First Person Film', organized by Alisa Lebow, Tony Dowmunt and others in the UK over the past several years. Catherine Russell's excellent book, *Experimental Ethnography* concludes with a fertile investigation into 'autoethnography' which she entitles 'journeys of the self' (1999: 275–314). Finally, an increasing number of sessions at the Society for Cinema and Media Studies and Visible Evidence conferences have, in recent years, been devoted to the investigation of autobiographical works.

2   The reference here is to Thomas Waugh's important anthology, *'Show Us Life'*.

3 For further discussion of Su Friedrich's *Sink or Swim*, see Renov (2004: 219–22).

4 See in this regard, Petric (1987).

4 ' ... To Leave the Confinements of His Humanness'

Authorial voice, death and constructions of nature in Werner Herzog's *Grizzly Man*

Thomas Austin

If, in the face of proliferating formats, hybridization and the interpenetration of modes of fiction and non-fiction, one can talk with any authority about a shared documentary project,[1] it might be tempting to characterize it as concerned with the retrieval of time: re/calling the past into the present, and preserving something of the past or present for future contemplation. Documentary could be seen to enact a search for, and testify to the continuing significance of, the 'then' in the 'now', or, as Bill Schwarz (2004: 105) puts it, 'the presence of the past within the present'.[2] This is already a reductive summary of documentaries' complex and multiple relationships to time, however. These will also include speculations and propositions about possible futures, as well as attempts to show audiences what is happening in the now, for instance, in the tradition of social problem films and television programming which may, however rhetorically, demand an urgent response in and beyond the moment of viewing. In any case, the endeavour of temporal recovery is in a sense doomed to be incomplete, imperfect, almost always less successful than intended. Yet it remains an abiding quest in much documentary output, and one which has also precipitated self-reflexive investigations of the mode's relationships with time and profilmic space, with how time has left (and will leave) its traces, however intermittently, on diverse places and bodies.[3]

The project of attempted retrieval brings particular formal and ethical dilemmas when a documentary deploys and recontextualizes material filmed by a now dead protagonist. How does the finally assembled text organize, mediate, and respond to the gestures and decisions of the original image-maker? In what ways might this posthumous figure's presence, in front of and behind the camera, both signal and refute their physical absence? And how do such questions become further compli-cated when the finished text circulates under the name of a living auteur?

In 2005, Werner Herzog's documentary *Grizzly Man* was released, gaining both critical acclaim and commercial success.[4] It portrays the life and death of amateur wildlife expert Timothy Treadwell, who spent 13 summers among grizzly bears in

Alaska, until he was killed by one. This chapter explores the ethical and formal dimensions of the representation of Treadwell's death, and how *Grizzly Man* engages with differing constructions of nature, via the coexistence of optimistic/'sentimental' and pragmatic/'realist' orientations towards the natural world as relayed in the film. But I begin my analysis by considering Herzog and his collaborators' framing and mediation of video footage shot by Treadwell, and the consequent 'double authorship' of the final film.[5] This includes an interrogation of Herzog's performance of authorial intervention and persona, via extratextual activities including promotional interviews, and his voice-over and an onscreen appearance within *Grizzly Man* itself.

Double authorship

Grizzly Man opens with the sound of nondiegetic guitar music, slowly fading out, and a long shot from a static camera of two bears grazing on all fours, mountains visible behind them. Wearing sunglasses and dressed in black, a blond-haired man (later revealed to be Treadwell) walks from behind the camera into the foreground of the scene, kneels down and starts talking direct to camera:

> I'm out in the prime cut of the big green. Behind me is Ed and Rowdie, members of an up-and-coming sub-adult group. They're challenging every-thing, including me.

Throughout the film, Treadwell's mode of self-presentation oscillates between the confessional and intimate style of a video diarist and the more obviously performa-tive register of a would-be television presenter, asserting his familiarity with the animals and his own endangerment. To borrow terminology from Michael Renov's discussion of autobiography and documentary (2004: 185–6), Treadwell is both 'looking out' (at the bears and their wilderness) and 'looking in' (at himself). With its threats and opportunities for (self-)discovery, nature functions here as a solace and retreat from human society, but also as a testing ground, energizing and validating Treadwell's sense of self.[6]

It is never entirely clear how much of his self-memorialization was intended for private use, and how much was amassed for some never-realized media project.[7] The opening sequence tends more towards the latter, but remains somewhat ambiguous. On the one hand, the footage is remarkable for its close and sustained visual access to the bears, perhaps 40 or 50 yards from Treadwell. His delivery, while increasingly idiosyncratic, is also coherent and eloquent, and not especially odd to television viewers used to celebrity specials and 'action man' series like the late Steve Irwin's *Crocodile Hunter*.[8] On the other hand, the images are constrained by reliance on a single, static camera, with none of the multiple angles, editing patterns, or use of slow motion to be expected from 'professional' wildlife coverage on film or television. In addition to these technical limitations, Treadwell is evidently working alone. His location on screen right obscures one of the bears, and he has no colleague to advise him on repositioning. But the sequence never displays the utter amateurishness of, for example, the home video material used at the start of Andrew Jarecki's *Capturing the Friedmans* (US, 2003).

As Treadwell proceeds with his monologue, the subtitle 'Timothy Treadwell (1957–2003)' appears on screen beneath his image. Addressing the camera and his presumed audience, Treadwell continues, with a smile:

> Goes with the territory. If I show weakness, if I retreat, I may be hurt, I may be killed. I must hold my own within this land. For once there is weakness they will exploit it, they will take me out, they will decapitate me, they will chop me into bits and pieces, I'm dead. But so far [saluting the camera with a finger] I persevere, persevere.

After two minutes of monologue, Treadwell smiles, blows a kiss to the bears and walks back to the camera. From offscreen space his disembodied voice says, 'I can smell death all over my fingers.'

The film fades quickly in and out of black to show another scene of seven bears, with the camera – presumably operated by Treadwell – occasionally panning and zooming to concentrate on two bears in particular. Over the images, a new voice makes itself heard, declaring:

> All these majestic creatures were filmed by Timothy Treadwell, who lived among wild grizzlies for 13 summers. He went to the remote areas of the Alaskan peninsula believing that he was needed there to protect the animals and educate the public. During his last five years out there he took along a video camera and shot over 100 hours of footage. What Treadwell intended was to show these bears in their natural habitat. Having myself filmed in the wilderness of the jungle I found that beyond a wildlife film, in his material lay dormant a story of astonishing beauty and depth. I discovered a film of human ecstasies and darkest inner turmoil, as if there was a desire in him to leave the confinements of his humanness and bond with the bears, Treadwell reached out, seeking a primordial encounter. But in doing so he crossed an invisible border line.

This is the voice of Werner Herzog, familiar to some viewers at least from his previous documentary works, and an appearance in Harmony Korine's *Julien Donkey-Boy* (US, 1999). The sound and image tracks are synchronized here, so that when Herzog speaks of Treadwell reaching out, this is timed to coincide with footage of him doing just that, moving his hand carefully from behind the camera towards the snout of an inquisitive bear. The effect is to prioritize the voice-over at this point, producing the images as illustrations of the spoken word.

Bill Nichols (1991: 223–4) has noted the controlling function of voice-over commentary in ethnographic films, one that may also pertain in a wider range of documentaries: 'Voice-over commentary recuperates images that defy mastery ... The description stands in for the described, erasing any gap between form and meaning.' However, the role of voice-over is not quite so straightforward in *Grizzly Man*. Most obviously, two voices (Treadwell's and Herzog's) are foregrounded, offering interpretations and commentaries throughout the film. Sometimes they are in agreement, sometimes in opposition.

These first scenes, with their two distinct voices, thus establish the dual authorship of *Grizzly Man*, and effectively announce its double mediation of the bears and their wilderness: through the interventions made by Treadwell – via his profilmic actions, his video footage and frequent use of direct address to camera – and by Herzog and his collaborators – via the selection from and arrangement of footage shot by Treadwell, use of interview and archive material, the imposition of music, and, most notably, voice-over commentary. The latter is both opinionated and authoritative but also subjective, grounded in personal experience and perception. The two voices, the two sets of interventions, the two claims to authorial status, coexist in an unequal relationship. Herzog's decisions frame those made by Treadwell. Herzog's voice is empowered to comment on that of Treadwell, while the latter, by contrast, has nothing to say about Herzog's commentary and can offer no critique of his work.

The privileging of Herzog's voice – and later his physical presence – produce in the text a second locus of authority and possible audience investment beyond the figure of Treadwell. It also constitutes an invitation to approach *Grizzly Man* as an authored work. This invitation was taken up by much critical coverage of the film, including a feature in *Sight and Sound* magazine, which noted Herzog's tendency in the last decade or so to focus on 'extreme stories of human endeavour – of ecstasy, death and transfiguration' (James 2006: 24), and identified *Grizzly Man* as the latest instance of this.[9]

An auteurist approach might also trace some significant continuities between Herzog's fiction films of the 1970s and *Grizzly Man*. For instance, Gideon Bachmann's (1977) description of a typical Herzog plot seems to anticipate Treadwell's trajectory, at least as represented in the film:

> An innocent is thrown into the world, unprepared, encounters despair and destruction and loses, leaving behind an emptier, more desperate landscape. This in a nutshell, has been the story line of each film Herzog has made ... the films are all records of doomed struggles. But hardly ever in the history of cinema has the depiction of doom carried so strong a message of life.
>
> (1977: 2)

Herzog's status as auteur is (re)asserted by intratextual elements within *Grizzly Man* (principally his voice-over commentary and single on-screen appearance) and also by extratextual appearances and citations. The latter function both as satellite texts put into circulation around the film for promotional purposes, and as more autonomous constructions of Herzog which may not necessarily be encountered as ancillaries to *Grizzly Man*.[10]

Much like film stars, whose extrafilmic manifestations and promotional labour have long been recognized and investigated by scholars, directors-as-stars need be conceived of as discursive, cultural and commercial phenomena that are constructed across a range of media outlets not restricted to their films. For instance, Timothy Corrigan has suggested that the media interview 'is where the auteur, in addressing cults of fans and critical viewers, can engage and disperse his or her own organising agency as auteur ... writing and explaining ... a film through the promotion of a certain intentional self' (Corrigan 1991: 108–9, cited in Grant 2000: 103).

Herzog's particular performance as auteur, via extratextual and intratextual cues to the viewer and/or reader, is an unmistakably physical one. Certainly, his voice, and the body from which it originates,[11] are more central to his persona, as a tool of his filmmaking and its promotion, than that of, say, Steven Spielberg or art cinema peers like Wim Wenders. While relatively unremarkable in themselves,[12] Herzog's body and voice have become freighted over time with a particular and complicated set of connotations that could be summarized as centred on notions of endangerment, empathy and intensity.[13]

Clearly, commentators, journalists and critics have all played their parts in the discursive construction of Herzog's reputation. But the director himself has also participated in the fabrication of his persona since the early years of his career. Much like Treadwell, Herzog repeatedly presents himself in the role of the male adventurer. For instance, in addition to filming in remote locations and extreme conditions, from the Amazon to the Sahara, he has performed a number of feats of endurance and risk-taking which (whether or not intended as such) are readable as acts of self-dramatization. These include walking from Munich to Paris in 1974 to visit Lotte Eisner (recounted in his 1981 book, *Of Walking in Ice*), and walking 2,000 kilometres around the German border in 1984.[14] In 1978, Herzog literally made a spectacle of himself by eating one of his shoes live on stage at UC Theatre in Berkeley, California, in honour of the premiere of Errol Morris' debut film *Gates of Heaven*, as captured in Les Blank's short film *Werner Herzog Eats his Shoe* (US, 1980).[15]

More recently, during a televised interview to promote *Grizzly Man* conducted on a hillside in Los Angeles, Herzog was shot in the stomach by an unseen assailant with an air rifle. This event became rapidly incorporated into the mythology of the director as risk-taking visionary. The footage, including the incredulous response of interviewer Mark Kermode when Herzog reveals his blood-stained boxer shorts ('You're bleeding! Somebody ... created a wound in your abdomen!') and Herzog's relaxed reply ('It's not significant. It's not an everyday thing, but it doesn't surprise me to be shot at'), was screened on BBC2's *The Culture Show* following an introduction that noted 'even meeting Herzog isn't without its risks'.[16] The broadcast sequence concluded with Herzog telling Kermode:

> I think the bottom line is, the poet must not avert his eyes. You have to take a bold look at what is your environment, what is around you, even the ugly things, even the decadent things, even the dangerous things ... I've done good battle and I've been a good soldier of cinema, and that's what I want to be.

To return to the film, as previously noted, Herzog's voice is privileged as a locus of authority throughout *Grizzly Man*, even while it avoids the conventional claims to objectivity of the documentary 'voice of God' by repeatedly stressing the subjectivity of the speaker. Most obviously, the commentary develops his own interpretation of Treadwell's life and work. For example, in one sequence, Treadwell has completed his address to camera when a fox that he has named Spirit runs into shot from some bushes in the background, followed by her cubs. The aleatory nature of this footage and other shots is foregrounded by Herzog's voice-over, which notes 'as a filmmaker sometimes things fall into your lap that you couldn't expect, never even dream of. There is something like an inexplicable magic of cinema.'

In a later instance, speaking over footage shot on a tripod-mounted camera left by Treadwell as he climbs a wooded hill in preparation to descend in one of his 'wild

Timmy jungle scenes', Herzog comments: 'In his action movie mode, Treadwell probably did not realize that seemingly empty moments had a strange secret beauty. Sometimes images themselves develop their own life, their own mysterious stardom.' The beauty of grasses and trees blowing in the wind in this scene retains something of the 'harnessing of spontaneity' which Dai Vaughan has located in the films of the Lumière brothers via the visual capture of non-human movements (plants, leaves, water), to which one might add the motility of animals.[17] But an auteur-oriented viewing strategy might also recall the shots of windswept trees and fields in Herzog's *The Enigma of Kaspar Hauser* (West Germany, 1974). Seen via this interpretive prism, Herzog's selection of such a sequence from Treadwell's footage, and the foregrounding of his particular reading of it via commentary, become yet more evidence of his auteurist stamp. The intratextually-cued recontextualization of the shot results in the production of 'Herzogian' imagery even when derived from another's filmed material, reaffirming Herzog as *Grizzly Man*'s dominant author figure.

The prefigured end: Treadwell's death

In addition to possible auteurist readings of the film, *Grizzly Man* can be placed in the context of popular screen representations of scenarios of (usually male) endangerment. Herzog's own documentaries *Wings of Hope* (Germany, 2000) and *Little Dieter Needs to Fly* (France, UK, Germany, 1997, remade by Herzog as *Rescue Dawn* (US, 2007))[18] are relevant here, as is the best-selling memoir and documentary adaptation *Touching the Void* (UK, 2003), along with a host of fiction films. The template has been reworked in the influential US reality television programme *Rescue 911* and a host of imitators across the world.[19] But all these examples have happy endings, concluding with acts of rescue and/or survival against the odds, which are crucial to their appeal.[20] Treadwell's trajectory is very different, and is signalled as such almost from the beginning of the film, as well as in the trailer and associated promotion. Furthermore, while the extent of the profilmic threat varies across these other instances, many of which employ reconstructions, its existence is repeatedly stressed, even perhaps exaggerated, in Treadwell's monologues and self-promotion, and certainly imparts to much of his footage an undeniable element of what André Bazin called 'the inimitable ... that which of its very nature can only occur once, namely risk, adventure, death' (1967, 2005: 158).

 Grizzly Man's narrative pattern of gradual and interrupted progress towards an anticipated moment of climax – Treadwell's death – is consistent with canonical narration in fiction film. As David Bordwell (1985: 159) has noted, the mechanisms of retardation and delay that manage movement towards an expected ending are central to textual attempts to organize audience involvement and response. But these structures produce particular impacts when the climax is a non-fictional death. The first gesture towards Treadwell's end is the early subtitle revealing the date of his death at 46 years old. Subsequent to this, the repeated references to endangerment and possible death in his monologues further sensitize the issue and raise expectations of the presumed denouement. Treadwell's active visual and aural presence is overlaid with the knowledge that he is (will soon be) dead, recalling Roland Barthes' celebrated phrase, 'He is dead and he is going to die' (1980, 1984: 95).[21]

In interview, a friend of Treadwell's relates hearing the news of his death. Then, a quarter of an hour into the film, Willy Fulton, a pilot and friend who flew Treadwell to and from his summer base every year, describes finding the bear that killed and ate him and his girlfriend Amie Huguenard, before returning with others who shot the bear. Following this, the immediacy of video footage of Treadwell recorded ten days before his death, crouched on the bank of a river, while 'Olie', a 'big old grumpy bear' that may have killed him, wades through the water looking for salmon only a few feet away, takes on a neuralgic and voyeuristic charge that it might not otherwise have had. Treadwell comments:

> It is the old bear, one who is struggling for survival, and an aggressive one at that, who is the one that you must be very careful of, for these are the bears that on occasion, do, for survival, kill and eat humans. Could Olie, the big old bear possibly kill and eat Timothy Treadwell? What do you think Olie? I think if you were weak around him, you're going down his gullet, going down the pipe.

One consequence of Herzog's placement of this material is that Treadwell is effectively shown anticipating and prefiguring his own death. This kind of performance of endangerment is not uncommon in 'action man' wildlife shows such as Irwin's *Crocodile Hunter*, but what makes the routine qualitatively different in this instance is the viewer's suspicion that Treadwell will indeed be killed by this bear.[22] The sequence is followed immediately by still photographs of armed men on the hill where Treadwell and Huguenard died, accompanied by Fulton's voice-over describing finding 'what was left of Tim's body'.

Around the mid-point of the film, Franc Fallico, the coroner who examined Treadwell and Huguenard, mentions the existence of an audio tape recording of their deaths, made with Treadwell's camera, which was running with the lens cap left on. Fallico gestures with his hands and looks urgently into camera as he half recounts, half re-enacts the voices on the tape: 'We can hear the sounds of Amie screaming and the sounds of Timothy moaning ... and I hear Amie beating on the top of this bear's head with a frying pan, and Timothy is saying "Run away, let go, run away, Amie, run away". ... Amie, we know, fought back for approximately six minutes.' The audience is reliant on Fallico's mediation of the tape here, and this process is extended in the next sequence.

Largely redundant in narrative and argumentational terms, the scene is crucial in further spectacularizing the two deaths, and also in developing Herzog's presence in the film. He is shown listening via headphones to the tape while Jewel Palovak, Treadwell's business partner and ex-girlfriend, holds his video camera on her lap. A slow zoom in past Herzog frames Palovak frontally in medium close-up, looking with an astonished and concerned expression at Herzog, as he says, off camera, 'I hear rain and I hear Amie "get away, get away, go away".' The camera then pans slowly back to a close-up of Herzog's head, shot from behind his shoulder. With his hand over his eyes, he is silent for several seconds. There is a cut to the initial two-shot framing and Herzog asks Palovak, 'Can you turn it off?' He removes the headphones and swallows, then Palovak starts to cry quietly. 'Jewel, you must never listen to this.' 'I know, Werner, I'm never going to.' After another cut, Herzog hands Palovak the empty videotape box and advises her to destroy the tape. The screen fades to black.[23]

In this exchange, the responses of both Herzog and Palovak provide both verbal and non-verbal cues to the viewer as to the traumatic content of the audio tape. While both are clearly affected by it, it is notable that Herzog, with primary access, is less emotionally demonstrative (and more authoritative, directive) in his reaction than Palovak. This gendered distinction is partly facilitated by the positioning and movement of the camera, which foregrounds Palovak's face as the ground on which emotion is rendered visible. And it is impossible to tell to what extent editing has compressed the duration of the scene in order to focus on her tears. Thus, the deaths of Treadwell and Huguenard, having occurred beyond visibility, are multiply mediated via the (unheard) sound recording, Herzog's verbal and physical gestures, and those of Palovak – their impact ultimately exhibited, embodied and spectacularized via the responsive female body.[24]

Heather Nunn has suggested that 'death is a fetishized object for many documentary filmmakers because in their desire to capture the real, whether in objective or subjective form, death can both "powerfully convey a sense of reality" but "it is also the place where the real ends" ' (Nunn 2004: 422, citing Fetveit 1999).[25] *Grizzly Man* exemplifies just such an ambivalence in its doubled movements of approach towards, and retreat from, the moment of death.[26] These play out through a series of suggestions and deferrals. Ultimately, in the absence of any more direct visual traces of violent death, Herzog keeps the sound recording of this final event at one remove, even while staging an indirect demonstration of its power via the filmed responses of Palovak and himself.

What, then, are the ethical consequences of this re-presentation of the deaths of Treadwell and Huguenard?[27] Bill Nichols (1991: 82–9) proposes a taxonomy of the relations between camera/subject/viewer which pertain when death is filmed and watched, codifying them as a series of gazes. These formal-ethical issues become further complicated in a case like *Grizzly Man* where the filmmaker has recorded his own death (and that of another) but a third person has assembled the finished film into which this event is inserted.

In its lack of images, Treadwell's sound recording carries marks of contingency which Nichols associates with an 'accidental gaze' (1991: 82–3). The orientation towards death mobilized in *Grizzly Man* as a whole also has something in common with Nichols' concept of a 'humane gaze', and might be termed a *retrospective* humane gaze. The humane gaze is characterized by Nichols (1991: 86) in terms of its stress upon 'a form of empathetic bond across the barrier between the living and the dead (or those whose death is imminent and those whose death is, as yet, unforeseen).' I shall argue below that Herzog's approach to Treadwell remains fundamentally empathetic, despite his clearly stated disagreements with Treadwell's understanding of the natural world.

Nichols locates the humane gaze in 'cases where death cannot be prevented by intervention' and suggests that 'Like endangerment, the display of a humane gaze may absolve the filmmaker of fault for seeking out and gazing at the death of others'

(1991: 86). Of course, whether or not this absolution works for *Grizzly Man* will depend on the dispositions and responses of any given viewer watching the film. However, it is fair to say that the distancing mechanisms of both chronological remove (this death had already happened before Herzog and his crew began to make their film), and the deliberate withholding of the sound recording, may have a mitigating effect upon the guilt of filmmaker and viewer. They also tend to emphasize the pastness and irretrievability of the final outcome.

In the sequence under discussion Herzog and Palovak function as emotional relay points for the audience, who are invited to empathize with Treadwell at the moment of his death as well as being asked to acknowledge and understand his fantasies and motivations through watching and listening to the film as a whole. As the critical but ultimately empathizing auteur, Herzog channels and mediates the extreme experiences of Treadwell's adventures and death, both through his body (listening to the tape and telling Palovak and the audience about it) and through the film that he has assembled and promoted. This dual role is perhaps what Nick James (2006: 26) was responding to when he described Herzog as 'the avatar of intensity' in his own documentaries. Yet Herzog's auteurist empathy can only be realized via reliance on, and at the expense of, Palovak: positioned, incited and produced as the expressive female body, which indirectly renders manifest the otherwise invisible, unrepresentable trauma of death.

Anthropomorphism and the evacuation/return of the female

Herzog's decision to withhold the audio of the bear attack perpetuates the silence of Amie Huguenard, who remains a voiceless and peripheral presence in Treadwell's footage. The latter's hyperbolic performance of masculine self-reliance on camera led him to minimize his collaboration with female colleagues and companions. (In addition to Huguenard and Palovak, *Grizzly Man* features an interview with Kathleen Parker, a friend who provided a base for Treadwell from which he flew with Fulton to the area of national park that he called the Grizzly Sanctuary.) In a voice-over, Herzog describes Huguenard as 'a great unknown of this film'. Her family refused to be interviewed 'and Amie herself remains hidden in Treadwell's footage. In nearly 100 hours of his video she appears exactly two times ... Only through Treadwell's diaries do we know that she was frightened of bears.'

In Treadwell's material, this deliberate evacuation of the human female is paired with an anthropomorphizing attitude towards the bears that mobilizes gender stereotypes in both naming them and describing their actions. For example, here is some of Treadwell's 'post-fight' commentary on a clash between two male bears:

> the fight between Sergeant Brown and Mickey for the right to court Saturn, the queen of the Grizzly Maze. We love that bear Mickey, we love him! We love him. But Mickey, I've been down that street, I've been down that street. You don't always get the chick you want, let me tell you.

Thus far, Treadwell's footage offers another instance of a well-established tradition of delivering gender clichés in wildlife documentaries. As Barbara Crowther (1995: 130) has noted, one consequence of anthropomorphism may be the effective naturalization of human gender norms via depictions of animal behaviours, particularly male rivalry, sex, reproduction and the 'survival of the fittest'. But Treadwell then shifts from his investment in, and identification with Mickey to a playful declaration of romantic interest in Saturn, relayed to Mickey as if he were a friendly male rival:

> And I'll tell you something, if Saturn was a female human, I can just see how beautiful she is as a bear. Wow! I've always called her the Michelle Pfeiffer of bears out here ... You lay there, I'm gonna go off with your girlfriend. Don't beat me up over it! Things are bad with me and the human women, but not so bad that I have to be hitting on bears yet.

The figure of the elided female has returned in the flow of Treadwell's monologue, which moves from the male bears to the object of their rivalry, to his own relations with women back in the human world.

A daydream

Grizzly Man can be seen to offer a commentary not just on Treadwell as a particular individual who employs both anthropomorphism and zoomorphism in his 'work', but also on wider cultural trends and strategies in the representation of human/nature/animal relations. Jean Baudrillard has pointed to the ways in which the muteness of animals provides something like a *tabula rasa* on to which human desires, anxieties and expectations are readily projected. He writes:

> They, the animals, do not speak. In a universe of increasing speech, of the constraint to confess and to speak, only they remain mute ... they only furnish the responses one asks for. It is their way of sending the Human back to his [*sic*] circular codes, behind which their silence analyzes us.
>
> (1994: 137–8)

Baudrillard's argument is pertinent to the representation of Treadwell in *Grizzly Man* insofar as the latter's escape from what Herzog calls 'the people's world' and his hopes for a transcendental bonding with nature and its wild creatures are so clearly and avowedly driven by his own particular experiences, disappointments and aspirations.[28] Moreover, Herzog presents some of Treadwell's attitudes as symptomatic of the wider significance of human desires in shaping constructions of the natural world.

In his influential essay, 'Why look at animals?' John Berger writes:

> Nature ... acquires the meaning of what has grown organically, what was not created by man, in contrast to the artificial structures of human civilisation. At the same time, it can be understood as that aspect of human inwardness which has remained natural, or at least tends or longs to become natural once more. According to this view of nature, the life of a wild animal

becomes an ideal, an ideal internalised as a feeling surrounding a repressed desire. The image of a wild animal becomes the starting point of a daydream.

(1980, 1991: 17)[29]

Berger proposes that the animal image, the starting-point of the daydream, is 'a point from which the day-dreamer departs with his back turned'. He illustrates this prevalent state of 'confusion' about wild animals with the following news story:

> London housewife Barbara Carter won a 'grant a wish' charity contest, and said she wanted to kiss and cuddle a lion. Wednesday night she was in a hospital in shock and with throat wounds. Mrs Carter, 46, was taken to the lions' compound of the safari park at Bewdley, Wednesday. As she bent forward to stroke the lioness, Suki, it pounced and dragged her to the ground. Wardens later said 'We seem to have made a bad error of judgment. We have always regarded the lioness as perfectly safe.'[30]

The impulses, desires and situations behind this kind of 'daydream' – an idealization of nature that is often impractical and sometimes dangerous, but is widely promoted via some mediations of nature – need to be interrogated further, rather than being ridiculed or pathologized. This is precisely what *Grizzly Man* achieves. Herzog's voice-over commentary repeatedly registers his disagreements with Treadwell's attitude to nature. For example: 'Here I differ with Treadwell. He seemed to ignore the fact that in nature there are predators. I believe the common denominator of the universe is not harmony, but chaos, hostility and murder'; 'what haunts me is that in all the faces of all the bears that Treadwell ever filmed, I discover no kinship, no understanding, no mercy. I see only the overwhelming indifference of nature.' But the film as a whole never loses sympathy for Treadwell, or consigns him entirely to the realm of the Other. Instead, it proposes similarities between him and 'us', as well as points of difference. A different treatment of the story might have diagnosed Treadwell's 13-year 'daydream' from a more comfortable distance, positioning him as the Other to be pitied, ridiculed or judged.

Herzog's last voice-over, accompanying Treadwell's footage of bears chasing along mud banks, asserts not difference but similarity, and constitutes an attempt to connect despite disagreement:

> Treadwell is gone. The argument how wrong or how right he was disappears into a distance, into a fog. What remains is his footage and while we watch the animals in their joys of being, in their grace and ferociousness, a thought becomes more and more clear. That it is not so much a look at wild nature as it is an insight into ourselves, our nature. And that, for me, beyond his mission, gives meaning to his life and to his death.

The last line of this commentary is run over a shot of Treadwell, followed by two foxes, walking away from the camera across a sunlit meadow. Then there is a cut to Willy Fulton in his plane, singing along to Don Edwards' song 'Coyotes'. The role of music here (and in earlier moments) is significant in inviting sympathy and empathy with Treadwell. This is made explicit in this valedictory sequence, where Treadwell's friend sings along to the only vocal music track in the film, substituting Treadwell's name at one point in the litany of loss: 'Now the longhorns are gone and the drovers are gone and the Comanches are gone and the outlaws are gone …'. The lyrics continue 'this is no place for an hombre like I am, in this new world of asphalt and steel', as the last images of Treadwell show him walking along the side of a river, moving, apparently irretrievably, away from the camera, followed by two bears splashing in the shallows. In these sequences sound and image function together to both propose and acknowledge feelings of mourning and loss – including the loss of connections to 'nature', even if these are more imagined than real – not to dismiss them as (only) sentimental or absurd.

Conclusion

Ultimately, *Grizzly Man* constitutes an interrogation of both prevalent attitudes to nature in the west and the functions of documentary. Writing on documentary has long grappled with the relationship – often proposed as dichotomous – between evidentiality and aestheticization, accommodated in a much-debated balance in John Grierson's famous phrase 'the creative treatment of actuality'.[31] For instance, Siegfried Kracauer argued that aesthetic 'beauty' and evidential 'truth' stand in mutual opposition: 'it is precisely the snapshot quality of [most newsreel and documentary] pictures that makes them appear as authentic documents'.[32] However, for Herzog, artifice in documentary does not stand in opposition to truth. On the contrary, it may indeed be necessary in order to arrive at a higher truth, beyond cinema-verité's 'merely superficial truth, the truth of accountants'.[33] In 'The Minnesota declaration: truth and fact in documentary cinema', Herzog wrote: '… there is such a thing as poetic, ecstatic truth. It is mysterious and elusive and can be reached only through fabrication and imagination and stylization.'[34] This is indeed what Treadwell – as re-presented by Herzog, that is – achieved, even in his 'kind warrior' posturings and naive sentimentality. Of course, the film also operates as a critique of such attitudes and their inculcation via the media.[35] But (unlike Berger) the critique presented in *Grizzly Man* never loses sight of the power and promise of the 'daydream' in its urge to judge it.

Acknowledgements

Thanks to Charlotte Adcock, James Montgomery, and Silke Panse.

Notes

1 Of course, such a move is not unproblematic, even as a rhetorical gesture. This would have been as true of earlier moments in history as it is now, in what John Corner (2002: 257) has termed the era of 'postdocumentary' culture.

2 For a wider-ranging consideration of 'the preservative obsession' (Schwarz 2004: 87), encompassing museums, theme parks, cinema, and the processes of historiography itself, see Rosen (2001).

3 For instance, although very different in form and content, both Claude Lanzmann's *Shoah* (France, 1985) and Errol Morris' *Mr. Death* (US, 1999) stage self-reflexive considerations of time and space, history and evidence, in relation to the Holocaust, interrogating how landscape functions as a visible, filmable, but hugely insufficient index of this event.

4 *Grizzly Man* grossed $3 million in three months in the US. Source: imbd.com. The film was produced by Discovery Docs for theatrical release and subsequent television screening on the Discovery Channel, and distributed theatrically in the US by Lions Gate Films. To this extent, it was an early beneficiary of Lions Gate Entertainment's move into documentary distribution following its successful involvement in the release of Michael Moore's *Fahrenheit 9/11* (US, 2004). In March 2006, *Grizzly Man* was screened on the Discovery Channel. The film was followed by a 30-minute 'companion special' that considered 'controversies such as claims of fictitious interviews in *Grizzly Man*'. Sources: www.grizzlyman.com. production.html, http://dsc.discovery.com/convergence/grizzlyman/about/ discoverydocs.html, both accessed September 2005, and www.discovery channel.ca/on_tv/releases/grizzly_man, accessed November 2006.

5 The rights to use Treadwell's video footage were granted by Jewel Palovak, his business partner and co-founder of Grizzly People. Herzog asked to direct the film while the project was already in development for Discovery, which had produced a television special on Treadwell in 1999. Source: www.wernerherzog.com, accessed July 2007.

6 The conventions of retreat and testing ground are of course commonly deployed tropes in western representations of nature, and in depictions of the difference and energizing danger provided by 'other' environments, societies and peoples.

7 Treadwell also visited schools to talk to children about his time with the bears, and showed some of his footage in these settings.

8 *Crocodile Hunter* became the most watched programme on the Animal Planet channel in the late 1990s (Cottle, 2004: 91–2). Irwin died in 2006 while filming a bull stingray, when it spiked him in the chest with its barbed tail. For an analysis of Irwin's self-promotion and some of his shows, written prior to his death, see Berrettini (2005).

9 For other auteurist readings of *Grizzly Man*, see several of the reviews listed at imdb.com.

10 On the degrees of autonomy that auteurism as a discourse and consumer practice can have from film texts brought under this heading, see Corrigan (1991) and Grant (2000).

11 Steven Connor (2000: 3) provides a useful reminder of the corporeal source of the voice, and its effect in producing the speaking subject when he notes:

> My voice comes from me first of all in a bodily sense. It is produced by means of my vocal apparatus – breath, larynx, teeth, tongue, palate, and lips. It is the voice I hear resonating in my head, amplified and

modified by the bones of my skull, at the same time as I see and hear its effects upon the world ... giving voice is the process which simultaneously produces articulate sound, and produces myself, as a self-producing being.

12 A recent *New Yorker* feature on Herzog paid most attention to his physical exploits, but did note in passing 'his sonorous voice, which, in his heavily accented English, suggests a Teutonic Vincent Price' (Zalewski 2006: 126). Thanks to Garth Twa for providing me with a copy of this article.
13 These associations are markedly different to that of perhaps the most famous directorial body in Anglophone cinema, 'Alfred Hitchcock'. This body was commodified and exploited as something of a trademark via the director's signature self-portrait sketch and cameo appearances in all his films for 50 years following *The Lodger* in 1926, yet also became readable as an immobilizing bulk that placed him on a par with certain of his voyeuristic characters. On Hitchcock's cameo appearances and the signature sketch, see Kapsis (1992: 20).
14 See Herzog's discussion of both these events in Cronin (2002: 278–82).
15 Blank's subsequent documentary *Burden of Dreams* (US, 1982), on the making of *Fitzcarraldo,* extended Herzog's reputation for risk-taking. Shot in the Peruvian rainforest, *Fitzcarraldo* (Peru, West Germany 1982) tells the story of a white rubber baron who has an enormous boat dragged across a mountain from one river to another. Herzog has said 'Though the film is set in an invented geography, I knew from the start that in telling this story we would have to pull a real boat over a real mountain.' He commented on Blank's film:

I do like *Burden of Dreams,* though it did cause some problems for me. For example, at one point in the film I talk of how people have lost their lives, but Les did not include my explanation of the circumstances in his film. He just cut it out, and so all of a sudden it sounds as if I had risked lives for the sake of a film. This stench followed me for a whole decade.

(Cronin 2002: 172, 185)

For a detailed discussion of the controversy caused by the film, and Herzog's response to a range of accusations, including megalomania and self-promotion, see Cronin 2002: 169–90).
16 *The Culture Show*, presented by Verity Sharp, BBC2, 2 February 2006.
17 Vaughan (1981, 1990: 65) writes: 'The movements of photographed people were accepted without demur because they were perceived as performance, as simply a new mode of self-projection, but that the inanimate should participate in self-projection was astonishing.'
18 For an account of the difficulties encountered in making this, Herzog's 'first Hollywood-funded feature', see Zalewski (2006).
19 On *Rescue 911* and its imitators, see Bondebjerg (1996). On *Touching the Void*, see Austin (2007).

20 An exception to this tendency for happy endings is Jon Krakauer's *Into Thin Air*, a first-hand account of a disastrous attempt to climb Everest in which eight people died, adapted as a television movie in 1997. Thanks to Peter Kramer for this reference. Another instance is the sailing documentary *Deep Water* (UK, 2006), where the breakdown and suicide of Donald Crowhurst stand in contrast to the survivability of the male adventurer figure in *Touching the Void*.
21 Barthes is writing about a photograph of Lewis Payne, awaiting his own hanging in 1865.
22 Ultimately, the film makes clear that Treadwell was killed by a bear that was unknown to him, and hence unnamed. Herzog refers to it as number 141, based on the tag that park staff had placed on it when it was younger.
23 On his website, Herzog states: 'Once I heard [the tape], I didn't waste five seconds to know: this will not be published, not in my film. Period. Even if Jewel had given me the permission and had asked me to include it, I wouldn't have done it.' Source: www.wernerherzog.com, accessed 9 July 2007.
24 In his own enactment of the audio recording, it is largely Fallico's move beyond the role of detached (male) professional that renders him grotesque.
25 Nunn also quotes Vivian Sobchack's observation that 'while death is generally experienced in fiction films as representable and often excessively visible, in documentary films it is experienced as confounding representation, as exceeding visibility'. Nunn, quoting Sobchack, cited in Nichols (1994: 48).
26 The (unheard) audiotape recording of the deaths of Treadwell and Huguenard is played just over halfway through the film. The remaining screen time is devoted to interviews with Treadwell's family and friends, and more of his footage, before the film doubles back on itself via a video that Treadwell shot two days before his death, where, Herzog suggests, 'he seems to hesitate in leaving the last frame of his own film'.
27 Note the latter is subordinated to the former throughout the film.
28 In the film, Treadwell, his family and friends mention his disappointment at a failed acting career, his use of drugs, and heavy drinking, from which, Treadwell suggests, he was saved by a new enthusiasm for the natural world. To this extent, *Grizzly Man* can be seen to provide a more overtly confessional version of the psychological tendency which Bazin located in post-war exploration films, whereby 'the behaviour of the members of the expedition and their reactions to the task in hand constitute a kind of anthropology of an explorer, the experimental psychology as it were of an adventurer' (Bazin 2005: 156).
29 Building on Berger's work, Akira Lippit has written:

> Modernity can be defined by the disappearance of wildlife from humanity's habitat and by the reappearance of the same in humanity's reflections on itself: in philosophy, psychoanalysis, and technological media such as telephone, film and radio ... Technology and ultimately cinema came to determine a vast mausoleum for animal being.
> (Lippit 2000: 25, 187, cited in Burt 2002: 27)

30 Berger (1980, 1991: 17).
31 Rotha (1952: 70). For further discussion of this slippery phrase, see Winston (1995), especially pp. 11–14 and 24–9.
32 Kracauer, cited in Arthur (1997: 3). A similar binarism has been labelled by some filmmakers the 'Zapruder quotient'. 'If you had a very high quotient of total amateurism in terms of technique, but the content was superb, what you were filming was absolutely riveting, that was 100% on the Zapruder curve.' Mike Wadleigh in *Late Show Special*, tx BBC2, 22 November 1993, cited in Chanan (n.d.), accessed online at: mchanan.dial.pipex.com/zapruder.htm.
33 Cronin (2002: 301).
34 Cronin (2002: 301).
35 To this extent, *Grizzly Man* stands in marked contrast to the anthropomorphism and sentimentality of the highly successful *La Marche de l'empereur/ March of the Penguins* (France, 2005).

5 Collective Subjectivity in *The Children of Golzow* vs. Alienation in 'Western' Interview Documentary

Silke Panse

This chapter explores the differences in approach to the documentary interview in opposing ideological systems via a case study of Winfried and Barbara Junge's *The Children of Golzow* (1961–2007). The longest-running documentary serial in film history, it chronicles the lives of the first generation brought up according to socialist ideals in the German Democratic Republic. Starting in August 1961, when the wall between East and West Berlin had just been erected, it follows the life-stories of a class of pupils from their first day of school. After the collapse of the socialist regime in 1989, the filmmakers accompanied the former GDR citizens into unemployment, re-education and to other countries. In the course of the 20 films, the style of filmmaking became progressively self-reflexive after starting out as expository and observational. The serial's self-reflexivity peaked after conversion from state socialism to a market economy. With the transformation from a socialist to a capitalist system, the process of individualization extended into the filmic representation, generating biographies about individuals instead of group portraits. Confronted with the same protagonists – first as stable GDR citizens and then as decentred subjects in the Federal Republic of Germany – we witness how the socialist interviewees react differently to interviewees used to a market society, how the former socialist subjects experience themselves as capitalist subjects, and how they change in their response to being filmed.

The sympathetic distance of the Junges' 'socialist' approach to interviewing, as well as the accepting reactions of the GDR subjects, contrasts with the sought provocation of the interviewee in popular documentaries made in a capitalist context. While 'Western' interviewees often react defensively to a provocative interviewing strategy, Winfried Junge's probing questions to his protagonists did not alienate his subjects. Even though the filmmaker tries to provoke his GDR subjects when he teases them about their weight or choice of marriage partner, his interventions are not confrontational and are not taken as such. In a society guided by the concept of the collective, the filmmakers were always already on the same side as their subjects. My analysis highlights the differences in perception of what might constitute documentary subjectivity and objectivity under both systems, arguing especially that the idea of 'distance' – foundational for objectivity in the West – was deemed neither threatening nor scientific under socialism. Moreover, I argue that the Golzow serial intrinsically differs from the more structured British television series *7-Up* (Michael Apted, 1964–) (Bruzzi 2007: 1) to which it is often compared.[1] Both long-term documentary projects portray their subjects in a manner converse to the apparent ideologies of their political systems. In the British series (set in a dynamic capitalist system that seeks change as necessary for market growth), change is only represented, whereas the GDR serial (set in state socialism, where change, like everything else, was planned and could therefore only be represented in retrospect) reflected progressively more change in becoming more self-reflexive.

The Children of Golzow follows a class of pupils born 1953–55 in the village of Golzow in the former GDR. Unlike the *7-Up* series with its set structure of re-visits every seven years, the Golzow documentaries are not ordered according to a pre-planned schema of visits in intervals and intentionally rely on invitations of the protagonists to be interviewed or filmed at diverse personal and public events. In addition, the release dates of the films are irregular. The first documentaries were short studies of the class. These were screened in cinemas as a supplement to the newsreel and fiction film. Only the third film, in 1966, announces in the credits that it would follow its protagonists for the next 25 years. Due to the children leaving the school and thus the class as a group formation, the course of their lives parted and the filmmakers had to follow the former children as single characters. Nevertheless, the protagonists were still collective members of each documentary and the single portraits were assembled into the blocks of a group film such as *Biographies* (GDR, 1980). The ideology of state socialism was against the portrait of a life as that of an individual. After reunification, the multiple lives were separated into individual biographies, not only as a result of the vast amount of material assembled over time, but also as a result of the short-term funding methods in a market economy. After reunification, the 'heroes' of the Golzow cycle – nicknamed 'Dallas East' by the DEFA[2] studio – starred in their own spin-offs. *Screenplay, The Times* (FRG, 1992) became the last group portrait for the next 14 years. Intended to draw the serial towards an end, only the penultimate film *And if They Haven't Passed Away* (FRG, 2006), with the somewhat pre-emptory subtitle *The End of the Infinite Story*, is an assemblage of biographical blocks again.[3] The format changed to individual biographies reflecting a process of individualization in the new capitalist system. The representation of the former members of the socialist group as separate individuals therefore is characteristic, not necessarily of 'free' human beings, but of free enterprise.

In the classless society of the GDR, the individual features of the protagonists' personalities emerge paradoxically as much more important in determining their paths in life and the structure of the films. Even though the classmates in school were also members of the same social class, since only one class officially existed in the socialist state, the structure and style of the films about them depend on their individual developments (and on the individual material that was shot). The structure of the films reflects the personalities of the protagonists as they appear in that footage. In that respect, *The Children of Golzow* differs not only from the *7-Up* series, whose structure is pre-determined and independent of the protagonists, but also from the ideology of a socialist state that does not allow for unplanned and individual development. The socialist participants, as presented in this serial, were less substitutable singularities as part of a collective than the individuals in the market economy in *7-Up*.

The serial became gradually more self-reflexive under socialism first, but then peaked shortly after reunification. The films made in the years after reunification manifested a pressing desire – and a pressure – for the filmmakers and the protagonists to be self-reflexive. Reasons and causes were individualized and the former socialist citizens were taught self-realization and self-motivation. After reunification, the serial's increased self-reflexivity was also the result of having to be justified to investors interested in commissioning further instalments. Barbara Junge describes the serial's trajectory of self-reflexivity:

> There was a brief moment in which things had opened up. We had interviewed most of them [as GDR subjects] and noticed that the attitude was receding beforehand: 'We can't do anything about the political state of things or what surrounds us anyway'. And so, people withdrew into the private and spoke more about the private, and so suddenly [just before reunification] people could get things off their chest. One can see that in the interviews which were made 1989/1990 ... These were issues that arose from that time. And when things then moved towards reunification, it ebbed away. Everything went much more quiet. One could feel that the steam had been released now.
>
> (Panse 2003)

To focus on the private in the GDR resulted from the blockage of debate about public politics. In contrast to a market economy, work in the 'republic of workers and peasants' was located in the same discursive space as the private realm. Both were open for discussion, whereas to object to the state was taboo. Winfried Junge (Schenk 2004: 64) observes: 'The people from Golzow were the most willing when we wanted to film their work. They felt comfortable with that. They could show what they were able to do and spoke quite openly about their problems.'[4] With unification, not only did the project become more self-reflexive, but its protagonists became more self-conscious. As GDR subjects, some of the children of Golzow were as untroubled about their careers as they were by their image on film. After conversion from state socialism to democratic capitalism, their affirmations under the eye of state censorship were replaced by fear that a company superior could see them. Whereas the GDR citizen did not say anything against the state but complained about work, the former GDR subject who is lucky enough to be employed in the FRG is under pressure to keep quiet about their employer, though they now can criticize the government. Winfried Junge (Panse 2003) points out: 'Now everything is great, because employees fear that they will lose their employment if they get bolshie. This is a new experience. Only people without work complain now; but about politics you can complain.' Not only did the emphasis shift, but the paradigms were reversed. After reunification, what was rewarded under one system was punished under the next. Thus for several reasons and in certain ways some of the reactions of the adults of Golzow and their filmmakers changed after the incorporation of one German state by the other.

The representation of change

The Golzow films fundamentally differ from the more structured British television series *7-Up*, most significantly in how change is negotiated and what idea of difference is involved in that change. ('Representation' and 'change' here are set up as antithetical.) Barton Byg (2001: 136) argues that the directors of the Golzow films and the *7-Up* series alike 'emphasize the timeless and immutable nature of human life in their subjects' and that both series 'emphasize[s] the unchanging'. On the contrary, we indeed find change to be experienced in *The Children of Golzow*. In the socialist serial, changes on a mundane level are subtly noted as responding in material ways to larger historical changes, whereas in the interviews of the *7-Up* series through the pattern of re-visits and the structure of the films, as well as the nature of the interviews, change is merely retrospectively represented. The unquestioning form of representation that *7-Up* uses – of the protagonists summarizing their time passed, for instance, and the employment of images as illustrations of statements – marks the project as a representative sociological experiment. This is, however, without attention to context. Winfried Junge (Schenk 2004: 82) agrees that the *7-Up* series is representative, whereas his serial is not, since *The Children of Golzow* operates (unlike the socialist state) less according to a plan, but grows out of situations. The Golzow films even convey the differences in change between the former socialist subjects in their transition from one political context to another. The lack of evolution in the *7-Up* series mirrors the determination of the British class structure at the time, more than the dynamics of a market society. The portrayal of lives as pre-determined was not only an effect of class in Britain, however, but of the aesthetics of the documentary series itself. In this sense, the *7-Up* series is analogous to the early 'capitalist representations' that Gilles Deleuze and Félix Guattari critique as overdetermining through structure. The subordination of the signified to the signifier is said to be similar in the early capitalist '*Urstaat*' and in Saussurian structuralism (Deleuze and Guattari 2000: 241–3). In both cases, a signifier would overcode the flow (Deleuze and Guattari 2000: 240).[5] Although not structuralist *per se*, in *7-Up*, the presentations of the protagonists' lives are overcoded by the representative format they are filmed in. The structure of the documentary reflects and produces ideology.

Because the Golzow serial already reflects on the limits of representation through its commentary, and the protagonists' development through its structure, the task of representing does not have to be carried by the documentary subjects being and narrating 'the way they are', as it does in the *7-Up* series. While the *7-Up* participants were asked how the repeated filming had affected their lives, the voice-over narration does not reflect on how the act of filming has affected the films' content and style. The *7-Up* series largely does without textual and directorial self-reflexivity. Instead, the protagonists are charged with the responsibility of representing their own development. Even though this individualizing of reflexivity goes hand in hand with an ideology of the market, the *7-Up* participants, in representing themselves without reflecting on their former representations, are rather 'rememorizing' in the Hegelian sense of, as Slavoj Žižek (2004: 13) puts it, 'reflectively returning to what the thing always already was'.[6] While one might expect that this returning to what was always already there, would be more likely the case in a documentary following the lives of socialist subjects in a socialist state based on a Hegelian model, it is the socialist documentary that not only witnesses but allows and acknowledges change. In *7-Up*, by contrast, change is represented as negative and only seen as a deviation from the previously outlined future. Tony is successful in the fulfilment of his working-class type as a taxi-driver. In this vein, he asserts symptomatically in *28-Up*: 'I don't wanna change. If I am ever going to change, it proves that the other Tony Walker was a fake.' And the upper-class John and Andrew are successful because they have fulfilled their past predictions for their future, predetermined by class expectation.

In the *7-Up* series, the model that produced substitutable particulars for the same generality – as Deleuze would phrase it – was 'class'. Whether we move forward or look backward does not matter, since life is just a fulfilment of a prediction, and thus the retrospective cannot differ from the forecast – this critique of the *7-Up* series could be mistaken for the temporal model of a socialist state. When Winfried Junge was asked about the serial's most socialist realist documentary, *When You Are 14* (1969) – apart from *These People Of Golzow – Analysis of the Circumstances of a Place* (GDR, 1984) the only Golzow film for which the filmmakers had to submit to state intervention, (Schenk 2004: 98) – he replied the following to the question:

> Schenk: 'You wanted to film a utopia and did not find it?'
>
> Junge: 'You say that today. But since Marx, we did not speak of socialism as an idea, but as a scientific world-view that was also supposed to be put into practice step by step in the GDR. The film had to find examples for it. And if it failed, one had simply been looking for them in the wrong place.'[7]
>
> (Schenk 2004: 32)

The term 'utopian' used in Western terminology to discredit Marxist ideas as a fantasy, assumed a different temporal trajectory in the socialist state: with reality being planned and not evolving, the future was just the realization of what had been thought before.

It is, however, in the British series, that we merely see older versions of the same model, but no transformation of the model itself. What change there is for the subjects in respect of their expectations, is represented as dramatic failure. This is exemplified in the figure of Neil. He is a failure, *because* he has changed and this is marked by a downward trajectory. Neil became the most tragic figure of the *7-Up* series, therefore generating the most audience response. By contrast, Winfried Junge rejects building the narrative structure of the Golzow films up towards the tragic elements in the protagonists' lives and to thereby heighten their struggles in the films for dramatic purposes. News, of course, is supposed to be about what is 'new'. In a market society, change itself is part of a commodity culture and interpreted as newness. The commodification of 'newness' for the sake of consumption was criticized by Marxist thinkers, who argued that something new does not just suddenly appear, but develops dialectically from the old. George Lukács (1949: 17), for example, noted: 'It would be a mistake to contrast socialist realism as something "radically new" to everything that is "old." Its essence develops dialectically.'[8] How can there be a change acknowledged, then, without this being about the New? By insisting on the value of showing, or telling, what apparently has not changed, the filmmakers have determined the Golzow serial as a documentary film distinct from actuality television. Categories such as job, wife, and place remain the same, so allowing more minor material changes to take place, or even letting us see how the protagonists cope with a 'lack of change', *The Children of Golzow* has thus allowed change to become evident, not only historical change (as one would assume to be the case in a state subscribing to historical materialist ideology), but material change in the everyday.[9]

The rise of documentary subjectivity – which has so far been regarded as a progressive development (Renov 1999: 84–94) – works well in a market economy that is based on individualism. This is even pointed out in *The New Yorker* (MacFarquhar 2004: 133) with respect to Michael Moore's documentaries: 'For Moore, though, everything is personal. He's not angry with capitalism, or even with companies; he's angry with Roger Smith, the C.E.O. of General Motors, and Philip Knight, the C.E.O. of Nike. He doesn't fight against war; he fights against Rumsfeld, Cheney, and Bush.' The form of subjectivity encouraged in his argument-based documentaries is one that criticizes other individuals, but not one that challenges the system. In that way, their self-reflexivity is also contained. Even though the reaction of Moore's subjects constitutes a main part of the documentaries, the making of the films themselves is not reflected upon, which has set Moore up for accusations of being hypocritical. By contrast, the Junges do not set out to make an argument, but regard themselves as chroniclers. With respect to *The Children of Golzow*, Bill Nichols' definition of documentary as making an argument does not apply (Nichols 1991: 125). It is rather that things only fall into place in retrospect. Thus, the serial is rather impressionistic. This enables the importance of events to be determined in retrospect – which is the reverse of socialist pre-planning. What was ordinary at the time is given the chance to become extraordinary only through time passed, as Winfried Junge points out (Richter 2003: 34): 'To make a film about nothing else than the non-dramatic everyday and typical ordinariness has been a motivation for us. Through the time-lapse effect of a film covering 41 years, the non-sensational sometimes gains importance.' Ordinariness would thus be a feature of the present. Profoundness only emerges in retrospect. What transpires through the longevity of the *Children of Golzow* chronicle is that a change of context, as defined through temporality rather than space, effects a change of meaning. Newness or change arrives in the serial as that which is not pre-determined. That the importance of events can only be acknowledged in retrospect is another feature of the serial that differs from the forward trajectory of state socialism. In contrast to the socialist realist style of the socialist state that had frozen its heroes in either plans, poses or scripts, *The Children of Golzow* serial realized the presentation of change.

Distance as objective in capitalism and as subjective in socialism

In *Jochen – a Golzower from Philadelphia* (FRG, 2001), in what could be interpreted by the viewer as an unstaged scene, we see Jochen's family entering the living room and assembling around the table. However, Winfried Junge's commentary discourages any notion of this being an observed 'authentic' situation, and with the same stroke marks the image as inherently prone to deception:

> Now the lighting has been set up in the parlour and that means: now do your directing. That is difficult when there is actually nothing to film, though we have the camera, which on days when something really does happen is often missing. It only remains to have them be seated for the unpopular 'interview' and converse about what was, is, or will be.

Through its self-reflexive commentary, the Golzow serial acknowledges that with a project covering such a long time, the visits of the documentary team can only ever represent the protagonist's life and never 'catch' lives unawares. What Junge says here not only means that the documentation has inevitably missed opportunities, but it also suggests that it has documented the missing of opportunities. In the serials' trajectory towards self-reflexivity, the off-screen narration later changes from commenting on what we see in front of the camera to commenting about what has gone on behind the camera or between the filming.

The relationship between the commentary and the image had specific implications in the GDR. The commentary was supposed to provide the mundane appearance of socialist reality with the official rose-coloured tint of socialist realism. After the filmmakers abandoned the expository and observational style of the first films, which only had a descriptive and quite positive narration, Winfried Junge's commentary and questions, however, often cast doubt on this illusory coherence of the world. The filmmakers' conscious insistence on off-screen narration becomes apparent in the commentary of *Screenplay: The Times*, the group portrayal of the Golzow films, which is the most self-reflexive. The film begins as such with Winfried Junge's voice-over narration: 'This film – will have a commentary, which I know could cost it sympathy.' The serial continued to be criticized for its dependence on the commentary, for telling more than showing: 'The people are never shown eating, celebrating or procreating' a West German newspaper (Becker 1999: 24) complained. While Western observational documentary – imbued by a scientific ethos of gaining objectivity through detachment and non-intervention – argued against narration, the alternate documentary route, of narration revealing an underlying, more 'objective truth', which was also practised by Western non-fiction television, was again not available to the GDR filmmaker. The interpretation of the documentary image in the GDR was predefined by the ideology of the state. Whereas in Western journalistic programmes, the commentary of the reporter would provide background revelations to question an apparently superficial external reality, the GDR filmmaker could not individually disclose a more objective truth. The individual comment could only be subjective. The images were, after all, depicting a reality that had been shaped by socialism. It is for this reason that Winfried Junge interprets his questioning comments as subjective, whereas a West German reporter would have interpreted the same narration as objective.

Alienation as surplus value

If something is presented as alienating in the *Children of Golzow,* it is not the interviewees, but the context. In many popular Western-style interviewing documentaries, by contrast, it is the interviewees who are intentionally alienated as well as presented as alienating to the viewer. Symptomatically, interviewees questioned in the context of a market economy also often react defensively to a provocative interviewing strategy, for example, that employed by Anglo-American documentarists such as the earlier Nick Broomfield (in, for instance, *The Leader, His Driver and the Driver's Wife,* 1991), Michael Moore and even Louis Theroux. Their interviews, as diverse as their individual approaches might be, are typically conducted in styles that rely heavily on irony. Deleuze and Guattari (2000: 225) situated modern capitalist society in an 'age of cynicism' where 'cynicism is capital as the means of extorting surplus labor'. With respect to these interviews conducted in a capitalist system, one could ask: what is the surplus value of the product 'documentary interview'? Even though the interviewers might be more leftist (and less politically cynical) than their interviewees, the way in which these documentaries generate revenue and establish a reputation for the filmmaker is through the addition in value through the interviewees' alienated and immaterial labour of defence.[10] This is then employed in the argument of the documentary for the moral superiority of the viewer who identifies with the filmmaker. The surplus here is reciprocal to the alienation of the 'worker-interviewee'. Provocation serves as a means to generate productivity. The filmmaker in these interviews functions as the capitalist, and the interviewees as the workers – unpaid because they apparently act merely as 'themselves'.

Alienation, in the context of these Western-style documentary interviews, has become a tool for identification with the interviewer against the interviewee, thus differing vastly from what the Marxist playwright Bertolt Brecht had intended with his alienation effect. Brecht (1964: 91) embraced the alienation of the viewer as a consciously sought artistic strategy intended to hinder the audience from identifying with the characters in a play. We as the audience consume the polemics of the interviewer in a way Brecht would have opposed, since the alienation of the interviewee here is for our entertainment (a famous example of an alienated interviewee being that of Charlton Heston in Michael Moore's *Bowling for Columbine,* 2002). Alienation effected in the documentary interviewees fosters their objectification for the viewer's consumption. Brecht took into account the distancing between actors, their roles and the audience in a fictional context, but not between the diverse levels of realities and the impact of agencies in a documentary set-up. Here, one party is delegated to play themselves (the interviewee) whereas the other (the interviewer) not only has the authorial control, but furthermore is rewarded by the audience's identification and cinema ticket.

Brecht wanted to de-familiarize the familiar of the everyday. *The Children of Golzow,* by contrast, appreciates the everyday and de-familiarizes documentary film-making by making the everyday strange through being self-reflexive about the filming of it. Unlike in Brechtian theatre, where what is shown is what is criticized, Junge might de-familiarize, but he does not criticize his documentary subjects. Due to the specific situation of the documentary interview, Brechtian distancing does not apply to the documentaries' reflexivity – even though the filmmakers share many of Brecht's concerns. Indeed, the seventh Golzow film, *Spare No Charm and Spare No Passion* (GDR, 1979), takes its title from his *Children's Hymn* and, through its repetitions in diverse contexts, became a sort of theme tune for the serial. It is more accurate to say that the Golzow documentaries follow in the humanist line of early Marx and Engels. While Marx (1973: 107) and Engels opposed making 'individuals into mere mouthpieces of the spirit of the times' as 'Schillerizing', a strategy that Friedrich Schiller employed in his novels, Brecht's pedagogic exercises exaggerated exactly that, while they were criticizing what they represented. Winfried Junge affirms: 'In our films, which always try to grasp the whole personality of a person, a presentation of the individual under only one specific aspect is inappropriate' (Schenk 2004: 174).[11] *The Children of Golzow* has a sympathetically distanced commentary and style of interviewing, but it is not distanced in the 'Western' sense of scientific observation nor is it distanced in the Brechtian sense of alienation.

The ethics of socialist aesthetics

After the first film, the filmmakers renounced the ostensibly 'hidden camera'. For *When I Finally Go to School* (1961), the film team looked into the class through the windows from outside, but the pupils were obviously under full 35mm lighting. This method was dismissed as it created distance and was not likely to cultivate trust. The socialist notion of the collective is one of the reasons why Junge had abandoned the earlier exercises in observation. In the socialist context, 'pure observation' was regarded as non-collective and was rejected in favour of filmmaking as a joint effort of the team and the protagonists. Winfried Junge stated: 'We are filming "our" film here. This is utterly different from us either hiding with the camera or directing next to the teacher from in front of the class' (Schenk 2004: 39).[12] As an effect of collectivity in socialism, the interviewing style in *The Children of Golzow* did not provoke the alienation of the interviewees, as is the case in many 'Western' documentaries and television formats. Questions that might be understood as malicious intrusions in a market society of individuals were not perceived as such by his GDR subjects, who appear unperturbed. Often it sounds as though the filmmaker wants to stir up trouble between the former children of Golzow and their partners, as in this sequence first filmed for *Biographies* (GDR, 1980) and later commented on in *Screenplay: The Times* (FRG, 1992). Winfried Junge mischievously applies the crisis tactics of American *direct cinema* – to film a person when their attention is directed elsewhere – to the conducting of an interview. But unlike observational filmmakers, Junge does not want to remain unheard and makes his questions more provocative to counter the distraction, here supplied through television. Jürgen is drinking beer while watching the World Cup and his wife Anita sits disengaged next to him, while Winfried tries to provoke the football fan into talking about the couple's lack of dialogue:

>Winfried narrating: My probing will be a nuisance too. I chose this moment to start up a conversation; and not about football.

>[...]

>Winfried interviewing: Will Anita get used to you being a football supporter?

>Jürgen [smiles]:   Not her.

>Winfried: Why not?

>Anita: Am not interested. Don't understand it.

>Winfried: You'll have to share a hobby or you'll have problems.

>Anita: Yeah, but not football.

>Winfried: What then? Fishing?

>Anita: Yeah, we go along sometimes.

>Winfried: Then you can enjoy the silence together.

>[...]

>Winfried: You are good at being silent together, aren't you? Or have you got nothing to say?

>Jürgen: If one sees one another every day, what does one have to keep talking for?

>Winfried: You're not a great talker, are you? And you found the right person for it.

>Jürgen: Yeah. But I talk a bit more than her.

>Winfried [in disbelief]:   More?

>Winfried narrating: For Jürgen, talking to each other seems to be even less important than being there for each other. How could he realize that I am trying to provoke him? Was I being fair to him? He stands on his ladder all day and deserves his sofa in the evening. He hasn't had one for long. Now he wants a little peace and quiet.

Even though to show something negative about a protagonist – in Jürgen's case apart from the marital silence also the fact that he was drinking alcohol – would perhaps have had a negative impact in turn on the protagonist's life, in the Golzow serial, *not* to show something, would have provoked a negative reaction in his peers. Jürgen did not find these questions objectionable, as Barbara Junge (Panse 2003) emphasizes:

Jürgen said, no, this [the alcohol issue] is part of my life and it has to be shown as it is. One has to realize especially that the film is going to be shown to his neighbours and the people of the village, and when this is not shown or mentioned they will say: we can't believe anything they say. In this sense it was important that he stood by it and that we could use it in the film.

Winfried Junge's stance against observation, steeped in the ethics of a collective, did not change after reunification:

But we are in the same situation as the people of Golzow. We might be a different generation, but we have lived in this eastern part of Germany, which was a state, that has now collapsed, and we are all affected. Now I cannot just exhibit them in the shop window and pretend that I don't exist with my stance ... In this respect, I put the political first and the formal in second place. Not everyone appreciates this. The audience thanks us for it.

(Panse 2003)

The filmmaker describes his approach to documentary filmmaking with a phrase merging ethics and aesthetics:

In documentary film, it is always the content that decides the form. And nothing else. And I don't want to philosophise about aesthetics in this form of documentary. In that respect a unique aesthetics has developed ... Documentary films need the *aesthetics of trust*. It is not possible in any other way with people in front of the camera ... with whom one wants to continue filming.

(Panse 2003)

Winfried Junge's (1995: 133–45) 'aesthetics of trust' respects the subjectivities of the protagonists as parts of a collective manifested in a film text that includes the filmmakers. Whereas the English subjects in *7-Up* are generally not only dispersed as individual adults in terms of location, but also socially since they were chosen from different classes (in both senses of the word), it is because the former children of Golzow still think of themselves as a group that they have more power over their representation. The filmmakers know that if they alienate one, the others would follow and they would stop participating in the serial. The ethical argument for an 'aesthetics of trust' in this long-term documentary thus has practical reasons as well. As Barbara Junge (Panse 2003) observes: 'You cannot of course record something about someone, which they themselves don't like. They would have such an expression in front of the camera that it would be impossible to use it.' When asked their opinion, the Golzow protagonists often refer back to the films. To the question from the audience 'What will you tell your grandchildren about the GDR?' Petra, the wife of Bernd in *Actually I Wanted to Be a Forester – Bernd from Golzow* (FRG, 2003), responded: 'I will show them the film.'[13] Contrary to 'Western' expectations – and evidence that the 'aesthetics of trust' works – the protagonists support the documentaries and brush off any suggestions that the filming has had a (negative) impact on their lives.[14] As the filmmaker's namesake Winfried remarked shortly after reunification in *And if They Haven't Passed Away Yet* (FRG, 2006): 'If you started the film today, it would look different. Perhaps half of the people would not have participated.'

In the section on Jürgen in the group portrait *Screenplay: The Times* (GDR, 1992), and in the biography *The Life of Jürgen from Golzow* (FGR, 1994) we see Jürgen and his wife Anita being interviewed on a bench in front of their house, but we see the filmmaker in the image as well:

> Winfried: How do you feel about me sitting here with you and having myself filmed? Do you think it's right?'
>
> Jürgen: It's fine.
>
> Winfried: Why?
>
> Jürgen: Well, people should see who undertook this with us here, right?
>
> Winfried: Well, I can't always hide behind the camera, right.
>
> Jürgen: It's easier to talk.
>
> Winfried: Do you think so?
>
> Jürgen: Yes.
>
> Winfried: Do you feel better when I'm sitting here with you?
>
> Jürgen: Yes.

The protagonists objected that – by documentary tradition – they always had to be unprepared with their answers, while the filmmaker was prepared with his questions. Winfried Junge reveals:

> We then arrived at the opinion, that we need to emerge from behind the camera and should sit next to them. And they confirmed this. Jürgen said: 'We can talk better, when he [the filmmaker and interviewer] is in the same situation as I am. He is always in the shadow and behind the camera and does not come forward.' Everyone found this unfair, that they are always the ones, who have to answer without any preparation while I come properly prepared.
>
> (Panse 2003)

This is an attitude shared by the filmmaker himself when he is an interviewee. At the beginning of our interview (Panse 2003), he remarks that now has to improvise. The Junges try to keep some editorial control over the articles and interviews that are published about them. However, this stance derives from a belief in a dialogue among equals and a rejection of 'speaking about' as a superior form rather than from image control. Winfried Junge's reaction to an academic text about *The Children of Golzow* confirms this: 'Well, I know of course what Barton Byg wrote. But we have never discussed this, because he does not engage me in the discussion. He travels through Germany and tells this to everyone and I have no opportunity to object' (Panse 2003). The Junges respect their interviewees as their equals as far as is possible in a set-up where they are still the filmmakers. They are shown the near final cut and are given the option to veto scenes. Winfried Junge explains:

> When it is noticed that these [ethics] are the reason for the camera, then to pull back to a long shot in which one sees me sitting there, then it's not a matter of me being so vain and now wanting to be in the picture too, but because, as Jürgen happily confirms, a dialogue is easier when the other person is also included in the image. Really, I should have sat down with them on the same bench. But that would have meant that I would have been always in the frame, with every sentence, and that is not good either. So if [the camera is to pull back], then it is to make clear that I am sitting there, asking the questions; but then it's back to him, one needs to close in again, and it's only him again.
>
> (Panse 2003)

The filmmaker makes a further important point here by relating the degree of self-reflexivity to the framing of the image through the zoom. A long shot includes the author and with him the context and thus allows for more 'collective self-reflexivity'. A close-up blinkers out self-reflexivity by focusing on only one person.

The limit of self-reflexivity

The limit of self-reflexivity is for the Junges the point when the filmmaker becomes the main subject of the film. And the filmmakers' reservation about the wish of Jürgen for Winfried to be always in the picture as well, makes sense:

> He [Jürgen] thinks, sitting on the same bench [and in the same frame] would make us wholly equal; that this would be the best. But this really is not possible. Then I would be the main hero in all of the stories because I am always with them – and we now have thirteen. And that is just not possible.
>
> (Panse 2003)

Here, it is argued that equality between filmmaker and subject, or the interviewer and the interviewee, is ultimately impossible. It could also be extended to suggest that equality, as in socialism, is not possible. Junge's stance of believing in a kind of equality that nevertheless insists in non-substitutability is distinct, for instance, from that of the Dutch documentarist Joris Ivens, who worked internationally as well as in the socialist context. In a speech at a film festival in Warschau in 1955, Ivens (1955: 251) stated that at the end of a documentary on a movement for farmers' collectives in the USA, he would have liked to have exchanged his profession with that of his subjects. To let the filmmaker into the image can only be the exception that proves the rule.

Whereas Anglo-American documentary has developed a subjective and deconstructive reaction against an overly 'objective' and impersonal observational mode, in the GDR the ordinary subject had to carry the burden of objectivity. This contrasts with the image of the marginalized populace at the bottom of a capitalist society, who

eventually had their voices heard in 'minor' documentaries or through identity politics. Symptomatically, in 'Western' market economies the most individualized way of filming, to film oneself or one's impact on the world, in autobiographical and performative documentary, became regarded as an important subversive movement. Barbara Junge opposes this option: 'For me it would be too vain, because it would look as if we wanted to place the roles we played in the foreground in the final film. And Winfred couldn't of course always be there in front of the camera or he'd be the main protagonist' (Panse 2003). The kind of self-reflexivity at play in *The Children of Golzow* remains grounded in a collective notion of 'self'. Frederic Jameson describes what is at stake as follows:

> In the 1960s many people came to realize that in a truly revolutionary collective experience what comes into being is not a faceless and anonymous crowd or 'mass' but, rather, a new level of being – what Deleuze, following Eisenstein, calls the Dividual – in which individuality is not effaced but completed by collectivity. It is an experience that now slowly has been forgotten, its traces systematically effaced by the return of desperate individualisms of all kinds.
>
> (1998: 10)

With their view of rejecting too much emphasis on their own 'selves', the Junges are in line with the socialist stance for the group and against the elevation of the one or the few. Winfried Junge (Panse 2003) sums this up:

> It is about the lives of these 10 people from Golzow. What opinions we might have, or whatever we have thrown in of ourselves – all this takes second place. It really isn't important. What is important is that it is clear, to a certain degree, what the relationship was like with the subjects; how we made it.

The space of contact as manifested in the documentaries about the previously socialist subjects perhaps constitutes what Michael Hardt and Antonio Negri (2000: 395) describe as 'a singularity that is a reality produced by cooperation'. Contrasting with Jay Ruby's definition of reflexivity as making 'his or her awareness of self a public matter and convey[ing] that knowledge to the audience' (2000: 155), in the Junges' practice of self-reflexive filmmaking it is not the exposing[15] of the filmmakers' or the protagonists' autobiographical selves that matter, but the new joint entity of the relationship between them. While in art, 'relational aesthetics'[16] between diverse materials and media became popular at the same time as documentary, *The Children of Golzow* manifests an aesthetics and an ethics of relations *within* documentary.

Notes

1   In Britain, the *7-Up* series continues to be regarded as the earliest of its kind: 'Michael Apted's long-running documentary series is identified by many as the earliest predecessor of reality television' (Gibson 2005).

2   Acronym for the *Deutsche Film Aktiengesellschaft*, the state film corporation of the German Democratic Republic.

3   In 2007, the Junges were working on what they hope to be the last instalment of the serial.

4   My translation.

5   The British artist Gillian Wearing has emphasized the containing effect of *7-Up* as the basis for her video piece *10–16* (1997) with a somewhat different result. In *10–16* adults are miming to audio statements by children of that age. Rather than suppress the manifestation of personal development of an 'original' subject, her videos create new subjects through a rigorous, artistic imposition of the signifier: the visible adult protagonists are 'being spoken' by the previously recorded utterances of children.

6   Žižek here sums up Søren Kierkegaard's and Deleuze's reproach of Georg Wilhelm Friedrich Hegel.

7   My translation.

8   My translation.

9   Brian Massumi, following Antonio Negri, notes that in the dynamic of capitalism normality is lost (Massumi 2002: 224). Naomi Klein also takes up the line that capitalism needs crises (Klein 2007).

10 Michael Hardt and Antonio Negri classify the production of affect, for instance, as immaterial labor (2000: 108–9). However, their focus is on the production of positive affect – service with a smile – that employers and families seek, not on the evocation of a negative response discussed here.

11 My translation.

12 My translation.

13 Petra Oesterreich, the wife of the main protagonist, said this in the Q&A following the premiere of *Actually I Wanted to Be a Forester – Bernd from Golzow*, London: Goethe Institute, 11 December 2003.

14 Bernd and Petra Oesterreich defended their participation after the screening of *Actually I Wanted to Be a Forester – Bernd from Golzow*, London: Goethe Institute, 11 December 2003.

15 Ruby's essay is symptomatically titled 'Exposing Yourself: Reflexivity, Anthropology, and Film'.

16 Relational aesthetics, made popular by Nicolas Bourriaud (2000), were criticized for their lack of ethics and empowering of institutions by Claire Bishop (2004).

6   Documentary as Critical and Creative Research

Mike Wayne

Much of the attraction of and debates and controversies around the documentary genre derives from it being a hybrid form, straddling both conflicting paradigms within the traditional social sciences, on the one hand, and the aesthetic dimensions of art and entertainment, on the other. Mixed in with these cross-currents, the question of the political or ideological nature of documentary as research, its 'critical' or 'uncritical' nature vis-à-vis dominant institutions, power relations, common-sense frameworks of explanation, interpretation and embedded cultural assumptions, are never far away. This chapter is about this trinity of terms as they pertain to the documentary: critical, creative, research. It asks what it means to discuss documentary as a mode of research, i.e. to what extent this audio-visual-based genre overlaps with issues around knowledge production associated with the social sciences; what it means to discuss some documentary films as critical practices, i.e. to define what 'critical' might mean for the media generally in the present contemporary context of unleashed global capitalism and how it might best be related to documentary; and this chapter asks what it means to discuss documentary as a 'creative' practice, i.e. one in which aesthetics plays a key role in its production and consumption. Finally, this chapter explores the relationships between the critical, creative/aesthetic and research aspects of documentary.

Documentary as research

What kind of research practice is documentary? Documentaries can of course draw on the quantitive methodologies of statistical analysis that are associated with what is known in the social sciences as the positivist paradigm. In the opening pre-credits sequence to *Super Size Me* (Morgan Spurlock 2004), a voice-over narrator (Spurlock) provides us with among the following statistics: that 100 million Americans are overweight or obese (some 60 per cent of the adult population); that the fattest state in America is Mississippi where one in four people are obese; that obesity is second only to smoking as a causal factor in preventable deaths (over 400,000 a year); that one in four Americans visits a fast food restaurant everyday; that McDonald's operates over 30,000 restaurants in over 100 countries across six continents; that it feeds 46 million people per day and that it controls 43 per cent of the fast food market in America.

As Graham Murdock reminds us, counting and measuring – the key tools of analysis for positivism – can tell us a lot about trends or the true scale of events. The sort of knee-jerk dismissal of such methods by positivism's antagonist within the social sciences, the interpretive paradigm, is unhelpful (Murdock 1997). The positivist paradigm is concerned to uncover statistical regularities in observable phenomena. It is strongly marked by its origins in the nineteenth-century natural sciences, hence its investment in the observation of empirical phenomena, its belief that reality (whether natural or social) is made up of universal laws, that 'proper' science is value-neutral and that the object of study is not or should not be influenced or changed by the studying subject (Hammersley 1995: 2). One can immediately see that philosophically at least, positivism has influenced certain traditions of documentary filmmaking, especially the appeal to the 'objectivity' of the subject-researcher (in the sense of value-neutrality) and the belief in the absolute objectivity (in the sense of being dichotomously independent from and uninfluenced by the researcher) of the phenomena that is being studied (Wayne 2003: 225–30). In relation to film, positivism grounds itself in the *iconic* nature of the visual sign (the image resembles that which it represents) and the *indexical* relationship implied (at least before digital technology) that the reality captured by the image must once have been there, present before the camera (itself often conceived as an objective, mechanical recording instrument).

Documentary sits at the intersection of contradictory philosophical streams and manifests this in its theory and practice. While positivist attitudes are common, the dualistic split between subject and object typical of positivism is challenged by the fact that documentary filmmaking involves *engagement* with *value-laden* contexts and people, begging the question of the documentary filmmaker's own evaluative responses to these people and the political and ethical conditions of intervention into these contexts. Thus, on the one hand, the Griersonian tradition of British documentary in the 1930s and 1940s stressed that documentary involved the 'creative treatment' of actuality footage (Grierson 1946: 78–89), which suggests a strong subjective engagement with material taken to have some sort of relationship to the real world. But at the same time, its vision of the world was one of controlled, well-ordered industrial and social processes and the conflict-free operations of Empire, illuminated by an authoritative middle-class 'objective' voice-of-god narration that smacks of positivism's confidence that society is a well-oiled system of universal laws. The direct cinema practitioners of the 1960s similarly stood at the confluence of contradictory philosophical streams: they were the 'direct descendants of the natural science paradigm' as Banks notes, due to their investment in value neutrality and belief that their presence did not change what they were recording, but at the same time this very separation and distance produced a mode of filmmaking 'sympathetic, even empathetic, with the rhythm of life as it was lived, and to be as reactive as possible to actual events in people's lives – the camera following, rather than dictating action' (Banks 1998: 18). Thus life became a little messier and more untidy than within the Griersonian paradigm.

Where the positivist paradigm involves controlled laboratory conditions and/or quantitive analysis of standardized regularities ('facts'), the interpretive paradigm by contrast places emphasis on qualitative analysis. Its focus is on the variability of meanings, which are understood to be context-dependent rather than universal and standardized. It is clear then that while some documentaries may be philosophically influenced by elements of the positivist tradition and while they may draw on knowledge generated by its characteristic quantitive analysis, the contribution of documentary film itself towards knowledge production, tends to be overwhelmingly qualitative. The documentary provides an audio-visual record of *particular* people, *particular* places and *particular* events. The statistic-heavy introduction in *Super Size Me* concludes with the narrator now appearing before the camera for the first time as if to say that while all those statistics have given some sense of the scale of the problem, it will only really become *meaningful* by grounding it in a particular case study. The film's original contribution to knowledge production is anchored in the chronicle of what happens to Spurlock's body and health when he goes on a McDonald's-only diet for one month. It is clear though that this experiment, which is monitored by three health experts, is designed to vividly illustrate the more general issue of the deleterious consequences of eating too much fast food. Thus the particularity of the stories which documentaries tell do not preclude investing those particularities with a broader social or historical meaning.

As a mode of qualitative research, we can identify a number of research tools or *methods* available to documentary: the interview (widely used, although in different ways, across both the positivist and qualitative/interpretive paradigms of social research), narration (equivalent to the researcher's own sequencing and analysis of their results in written texts), archival footage (again used by sociologists and historians) and dramatic reconstruction (perhaps more unique to documentary). All these methods can be mobilized in very different ways. Literary and historical allusions and free association characterize the narration of Patrick Keiller's *Robinson in Space* (1997), for example, and is very different from the sort of linear cause–effect account that predominates in many documentaries. The method of narration in *Robinson in Space* is mobilized using a surrealist *methodology*, designed to discover unexpected connections and reveal concealed realities. A more linear narration in which the image track has the role of illustrating (rather than provoking) what the narration is saying, uses what Bill Nichols calls an expository methodology (2001: 105–9). This distinction between methods and methodologies is widespread within the social sciences. A methodology refers to the more or less coherent principles and values that organize the use of the research methods: different methodologies stress different approaches to knowledge generation.

Examples of methodologies within the interpretive paradigm are symbolic interactionism, phenomenology, hermeneutics, psychoanalysis and ethnography (Sarantakos 1998: 33). Despite their differences, all these methodologies share an emphasis on the way human subjects creatively imbue their activities and interactions with culturally constructed meanings. Audio-visual methodologies may be rather less clearly defined than in the social sciences, more numerous, more prone to intertextual co-mingling with each other and there may be more of a case in some instances to think of a documentary having elements of its own methodology (what we would call authorship in film studies more generally). But let us just consider the case of the interview method in a little more detail.

While the positivist paradigm will use interviews organized around a standardized questionnaire that predetermines the range of responses the interviewee can give, the qualitative paradigm pays attention to the particularity of the subject, their audio (and visual) contribution being distinctive to their particular experiences/ background as a participant, expert or observer. 'Qualitative interviewing', suggest Rubin and Rubin, 'is a way of finding out what others feel and think about their worlds' (1995: 1). It turns everyday conversational skills into 'a tool of research, an intentional way of learning about people's feelings, thoughts and experiences' (1995: 2). Qualitative interviewing can be focused either on the cultural milieu of the interviewee(s), exploring in ethnographic manner, their norms, values, understandings and the taken-for-granted rules of behaviour of a group or society, or they can be more topical based (Rubin and Rubin 1995: 28), focused on an event or process which the interviewee has some direct and immediate experience of or else in the case of 'expert' testimony, some professional knowledge of. Qualitative research focuses on the variability and complexity of context-sensitive meanings generated by social practices. Of course, in practice, interviewee responses that give details on particular events may also give us insights into the cultural milieu of a particular group of people operating within given institutional, social or historical contexts.

Errol Morris' *Fog of War* (2003) is unusual in that while most documentaries use the comparative method to juxtapose the discourse of different interviewees, this film has a single interviewee only: Robert McNamara, former Secretary of Defense (read War) under both President John F. Kennedy and Lyndon Baines Johnson during the US occupation of Vietnam in the 1960s and early 1970s. The comparative method is often used to explore contrasting views on points of fact and values and Morris explored this brilliantly in his earlier documentary, *The Thin Blue Line* (1988) which both acknowledges the subjectivity of testimony while also working towards an adequate account of what really happened in a murder case. The film helped overturn a wrongful conviction, a good example of a documentary making an original contribution to knowledge. The very title, *Fog of War* places the question of subjectivity, judgement, knowledge and self-knowledge to the fore. Indeed, in terms of our two paradigms, *Fog of War* charts the shift in McNamara's thinking from a positivist to an interpretive paradigm.

McNamara was a Harvard professor with a background in data analysis, who begins his experience of war during the Second World War as the epitome of a morally disengaged, positivist calculating machine, whose analysis of bombing raids over Japan (sorties, tons of bombs dropped, targets hit, etc., illustrated with a rapid montage of reports, graphs, percentage figures, and so forth), helped influence General Curtis Le May to firebomb Tokyo and other cities to destruction. The intertwinning of murderous scientific rationality and modern technological destructive power is wonderfully illustrated by a special effects shot that shows not bombs, but numbers, dropping out of a plane's bomb bay doors to the targets below. The limitations of McNamara's reflections are illustrated when he discusses the 'proportionality' of the American atom bomb attacks on two Japanese cities. Here he is evasive and refuses to condemn senior military and political figures behind the decision. The film itself underscores this visually with a series of jump cuts and black screen punctuations suggesting his torturous rationalizations.

Morris is well known for using his own specially designed interview technology: the Interrotron. This places an image of himself under the camera lens (like an auto-cue machine) and interviewees address themselves directly to the camera and therefore the watching viewer. This produces an unusually intense relationship between viewer and interviewee. While it might seem to offer McNamara a commanding platform on which to provide a self-legitimating account of his role in the Vietnam War, it also subjects his account to microscopic scrutiny, where we find various hints and clues (often in little details and throwaway remarks) that suggest that here is a profoundly narcissistic man with extremely limited powers of self-introspection and amazing detachment from all the death and destruction he was involved in propagating.

Later in the film, in the context of the Vietnam War, which saw increasing opposition within the US, McNamara's discourse shifts away from the positivist certainties which characterized his number-crunching days during the Second World War, and now he begins to stress the role of subjective perspective in inter-nation conflict. It is less clear, however, to what extent the film itself shares some of the more humanist, subjective and cautious reflectiveness of the later McNamara. As with his discourse, so within the film itself, there is little indication of the powerful economic interests of American capitalism that lay behind a war McNamara now sees as some sort of unfortunate misunderstanding between nations. The morally dubious nature of McNamara ought not to be reduced to the level of the individual, but rather should be seen as symptomatic of the broader structures of power in which he operated. As we shall see later, structures of power can be concealed as much within the interpretive paradigm as the positivist paradigm.

While *Fog of War* interviews its single protagonist in an anonymous studio setting, *Mondovino* (Jonathan Nossiter, Argentina, France, Italy, US, 2004) makes great use of the environments in which subjects are interviewed (as well as the comparative method to bring out contrasting viewpoints and values) to tell us something about them, to locate their subjectivities (and therefore their perspectives and values) in a social context. The film charts the global battle in the wine business between small-scale producers who use artisanal working practices and for whom winemaking is an art and above all what Marx called a use-value, and large-scale producers who operate globally using mass production methods and for whom the commercial value of wine (or what Marx called exchange-value) ultimately trumps its use-value. For example, in the early part of the film the small-scale wine growers are usually interviewed outside on hillsides (close to nature and production) while the wine consultant and the mass producers he advises are shot mostly in interiors (cars, houses and inside sheds where machinery is used to oxygenate wine). Later in California, the filmmakers interview one large-scale wine producer next to his swimming pool. He is talking about how he and his wife designed their garden and brought their trees, shrubs and bushes from Italy. This, we are told is a statement, a 'showcase for our wines, our lifestyles, our commitments to charity'. On the word 'charity', there is a wonderful cutaway to an automatic machine swimming around the pool, evidently cleaning it. This cut hints at a level of luxury and commodity fetishism that works to counterpoint the philanthropic image being projected by the interviewee and his wife.

In another interview with a CEO of a large French company that markets a Californian wine, the main subject occupies the centre-right of the image but is out of focus even while he is talking. In the background, silent but in focus, a worker in company overalls is up a ladder attending to some problem or the other. This nicely illustrates the hierarchical working practices that characterize the large commercial concern in contrast to the small-scale family-run business. This image of the worker in the margins, in the shadows or in the background is also repeated in the California location sequences. Interviewing another merchant of globalization, the film cuts to a series of pictures on his office wall: former US President and emblem of de-regulated capitalism Ronald Reagan is seen holding a glass of wine, then later the camera zooms in on an example of facile visual exploitation with a picture of three black kids in shorts playing and laughing in the sand around a bottle of red wine in some generic 'underdeveloped' context, lending their connoted 'natural' happiness and authenticity (as constructed by the West) to the carefully calculated commodity (Barthes 1993). In such ways *Mondovino* picks out visual elements of the subject's social environment to comment on or add a revealing dimension to their verbal discourse.

Documentary as critical practice

I want to now broach the methodological developments in qualitative analysis that came out of an increasing awareness of the significance of culture generally and mass-mediated visual culture specifically from the 1960s onwards. Semiotics (Barthes), structuralism (de Saussure, Lévi-Strauss, Eco), post-structuralism (Barthes, Derrida, Foucault), psychoanalysis (Freud, Lacan, Žižek), and postmodernism (Baudrillard, Lyotard, Jameson) have all significantly enhanced our understanding of the fundamental lessons of the qualitative paradigm already established by such social science methodologies as phenomenology and symbolic interactionism. Interactionist sociology, for example, treats the actions of actors as symbolically constructed signs in relative flux and requiring active interpretation by all participants. But where the object of analysis in symbolic interactionism is face-to-face interactions, verbal conversation and social role play, the 'new' qualitative methodologies constituted a 'linguistic turn', focusing above all on written language and visual (mass media) signs. Interestingly, they also emphasized 'structures', displacing individual subjectivity just as the positivist macro-focused social sciences did. But unlike the positivist social sciences, here the 'structures' in question were the structures of language and meaning making itself, rather than social reality 'out there'. Despite these differences between the social science qualitative methodologies and those of the linguistic turn, strong continuities remain. Locating and integrating these post-1960s methodologies as branches of a paradigm *already established* within the social sciences is useful because it may help to call into question the currently dominant understanding and self-constructed history within cultural studies that these methodologies represent a radical, fundamental and hitherto unexplored means of knowledge production. Indeed, these are the methodologies that would be typically understood as *the critical methodologies* of our time (for example, see Easthope and McGowan 2004). But the word 'critical' tends to function merely as a convenient umbrella term for these methodologies and an implicit rebuke to either the humanist orientation of earlier qualitative methodologies and the more positivist or empiricist methodologies which assume that concepts, language and representations generally can have a more or less unproblematic correspondence to or reflection of the real world. But most of the main figures (given above) associated with the 'linguistic turn' have not explicitly characterized, discussed or defined their theories as 'critical' at all.

For all their undoubted strengths and contribution to developing our conceptual apparatus for decoding signs, the new qualitative methodologies associated with the linguistic turn also share with their social science cousins a weakness that runs through all the methodologies in the qualitative paradigm: namely a tendency towards subjectivism (where the real world as a set of material forces shaping the values and perceptions of the subject disappears) and relativism (where one point of view, one set of values is as good as any other and there are no grounds for making evaluative judgements between different value systems and perspectives). If Errol Morris's problematization of testimony and perspective had collapsed altogether into subjectivism and relativism in *The Thin Blue Line*, then in all probability, a wrongful conviction for murder would not have been overturned. Postmodernism, which is the logical culmination of this subjectivist and relativist trend, helped to so undermine our capacity to provide critiques of massive centres of power and propaganda that Christopher Norris was moved, shortly after the American-led attack on Iraq in 1991, to write a book called *Uncritical Theory, Postmodernism, Intellectuals and the Gulf War* (1992). Norris' complaint was that subjectivism and relativism had so undercut the confidence of intellectuals to make truth statements about the world, that the arbitrary and deeply self-interested exertions of state power (and media representations) involved in Gulf War I, were being given a free ride. With the consequences of Gulf War II (2003) still playing itself out (and the subject of a number of documentaries) it seems we need to look elsewhere if we are to get a proper handle on this term 'critical'.

We could do worse than return to the tradition which first consciously worked out a research programme that was explicitly called 'Critical Theory'. The Institute for Social Research (sometimes called the Frankfurt School because of where it was founded) was established in 1923. The School was influenced by a number of philosophers such as Hegel, Nietzsche and Freud, but above all by Marx. At least up until the late 1940s, it developed (first in Germany, later in American exile from Nazi Germany) an approach to social analysis and a definition of what constitutes Critical Theory from which we can extrapolate, at the risk of over-homogenizing what were inevitably different approaches, judgements and interests among the key personnel, four features:

1. Critical Theory sought to overcome what it saw as a debilitating dichotomy between philosophy and science. Philosophy provided a history of thought 'oriented to the potentialities of man lying beyond his factual status' (Marcuse 1989: 66) but at the price of scholastic isolation from social reality as it was. Science, on the other hand, engaged in modern social, political and technological trends, but at the price of naturalizing society, treating science and its objects as neutral technical processes unconnected with 'the social process as a whole' (Horkheimer 1989: 54). For our purposes, it is easy enough to recast this dichotomy as the already discussed split between the positivist paradigm (with its tendency to take the social world as a given) and the interpretive paradigm, with the latter standing in for philosophy, as both place the emphasis on the realm of ideas, ideals, culture and the constructed meaning of action and behaviour. Among the methodologies of the linguistic turn, this emphasis is no longer grounded in the humanistic model of 'man', but instead projected into the very structure of language and signifying *systems*, but nevertheless, the emphasis remains on the process and construction of meaning making.

2. Critical Theory is also a reflexive theory, 'critical of itself and of the social forces that make up its own basis' (Marcuse 1989: 72). By contrast, although science is centrally concerned with 'a knowledge of comprehensive relationships' within its own specialist field, 'it has no realistic grasp of that comprehensive relationship upon which its own existence and the direction of its work depend, namely society' (Horkheimer 1989: 56).

3. The weakness of traditional theory (in both philosophy and science) against which Critical Theory defined itself was only one example of the impact of ideology, which is to be found as well in law, morality, religion and cultural institutions. 'Every human way of acting which hides the true nature of society, built as it is on antagonisms, is ideological' (Horkheimer 1989: 55). Thus Critical Theory practises ideology critique, exposing the way antagonisms generated by the dominant social interests of a capitalist society (capital and state) are concealed, displaced and rationalized.

4. The Critical Theorists followed (in theory) Marx's famous eleventh thesis on the German philosopher Feuerbach, which noted that philosophers have only *interpreted* the world but that adequate knowledge of it meant that it must test and be tested by transformative action (i.e. to change the world).

Douglas Kellner has suggested that there is a 'missed articulation' between Critical Theory and cultural studies (2002). By contrast, and without making the mistake of suggesting that documentary research today is a full realization of the principles of Critical Theory, there are nevertheless some interesting points of contact and similarity.

1. I have already suggested that documentary practices sit (sometimes uneasily) at the intersection of, and can in some ways integrate, the approaches of positivism and the interpretive paradigm. When Morgan Spurlock vomits up a McDonald's meal in *Super Size Me*, the link between that very particular incident, and visceral 'abject' image on the tarmac and a broader

critique of how corporate junk food penetrates the body and makes an increasing number of people sick in a more long-term and potentially fatal sense, has been secured at least in part by something like the sort of synthesis between research methodologies that the Critical Theorists advocated. It should be noted that the methodologies of the linguistic turn have been singularly uninterested in integrating qualitative modes of analysis with the sort of large-scale empirical data generated by more positivist methodologies.

2. A reflexive understanding of the social conditions of knowledge production is also increasingly part of a broader popular understanding of the way the media operates in society. Rather than insisting that every documentary interrogate its own conditions of production, we ought to recognize the broader self-reflexive knowledge about media culture that is now in play. The economic underpinnings of the news media, their closeness to the state, the limits in their repertoire of conventions, is in uneven, doubtless partial, but indisputable general circulation. Media criticism is in the mainstream. This is evident from both popular culture representations of the news media, from Hollywood films such as *Network* (Sidney Lumet, 1976) all the way to *Wag the Dog* (Barry Levinson, 1995) and beyond, television satires on television news and current affairs programming (the work of Chris Morris, for example) as well as documentaries themselves. Brian Springer's *Spin* (1995) utilized unbroadcast satellite feeds to reveal the disjuncture between off-air commentary and attitudes and on-air packaging of the finished product, while Robert Greenwald's *Outfoxed: Rupert Murdoch's War on Journalism* (2004) explored how the Fox news network in America is shaped around a strong right-wing agenda. Michael Moore's *Bowling for Columbine* (2002) about America's gun culture, featured an extensive critique of local television news, with its alarmist and disproportionate emphasis on crime, its racist reiteration of white victims and black perpetrators, and how a climate of fear nurses the sort of anxieties that help advertisers sell commodities that promise to make things better. This critique, in a film that broke box office records for a documentary within the US market, essentially mirrors academic criticism of US television news and brings it into the mainstream (see, for example, Klite, Bardwell and Salzman 1997). Moore's *Fahrenheit 9/11* (2004), the most successful documentary ever in the US market, opens with unbroadcast footage of the principal protagonists' or rogues gallery involved in propagating the war in Iraq. Here they are: Bush, Rumsfeld, Rice, Powell, Wolfowitz, all being prepared on separate occasions for the television cameras, prior to broadcast; microphones are being clipped on, make-up applied, hair brushed, and so forth. It's a series of shots over the credit sequence (including Bush making childish faces to the camera) that nicely makes the point about image displacing reality and the lack of critical interrogation of the pro-war case by the television networks. It should be noted that the qualitative methodologies of the linguistic turn, while they are reflexive within their own specialist field (the analysis of meaning making), have been in general

as uncurious about their own broader *social* conditions of existence as the science that the Critical Theorists critiqued.

3. The emergence of feature film documentary as a prominent player within the sphere of public opinion formation has evidently crystallized around the great assault on corporate capitalism, consumerism and globalization of market relations that has been such a welcome feature of the recent political landscape. A list of such documentaries would include: *Super Size Me, Mondovino, The Corporation* (Mark Achbar, Jennifer Abbott, Joel Bakan, 2004), *Fahrenheit 9/11* (Michael Moore, 2004), Robert Greenwald's *Outfoxed: Rupert Murdoch's War on Journalism, Walmart, The High Cost of Low Price* (2006) and *Iraq for Sale: The War Profiteers* (2006), *Czech Dream* (Vít Klusák, Felip Remunda, 2004), *The Yes Men* (Dan Ollman, Sarah Price, 2003), *Enron, The Smartest Guys in the Room* (Alex Gibney, 2005), *A Social Suicide* (Fernando Solanas, 2004), and *The Take* (Avi Lewis, Naomi Klein, 2004). These documentaries are critical precisely in their interrogation (sometimes confused or partial no doubt) of the dominant assumptions of everyday life under capitalism and its various institutions. They constitute an audio-visual example of that current of critical journalism that Philo and Miller compare favourably with the writings of media and cultural studies academics (Philo and Miller 2001: 74). In the field of cultural and media studies, the whole project of ideology critique (connecting ideas to social interests) has become progressively marginalizsed by the postmodernist critique of 'grand narratives' that have yet to catch up with the emergent story of the new anti-capitalist conjuncture.

4. Documentary belongs to the mass media (including today the Internet, which can be used for marketing, distribution and even fundraising) and speaks in a language that is generally less specialized and more open to lay publics than 'philosophy' or academia. The latter tend to be concerned largely with interpreting the world rather than changing it, as Marx put it. By contrast, a number of the documentaries listed above have been produced and disseminated as products that self-consciously come out of social struggles and with the aim of amplifying the critiques of groups struggling for progressive social transformation, spreading awareness and knowledge and being used as resources for activist networks. In the Marxist tradition, the integration of theory and practice, which is an essential pre-condition of adequacy for both knowing and doing, is called praxis.

Documentary as creative practice

Jon Prosser has noted that while the long hegemony of the positivist paradigm indirectly marginalized image-based research (the role visual technologies could play in anthropology, sociology, history, and so forth) reducing it at best to the role of cataloguing and documentation, orthodox qualitative researchers have 'undervalued and under applied' image-based research (Prosser 1998: 97). The anthropologist Kirsten Hastrup, for example, champions writing over the visual image. She bases much of her critique on a disappointing experience she had when she tried to photograph an Icelandic ram competition. But her critique suggests that successful image-based research requires a number of factors: technical competence with the medium, knowledge of its history of uses, imaginative capacity to mobilize that knowledge in given situations and preparation for the specific logistical difficulties of those situations. According to Hastrup, the visual image can: 'record only visible things; while we can take a close-up of the ram's private parts we cannot see its metaphorical expression of the owner's sexual abilities' (1992: 14). Hastrup's argument that photography cannot make connections, cannot capture the broader context, is too grounded in the particular and is devoid of the capacity to be suggestive, ambiguous or metaphorical suggests an absence of all the above preconditions for successful photography.

Creativity and imagination are certainly important elements in any kind of cultural production that aims to be rewarding for audiences. Many of the Critical Theorists, such as Marcuse, thought that imagination and fantasy were important resources for critical thinking, providing us with the ability to 'create something new out of given material[s] of cognition' (Marcuse 1989: 71). With the question of the pleasure and cognition to be derived from the creativity and competence in art and culture we pass over into the realm of aesthetics. Creativity may be an important element in critical thinking, but it is hardly the exclusive province of critical practice, as Leni Riefenstahl's documentary *Triumph of the Will* (1935) with its celebration of German fascism, taught us all those years ago. Aesthetics is indeed a terrain well booby-trapped with ideological mines. For one thing, within bourgeois ideology, aesthetics have often been conceived as a realm outside politics and ideology, transcendent art or 'mere' entertainment, but certainly not impacted by social interests. One particular way of figuring aesthetics as outside the realm of the social has been to interlace it with Nature itself. In this sense, a documentary like *Touching the Void* (Kevin Macdonald, 2003) uses the stunning environment of snow, mountains and sky to abstract what is a quite socially specific drama out of the realm of society altogether. Thus the contradictions of competition and co-operation that bind and separate the professional middle class in their struggle to ascend the career mountain is the real story that lies behind the phantasmagoric and pseudo-universalizing one told by the film, the audience for which were interestingly enough, overwhelmingly middle class (UK Film Council, 2004: 32). The film encourages the audience to ask of its central ethical dilemma: what would I do in such a situation? Would I cut the rope? But this is essentially an unrecognizable transposition of the question of *solidarity* that in rather less dramatic scenarios, actually confronts us here and now, where all too frequently, in our everyday practices, we are busy cutting the rope.

One way of engaging with the question of aesthetics while resisting its ideological lures and traps, is to re-ground it as a subset (albeit a 'special' one) of human labour generally. The aesthetic is not qualitatively different from other kinds of human labour (and so therefore does not transcend society). Despite all the creativity, play and experimentation that are routinely robbed of ordinary human labour, it still retains some residual subjectivity, that is human agency and consciousness that is potentially at least, in contradiction and conflict with capital. Capital demands, despite the new management discourses promoting the importance of 'worker knowledge' and 'human capital', the subordination of labour to the imperatives of profit accumulation. Because this demand is potentially limitless but human bodies are finite, there can never be the degree of integration of human labour (and cultural production) into capitalism that the Critical Theorists, Max Horkheimer and Theodor Adorno famously envisaged in a period of particularly dark pessimism (Adorno and Horkheimer 1977). Furthermore, to a *degree*, aesthetic labour is different from ordinary labour. Cultural materials, despite the controlling conditions they are made under, remain more pliable and plural in their possible uses, relatively less prone to absolute standardization (each film is a prototype), more open to authorial 'capture' by cultural workers and often vibrantly alive to registering shifts, changes and contradictions in the wider body politic than other kinds of labour.

The potential within the aesthetic for play, creativity, acutely attuned sense perception, experimentation and participation (for both producers and audiences) and a place where, potentially, thinking and feeling can come together, makes the aesthetic register a kind of prefiguring of the sort of world a critical theory like Marxism hopes to make a contribution to bringing into existence. It is after all the fundamental axiom of Marxism's critique of commodity fetishism that consciousness parts company with social being when the latter is constituted in ways that rob it of memory, agency, autonomy, creativity and our relatedness to others.

A nice example of how documentary labour sets into play a number of the above qualities of the aesthetic can be found in a short film by Sandra Ruesga on a Spanish/Catalan compilation DVD called *Between the Dictator and Me* (2005). The dictator in question of course is Francisco Franco who came to power in 1939 when the fascists won the three-year Spanish Civil War. Franco ruled Spain until his death in 1975, building his dictatorship on the grave of the experiments in socialism and anarchism which his forces had set out to crush. *Between the Dictator and Me* is made by young documentary filmmakers, recounting their earliest experiences of growing up in Franco's Spain. Ruesga's contribution works with, but also reworks and interrogates, the genre of the family video. The video camcorder has increasingly supplemented the use of photography as a means of providing a record of family history. What Richard Chalfen calls 'the home mode' of visual communication (1998: 215) has tended to reinforce the ideology of the private 'happy family'. Ruesga's home video footage is no different, with the occasion for documenting what the family is doing tending to revolve around birthdays, holidays, significant moments (such as christenings) and other activities of fun and leisure. This material constitutes the image-track of Ruesga's documentary.

The audio-track is made up of two separate telephone conversations between Ruesga and her mother and father as she seeks to make sense of their silence, apathy and accommodation towards the Franco regime. The motivation for the documentary is evidently her re-assessment of the family videos and the choices her parents were making. Specifically she asks them why they went on holiday at the Valley of the Fallen, where Franco is buried, or why they visited a fascist monument at Cerro de San Cristobal. Her parents were not fascists, but neither did they do anything to think or act critically in relation to the dictatorship. So the filmmaker plays as a child in the shadow of fascist monuments and understandably feels a painful gap between that time when she was kept in the dark and uninformed about the nature and history of the society she grew up in and her own emergent consciousness as a young adult about the dictatorship. These gaps between now and then are re-doubled in the gap between herself now and her parents' breezy rationalizations of their indifference to the nature of their society, articulated by the fact that the interviews are conducted by phone, which symbolizes *both* communication and distance. Ruesga's short nicely demonstrates the power of the aesthetic at work: the potential for critical evaluation (here of personal archives), for re-articulating the private and the personal with a political and public life it is often torn from, the potential to remake both cultural materials and re-evaluate the self and its social and historical conditions of existence. And all this is achieved by a few relatively simple but effective choices and juxtapositions made in the realm of documentary cultural production.

Conclusion

I have argued that documentary, as a mode of generating knowledge, is strongly grounded in the paradigm of qualitative research practices. The case study, inductive analysis, inferred typicality from the particular, predominate. Nevertheless, documentary can draw on the statistical data of positivist research to identify macro trends and scales. At a philosophical level, the recording capacities of film share with positivism something of its confidence that the data it is generating provide evidence of a real world 'out there' that is not reducible to perception and point of view, no matter how much it may be mediated by it. Overcoming the divisions between the naïve realism of positivism and the tendency towards relativism characteristic of the qualitative paradigm generally and the methodologies of the 'linguistic turn' specifically, was one of the ambitions of Critical Theory. While the methodologies of the linguistic turn may be *integrated* into a critical theory, whether they constitute a 'critical theory' in and of themselves is very much open to doubt in my view. Further, I suggested that within the *culture* of documentary films, there is a strand, articulated to a critique of capital and state power, which has many points of contact with Critical Theory and represents critical research practices rather more robustly than much contemporary film and cultural studies within academia. Finally, documentary is not just a research practice, critical or otherwise, but an art form, a creative practice that intersects with debates on aesthetics, which, properly understood, can see cultural production as a special prefiguring of what emancipated cognition and feeling might look like in future.

7 Reframing Ethnographic Film

Paul Basu

> *Ethnos*, 'a people'; *graphe*, 'a writing, a drawing, a representation'. Ethnographic film, then: 'a representation of a people on film'. A definition without limit, a process with unlimited possibility, an artifact with unlimited variation.
>
> (Eliot Weinberger, *The Camera People*)

Despite the broad inclusiveness suggested by an etymological definition of ethnographic film, it is clear that, through most of its history, this subgenre of documentary has had a more narrow usage. Like their textual counterparts, ethnographic films have not typically been concerned with representing all peoples equally – they are largely films made by 'us' (urban white Westerners) about 'them' (our non-urban, non-white, non-Western *Other*). For this reason, suggests Weinberger, it is not Louis Lumière, with his *actualitiés* of French factory workers and alighting train passengers, who is recognized as the first ethnographic filmmaker, it is his compatriot, Félix-Louis Regnault, who set up his Chronophotographe camera at the Paris Exposition Ethnographique de l'Afrique Occidentale of 1895 to film a Wolof woman from Senegal making clay pots (Weinberger 1992: 26; Rony 1992).

While the use of cameras to film moving images of ethnographic subjects may thus be traced to the very origins of cinema, ethnographic film as such has remained somewhat peripheral to the mainstream documentary tradition and, indeed, to anthropology, the academic discipline most closely associated with ethnographic research. Nevertheless, anthropology (by which I mean social or cultural anthropology) is one of the few social science disciplines to have seriously explored the use of cinematic, and, later, televisual and digital video technologies as both a tool of research and a medium for the dissemination of knowledge (Winston 1995: 170). Over the years there has been a sufficient number of exponents of 'visual anthropology' for an ethnographic film canon to emerge and innovation in form to occur, not least through the genre-defying work of figures such as Robert Flaherty and Jean Rouch, whose influence has been as significant to visual anthropologists as it has been to documentary filmmakers more generally.

Definitional debates

If the first real revolution in the popularization of ethnographic filmmaking came with the development of lightweight 16mm cameras and synchronous sound recording equipment in the 1950s and 1960s (the same technological impetus behind the *cinéma vérité*, direct cinema and observational documentary movements), today, in the era of low-cost, palm-sized digital camcorders, more anthropologists than ever are recording moving images as a routine part of their fieldwork, and there is a corresponding burgeoning of university training courses at which to acquire the appropriate technical skills, and ethnographic film festivals at which to show the results. Nor is there a shortage of writing on ethnographic film: among the more significant recent contributions to this literature are David MacDougall's *Transcultural Cinema* (1998) and *The Corporeal Image* (2006), Anna Grimshaw's *The Ethnographer's Eye* (2001), Jay Ruby's *Picturing Culture* (2000), Peter Loizos's *Innovation in Ethnographic Film* (1993), and Lucien Taylor's *Visualizing Theory* (1994). As well as providing a detailed account of the history of ethnographic filmmaking and positioning the practice within the broader subdiscipline of visual anthropology (Banks and Morphy 1997), this literature debates issues such as the relationship between written and filmic ethnography, the power inequalities between those controlling the means of representation and those represented in ethnographic films, and the innovation of more participatory filming techniques.

My intention here is not to rehearse these debates again, so much as to relate them to continuing controversies over the 'framing' of ethnographic film in televisual, academic and artistic contexts. In relation to the history of its production and consumption in these differing contexts, and in tandem with the changing object of anthropological inquiry, a question obstinately remains: just which films *are* ethnographic? And, crucially, for whom? These are not new questions. Indeed, many of the early commentaries on ethnographic film are largely concerned with defining the genre (e.g. Hockings 1975; Ruby 1975; Heider 1976). Their method is chiefly to assess films according to the established *textual* conventions of academic anthropology. Heider, for example, identifies as most ethnographic those films which most closely replicate the 'scientific enterprise' of ethnographic research and writing (1976: 5). Aside from disregarding the possibility of a distinctively *cinematic* anthropology (cf. Rouch 2003), a fundamental problem here is that the 'scientific' identity of the ethnographic enterprise is itself vulnerable to critique (e.g. Marcus and Fischer 1986).

More recently, Banks has returned to the question of definition, reminding us that the 'ethnographicness' of a film may be determined differently in relation to the various processes which together constitute the complete work. A film's ethnographic identity may thus be located in the intentions of the filmmaker, in the event filmed (including the event of filming), and in the reactions of audiences (Banks 1992). It is clear, for example, that not all documentaries shot in non-Western societies are necessarily ethnographic; what constitutes them as such may be the anthropological training of the filmmaker, the degree to which the circumstances of filming mimic the methods of ethnographic fieldwork, or the use of specialist vocabularies in voice-over narration. But, equally, a film may be perceived as being ethnographic by audiences who may themselves have only a limited knowledge of what ethnography is.

A second question emerges in relation to the discourse which surrounds ethnographic film (and I suggest that it is through this discourse that the ethnographic film 'canon' is established): we might ask why it is that, despite the current proliferation of the use of digital video by anthropologists as part of their fieldwork, very few works have emerged since the mid-1980s that have amassed a body of critical analysis equivalent to that generated by ethnographic films from earlier periods. Thus, the same few 'classic' films (and filmmakers) are discussed *ad nauseam* in the visual anthropology literature, while more recent works languish unviewed on bookshelves and computer hard drives after brief excursions on the ethnographic film festival circuit. The canonical filmmakers discussed in the above literature thus typically include Jean Rouch, John Marshall, Robert Gardner, Timothy Asch, David and Judith MacDougall, Gary Kildea, Ian Dunlop, and Melissa Llewelyn-Davies, all of whom established their reputations working on 16mm in the 1950s, 1960s and 1970s. Whereas new documentary filmmakers continue to graduate from noviciate obscurity, the question emerges as to why so few new *ethnographic* films and filmmakers have emerged since this period to contribute to, or challenge, the established ethnographic film canon. The answers are, no doubt, many, but I suggest that significant factors include the absence of formal innovation since this period, and, not least, the above-mentioned lack of definition regarding what constitutes an ethnographic film in the first place.

As a way of thinking about the contemporary framing and reframing of ethnographic film, I propose first to discuss the recent popular BBC television series *Tribe*, which, despite being identified as ethnographic by audiences and presented as such on an accompanying website, met with censure from academic anthropologists and was regarded as presenting a distorted image of anthropology to the wider public. Second, I shall consider the work of Kim Longinotto, whose documentaries, though not intended to be ethnographic, are nevertheless embraced as such by academic anthropologists and regularly win prizes at ethnographic film festivals. Finally, in a more speculative conclusion, I consider the contemporary 'ethnographic turn' in video art, suggesting that this represents one of the more exciting possibilities for the future of ethnographic film.

On (not) going tribal

In the UK, anthropologists sometimes mourn the passing of the 'halcyon days' of the 1970s and 1980s when documentary films with an explicit anthropological content were a regular feature of the television schedules. As Paul Henley has recently noted, in this period, 'perhaps as many as 100 hour-long television documentaries were made for British television based directly on the fieldwork of one or more consultant anthropologists' (2006: 171). Indeed, programmes made for Granada's *Disappearing World* strand, which ran intermittently from 1970 to 1993, are often still used in undergraduate anthropology teaching and are distributed for educational use by the Royal Anthropological Institute. Combining observational styles with subtitled inter-views and expository voice-over narration, these films were concerned with such issues as gender relations among the Maasai (*Masai Women*, 1974), gift exchange in the highlands of Papua New Guinea (*The Kawelka: Ongka's Big Moka*, 1974), and conflict and social change in the Columbian rainforest (*The Last of the Cuiva*, 1971).

They also reproduced a somewhat stereotypical public perception of anthropology as a discipline concerned with remote, tribal peoples, whose traditional ways of life were threatened with extinction. By the 1970s, most professional anthropologists would distance themselves from this outmoded 'salvage anthropology' paradigm, and yet the programmes had sufficient ethnographic credibility to gain a generally positive critical response from within the discipline (e.g. Loizos 1980; see Banks 1994, for a more negative critical view).

Since this golden age, anthropological programming has, as Henley (2006) quips, itself become a 'disappearing world' on British television. Contrary to this trend, in 2005, the BBC broadcast a series of six one-hour programmes entitled *Tribe* (the series was broadcast on the Discovery Channel in the USA as *Going Tribal*); a second, three-part series followed in 2006, and six more programmes are in production at the time of writing, scheduled for broadcast in 2007. Each of the programmes is concerned with a different indigenous group, and follows the trials and tribulations of the on-screen presenter, Bruce Parry, as he undergoes various initiations and seeks to 'go native' and live as the tribespeople do. Each episode follows a similar structure, which sees Parry travelling to a remote destination, meeting and interacting with members of the host 'tribe', learning about and attempting to participate in often stereotypically exotic cultural practices, reflecting on his experiences and on the endangered lifeworlds of his hosts, and eventually bidding his farewells and heading off for another adventure. While *Tribe* was not explicitly presented as an 'ethnographic' or 'anthropological' series when it was first broadcast, it is interesting to observe how it has been received as such by audiences and, indeed, how the programmes have been repackaged within this rubric on a BBC website devoted to the series (www.bbc.co.uk/tribe).

For each of the nine 'tribes' to feature in the first and second series, the website thus provides maps, photographs, clips from the respective episode of *Tribe*, links to related BBC, NGO and research websites, and written descriptions of everyday tribal life, customs, beliefs, and the challenges that each group is confronted with. Much of the textual content appears to be drawn from ethnographic writing. In addition to these 'tribe-specific' pages of the website, five further sections address more generic themes relating to indigenous populations under the titles: 'Knowledge', 'Issues', 'Daily Life', 'Language', and 'Location'. These sections also contain informative texts, clips from relevant episodes of *Tribe*, links to related websites (including links to an 'Online Anthropology Library' and the 'Anthropological Index of the Royal Anthropological Institute'), and reasonably comprehensive bibliographies comprised mainly of anthropological references. It is clear, then, that through the BBC's accompanying, education-rich website, *Tribe* is framed as a popular anthropology series, and, indeed, judging from viewer feedback comments posted in another section of the website, this would seem to be how audiences perceived the series when it was broadcast.

While viewers have praised *Tribe* as being 'informative and educational', providing 'insight into ways of life totally different to our own' and thus 'raising questions about our own culture', the series has been strongly criticized by professional anthropologists and characterized as a 'Victorian romp', 'more primitive, representationally, than the societies it purports to represent' (Hughes-Freeland 2006:

22). Much of this invective has been directed towards the macho antics of the on-screen 'front man' of the series, Bruce Parry, an ex-Royal Marine Commando and self-proclaimed 'adventurer', 'expeditioner' and presenter of 'extreme outdoors' television programmes. Superficially, Parry's persona in *Tribe* is that of the ethnographer: someone who travels to remote indigenous communities and who braves numerous discomforts in attempting to live as his/her local informants do, staying in their homes, eating their food, participating in their 'traditional' customs and so forth, as way of learning about their society. The superficiality of the resemblance to an ethnographic methodology is, however, drawn to our attention by the anthropologist Pat Caplan, when she reminds us that:

> (1) Parry is not a trained anthropologist; (2) he did not speak any of the local languages; (3) he spent only an average of a month in each area; (4) there was little or no reference to any previous anthropological research in the region; (5) the material presented lacked much in the way of social or cultural context.

> (Caplan 2005: 4)

Academic anthropologists, in contrast, are, generally speaking, trained post-doctoral researchers who learn the languages of those they are studying, engage in long-term immersive fieldwork (typically a year or more), explicitly position their work in relation to previous research in the region, and are at pains to contextualize the phenomena they are studying within the broader social, political, economic and cultural worlds in which they are embedded and from which they gain their meanings.

It is, of course, somewhat naïve of anthropologists to expect this kind of academic rigour from a popular television series. As André Singer, a prominent figure in both ethnographic film and mainstream television documentary production, has noted, the mass audience for whom *Tribe* is made probably wouldn't dream of watching the earnestly ethnographic works collected in the Royal Anthropological Institute's film library (2006: 24). But the stark differences between anthropologists' and popular audiences' experiences of the series are revealing of a more significant disjuncture between the popular perception of anthropology (such as it exists at all) and the realities of anthropological inquiry in the twenty-first century. The vehemence of the anthropological critique of *Tribe* may thus be explained by the fact that the series reproduces the very exoticist stereotypes that anthropologists have, for generations, striven to problematize and distance themselves from (MacClancey 2002). The problem is that, while anthropologists have long worked in much more diverse settings – including in their own and other complex urban societies – and are more interested in engaging with modernity in its multifarious, localized manifestations rather than collecting 'pre-modern', primitive survivals, in the popular imagination the discipline is still associated with nineteenth-century adventure and exploration, and with the investigation of exotic esoteria and tribal customs.

There is, however, a more profound issue here, beyond a lay misrecognition of the object of contemporary anthropological study. We might ask just why mass audiences are drawn to these stereotypical, 'primitivist' representations of indigenousness rather than to the more typical contexts of current ethnographic research. And here one encounters a tenacious myth, and one with which the discipline of anthropology is thoroughly implicated: that of the Noble Savage (Ellingson 2001). *Tribe* thus reproduces a romantic fantasy of the modern Western mind, which idealizes and constructs indigenous peoples as being closer to the 'natural' state of humankind, and innocent of the moral corruption which is perceived to blight modern, industrialized society. Connected still to their more authentic ways of life, their traditional customs and beliefs, the endangered tribespeople are portrayed as living in harmony with their environments, keepers of all that we have lost or destroyed. *Tribe* is, however, far from being 'Reality TV', insofar as the more complex realities of indigenous societies – realities which do not accord with the myth – are not filmed or are edited out, and thus, in a way, denied. While seeming to advocate social responsibility, the representational approach of *Tribe* reproduces a cultural evolutionist worldview, which may once have informed anthropological inquiry (Stocking 1987), but which has long since been discredited and found to be morally insupportable. I suggest, then, that a significant reason why *Tribe* so rankles academic ethnographers is that it represents an image of anthropology once exorcized from the discipline, but which forever seems to return to haunt it via the popular media.

Challenging traditions

The documentary filmmaker, Kim Longinotto, has an ambivalent attitude towards ethnographic film. On the one hand, she herself associates ethnographic film with the primitivist representations reproduced in *Tribe* and thus distances herself from the genre. On the other hand, Longinotto appreciates that many anthropologists also reject such outmoded stereotypes and are more likely to identify her own films as being ethnographic. Indeed, many of Longinotto's films are distributed in the UK by the Royal Anthropological Institute (RAI), and, as previously noted, they are regularly screened and win prizes at ethnographic film festivals: *Divorce Iranian Style* (1998), for example, won the RAI Film Prize at the 7th RAI International Festival of Ethnographic Film (a prize awarded 'for the most outstanding film on social, cultural or biological anthropology'), while *Sisters in Law* (2005) won the Audience Prize and received a special commendation for the Basil Wright Film Prize at the 9th RAI International Festival of Ethnographic Film (the latter being a prize awarded for 'films *in the ethnographic tradition* which exemplify the power of film to evoke a concern for humanity' (Benthall 1986: 1, emphasis added)). Drawing upon an interview I conducted with the filmmaker in October 2006, my interest in this section is thus to consider the anthropological community's framing of Longinotto's films within an 'ethnographic tradition', while recognizing that this does not necessarily correspond with how Longinotto would herself frame her films.

Adopting an observational filming approach first encountered under the tute-lage of Colin Young while attending Britain's National Film and Television School in the 1970s, Longinotto's films address contemporary gender-related issues such as female genital mutilation, domestic violence, divorce, and sexual politics in geo-graphical contexts as diverse as Iran (*Divorce Iranian Style*, 1998; *Runaway*, 2001), Cameroon (*Sisters in Law*, 2005), Kenya (*The Day I Will Never Forget*, 2002), and Japan

(*Gaea Girls*, 2000; *Shinjuku Boys*, 1995; *Dream Girls*, 1994). Most of these films have been commissioned by Channel Four Television or the BBC for their major documentary strands. At the core of each of the films, is a collaboration both with the subjects of the films (leading Longinotto to describe her approach as more participatory than observational), and with co-directors who have local language and cultural skills. In another context Longinotto has described her films as being about 'strong women, and particularly about women who are brave outsiders' – women who dare to speak out 'against customs that oppress them' (Geritz 2006). In this respect, whereas *Tribe* portrays change as a negative, external influence, capable only of damaging the supposedly harmonious balance of traditional lifeworlds, for Longinotto, tradition is often repressive, and change is regarded as emancipatory and empowering. 'I am interested in filming stories of change', Longinotto explains, 'and if a film can be a little part of that change, then I'm really proud.'

This departure from what are popularly understood as the 'traditional' objects of ethnographic study is consistent with changes within the discipline of anthropology itself, which has long championed the more critically engaged approach evident in Longinotto's films. Within anthropology, this shift has been explicitly signalled in ethnographic collections such as MacClancy's *Exotic No More* (2002), the contributors of which are 'dedicated to research which has socially beneficial ends', and pursue their anthropological engagements in 'non-traditional' fields such as biomedical research, environmentalism, human rights discourse, aid programmes, religious fundamentalism, and mass media (MacClancy 2002: 2). In his introduction to the volume, MacClancy also makes the point that this is not a recent innovation, and that anthropologists have been working 'at home', in Britain and France, for example, as well as in more exotic 'ethnographic' locations such as Papua New Guinea or West Africa, since the beginning of the discipline in the nineteenth century (2002: 1). It is, however, interesting to note that the period in the 1980s when anthropology went through its most radical 'crisis of representation', and when its contribution to cultural critique became a mainstream *raison d'être* (Marcus and Fischer 1986), coincides with what might be regarded as the ossification of the ethnographic film canon. Indeed, this moment is signalled by the release of Trinh Minh-Ha's 'anti-ethnographic' film *Reassemblage* (1982), with its rejection of virtually all ethnographic conventions and its avowed anti-representational intent: 'I do not intend to speak about / Just speak nearby' (Trinh 1992: 96).

In Longinotto's work, too, there is a rejection of ethnographic conventions: her films eschew both voice-over commentary and contextualizing exposition. The film *Sisters in Law*, for instance, which follows the lives of a number of Cameroonian women as they are encouraged to bring domestic abuse cases to court by two female lawyers, makes no recourse to such explanatory devices. Longinotto recalls being surprised at the critical reception of the film at a London screening: '"There's no context", they said. "You're making a film in Cameroon and we don't know anything about Cameroon. What's the history of the judiciary in Cameroon? How many women judges are there? What's the colonial history?" People wanted the film to tell them everything.' Longinotto's defence is that she is not making educational films, but that she is 'telling stories through other people's lives', and that the objective is to allow 'deeper truths' to emerge, 'truths about you and me, and truths about all sorts of other things ... emotional truths, really'. Longinotto explains that she does not want her audiences to think of her films 'as ethnographic': 'they aren't about customs or traditions or things that are exotic – I want them to be thinking that the women in the films could be their aunt, their daughter or sister ... they are about universal things'. This desire for her audience to see beyond apparent cultural differences and identify with the characters of her films is coupled with a respect for the audience's ability to contextualize the films' stories for themselves. Longinotto believes that the internet, in particular, will 'liberate film from the burden of giving information' – 'if people want to understand *Sisters in Law* in relation to Cameroon's colonial past, well, they can access a hundred articles on that; they don't need me telling them my interpretation of it'.

Longinotto argues that the presence of an 'intermediary or a commentary telling you what to think' in her films would act as a barrier, hindering the audience's involvement with what is happening on screen: 'What I am trying to do is plunge you straight in, so that there's nothing to save you from the experience.' Longinotto provides an example of this when she describes filming a scene in *Sisters in Law* in which a woman who is being prosecuted for mistreating her 8-year-old niece makes a dramatic plea for forgiveness: 'I remember when I was filming it, and I'm kneeling just by her, she gives this *huge* performance, and I'm filming it and I'm thinking, you know, people are going to *be here*, as if they are kneeling here, they're going to be seeing this first-hand like I am.' For Longinotto, it is this ability to transport audiences into the ethnographic *mise-en-scène* of the film that represents the real power of the medium. Without wishing to overstate the parallel, such 'immediacy' has clear resonances with the experience of ethnographic fieldwork, in which the researcher is similarly plunged into an alien context without necessarily having the social and cultural competences to make sense of it. Thus, as Longinotto states, as a viewer of her films, 'You are constantly surprised, you are constantly on your guard, you are constantly having to work things out like in real life ... that's what I want audiences to be doing in the films.'

While Longinotto insists that her films are 'documenting change that's already happening' rather than explicitly advocating change, it is also clear that they have an impact on the people and issues with whom and with which they engage. Unencumbered by academic anthropology's ethical and moral quandaries regarding advocacy (e.g. Hastrup and Elsass 1990), Longinotto is proud of the capacity of film to contribute to what she perceives as positive social transformation. Thus, whereas the anthropologist and filmmaker Melissa Llewelyn-Davies adopts a neutral stance on female genital mutilation (FGM) in the film *Masai Women* (1974), Longinotto has no qualms about the partisan perspective of her film *The Day I Will Never Forget*. And whereas the actual act of female circumcision is represented only elliptically in *Masai Women*, Longinotto was unhesitatingly encouraged by her Kenyan collaborators to film the event explicitly and retain it in the edit. Despite concerns that this would be sensationalist, Longinotto is convinced that this was the right decision and she cites an occasion when the criticisms of a pro-FGM group were silenced after a screening: 'How could they defend that practice after all of us in the audience – there were about

800 of us – have watched it?' Committed to championing what she regards as unequivocal human rights, Longinotto expresses some relief that she is not an anthropologist and hamstrung, as she sees it, by academic quandaries over cultural relativism or fears that her interventions might bring about social change rather than reflect it. If anthropologists are typically more hesitant when it comes to advocacy, Longinotto's films nevertheless raise ethical and moral dilemmas that they also regularly confront, and, indeed, as MacClancy's collection shows, many anthropologists have an equal commitment to directing their ethnographic means towards such socially transformative ends (2002: 2).

If one were to assess Longinotto according to the same criteria that Caplan applies to Bruce Parry, one would have to conclude that she also has few 'ethnographic credentials': she is not a trained anthropologist; she does not speak the languages of many of the people she films; her films are shot over a relatively short period (typically two or three months); and they do not refer to previous anthropological work in the area or provide much in the way of social or cultural context (Caplan 2005: 4). But whereas *Tribe* at best reproduces an inaccurate, though still popular, impression of anthropology as a Victorian romp, concerned with exotic customs and ennobled traditions, it is clear that Longinotto's films more closely reflect the realities of contemporary anthropological inquiry and are therefore often framed as 'ethnographic' by the discipline. While lacking the academic and cultural context that an academic monograph affords, Longinotto's stories of gendered negotiations of power in complex and dynamic social environments are played out across the same terrain as that with which anthropologists are typically engaged. This makes Longinotto's films particularly useful within undergraduate teaching, for example, where they speak to issues within the mainstream anthropology curriculum, and where a broader cultural context can be given by a lecturer. If an episode of *Tribe* is shown in such a teaching context, it is usually as an illustration of what anthropology may seem to be, but is not.

Ethnographic installation: beyond the narrative frame

From the foregoing, we may conclude that a fundamental incongruence exists between televisual and academic framings of ethnographic film. As might be expected, academic ethnographers are particularly keen to defend the integrity of their discipline against the outdated stereotypes and misconceptions that continue to be promulgated in the popular media. Their efforts are, however, largely contained within their own professional practices (e.g. critiquing popular television series like *Tribe* in journals such as *Anthropology Today*; appropriating for their discipline documentaries such as Longinotto's through the awarding of prizes at specialist festivals), and one assumes that popular television audiences remain unperturbed by such machinations as they continue to consume enthralling curios of exotic otherness under the guise of 'edutainment'. Meanwhile, academic ethnographic filmmaking remains as peripheral as ever to both popular audiences and, it must be said, to the majority of anthropologists: a genre in search of an audience.

What, then, of the future of ethnographic film? While I have suggested that the use of digital video as a routine part of anthropological fieldwork has become standard, I have also argued that this has not resulted in any significant addition to or revision of the established ethnographic film canon. The proliferating use of camcorders in the field can be explained by the new accessibility of digital video technology, but technological innovation in the means of production has not yet been matched by innovation in the manner in which ethnographic footage is articulated, disseminated and consumed. While television appears to be an unlikely medium for such innovation to now take place, inspiration may be found, I suggest, by considering alternative venues for the exhibition (if not *broad*cast) of ethnographic audio-visual material. The future of ethnographic film is, I maintain, therefore more likely to be framed by advances in the online archiving and distribution of digital video, by the increasingly sophisticated use of moving image media in ethnographic museum spaces, and, not least, by the incorporation of formal innovations evident in the so-called 'ethnographic turn' in contemporary video art installation.

What these venues provide is an alternative structure for the presentation of ethnographic audio-visual material: a structure that is, in many respects, more compatible with the anthropological project than conventional film or televisual narrative. Although space does not allow for a detailed analysis, I conclude this chapter with a discussion of this alternative structure as manifest in two recent multi-screen video installations, Ann-Sofi Sidén's *Warte Mal! Prostitution After the Velvet Revolution* (1999) and Kutlug Ataman's *Küba* (2004).[1] Exemplars of a broader trend in video art, I suggest that these exhibitions provide particular inspiration for the future reframing of ethnographic film.

In common with Longinotto's documentaries, Sidén's and Ataman's installations are not immediately recognizable as ethnographic works, since they are not concerned with stereotypically 'exotic', 'primitive' or 'tribal' others. As has already been discussed, however, such traditional objects of ethnographic study have long ceased to define the anthropological project. Indeed, the issues addressed in *Warte Mal!* and *Küba* – the culture of prostitution in the Czech border-town of Dubi, and social relations in a beleaguered urban enclave on the outskirts of Istanbul – are quite typical of the fields in which academic ethnographers are today engaged. Rather than their subject matter *per se*, however, what sets these works apart as examples of a new 'ethnographic paradigm' in art practice, is the methodology of their making. Thus, both installations entailed their makers conducting something akin to ethnographic fieldwork as they immersed themselves for appreciable periods of time in the communities which are the subjects of their work. In so doing, they developed the relationships with their informants that enabled them to assemble the video-taped narratives and life histories that form the core of the installations. Sidén, for example, spent some nine months living in Dubi gathering materials for *Warte Mal!*, including long periods staying at the Motel Hubert, a motel frequented by the prostitutes whom she befriended, and where rooms are rented by the hour to their clients.[2] In a similar manner, Ataman spent over two years living intermittently among the residents of Küba, forging relationships with informants and recording what he refers to as the 'research documents' which are at the centre of his artwork (Kent 2005: 8).

The candour of the conversational interviews resulting from this long-term fieldwork is key to the success of these installations. In contrast to the 'directed' nature of the journalistic interview, with its dependence on eliciting extractable 'sound bites', the ethnographic approach to interviewing adopted by Sidén and Ataman opens up an almost therapeutic space in which members of Dubi's and Küba's communities are able to tell their stories and voice their own hopes, fears and concerns (Nash 2005: 45). While such methodologies place Sidén's and Ataman's work firmly within an ethnographic turn in contemporary art practice, the mimicking of an ethnographic methodology is, as Banks (1992) notes, not in itself adequate in defining a work as ethnographic. Indeed, I suggest that *Warte Mal!* and *Küba* provide greater inspiration for the reframing of ethnographic film when one considers not only their subject matter or how their audio-visual raw materials were gathered (important though these factors are), but in how these materials are articulated within an 'exhibitionary context': a context 'in which the *work* of the work of art is activated' (Cummings and Lewandowska 2007: 134, emphasis added).

What characterizes this context in both *Warte Mal!* and *Küba* is the configuration of multiple video screens within the exhibition space. The visitor to *Küba*, for instance, is confronted by 40 'thrift store' television sets, each standing on a battered TV cabinet and placed in front of a sagging armchair (see page 11). On each television is played a loop of a lengthy, seemingly unedited interview with a different informant or group of informants, such that the room is filled with an array of 'talking heads', a hubbub of disparate voices. Totalling over 30 hours of linear viewing time, *Küba* is, as Nash points out, a work that is 'impossible to apprehend in its totality' (2005: 44). Rather, within a typical two- or three-hour visit, audience members are compelled to move physically from television set to television set, sampling what they can of the interview material presented according to their inclinations and stamina. At the same time, because of the spatial configuration of screens (and loudspeakers), they are made visually and aurally aware of the magnitude of what they are unable to attend to and thus ever conscious of the partialness of their experience.

While *Warte Mal!* has fewer screens (only 13), their configuration is even more architectural and immersive. The visitor to Sidén's installation thus enters a dimly-lit corridor, off which lead numerous cubicles, each equipped with benches, loudspeakers, and television monitors on which Sidén's interviews with Dubi's prostitutes, pimps and police officers are played. Elsewhere, onto screens and walls, are projected other video clips, stills photographs of Dubi's environment, and excerpts from Sidén's written diaries recording her experiences as an artist-ethnographer living among her informants. The spatial configuration of the exhibition echoes that of the Motel Hubert, with its labyrinthine corridors and anonymous rooms, but it is also evocative of a peep-show arcade or the 'shop windows' of Amsterdam's red light district. Unlike motel room or peep-show booth, however, the cubicles of *Warte Mal!* have transparent walls, and thus, as visitors move between the viewing booths of the exhibition, they watch with the unsettling knowledge that they are also being watched. In her contribution to a fascinating interdisciplinary discussion of *Warte Mal!*, the anthropologist Laura Bear remarks that, unlike conventional documentaries viewed in private or in darkened auditoriums, this intervisibility in Sidén's exhibition forces visitors to confront their own roles as 'consumers of images of others' lives', and reflect on their position *vis-à-vis* the images and lives they look at, listen to, and read about in the installation: are they witnesses, observers, or voyeurs? (Carolin and Haynes 2007: 160).

Reaching beyond the limits of conventional filmic grammar and narrative, Sidén's and Ataman's installations might be better regarded as 'archival' in character: open-ended collections of recollections, assertions, anecdotes, silences, songs, stories, faces and expressions that audiences must navigate and make sense of. 'Purposefully incomplete' (Kent 2005: 8), left unedited and uninterpreted, these spatially-distributed, immersive archives of interviews can be 'read' in multiple ways, each 'document' recontextualizing adjacent ones according to the varied navigations and attentions of each visitor. Indeed, it is only through the engagement of audiences that these works are in any way 'finished' – and, then, only ever partially so, since visitors are necessarily aware of the plurality of alternative readings/navigations that they might have made. Through such configurations, Sidén and Ataman extend the 'work' of the artist-ethnographer to their audiences. And, while the voices, words and faces they encounter are, of course, mediated by Sidén's and Ataman's video cameras, visitors are nevertheless immersed in social worlds other than their own in a deeply affecting manner. Made conscious of the limits of their knowledge when faced with such an excess of information, unsettled by their ambiguous position as 'observers', yet forced into *making* sense of the possibly contradictory impressions that they experience, visitors to *Warte Mal!* and *Küba* are transformed from passive viewers of the lives and worlds of others into reflexive researchers – 'audience-ethnographers', one might say – within the exhibition space.

If the archival structure of *Warte Mal!* and *Küba* represents a significant departure from conventional film grammar, which 'constrain[s] meaning through narrative chains of signification' and 'close[s] off plural readings' in its temporal flow (Pinney 1992: 27), this is not to say that no narrative process is at work in such installations. They are, after all, necessarily experienced in a temporal sequence by audiences as they meander through the various interviews, enacting a kind of 'spatial montage' (Fleck 2002: 132; see also Bal 2007). But, crucially, it is through the plurality of visitors' own sense-making paths that meaning is actualized in these exhibition spaces, and in this respect their semantic capacity is not reduced to serving the particular arguments or intentions of the artist-filmmakers. The issue is not only about displacing and redistributing authorial power, rather, it raises a key question regarding the fundamental compatibility of the narrative film form as an ethnographic medium.

Whereas the literary qualities of supposedly 'scientific' ethnographic research monographs have been exposed (Clifford and Marcus 1986; Geertz 1988), such monographs – which remain the dominant medium for the communication of anthropological knowledge – generally have a weak narrative structure. Characterized by ethnographic 'thick description' (Geertz 1973), in which descriptions of observations and intersubjective interactions are interwoven with analytical commentary, these texts are rarely read like novels from beginning to end, but rather rely on indexes, chapter headings and sub-sections for navigation. Like Sidén's and Ataman's exhibitions, they have an archival quality, which readers are able to explore and interrogate differently according to their interests. Needless to say, other than in its most didactic form, the filmic version of ethnographic thick description is not served well by the 30-minute, 60-minute, or even two-hour narrative film format. The future of ethnographic film – of the use, that is, of moving image technologies in the service of the anthropological project – lies, therefore, beyond the narrative frame that typifies the established canon, and rests, I suggest, in the continued experimentation with archival modes of articulation and distribution within online and offline exhibitionary contexts.

Notes

1   My comments are based on the London installations of these works, in 2002 and 2005 respectively, at the Hayward Gallery (*Warte Mal!*) and in a derelict postal sorting office on New Oxford Street (*Küba*).
2   The title of Sidén's installation, *Warte Mal!* (Hey, wait!), was inspired by the phrase that the prostitutes call out to attract the attention of drivers on the road passing through Dubi to Germany.

8 Transcendental Realism in Documentary

Erik Knudsen

Prologue: an introduction

What defines the documentary genre is also at the root of its limitations; an epistemology which ties it to the factual or empirical experience of life. The very term, documentary, itself has a strong association with the industrial age from which the moving image medium emerged: empirical proof, factual evidence, scientific methodology and psychological justification all serve to reinforce the role which the documentary genre is expected to play. The emergence of anthropology and sociology as pseudo-scientific disciplines has helped cement the notion of factual representation of reality.

Here, I shall call for a different perspective on the documentary form: not with a view to discussing what documentary is, but to make some suggestions of what it could be. I hope to speak as a filmmaker and not an academic; for the motive is to try and understand how, in practice, one may evolve the documentary form – indeed, the cinematic form, generally – in such a way as to deal with experiences not sufficiently touched by the form as it is currently generally practised.

At the heart of such an exploration lie a number of questions. How can one employ a practical approach to cinematic documentary narrative which goes beyond the dominant paradigm exemplified by elements such as cause and effect, conflict and resolution, and psychologically explicable situations, character motivations and narrative motivations, to reveal qualities of spirituality and transcendence without reducing these elements to fit a rationale that ultimately contradicts the very nature of these transcendental and spiritual qualities? Within this context, how can one practically create a cinematic documentary narrative that is essentially driven by the experiential rather than by meaning, representation or the illustrative? While certain genres within fiction may bring together some of these elements in an agreed fictional paradigm, how can one bring such elements together within forms of fact?

Why should this be necessary? There are three broad reasons I feel that make such an exploration necessary. First, there is a long-term danger in reducing our reflections on life and our lives to dimensions which only exists in planes of material cause and effect. A society and culture will be starved, wither and eventually die if it cannot also breathe in paradigms of the infinite, eternal, mystical and unconscious movements of existence. Knowledge is something we all seek, yet there are many layers of knowledge which should not be limited by particular kinds of methodology.

T.S. Elliot suggests that:

> We shall not cease from exploration
> And the end of all our exploring
> Will be to arrive where we started
> And know the place for the first time.

(Eliot 1944: 48)

If knowledge and awareness were key motivations in creating documentary work, then it is not merely a question of showing the outside world, and its immediate layer beneath, but about getting into the very heart and soul of who we are and what we are.

Second, and in a sense arising from the first point, there are many issues and problems that we face that cannot be adequately solved or moved forward exclusively by looking at them in terms of material, sociological or psychological interactions. We need to look at such problems in a deeper, more holistic light, bringing into the fray the spiritual and transcendental.[1]

Third, if the language of documentary does not evolve and change, there is a real danger that the form will become a hollow expression, built on clichés and that it will cease to be an effective tool of understanding and knowledge.

While in early British documentary, there were some attempts to discover the poetry of documentary,[2] much of contemporary documentary is confined to a perspective on life in which the factual is primarily what can empirically be observed, then supported by the psychologically explicable. Social realism, observational documentary and interview-based documentary are examples of variations of a genre which broadly lives within the same classical paradigm of cause and effect, conflict and resolution.

There are a number of, usually, non-UK examples of documentary which have attempted to break away from this paradigm: the late Jean Rouch, for example, whose work in Africa shows how the documentary has the potential to go beyond the material surface of the world to reveal a spiritual dimension; or Dvortsevoy, whose work[3] sees him move away from any notion of cause and effect, conflict and resolution, in order to reveal a dimension of life which social realism cannot adequately reveal or portray.

While most of the world rushes headlong into embracing a largely materialistic engagement and perspective on life, some parts of the world still have remnants of cultures in which the spiritual, the mental and the physical occupy equal status in epistemology. In African and Latin American literature, for example, we often hear commentators from the developed world using terminology such as 'magical realism' to describe a seamless blending of realism, mysticism, magic, fact, history, politics and morality in the creation of cultural product. For the traditional African, though, the label is irrelevant; for it is all fact, all true. While African literature grew out of existing oral traditions and has never required the up-front investment that film has required, it has been able, to a large degree, to reflect more accurately the spiritual and transcendental qualities of African life, there is little or no evidence of African documentaries having done so.

Nor is there much evidence of British documentary consistently attempting to reflect the spiritual and transcendental aspects of the British. Arguably, British documentary has generally been in decline during the latter two decades of the twentieth century, in terms of the breadth and depth of what is produced. The commercial climate of contemporary television, the traditional funder of much important documentary work of the past, has seen an increased dependence on formulas which reinforce the need for drama, conflict and explicable cause and effect.

The problem, and the solution, to the different kind of documentary I am suggesting in this piece start with the question of reality and the question of why we are making documentaries in the first place.

The beginning: reality as experience

To me, filmmaking, including documentary-making, is an art. And art has an important function in society. As Hamlet put it:

> For anything so overdone is from the purpose of playing, whose end, both at the first and now, was and is, to hold, as 'twere, the mirror up to nature, to show virtue her own feature, scorn her own image, and the very age and body of the time his form and pressure.
>
> (Shakespeare 1970: III, ii)

Add to that a sense of duty, in which the artist must 'send light into the darkness of men's souls' (Kandinsky 2006: 10) in order to help the viewer understand more and become more aware of themselves and the world in which they live.

The assumption often is that the physical world creates the emotions and feelings that psychology then frames into a context of explicable cause and effect built on a scientific paradigm. But what if it were the other way round? What if one had the worldview that the physical world is a product of feelings, some of which are so deep, mysterious, inexplicable and beyond the individual, that encourages a different kind of interaction with reality?

It is not my intention here to go into a complex discussion of the nature of reality, but simply to pose some questions and raise some issues that might make us look differently at how one might approach the documentary form. Nevertheless, since the documentary form is steeped in debates and discussions about fact, fiction, proof, imagination and reality, it is important to at least question what we mean by reality. Where, for example, does the reality lie in a process that involves manipulating form?

Many documentary makers get very hooked up on issues of authenticity in order to justify the genre: that the process adheres to certain conventions in order to justify the finished form as being some kind of fact. This is a dogma with which our Western mode of thought is particularly obsessed. As Jung puts it:

It is a rational preposition of ours that everything has a natural and perceptible cause. We are convinced of this. Causality, so understood, is one of our most sacred dogmas. There is no legitimate place in our world for invisible, arbitrary and so called supernatural forces ... We distinctly resent the idea of individual and arbitrary forces, for it is not so long ago that we made our escape from that frightening world of dreams and superstitions, and constructed for ourselves a picture of the cosmos worthy of rational consciousness ... We are now surrounded by a world that is obedient to rational law.

(Jung 1961: 149)

If we, in documentary, restrict ourselves to a dogma of reality which only exists within the rationale of cause and effect, then, of course, it makes sense that a methodology has been built on process and consequent outcome; a methodology that legitimizes this outcome within the confines of rational cause and effect. This is the reality of science[4] and does not necessarily reflect the full range of experiences people have of life, for which we have somewhat inadequate terminologies such as the spiritual, transcendental, the soul, the heart, and so on.

Such pursuit of justification leads to dogmatic notions of reality being present in the process and the form.[5] But if one were to think of reality as including elements of experience that lie outside the construct of what Jung calls 'rational law' to include the many experiences and feelings people have that cannot be adequately identified or explained within this rational law, then the documentary filmmaker is faced with a number of problems relating to process and form. If one looks at traditional African cultures, for example, and looks at their way of dealing with the reality around them, there is little separation of fact and fiction, or reality and imagination, in the stories they use to reflect this reality.[6] If we, as human beings, are made up of mind, body and spirit working seamlessly together with such faculties as logical thinking, imagination, feelings, emotions and a propensity for mystical reflection and superstition, why should all of this, in its totality, not be considered as part of the reality of the real world?[7]

The reality, then, perhaps lies somewhere else, when we talk about documentary, or indeed any artistic expression. Perhaps the reality lies not in the form and the process – the very things that define documentary – but either side of that. In other words, perhaps the reality that we want to reflect ultimately lies in the feelings that prompt and necessitate the expression and then in the feelings and experiences that result from this expression. If this is the case, then the legitimacy of the form and process becomes irrelevant.

In most cases, I would imagine that the documentary filmmaker is driven by a need to express something they feel, even if that feeling can find a connection with the world around them. It is hard to determine if that feeling is caused by events, or whether that feeling finds an affinity with events. Why try and separate the two? What is relevant is that the filmmaker is prompted by something and feels it necessary to express that something and that they see the means to do so in events and imagery going on around them. We may rationalize why we want to do something, but perhaps the rationale cannot give the full picture. In this sense, is the documentary filmmaker any different to any other kind of artist? 'The idea simply comes', says T.S. Eliot (Burnshaw 1970: 153). 'My ideas come as they will, I don't know how', says Mozart (Burnshaw 1970); 'When your daemon is in charge, do not try to think consciously. Drift, wait, obey', says Kipling (Burnshaw 1970).

The codes of film forms evolve over time. While two distinct broad genres – fact and fiction – developed to reflect the dichotomous thinking of our Western culture, reflecting our strong tendency to compartmentalize, there is no doubt that much cross-fertilization between these two genre has taken place. Such films[8] tend to use this blending of genres predominantly as stylistic devices and remain firmly within the paradigm of classic narrative.

Dreams, imagination and intuition can and should be as much a part of documentary, as factual observations can and should be a part of fiction. Rather than thinking of simply merging or blending the two – through stylistic accentuation – perhaps one should be thinking of transcending these genre distinctions in a more fundamental way.

The reality – and the truth – ultimately rest within feelings and experiences of the viewer. Documentary needs to find ways in which it can move the viewer in such a way as to also address their spiritual and transcendental reality. Within fiction, there are clearer examples of filmmakers whose oeuvre specifically addresses transcendental form.[9] Documentary, on the other hand, has too often been bound by boundaries of fact and authenticity.[10]

The middle: emotions, feelings and cinematic narrative

I would like to explore a little further what is meant by 'move' the viewer transcendentally, to contrast this with how they are moved psychologically in the classical documentary or fiction film and then to look, briefly, at some broad elements which might affect how the filmmaker would proceed to make a documentary that reaches the other sides of our experience of reality.

Stanley Burnshaw, when talking about how poetry works, pointed out the following:

> Poetry begins with the body and ends with the body ... So immense are the possible combinations of external forces alone that it seems ludicrous to discuss them in terms of what we now know or in time hope to know. The more promising course has been to learn our bodies and then from within to look outward. And we have come across one finding with which all that may be discovered will have to accord: the entire human organism always participates in any reaction.

(Burnshaw 1970: 10)

Arthur Koestler talks extensively about this notion in his book on creativity, *The Act of Creation* (1969). We are overwhelmingly dominated by our emotions and feelings, much more so than by our intellect.[11] When we respond emotionally or feelingly to stimuli, our whole physiological body is involved in the process. Wherever one believes the source of these stimuli to be – psychological, spiritual, physical, tangible or intangible – they manifest themselves in powerful actual form in the individual's mind and body, simultaneously.

In physiology, there are two contrasting and opposite manifestations; one associated with emotions, the other with feelings.[12] Emotions are associated with an adrenergic[13] response in our bodies. In the extreme, such a response often relates to survival, or 'fight or flight' situations and the emotions associated with this Koestler calls self-assertive[14]. Such emotions include, by way of some simple examples, fear, rage, anger, sexual attraction, anxiety, excitement, jealousy. They are self-assertive in nature because they re-assert our individuality, separate us out from our surroundings, put the body in a ready state to deal with problems, enable us to laugh at other's misfortunes or take sides, as necessary to 'defend oneself', or to re-assert one's own superiority. Feelings, on the other hand, are associated with a cholinergic[15] response in our bodies. Such feelings relate to the participatory in us, the tendency to dissolve one's ego into a greater whole. Some such feelings might include awe, grief, love, joy, longing, and sorrow. They are participatory feelings because they help us dissolve into a greater whole by, in contrast to emotions, opening up to participating in something greater than ourselves.

Where the self-assertive emotions drive us towards individual action and reaction, the participatory feelings drive us towards stillness and inaction; where the self-assertive emotions demand we are alert, the participatory feelings encourage us to relax;[16] where the self-assertive emotions engage us, essentially, in issues of survival, the participatory feelings encourage us to engage with the transcendental (see Figure 8.1).

Forgive my digression into this brief and simple description of the physiology of feelings and emotions, but for me they confirm impressions I already have as an artist; namely, that there are different sides of me that respond differently to stimuli – and in this discussion we are, of course, talking about the stimuli of a cinematic narrative. My contention is that these emotions and feelings are the primary way in which the filmmaker engages the viewer and in that sense moves them. The intellect primarily reflects on these emotions and feelings and tries to make sense of them. However, even if the intellect is unsuccessful at making much sense of the emotions and feelings, this does not mean one has not been moved. Music – for me the most powerful of all the arts – is a good example of a form, considerably abstracted, which can move without one's intellect necessarily being able to understand why or how.[17]

The materialistic cultures of the developed world lean heavily towards a preoccupation with survival and the self-assertive; the survival instinct drives us, anxiously, to assert our individuality and its base needs by accumulating more material wealth and superiority over nature and this instinct has strong roots in the emotions of fear. The measure of our achievements is quantified in external actions, in material manifestations and is framed within a paradigm of psychological cause and effect. We look back in time, or across at more 'primitive' cultures, and define cultures which prioritize, or prioritized, their relationship to life differently as under-developed.

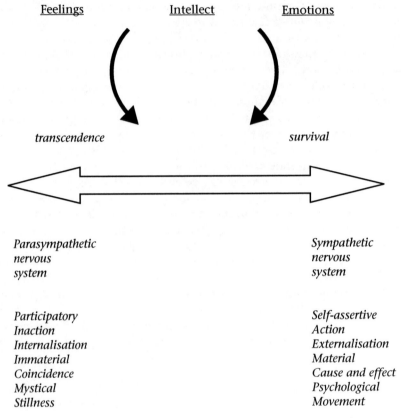

Figure 8.1 Comparison of self-assertive emotions and participatory feelings

But perhaps the more, so-called, 'primitive' culture has, or had, different priorities. In sociology and anthropology there was a tendency to use the paradigm of psychological realism – the cause and effect of rational law – to explain under-development. It was always assumed that so-called 'primitive' cultures were preoccupied with survival. However, this assumption says more about our own culture than it does about cultures in which a different emphasis is at work. The differing priorities of such cultures were not understood. Such priorities may have included a more transcendental relationship to nature; one in which the priority was not about asserting individuality, but about placing that individuality within a larger spiritual and mystical context, for example, of the dead and the yet to be born. With an emphasis on the participatory, the collective interaction with nature is, or was, not one of ruling over it, but assimilating with it, where what we call coincidences and mysticism form part of a pattern outside the scope of the rational mind, where stillness and inaction are revered, and where the priority is not to gain materially, but to transcend attachment to the physical world.

The relative balance between these two tendencies within the individual and his culture has a profound effect on how stories are told. Stories are fundamental to our engagement with life[18] and the structure and mode of story-telling are a reflection of our direct experience of, and attitude to, the world within and around us. The classical narratives of the Anglo-Saxon[19] influenced cinema – both fiction and documentary – are heavily steeped in the psychological realism of self-assertive emotions. The vast majority of work is designed to engage our emotions – as opposed to our feelings – and perhaps it is no coincidence that at the extreme end of fiction, for example, there is little difference between the experience of a movie and that of going on a rollercoaster in a theme park. The purpose is clear in such cases: to have you, the viewer, sitting on the edge of your seat, adrenaline pumping around your system, engaged with issues of survival, alert, ready for 'fight or flight' action, consumed by fear.

Thankfully, few documentaries reach these extremes. Nevertheless, most Anglo-Saxon documentaries do, in more subtle and sophisticated ways, predominantly solicit the self-assertive emotions. In fact, it is the dominant mode of engaging the viewer. The establishment of a protagonist, or protagonists, with a problem or an aim, the psychological justification of this with a premise of some sort, showing the obstacles that provide a challenge for the protagonist(s), then taking this challenge to a decisive situation or moment and then finally wrapping up the journey in some sort of resolution provides the basic narrative skeleton of most documentary films. Ultimately, they lean towards issues of the survival of something palpable, something psychologically explicable, or even something physical, such as a human life. It could also be about the survival of an idea, a culture, certain values, even the survival of someone's sanity. The protagonist's aims are usually always psychologically explicable, as is the premise. The challenges, likewise, need not merely be physical, but could be mental. The emphasis is on action, externalizing the issues into palpable form, usually through the creation of conflicts, establishing clear causes and effects and a tendency to exaggerate movement (be this physical movement of or within the frame, or the movement of the narrative arc). No matter how subtly or creatively presented, these elements provide the bedrock of the dominant classical mode of documentary story-telling; one with which most people are very familiar and one with which most can readily engage, because it so closely mirrors our culture's preoccupations.

A good, and very effective, example of such a documentary would be Phil Agland's *Serial Killer*.[20] Part of the television series *Shanghai Vice*, which revolves around the work of the Shanghai police in a rapidly developing and expanding metropolis, this film is concerned with the police's efforts to catch a serial killer. The subject itself, of course, immediately helps to engage our self-assertive emotions. Ostensibly a strictly observational documentary, Agland, nevertheless, heavily incorporates the codes of the classic fiction thriller: the darkly moody lighting of many of the key scenes; the suggestive night time cityscape interludes linking the key sequences; the action editing of dialogue scenes; the use of informational devices, such as the telex machine in an empty police office announcing the next victim; and, importantly, the juxtaposition of the police efforts with a subplot of two innocent women – potential victims? – concerned with improving their sex lives – to name but a few examples – all contribute to generating an engagement with our self-assertive emotions, such as fear and anxiety. Add to these codes the classic narrative elements of: the protagonists – predominantly the police, who have the aim of apprehending the serial killer before potentially innocent women, such as the ones in the sub-plot, get sexually abused and killed; the premise – Shanghai's economic boom and the social problems this brings with it; the obstacles – the various challenges of the investigation, complicated by the burgeoning city with its consequent social problems; the climax – the apprehension and interrogation of the serial killer (have they got the right man and will he confess?); and the resolution, which ties together some loose ends, reflects on the outcome and suggests new challenges. Not only are we engaged with the literal survival of potential victims of the serial killer, but at stake is also the survival of social cohesion and social values in a rapidly changing metropolitan environment. Our self-assertive emotions are engaged with the narrative form, reflecting and shaping the reality we experience, re-affirming the paradigm of psychological realism.

But what about those of us – viewers and filmmakers – who want to engage with transcendental reality? How can the documentary form help us reveal and mirror this reality – either in addition to psychological realism, or leaning more specifically towards the transcendental? In fiction, as mentioned earlier, there are examples of filmmakers specifically working to this end. In other art forms, the idea of transcendental realism is well established.[21] Somehow, the documentary form lags behind, hampered by pseudo-scientific notions of realism, authenticity and fact.[22]

If the aim of the construction of the classic narrative forms is to primarily engage our self-assertive emotions, then the aim of the transcendental narrative forms is to engage our participatory feelings. Awe, sorrow, joy, longing are feelings that require a different approach. Perhaps even the process of creation itself, with less reliance on rational laws and rules about narrative structure, comes into play:

> Things are beautiful where they are inevitable, that is, when they are free exhibitions of a spirit. There is no violence here, no murdering, no twisting-about, no copying-after, but a free, unrestrained, yet self-governing display of movement – which constitutes the principle of beauty. The muscles are conscious of drawing a line, making a dot, but behind them there is an unconsciousness. By this unconsciousness nature writes out her destiny: by this unconsciousness the artist creates his work of art. A baby smiles and the whole crowd is transported, because it is genuinely inevitable, coming out of the Unconscious.
>
> (Suzuki 1996: 281)

This very notion carries itself into the way one might deal with events in a narrative; a notion that the narrative events are not tied by some explicable series of causes and events, but by some other forces that one can only call mystical or coincidental. While in the classic narrative, events generally follow some sort of line governed by palpable causes and effects, in the transcendental narrative such events may be governed by motivational forces which lie outside of what is psychologically explicable. In the extreme, they might even appear random, a term we attribute to events to which we are incapable of attributing causes. Such coincidences may be tied to other elements of the narrative in a loose binding web in which the viewer would be asked not to make cognitive sense, but to transcend the need for causes and to experience these connections in a state of, for example, wonder or awe. The scenes may not follow, one from the other, along classic narrative's lines, but the viewer may be asked to submerge themselves in scenes and sequences, to linger on things that seem, to the logical or psychological mind, irrelevant, or to suspend their need for consequential organizing of events and scenes. Detail becomes an important feature; for it is often through the immersion in detail that new links and connections are made that lie outside the paradigm of cause and effect.

The notion of having a protagonist, with aims, premise, obstacles and resolution, becomes less and less important. Indeed, the possibility of having no protagonist at all becomes perfectly viable; for, perhaps, the observation of so-called coincidental or random events in themselves can provide the catalyst for an engagement rooted in participatory feelings. Stillness, both in terms of the movement of, or within the frame, and the movement of the narrative arc, provides more opportunities for the viewer to fill an empty bowl with their own feelings, as opposed to being presented with a full bowl for digestion and reaction. When the rational mind is suspended, engaged with scenes that link by way of coincidence and detail, the relationship with the narrative starts to become one of meditation; a state in which one could, perhaps, start to see things that one would not otherwise see, feel things that one would not otherwise feel.[23]

Internalization – for lack of a better expression – and reducing the role of external actions, is another important feature of the transcendental narrative. Reducing conflict and dramatic events as an expressive tool helps to create internal spaces within which the transcendental narrative can achieve its aims of engaging with the viewer's parasympathetic feelings.

By its very nature, this irrational and mystical part of our experience of life is very difficult to qualify. The notion of constructing rules, fixed patterns and solutions goes against the very grain of how it works. I hope to have suggested elements, rather than specify them, as I believe what D. T. Suzuki says above about the unconscious movements of the creative process to be correct.

A good example of a documentary leaning towards the transcendental would be Sergei Dvortsevoy's *Bread Day* (Russia, 2001). Set in a remote Siberian settlement depleted of the young and leaving a population of older people, the film is uncompromisingly observational. But there are few elements that one could say would fit in with classic narrative forms. First, there seem to be no protagonists and consequently no aims. There might be a hint of a premise, in that the film is structured around the delivery of a train carriage with bread for the settlement. This is clearly a weekly event, and therefore nothing unusual, but Dvortsevoy uses this delivery to provide a basic structure: the bread is collected by some of the residents, brought to the settlement; observation of the settlement; the empty carriage is prepared to be returned, suggesting that the cycle is about to start all over again. This tri-partite structure is reminiscent of the Zen narrative structure one might see in much of Ozu's later work;[24] normality – disparity-normality/transcendence.[25] In such a narrative, nothing need superficially change; the change occurs in the viewer as a consequence of going through the experience and where the situation remains exactly the same at the end, as it was in the beginning, there is, nevertheless, a different transcendental relationship with that situation.

The imagery and events, in the context of psychological realism, seem random in *Bread Day*: we are not following any particular character; we are not following any line of events, one following on from the other; we are as interested in the activities of the animals as the people; we are as likely to be observing a collapsed shed, or space that a person or animal has vacated, as we are to be observing what happens to the bread in the shop; long panning shots move from one thing to another, without apparent motivation; tit-bits of conversations are picked up on the wind. There are, of course, connections, but they are tied together in a transcendental web through our participatory feelings; coincidental links allow us to engage with the imagery and the narrative in a completely different way than if more classical elements had been employed.

Add to this Dvortsevoy's approach to detail and pace. Stillness – in the frame, of the movement of the frame and in the arc of the narrative – lies at the heart of his cinematic approach. We are being encouraged to meditate on what we are seeing, rather than to seek causal links. The opening shot, for example, must be about 10 minutes long: uncompromisingly, we follow half a dozen elderly people pushing the decoupled rail carriage along the train track to their settlement. Not much is said, for it is hard work. In the classical approach, once the causal significance of this action had been established, the temptation would be to cut to the next scene. Dvortsevoy, on the other hand, lingers and we start to become immersed in the detail of what is happening; not in search of its material or psychological significance, but almost as a meditative experience. We come to feel the scene, as opposed to responding to it emotionally.

This approach gives us a very different view of reality; it is not a sociological reality, nor a factual reality in the traditional sense (there is very little factual information from which I can build a psychological picture); there is no exposition, no explanations, no back story, no obvious conflicts, no climax. Nevertheless, there is a strong reality; but it is another side of reality than we are used to seeing. It is more mystical, transcendental, as it fills us with feelings of awe and sorrow.

The end: a call

The heart of the process of making films, for me, is intuitive.[26] An inner necessity, which I cannot explain, drives me to make them. I would even go as far as to say – as Rodin said about his relationship to stone and sculpture – that the stories I tell already exist. My job, as an artist, is to see these stories and then to bring them into a tangible form. Intellectual reflection is just that: intellectual reflection. For me, the act of creation is not an intellectual act, but an act of inner necessity, faith, feeling and craft.

Intellectual reflection is, of course, in its proper place, very useful. Reflecting on my work in the context of research has helped me become aware of unconscious and intuitive tendencies, impulses and directions. It is not for my intellect to rule these impulses and tendencies, but to try to understand them, while allowing them free rein to take me where they want to take me, in order to, as Schumann says, 'send light into the darkness of men's hearts' (Kandinsky 2006: 10).

In my own work,[27] I try to achieve this by exploring this notion of transcendental reality. For me, the spiritual poverty that pervades in the rich Western world is a serious problem:

> Never before has ignorance reached such monstrous proportions. This repudiation of the spiritual can only engender monsters. Now, as never before, we have to make a stand for everything that has the slightest relevance to the spiritual.
>
> (Tarkovsky 1994: 22)

And the documentary genre should, and can, play its part.

Notes

1 In the liberal, consumer-led societies of the developed world, we have a tendency to link our material success with progress. However, one need only look at the immense interest of many people from these so-called successful societies in so-called 'primitive' cultures' relationships to nature and the spiritual as indications that many people feel a sense of alienation from key aspects of their lives.

2 The work of Humphrey Jennings, for example.

3 *Bread Day* (Russia, 2001) or *In The Dark* (Russia, 2005) are good examples. Additionally, *Tische* (Victor Kossakovsky, Russia, 2002) serves as another example. Neither filmmaker uses a term such as 'transcendental realism' to describe their own work, but there are hints and similarities in intention. See Kossakovsky's discussion with Maxine Baker (Baker 2006: 177).

4 I include in science, the 'sciences' of sociology, anthropology and psychology.

5 Notions of how a documentary can be shot, interactions with participants, notions of proof and evidence and a range of conventions that tell the viewer that 'this is real' and, by inference, therefore also 'true'.

6 I recently made a documentary, *Heart of Gold*, in Ghana about this subject, part of a research project funded by the Arts and Humanities Research Council, entitled 'An Exploration of African Story-telling Techniques: Possible Uses in Documentary Form'. See www.onedayfilms.com/films/heartofgold, for further details.

7 In fact, why do we think of documentary and fiction as fundamentally different?

8 Examples might include, *Tina Goes Shopping* (UK, 1999) and *Medium Cool* (US, 1969).

9 Bresson, Ozu and Dreyer are three examples that Paul Schrader talks about in his book, 'Transcendental Style in Film' (1972). Add to this, Andrey Tarkovsky and Victor Erice, whose *Quince Tree Sun* (Spain, 1992) is a good example of a film transcending both documentary and fiction.

10 Krzystof Kieslowski is another filmmaker whose work one could call 'transcendental'. He has been rather circumspect about why exactly he gave up documentary making after 20 years to concentrate on fiction. However, his fiction films clearly have a strong symbiotic relationship with his earlier documentary approaches.

11 In fact, Koestler's *The Ghost in the Machine* (1967) is all about how the lack of understanding of how powerful our self-assertive emotions are is a serious problem for mankind.

12 The distinction between emotions and feelings is one that I am making for the sake of this exposition and not one generally made within physiology, where all these responses tend to be referred to as emotions.

13 The release of adrenaline, which is connected to the sympathetic nervous system.

14 See *The Act of Creation* (Koestler 1969: 10–14).

15 The release of acetylcholine, which is connected to the parasympathetic nervous system.

16 This may, for example, include meditation. Also, sleep, the ultimate relaxation physiologically, is the antithesis of self-protective alertness, as it is a state in which the individual is at his most vulnerable.

17 There is, perhaps, another discussion to be had about semiotics and its relationship to the process of engaging the viewer, but this must be left for another time and place.

18 'The universe is made of stories, not atoms' (Rukeyser, quoted in Feldman and Kornfield 1991: i).

19 I include in the Anglo-Saxon cinema that of the US and other cultures adopting the story-telling modes of these English-speaking cultures.

20 Channel Four, UK, 1999.

21 See the work and writings of Cezanne, Kandinsky, Mozart, Karl Jenkins, or Bill Viola to name but a few.

22 Perhaps it is important to point out at this stage that I am not suggesting that psychological realism and transcendental realism are separate entities that do not work and interact with each other. On the contrary, a number of films will have elements of both. I am discussing these elements in terms of relative balance, emphasis and tendencies.

23 For more extreme examples, the reader may want to see *Empire* (Andy Warhol, US, 1967) or, more recently, Bill Viola's work, which often has its roots in factual research. An example of his work, and his discussion of some of his themes, can be seen at www.billviola.com or www.tate.org.uk/onlineevents/webcasts/bill_viola/default.jsp.

24 *Tokyo Story* (Japan, 1953) being a supreme example.

25 See Paul Schrader's discussion of this in *Transcendental Style in Film* (Schrader 1972).

26 Was it not André Gide who said, 'Art is a collaboration between God and the artist and the more God has to do with it, the better'?

27 Such as the fiction films *Brannigan's March* (UK, 2004) and *Sea of Madness* (UK, 2006), or the documentaries *Bed of Flowers* (UK, 2001) and *Heart of Gold* (UK, 2006).

9   Filming 'the Invisible'

Michael Chanan

I

When I first taught filmmaking in the 1970s – before video had properly arrived – I was junior to an old hand, a former BBC man called Ron. We got on very well, but we had almost opposite approaches to shooting documentary, a difference which was symbolized by the question of the tripod. Ron taught that you should always keep the camera on the tripod except when there was an overriding reason for taking it off. I, on the other hand, was a newcomer who came to the medium at the end of the 1960s. I naturally had a penchant for what is loosely called *cinéma vérité*, which went with a camera style that the oldies among BBC cameramen called wobblyscope – they were all men, and I'd worked with some of them.[1] But I'd also had the good fortune of working with a couple of younger cameramen (freelancers, as we used to call them), who moved with great agility, always smooth and steady, and with this as my model, I taught that you should keep fit and shoot documentary hand-held, and only put the camera on the legs when there was good reason to do so.

We decided the sensible thing to do was debate the question in front of the students. Another thing Ron said on one of these occasions – another old BBC adage – was that you can't shoot a black cat in a coalhole, a warning against trying to shoot documentary in dark places without lights. This was another growing predilection of the time, another possibility introduced by the new lightweight gear, which included better lenses and faster film, portable tape recorders and directional microphones, and allowed the camera team the more easily to cross the boundaries between public and private. As Brian Winston (1995: 230) neatly puts it, 'Paradoxically, because the new equipment made filming so much less intrusive than it had been, the finished films were far more so.' In short, the new documentary placed the old definition of privacy in crisis precisely because it created new ways of trespassing on privacy. In the process, the documentary camera began to enter the private places and even intimate spaces of everyday social life whose portrayal was previously the privileged province of fiction.

My own instinct was not to intrude but to try things out when the opportunity arose. I would say, if you can see it in the viewfinder, shoot it, and then 'push' the film stock, as it was called – the practice of processing the film in the laboratory as if it were faster than it was rated; this produced a more grainy image, but allowed the filmmaker to shoot spontaneously under available light. But Ron's phrase stuck in my mind for another reason – for its metaphorical possibilities: to speak of things you can't shoot because you can't see them, things that are invisible in some way other than lack of light. For example, in the sense that Walter Benjamin (1979: 255) indicated, in his 'A Small History of Photography', when he cited Brecht's (2000: 144–5) remark that the simple reproduction of reality says very little about what it shows, and a photograph of, say, the Krupp works or AEG tells us almost nothing about these enterprises, because it cannot reveal the reification of human relations which is produced within them.

I was thinking about this question all the time I was writing *The Politics of Documentary* (Chanan 2007), but a way of broaching the issue there escaped me, and so this is the subject I want to take up here, as a kind of supplement. What I propose is not at all a definition of the invisible, but some notes towards the deconstruction of the language game of invisibility.

II

Let me start with some examples. First, a literal instance. In 1981, I filmed with Peter Chappell in El Salvador, during the uprising of the Farabundo Martí Liberation Front.[2] We had secured a commission from West German television to go behind the guerrilla lines and report on what life was like in the liberated zones. In other words, we weren't shooting the military clashes and actions – but we couldn't entirely avoid getting caught up in them. This happened once, during the daytime, when the encampment where we were billeted came under a pounding from across the valley – but the shells were landing much too short. (Anyway we knew that if it got dangerous, our friends would pull us back.) The problem was how to film the incident. Since the shells were few and far between, you could run the camera for minutes at a time without seeing anything, and when the next burst of fire came, you might be looking in the wrong direction. We didn't have enough film stock for that, because we had to carry it all with us, so we fell back on a handful of shots of the scene, the fighters on the alert. Later, we incorporated these shots into a montage to accompany a song sung by the guerrillas at night under the stars, which we couldn't film but did record. A day or two later, we were invited to accompany a small troop going out on a raid, but we had to decline: they were leaving at sundown, and that night there was no moon, so there wouldn't have been any light to film by (I'll confess we were relieved). But our shots of the fighters marching out of the village in the beautiful colour of the setting sun suggested the narrative shape of the film, and became the final sequence. The effect was to keep the film from closure, because this ending was the opposite of the heroic cowboy riding off into the sun after a happy ending. Here there was no happy ending, the struggle continued.

Second example, of a different type. Later the following year, again with Peter, our small film crew (this time there were four of us) arrived in Panama to shoot a sequence for a documentary we were making for Channel Four about Latin American Cinema, only to discover from the friends who met us at the airport that a coup had taken place just a few hours before we'd arrived.[3] Our immediate thought was, how do we film what's going on? There's nothing to film, said our friends. It was a palace coup – no disruption, not even any soldiers on the streets. Nor was there anyone who was willing to tell us anything, and certainly not to talk on camera, because they didn't know which way the wind was blowing. (Just as well, since a few days later the new interim president sent in his hoodlums to smash the offices of the country's leading newspaper.) So we dropped the idea and went back to our original schedule. But my mind went back ten years, when I was on a trip to Bolivia and there was an attempted coup in La Paz, where I didn't see anything either; but in La Paz you could hear things, because the city lies in a steep valley, and the sound of gunfire ricocheted back and forth.

To film events like these you have to be in the right place at the right time (or the wrong time). Like the Irish filmmakers Kim Bartley and Donnacha O'Briain, filming a profile of Venezuelan president Hugo Chávez in April 2002, *The Revolution Will Not Be Televised*, when there was a coup attempt against him. When the crisis broke, they were with Chávez in the presidential palace; when he was whisked away, they stayed there for the duration of the crisis, capturing an extraordinary record from the inside, until the moment when he returned two days later (whereupon, as he strides triumphantly into the palace, he greets the camera crew as old friends). When you see this kind of footage, showing something we never normally see, the viewer's astonishment takes over, and all the other stuff that still remains out of view, because it was dropped in the editing or didn't get captured by the camera in the first place, falls out of the picture. Not for long, however, since the film met with a hostile reception among Chávez's opponents, who quickly began tearing it apart for everything it doesn't show, or which they claim it distorted by tendentious selectivity.

Many of these criticisms miss their mark because they misconstrue the power of documentary as testimony. This is a film with a strong point of view because, as Pasolini (1980: 5) once put it, 'It is impossible to perceive reality as it happens *if not from a single point of view*, and this point of view is always that of a perceiving subject.' But here we need to add a number of riders. First, the truth is that there are *always* other things which remain out of view, and this gives rise to a crucial characteristic of documentary: the documentary that you see is only one version of the film it might have been. Why? First, because the other versions are lying on the cutting room floor, as we used to say. Second, also because the documentary that was shot is only one version of what could have been shot, if the camera had been running at different moments or pointing the other way. This is one of the areas where documentary practice differs from fiction, which is constrained to follow a script. What the documentarist shoots isn't arbitrary, because it is undertaken with some degree of preparation and a certain set of expectations, but the art of the thing is to improvise around the unforeseen; otherwise what you get is the formulaic and stereotyped conventional wisdom which makes up the bulk of television current affairs. The wager of so-called 'creative' or 'authored' documentary is that whatever you film is going to be at least characteristic and even symptomatic of the subject under investigation; the challenge is that you have to be very much on your toes, you have to think about how you're interpreting the situation and why you choose to film this or that, what to follow as events unfold. But in all cases, there is always whatever was going on behind the camera at the moment of filming, whichever way you point the camera, and which you are therefore *not* filming.

The result is that watching a documentary corresponds rather ironically to something like the Donald Rumsfeld scheme of the world, in which there are 'known knowns' ('the things we know that we know'), 'known unknowns' ('things we know that we don't know'), and then there are 'unknown unknowns' ('things we don't know that we don't know'). In other words, the documentary is always built on structuring absences, which are normally suppressed in the process of editing, that is, of achieving narrative or discursive or poetic coherence. This indicates another kind of filmic invisibility altogether, the myth of invisible editing, which supposes that the best editing is the kind that the viewer doesn't notice – except for cuts designed to draw attention to themselves. But even when they do, the labour of editing, the weeks of chipping away at the shots and moving them back and forth, remains beyond the ken of the viewer; hence the ironic title of Dai Vaughan's study of Humphrey Jennings' editor, Stuart MacAllister, whom he called 'The Invisible Man'.

Invisible editing has its counterpart in the invisibility of the camera, and another myth – that the most 'objective' kind of filming is 'fly on the wall', where the camera observes but never intervenes, and the subject agrees to ignore it and sometimes indeed forgets its presence. This is a complex question about the self-presentation of the subject, with or without a camera present, or what Erving Goffman (1971) called 'the presentation of self in everyday life'. There is evidence about this in the case of JFK, the principal subject in three classic films of direct cinema in the early 1960s produced by Robert Drew. Kennedy was a willing accomplice, at least to begin with, and *Primary*, the first of them, came about in part because Kennedy, whose father after all was an erstwhile movie tycoon, was well prepared to take on the rapidly evolving media as a condition of political success. Although according to one account (Watson 1989), Kennedy was somewhat uncertain about what he was letting himself in for, *Primary* was a critical success, but when Drew went back to him in 1961 to persuade him to let himself be filmed in the White House going about his business, Kennedy wasn't certain the experiment would work. 'If I can actually lose consciousness of the camera', he said, 'and it doesn't intrude, we might be able to do something. If the camera is bothersome then we can't.' The modest results were seen on ABC television under the awkward title *Adventures in Reporting: Adventures on the New Frontier*. Drew decided he wanted to try again. He had come to the conclusion that mere observation wasn't enough, and reasoned that in order to avoid a string of uneventful scenes, your subjects needed to be caught up in testing circumstances which would allow them to forget the presence of the camera and at the same time provide the film with narrative drive – the dramaturgy of what came to be called the 'crisis' scenario, after the title of this third film with Kennedy (*Crisis*, 1963). But this time, after seeing it shortly before his assassination, it seems that Kennedy had changed his attitude, and Pierre Salinger recalled that he was quite upset about it: 'He thought he'd gone too far ... He said he had forgotten the cameras were there. He was not sure that the image he gave was the right image.'

Kennedy's ambivalence finds its counterpart in the ambivalence of the viewer, who often cannot believe in films like this that the subject is not in some way acting themselves for the camera, that is, acting up, putting on a performance. When Don Pennebaker was criticized for this over his portrayal of Bob Dylan in *Don't Look Back*, he replied, if I recall correctly, that of course Dylan was performing, 'he was playing himself, and doing it very well'. But this is a film which also offers a paradigm of situations where the camera's presence does not significantly affect what its going on, namely, musical performance. The musician making music is already performing a role which the camera can observe without affecting it, because making music already involves the whole person in an act of communication which the filmmaker can shape, but which is given by the performer as a gift. Like the scenes in *Don't Look Back* where it can be said that Dylan isn't acting for the camera because he's focused on making music, performing in concert for the audience, or else privately for himself, or with his companions. These scenes, observing musicians sharing their music away from the audience, are among the most satisfying; this is where Dylan appears to be most completely himself, doubtless aware of the camera's presence, not performing for it, however, but happy for it to do its job.

Many of the problems about representation in the documentary arise from peculiar (and invisible) tensions between the film we see and the unseen film it might have been. This is not to say that documentarists simply have to live with the problem in the hope that the viewer won't notice (this is how the hacks behave). Many filmmakers, going right back to Vertov in the 1920s, have developed techniques of self-reflexivity designed to remind the viewer that this is not reality as such but its double, selected and recombined, with everything this might imply. These include films I discuss in the book, like Michael Rubbo's *Waiting for Fidel* (1974), and Raúl Ruiz's *Of Great Events and Ordinary People* (*De grands événements et de gens ordinaires*, 1978), in which the same Rubbo appears as himself in his real-life role of Canadian filmmaker shooting abroad. Both films break open and render visible the conventional forms of construction of documentary discourse, exposing the codes which normally determine the reading of the representation. And then there's a neglected film from an unlikely source, an Iranian documentary dating from 1967, *Story of a Boy from Gorgan, or, The Night it Rained*, by Kamran Shirdel. A playful satire on the condition of documentary, we are watching the expedition of a film crew despatched from Tehran to investigate an incident in the news, in which a teenage boy is said to have averted a catastrophic rail crash near the town of Gorgan, only to discover that the 'heroic' act may be in question. The first self-reflexive gesture comes at the outset, in the commentary: instead of addressing the audience in the cinema, this voice addresses the head of the studio back in Tehran for whom the film is being made, by way of explanation of the confusing material they've come up with. They have filmed interviews with everyone involved they could find, but can only present them in the order in which they found them (of which one result is that the boy himself comes late in the process). The result is summed up by Hamid Naficy (1981: 41–6):

> The viewer is faced with a bewildering range of accounts of what was done by whom and when. A salient comment on reality and perception, this film was banned for years before winning the 1974 Tehran International Film Festival as best short film.

What's going on here is that the film plays into an ideological quagmire in which one ambiguity compounds the next, and of course this is maddening to authority. A relentlessly teasing film, which makes you suspect that reality cannot be grasped, it's too elusive, and not to be got at by such blunt instruments as the mass media, documentary included; the result is both a commentary on the intractability of reality, and a deconstruction of the representation of 'truth', that is to say, the official regime of truth. No wonder that after its delayed festival prize, it was suppressed again.

III

If the invisible hides itself away, then as soon as one begins to ask what it is, why you can't film it, how it impinges on what you can and do film, it turns out to have a number of different properties, to be invisible in different ways. Perhaps we need to posit different levels, or maybe zones of invisibility. Something can be invisible because it's overlooked, or difficult to access, or it happened off camera. Or it can be invisible because it is heard but not seen, like the disembodied voice of the commentary. Perhaps it's invisible because it's a physical thing but without a visible form, like a taste or a smell. Perhaps it's an event which has already taken place.

Here I think first of two films by Joris Ivens about the wind, *Pour le Mistral* (1965) and his last film, *A Tale of the Wind* (1988). The first of these is a lyrical portrait of the wind which sweeps across the photogenic Provençal landscape, a bold experiment which requires two projectors, not simultaneously but one after the other: it begins in black and white, in the old standard academy ratio, and halfway through suddenly switches to colour and cinemascope. The effect produces a powerful frisson which transcends the photogenic and brings a physical sensation of the wind blowing in the contours of the landscape and even around your own body. (Ivens (1969: 37) said about his early film, *Rain*, that he was very happy when he noticed at the end of one of the first screenings 'that the audience looked around for their raincoats and were surprised to find the weather dry and clear when they came out of the theatre'). The second, co-directed with his wife, Marceline Loridan, is equally lyrical but constructed through metaphor. The 90-year-old man goes back to China where he first filmed half a century earlier, and then again in the 1970s, in order to film the impossible: the wind in the Mongolian desert. This time, however, he's not making political reportage, but a cryptic meditation, mixing childhood reminiscence, fantasy images, dance, dream sequences, and direct shooting, which in his own words, occupies 'a no-man's land somewhere between reality and imagination' (quoted in Stein 2002). All his life, Ivens has suffered from asthma, and the quest is a very personal one, not only a strong metaphor for the breath of life, but through the constant presence of the Chinese dragon, the mythical representation of the wind, it also becomes a metaphor for the freedom of the artistic imagination. (But this is of course a political statement too.)

If the wind is invisible, it is certainly physical, but there are also things in the world which are very real but not physical objects at all. For example, a social or historical process which cannot be observed directly but can be read in its signs, like archaeological objects or architectural ruins. Or the garbage generated by modern consumerism, a subject of films like Agnès Varda's *The Gleaners and I* (France, 2000), Eduardo Coutinho's *The Scavengers* (*Boca de Lixo*, Brazil, 1993), and a short parody by Jorge Furtado called *Island of Flowers* (1989). All of these are examples of an aesthetic of garbage of which Robert Stam (1998: 19) has observed that the rubbish tip can be seen as an archaeological treasure trove 'because of its concentrated, synecdochic, compressed character' as 'congealed history', like 'a gooey distillation of society's contradictions'. Thus the garbage dump becomes a critical vantage point which reveals the social formation as seen 'from below', a place inhabited by marginalized, rejected, downtrodden and forgotten people, people who for most of the time remain invisible to us. But here we slip into another kind of invisibility, that of exclusion from the world of representation, the ideological imagery of the world projected in the mass media, in which, as Siegfried Kracauer once remarked about illustrated magazines, the public sees the world whose perception of it is hindered by the illustrated journals themselves. Television raises the stakes, of course, as evidenced by *Bus 174* (Brazil, 2002) by José Padilha and Felipe Lacerda: a bus is hijacked in the centre of Rio de Janeiro, a solitary gunman holds the passengers hostage, the television cameras get there as fast as the police, and the whole tragic event is broadcast live. Investigating the identity of the hijacker, the film presents us with a figure from Rio's urban underclasses, who as Walter Lima Júnior (2002) put it, 'craves for visibility': 'he desperately wants to be seen and tells everyone that "this is not a film, it's real".'[4] This is also the problem which concerns the Cuban filmmaker Julio Garcia Espinosa (2005), when he says that Latin American countries are invisible, and a country without an image is a country which does not exist, where death is therefore less painful.

If the underclasses remain invisible, except in their most stereotypical aspects, because the universe of images ignores them, at the other extreme, what is hidden away from us, because we don't usually have access to it, because it goes on behind closed doors, is the intimate character of power and authority, the way its holders behave in private (in what Goffman called the 'backstage' areas of everyday life). Even on those rare occasions when the camera gets access, what remains invisible is power and authority as a system, in which this behaviour is embedded, its social actors 'interpellated', because a system as such is not a physical object, a material thing, and all we can see are its symbols and symptoms. As Thomas Hobbes once observed, power lies in the reputation of power. And yet these visible signs can be subtly indicative. Here I think of a film which Peter Chappell made ten years ago, called *Our Friends at the Bank* (France, 1997), which follows a round of negotiations between Uganda and the World Bank over a period of 18 months. Access like this to affairs normally conducted in secrecy is extremely rare, and the film came about because of the Bank's concern over the bad shape of its public image. As a result, instead of the conventional format for this kind of subject – press conferences, interviews, the speculations of experts and journalists – here we enter the discursive universe of the negotiators themselves, we discover how they really talk to each other, how their different agendas are encoded in their verbal communication. As one reviewer (Ugwumba 2001) saw it, politicians, functionaries, bureaucrats, economists and civil servants of several different nationalities are 'almost [like] chess pieces', shuffling between meetings 'in a game played on a shifting board' – sometimes Uganda, sometimes New York or the Bank's headquarters in Washington – and as negotiating sessions alternate with private meetings often characterized by jokes and jibes. Not only that. The quiet observational filming helps reveal the power structure not only through their speech but also their body language. An institution like the World Bank is interesting, says Chappell, because it often brings people into a proximity with others which would be unusual in their own cultures. And this is not invisible, it is more a question of how you film the scene and the space where it's unfolding. The effects are apparent, for example, in differences of deference or self-confidence which the same person manifests in different situations and places, like the Ugandan Minister of Finance a little overawed by New York compared to his self-assurance back in Kampala. This you can show, but the signs do not interpret themselves: they have to be seen in context, and this is the job of montage and editing. The problem of context, however, is that behind every context is another context. (And the problem of the mainstream media is the way they rob the information even of the immediate context, and certainly render the wider context quite invisible.)

Patricio Guzmán, talking about the filming of what became *The Battle of Chile*, an extraordinary record of the events leading up to the coup against Salvador Allende in 1973, explained how the group decided on their approach to documenting the unfolding events. They analysed the task and opted for a thematic treatment, because they realized, he said, that 'many events occur only as the result of a long process – a process that ... often seems invisible. What you are able to film is the culmination of the process, the final, visible event: the workers taking over a factory, for example' (Burton 1986: 57). Here the issue is the invisibility of history as process, a problem realized in the earliest days of cinema by one Boluslaw Matuszewski, who wrote a pamphlet in 1898 proposing an archive of actuality films for the use of historians. There would be certain limitations, of course. While the usual version of history offered by the cinema, he said, 'is composed of ceremonies arranged in advance and posed before the lens', there is one difficulty which 'gives us pause', namely, 'that a historical event does not always happen where someone is waiting for it' (Leyda 1964: 15). But even if the camera were there – like Mr Zapruder on the grassy knoll when Kennedy was assassinated – it wouldn't help. History, as Bill Nichols (1991: 142) put it, is the referent of documentary which always stands outside the filmic text, 'always referred to but never captured'. The film as such is always made up of images that are never more than fragments, in which history itself is invisible, an absent cause (as Fredric Jameson somewhere calls it) accessible only through textual reconstruction. This textual reconstruction is the work of montage.

If montage is the crucial process that turns camera footage into a film, there is a family resemblance between the classic montage theories of Eisenstein, Pudovkin and Vertov which is due to the shared influence of Marxist philosophy and the concept of the dialectic, which each interpreted freely according to their own predilections. It was left to Walter Benjamin, in another context, to speak of the 'dialectical image' as such, a concept he proposed in his unfinished Arcades Project, an account of Paris as the capital of the nineteenth century, for which he assembled over a thousand pages of research notes, which survived, and an album of images, which didn't. The idea, which he noted could be applied to film, derived from sauntering like the *flâneur* through the Arcades themselves, where it was possible to observe a kaleidoscopic and fortuitous concurrence of window displays and shop signs which created bizarre juxtapositions. Benjamin, according to Susan Buck-Morss (1991: 67), was drawn to concrete graphic representations in which images of particular phenomena or moments pointed to larger historical truths. He also thought that 'the technique of montage has "special, perhaps even total rights" as a progressive form because it "interrupts the context into which it is inserted" and thus "counteracts illusion" '. In short, he was interested in images as emblematic traces removed from the historical continuum, which could be reactivated through juxtaposition. The crucial quality of the dialectical image was its historical resonance. The concept is a fuzzy one, because the dialectical image is necessarily ambiguous, but it points to the space of history because the image represents a momentary aspect of a dialectical process – 'the figurative appearance of the dialectic, the law of the dialectic at a standstill' (Benjamin 1973: 171).

But in that case, the medium of film grants every image the capacity to become a dialectical image, and montage is the process of bringing the dialectic to life again. In this way the filmmaker can even overcome Brecht's objection that the photographic reproduction of reality says very little about that reality. Here a paradigmatic example can be found in Ivens' *Philips Radio* of 1931, where he contrasts the modern assembly line with the old-fashioned artisanal methods of the glass blowers with their cheeks all puffed out, an image he repeats in increasing close-up to make the effect even more grotesque. The film, as Philips wanted, was highly photogenic, but also widely perceived as critical of the system it portrayed. According to one reviewer, 'It raises the spectre of the physical and moral ruin which threatens those workers who are the victims of capitalist rationalisation.'[5]

IV

Let's recap. The documentary camera is limited by the fact that some things are invisible, but for different reasons (like cats in coalholes and palace coups). Some things can be shown through the visible signs of their effects (like the wind). However, the invisibility of social processes is something else altogether. Sometimes their effects are very visible – like slums and hovels and shanty-towns – but the process as such is not a physical object, nor indeed a singular thing, but more like history, which refuses to present itself promptly in front of the camera but remains an absent cause; with the consequence that the signs of those effects are at best amorphous, ambiguous, and open to interpretation. We can also speak here of concepts, including fuzzy ones, which defy visualization, like the infamous 'invisible hand of the marketplace'. Concepts, however, can sometimes be represented symbolically, like the machine once constructed by some Cambridge economists in order to show the flow of money through the economy, which Adam Curtis puts on the screen in his critique of economics in his television documentary *League of Gentlemen* (BBC TV, 1992). And sometimes a film can inscribe a verbal metaphor. One of the finest examples is Sergio Rezende's investigation of the (pre-HIV) blood trade in Brazil, *To the Last Drop* (*Até a Última Gota*, 1980). Most of the donors come from the ranks of the poorest of people, who resort to earning their meagre living by selling their blood on a regular basis. This is not very good for you. When it emerges that most of this blood is not for use in Brazil, where it is far too expensive, but is bought by multinational corporations to supply the United States, you get the clearest of metaphors of the way that economic imperialism bleeds the Third World dry not just figuratively but also literally.

To shift register, and enter the purview of philosophy, these observations raise a question of ontology, because if there are different types of invisibility, it follows that there are different types of thing, or thingness. Heidegger showed that the category of the 'thing' in Western philosophy is much more difficult to unravel than might be supposed, since it stretches from everyday physical objects like stones or shoes to works of art, and he tried to distinguish their thingness or thinghood, but in a metaphysical discourse that stretches at the seams and is hardly capable of expressing any kind of concrete meaning. Part of the mystery, the problem in thinking this through, is that occidental culture is caught up in a language which has a veritable bias towards objectification (or reification) which makes it difficult to escape from its logic. This is not necessarily true of other cultures and languages, and therefore philosophies. In Japanese, for example, there are two words for 'thing', *mono* and *koto*. *Mono* means thing or object in the usual Western sense of the word, although *mono* things are not only material objects, but also ideas, facts, and even emotions. *Koto* is more difficult to explain, because it is closer to thing as event, occurrence, or happening. According to Rein Raud (2002), a European authority on Japanese literature, modern Japanese philosophers of different persuasions are all agreed that these terms represent two different kinds of cognition. And as various linguists explain, *koto* indicates things that have a temporal duration, as opposed to *mono* where the temporal duration isn't relevant.

Raud gives the simple example of a railway station announcement, 'The train going to Shibuya is arriving'. Here, 'the train going to Shibuya' is expressed in one word, *shibuyayuki*, which he tells us is a verb that indicates the act or event of going to Shibuya; a bit like 'the westbound train' except that no actual train is mentioned, because it's implied in the context. Thus, both English and Japanese refer to 'things'; their difference, says Raud, lies in what kind of 'things' they consider to be fundamental. In Japanese, it's being Shibuya-bound. In Western languages, the focus is primarily on the train as such; its arrival at the station is an action that it performs, and where it's bound is a relevant, but contingent fact about it.

Western language, says Raud, is biased towards objects, and Western thought has traditionally privileged *mono*-type phenomena over *koto*, with crucial and profound effects on our culture and philosophies.[6] Japanese, by contrast, as well as Chinese and other, mostly Asian languages, is oriented towards events, and Japanese linguists see the *mono* and the *koto* as in dialectical interaction: anything perceived as *mono* can also be seen as phenomena in process of manifestation and therefore *koto*. But this places the whole problem of documentary representation in a completely new light. In this novel perspective, it seems to me that the same is true of the language of film, ever since the train steamed into La Ciotat in that famous first film of the Lumière brothers. On this reading, the image on the screen belongs to the world of *koto* precisely because the film image turns the object in the lens, the profilmic scene, into a self-manifesting phenomenon. What the screen reproduces is the event unfolding in front of the camera, sheer movement, almost regardless of what it is that's moving, and indeed in the earliest days of cinema this was quite enough to fascinate the audience. The sight of the film as it unfolds on the screen – like the movement of the waves in another Lumière film, *A Boat Leaving Harbour*, the rowing boat and the swelling sea – is not so much an object as an experience, a moment with temporal duration to be experienced as such, therefore not a *mono*, but a *koto*. (I also think of the 4-minute shot of a photograph of Che Guevara at the end of *The Hour of the Furnaces* (*La hora de los hornos*, Argentina, 1968) by Solanas and Getino, but thereby hangs a tale: projectionists who showed the single copy which was circulating in Britain, used to snip off a few frames as a souvenir; in the end, the shot was little more than a few seconds long, and no longer had the same effect.)

From a Western perspective, documentary is a form of discourse that by its nature speaks in particulars (that train arriving there on that particular day). Each shot is a unique event or occurrence, with the photographic image being taken as a guarantee of the ontological integrity of the object it portrays. But inevitably, at the same time, it also lends itself to being read as a universal ('The Arrival of a Train', with an indefinite object). As the subject on the screen, however, it comes alive in the special way that French theorists in the 1920s described as *photogénie*. In the writings of Louis Delluc, Louis Aragon and Jean Epstein, where film and modernism came together, *photogénie* means more than photogenic in English, or 'attractive to the camera'. It is more than the special beauty of certain faces or certain filmic effects, but also a sense of transcendence which film lends to the phenomena observed, a shimmering that gives us the impression of seeing things as we've never seen them before, as if endowed with a special intensity and inner life, or as Epstein put it, a personality of their own. This intensity operates not only through people, lending stardom to certain actors independently of their ability as actors (or sometimes lack of it), but also through objects. A close-up of a revolver, says Epstein, 'is no longer a revolver, it is the revolver-character … It has a temperament, habits, memories, a will, a soul' (quoted in Abel 1988: 317). Again, it seems to me that this existential quality belongs to the world of *koto*.

This shift of perspective also, I think, shifts the puzzle about filming the invisible, at least if we follow Hiromatsu Wataru, one of Japan's leading Marxist philosophers, who according to Raud (2002: 102), believes that at the level of the *koto*, the event is not closed to the rest of the universe – on the contrary, it opens out into a chain of relations, and in this way, even 'overcomes' the subject–object division that characterizes modernity. The best way to explain is one final example. There is a great *koto* moment at the climax of the Israeli film *Checkpoint* (2003), by Yoav Shamir, a singular exercise in observational reportage, filmed over the course of a year, at different times of day and in all weathers, at various checkpoints which control the movement of the Palestinians in the Occupied Territories. Nothing is staged and there are no interviews, but from time to time, people address themselves to the camera of their own accord, both Palestinians and Israeli soldiers, suggesting that they are perfectly aware of being filmed. Then here we are at the entrance to Ramallah after a heavy snow fall. A Palestinian man hands over his ID card with the words, 'Let us past this time, look at the weather.' An Israeli soldier walks away from the camera with the comment 'Let him film. What do I care? I don't care what people think.' A moment later, they're all throwing snowballs at each other, the Palestinians crying 'Allah Akbar', as one man shouts 'You can see that you went through an Intifada', and a voice replies 'Come on, we'll give you an Intifada'. The scene transcends itself to become a powerful, intensely poignant, and poetically ambiguous symbol of the physical violence of the conflict which throughout the film remains off-screen and invisible, but which the viewer knows is going on because it's always in the news. In the process, the scene exemplifies one of the most profound capacities of documentary cinema, which goes beyond the representation of the way things appear, to become a metaphor for what is going on behind and beyond the image which the camera is able to record. In a strangely understated kind of way, the snow-fight in *Checkpoint* is cathartic, precisely because it doesn't invent or fictionalize but simply points beyond itself to the wider and deeper tragedy.

In short, despite appearances, so to speak, documentary has a power, if not directly to reveal the invisible, nonetheless to speak of things that orthodoxy and conservatism, power and authority, would rather we didn't know and didn't think about. And this is exactly why we need it.

Notes

1 The term *cinéma vérité* is dreadfully misused, and, strictly speaking, should be differentiated from the practice developed out of New York and known as direct cinema, but to the old school BBC cameramen, all of it was wobblyscope.

2 We worked as a two-man crew, with myself recording sound and interviewing. Peter shot the film entirely hand-held – we were moving around on foot and needed to be agile, so we didn't even carry a tripod with us, but then Peter's camerawork is impeccable and he didn't need one.

3 31 July 1982, *golpe de estado* by Ricardo de la Espriella against Arístides Royo.

4 My thanks to Thomas Austin for reminding me of this example.

5 Léon Moussinac in *L'Humanité*, reprinted in Delmar (1979: 23).

6 Kimura, Raud tells us, points out that the subject is conceived by the Western philosophical tradition as a *mono* – 'a view with which he himself vehemently disagrees' (2002: 104). 'Quite obviously,' says Raud, 'object-biased languages also lend themselves easily for the expression of subject–object splits while event-biased languages are likely to leave the speaking subject more open toward the events it speaks about' (2002: 99). He concludes that 'modernity' can be seen as a socio-cultural paradigm in which object-oriented thinking is the norm (2002: 105).

Part II

The Changing Faces of Documentary Production

Hasta Siempre (UK, 2005). Courtesy Rice N Peas Films.

10 Developing and Producing a Feature Documentary

The case of *Deep Water*

Wilma de Jong

> I think the [documentary] production process is so much more full of risks ...
> things can happen, and they change the direction of the film, that it's not
> comparable to fiction.
>
> (Director 1, May 2005)

This chapter addresses the development and production process of the feature
documentary *Deep Water*, which was released in 2006 and subsequently won the
Greirson Award, the prize for the Best Documentary at the Rome Film Festival and
was one of two winners of the FOCAL (Federation of Commercial Audiovisual
Libraries) Award for the best use of archive footage in a feature-length factual
production.

My interest focuses on the positions, interactions and relationships of power in
the field of film production, and how these influence both the production process
and the final film text. My research consisted of regular semi-structured interviews
with the producers, the writer, one of the two directors and one of the editors, as well
as a single interview with representatives of each of the financiers and the distributor
of the film. As Simon Cottle states, a case study like this 'offers a rare glimpse into
how these wider forces [of production] are professionally managed and creatively
negotiated by programme makers working within a particular and differentiated
organisational field' (2003: 170). As was Cottle, I have been inspired by Bourdieu's
concept of the 'field of cultural production' to analyse the wider structures in which
small independent companies operate. Bourdieu defines a field of cultural production
as: 'A series of institutions, rules, rituals, conventions, categories, designations,
appointments and titles which constitute an objective hierarchy and which produce
and authorise certain discourses and activities' (Jenkins 2002: 21). This concept offers
a means of analysing the relationships between the different organizations operating
in the current field of feature film production. Although the concept of 'networks' is
often used to describe these relationships (Leadbeater and Oakley 1999: 11), this
conceptualization may underplay hierarchical and competitive relationships, which
for Bourdieu are the essential features of a field of cultural production. I have used
Bourdieu's concept of the 'field of cultural production' as a canvas on which to draw
the relationships between filmmakers, financiers and distributors, and to link this to
the actual process of producing.

Documentary production research

Documentary production studies have mainly focused on the production of documentaries in a television context (Silverstone 1985; Dornfeld 1998; Kilborn and Izod 1997), which, considering the long and solid tradition of documentaries broadcast on television in the UK, is not surprising. Within television's chain of command, documentary directors/producers have to answer to commissioning editors, series editors or the head of factual production, and at the end the documentary has to fill a certain slot within the schedule. These organizational differences obviously influence the constraints and possibilities of the director and producer in a variety of ways.

Production procedures of feature documentaries might be comparable to those of television documentary, but the relations of power involved are significantly different. These, I will argue, influence the final text in important ways.

Debates in media studies seem to emphasize the big media conglomerates (Cottle 2003; Tunstall 1994). As Hesmondhalgh has argued (2002, 2006) the predicted Americanization of media conglomerates has not taken place, as localized media production has proliferated and has become stronger. In 1999, Leadbeater concluded that the cultural independents were taking on an increasing share of the employment and output of some of the fastest growing sectors in the British economy, growing at twice the rate as the economy as a whole. The independents are a driving force. These small companies do not produce the lion's share of the films in the UK, but they are important for the number of people they employ (Hesmondhalgh 2002) and the possibilities they offer for aspiring directors, writers and producers. Research by Beacham (1999) among students at Goldsmiths College, London concluded that most students who had finished their degrees in media studies ended up in small independent production companies for their first jobs.

> You know, new talent can only come through because people take a risk on those people but the only people who are doing that is the independent production companies, I guess
>
> (Producer 1, May 2005).

In the case of documentary production, for instance, the much discussed documentary 'boom' (Austin 2007) of recent years – including highly successful films such as *Fahrenheit 9/11* (2004), *Bowling for Columbine* (2003), and *Super Size Me* (2005) all of which originated in the US, and *Touching the Void* (2003) from the UK – has led to more documentaries being produced and released for cinema distribution in the USA, Europe and the UK (Arthur 2005; Vicente in this volume). These mainly US developments seem to have paved the way for some financiers and distributors in the UK to finance documentaries in what could be described as the traditional fiction field of production. The UK Film Council, a major investor in fiction films, has also taken on investment in feature documentary:

> We [UK Film Council] were set up 6 years ago. As a New Cinema fund, there was no remit to make or finance feature documentaries initially, it was solely feature films … The head of the New Cinema Fund, and myself, decided to invest in feature documentaries. The first one we invested in was *Hoover Street*

Revival. Then this kick-started that process and became more significant. I guess in those terms we started very small, more of a completion fund. Now we generally as a rule of thumb do two feature documentaries a year – one to two a year.

(Representative of New Cinema Fund, UK Film Council, May 2006)

Deep Water was submitted for funding by APT Films, a small independent production company in London. The film tells the story of the *Sunday Times*-sponsored 1968 Golden Globe Race; a solo, non-stop circumnavigation sailing race. This major sailing challenge attracted sailors, adventurers and those seduced by the possibility of winning £5000. The race has become famous because of the sailor Donald Crowhurst, who notoriously 'conned' the media about his 'winning' position in the Atlantic Ocean. The newspapers heralded his achievements, but after some months of silence his boat was picked up 1,200 miles from Madeira and Crowhurst was assumed to have committed suicide. Of the nine entries Robin Knox-Johnston was the only finisher and won the prize but donated the money to Crowhurst's widow and children.

The producers and some of the financiers of *Deep Water* also felt that the times were in their favour and that the success of *Touching the Void* shaped the possibilities for *Deep Water*:

I remember coming off the tube and seeing a poster for *Touching the Void* and I remember thinking, OK – here's the first big adventure feature documentary with a proper budget and if that does well, we'll be fine.

(Producer 2, April 2005)

The UK Film Council, who also funded *Touching the Void*, made a clear link between the two films:

My pitch on it at the time, to attract financiers' interest, was to say 'It's *Touching the Void* on the seven seas.' You know, it's action adventure, danger, all of that. That was what came to my mind when I saw the archive I thought, that's what it is. And I think it's that kind of audience, who are into sport, who are real sea-faring enthusiasts.

(UK Film Council, May 2006)

Channel Four, working within a completely different remit as a broadcaster than the other financiers, was doubtful about the commercial potential of the *Deep Water* theatrically but had other reasons to co-fund the film:

I mean, one of the big reasons to this [commissioning] was that the family had agreed to talk. They had never spoken before. Clare Crowhurst and the son and the daughter had never ever contributed to any programme about Crowhurst before. So that's a massive factor. For the first time, we're in a position to make the Crowhurst documentary.

(Commissioning editor, Channel 4, June 2006)

Although research for the production of *Deep Water* started before *Touching the Void* had been released, it was clear that documentary production was gaining momentum around this time and that *Touching the Void* has been more than an inspiration, as most parties made direct comparisons with the documentary. It could be argued that a few big successes led to acceleration in documentary production and *Deep Water* was developed in just that period of 2003–4.

APT Films was set up in the 1980s and was part of the workshop movement initiated and encouraged by Channel 4. The background of APT Films still remains recognizable in the films they produce and most films have a 'social engagement edge'. But the company has successfully adapted its interests to contemporary market demands as a wide range of prizes for its films may indicate. APT Films, in line with its social engagement background, offered a different reading and analysis of Crowhurst's story, which led to a film concept in which it was not his 'conning' nature that was emphasized but what he had in common with a possible audience:

> I think basically people categorized him as a cheat and a conman and I think it's much more interesting to recognize that he was a person who responded, you know, like we all do, to a set of pressures that he experienced ... In some ways he's a sort of anti-hero ... you need to feel that you, you may well go there yourself.
>
> (Director 1, May 2005)

Crucially, this approach encouraged Crowhurst's widow and children to give permission to film their story, use their archive and to be interviewed for the film. Without doubt, a documentary such as *Deep Water* could not have been realized without this essential permission. One cannot underestimate the skills involved to manage such contacts; after all, the filmmaker roams around in the world of the family's intimate life history. This link between the storyline and the gaining of permission demonstrates the intrinsic relationship between production methods and text in documentary production.

For financiers, both in the public and commercial sector, a combination of creative and financial factors played a role in the commissioning process of *Deep Water*:

> Obviously we would always be attracted to a project in the first instance creatively. And then we would run various different systems of assessment, we would run numbers based on international sales, comparison films, what our level of equity input would be, and see how we can either pre-sell or do broadcasting deals or – there are so many different ways that we can 'cut it' if you like.
>
> (Pathé, financier and distributor, July 2006)

Although comparisons between *Touching the Void* and *Deep Water* may seem obvious and understandable as both documentaries address risk and adventure, the difference in documentary representation makes the comparison problematic. After all *Touching the Void* was a re-enactment of a story with interviews with the actual climbers involved in the original event, while *Deep Water* consists mainly of archive material and interviews with family and friends of the deceased protagonist. Archive material, shot with different intentions and in different circumstances, by its nature would never be able to create the same dramatic tension as a purposely shot dramatized story.

One producer commented on this difference early in the production process:

> Our film is very different because all our footage, or most of it, is going to be real ... it's not reconstruction. So that's probably the difference between *Touching the Void* and our film and why *Touching the Void* works probably is because it works as a fiction film, and our film will have to work on quite a different level.
>
> (Producer 2, May 2005)

Co-production

Within the field of cultural production, power relations between independent companies are played out partly in terms of which company has the symbolic capital to enter the competition for public as well as commercial finances. The symbolic capital – prestige, status and reputation – acts as a structuring device in the field, but it is acquired capital, which means it can also be lost. The originator of the film was very aware of her lack of 'symbolic capital' within the hierarchy of the field, and approached APT Films to co-produce this film:

> You know Stir-Fried Films[1] came to us [APT Films] because we have the relationships that were needed to make that film happen. I mean, we too have been to bigger film companies as well to more experienced producers.
>
> (Producer 1, June 2005)

There seems to be a continuously changing tiered system operating in the independent production field, where smaller companies will approach more experienced and bigger companies to co-produce films. They can then make use of the track record of the more experienced producers at these companies who also approach the major independents for certain projects. This means that the field is in a constant state of flux. To a certain extent, the field reorganizes itself depending on feasible ideas for films that emerge.

Development of *Deep Water*

A lengthy development period is necessary to find a form to tell the story (Grimsby and McClintock, cited in Kilborn and Izod 1997).

If there is one stage in the production process of a documentary which is under-analysed and under-estimated both in labour and in expenditure, it is the development phase. Hesmondhalgh (2002) argues that one of the factors behind the continued importance of the independents is development: 'the conception stage of texts remains small-scale and relatively inexpensive and still takes place in relatively autonomous conditions' (2002: 149). The link between development and independents is commonly made in the industry.

> I think that in Britain the independent production community is the powerhouse of the industry. I think it's the small, independent companies that come up with the ideas ... and the bigger companies often buy those.
>
> (Producer 1, May 2005)

For historical documentaries such as *Deep Water*, research is labour-intensive and therefore not inexpensive:

> We were doing a lot of research, so we were meeting with Robin Knox Johnston, we met with Chay Blyth. We tracked down Murray Sayles, one of the journalists who covered the race, and I started to look into the archive, and I remember about two years ago, I spent about three or four months just literally going through the archive libraries and starting to see what was out there in terms of newsreel footage or footage taken by the sailors themselves or newspaper articles.
>
> (Producer 2, April 2005)

If it is possible to write a treatment without research for fiction, then it is almost impossible for a documentary. Research, it could be argued, is one of the defining characteristics of documentary production, as many documentary filmmakers claim:

> Documentary filmmaking for me is a process of evolution. We will sit and talk about an idea, but after two or three months on the road the idea will still be there but a great deal will have changed. And a lot of our preconceptions will have turned on their heads ... Things have to grow. That's why the long development period is necessary.
>
> (Grimsby and McClintock, cited in Kilborn and Izod 1997: 6)

Considering that it took three years to get the film off the ground, the £14,000 of development money, which was obtained from Screen South, Media Plus and the UK Film Council, was hardly enough to cover labour and travel costs, access and copies of archive material and the clearing of rights. In the case of *Deep Water*, the long development process led to a change of genre, from fiction to documentary:

> To begin with, Producer 2 and Stir-Fried were working around the possibility of a fiction, and we got a bursary from Screen South to write a fiction treatment. In the process of doing that, we came across more and more interesting archive and it seemed to me that what was interesting about this story was that it was true ... and the amazing thing is that a lot of these sailors took cameras with them. There are very early 16mm films and there are audiotapes, which are a phenomenal archive, so I thought it was a more interesting story to tell through documentary.
>
> (Director 1, April 2005)

Finding a form to tell a story is a time-consuming creative process. After all, many interpretations of a 'real' event are possible.

Those involved in *Deep Water* at this stage of the production had other jobs or had accrued debt. The commitment and great time investment of 'creative independents' are remarkable features of the film production field.

The financiers, Pathé and UK Film Council, also mentioned the issue of time:

> In fact, it [development of documentaries] takes more time than it does when we do fiction. It's more time-consuming ultimately ... Initially, we were a little innocent and naïve in our assumptions that it wouldn't take as much time and would be quite a straightforward process, and then we found out it's not ... But we still want to do them [documentaries].
>
> (UK Film Council, May 2006)

One issue in this case is that the employees of funding bodies are being paid for this development time, while those who develop potential new films are not.

Management of time and risk in the field of production

Figure 10.1 illustrates the hierarchical and competitive nature of the field of film production. The split in the model is between the kind of organizations and their risks when operating in this field. The financiers are public bodies and commercial organizations, that employ specialists in film production, law and finance. In this model, those media professionals located in the middle shoulder the greatest risk during the development stage.

Independent writers, directors and producers invest significant time in the development of a film project with very limited remuneration:

> They [producer, writers] bridge the gap [between the financiers and the media professionals] but also manage the lot.
>
> But I normally see it as ... there are two different kinds of people in the film industry. There's people who do jobs and who earn money –
>
> *Interviewer:* 'Camera man and sound man?'
>
> Yeah and they're not going to work unless they're being paid a fair rate. And then there are people generally [in the middle] that are in the business of developing ideas, projects, and things in order to ... realize a vision. They hope that one day they'll get paid. Silly people!
>
> Really, it's the people in the middle [directors/producers] who are unpaid and the people at the top are paid a wage.
>
> (Producer 1, June 2005)

Both Blair (2001) and Smeaton (2003) report how since the 1970s employment practices in the film industry have changed. Self-employment has now been the dominant form of employment for the past 25 years. Both at the level of the independent company and at that of the crafts people, risk-reducing mechanisms are operating. Within APT Films, several directors and writers make films with the same producers, production staff and support staff. Faulkner and Anderson's (1987) research in this field demonstrated that successful producers and directors work together on a repeated basis in order to reduce uncertainty and increase profits.

FIELD OF CULTURAL PRODUCTION

FIELD OF FILM PRODUCTION

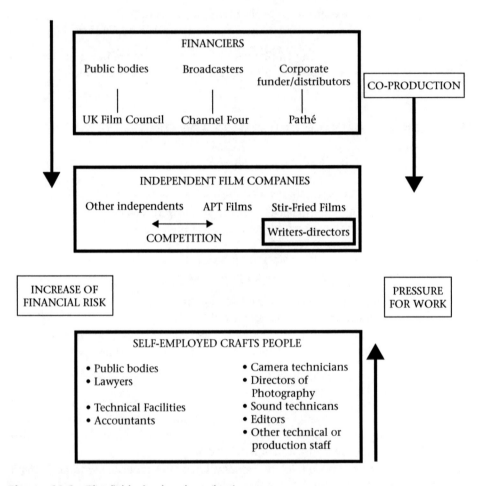

Figure 10.1   The field of cultural production

Blair (2001) notes that the same mechanism operates with groups of craftspeople – camera operators, editors, and production managers – who work in established groups and gain employment through that group membership. But the hours involved in working in the independent sector are excessive. Production companies tend to juggle a portfolio of films in development, as only a small percentage will be realized:

> I've worked longer hours than any of my high-earning lawyer friends. And it's not so much long hours as just that those hours never stop. It's kind of like no tomorrow ... we're out on holiday, I'll still take the phone calls

because there's, you know, it's like I'm juggling. I'm juggling at the moment kind of twelve or so films actively in development which are all moving along and none of them want to wait for me to be busy on another film or for me to be on holiday.

(Producer 1, May 2006)

Development should be considered one of the defining characteristics of documentary and a strength of the independent production field. Although risk-reducing mechanisms operate in the field, it could be argued that present developments, mainly in the broadcast industry, involving staff redundancies lead to increased risks for small independent companies. In a field with strong tendencies towards monopolization (*Guardian*, 1 April 2005), this could mean that smaller companies are entering a period of increased pressure on their existence.

Documentary: undoing the shackles with the past

Notwithstanding the popularization of a variety of factual formats, the word 'documentary' still seems to be for audiences what Macdonald and Cousins describe as 'the most dreary and off-putting of terms' (1996: xi).

Which is what I mean about the word 'documentary', it sounds like homework. It sounds like it's going to ask you for something rather than offer you something, I call them programmes or films.

(Commissioning editor Channel 4, June 2006)

Although documentaries have been highly successful, the 'dreaded image' still resonates in the discourse around its production:

It's interesting, we had a meeting [with financiers] recently and it was around marketing, and they said OK – we will never in our marketing campaign ever mention the word 'documentary' and we will never mention the word 'sailing'. Those are the two things – in the marketing of *Touching the Void* you never heard the word 'documentary' or the word 'mountaineering' – it's an adventure story.

(Producer 2, April 2005)

It's not only audiences who turned away from the dreaded image of documentary; for a long time documentary was seen as 'easier' than fiction by feature filmmakers and not really the real thing.

Grierson, the founding father of documentary in the UK, not only coined the term 'documentary' (Nichols 1991; Winston 1995) but also determined what it used to stand for: utilitarian, pedagogic, impersonal and serving a social purpose. Placed in the context of the 1930s and, above all, the funding regime of the semi-governmental framework Grierson was working within, it is not surprising that documentary texts developed the way they did. In contrast, recent popular culture has shaped new documentary formats and it has re-emerged in many forms and shapes to be, above all, more entertaining and therefore able to reach bigger audiences:

> I believe there's absolutely an appetite for documentary film. And I think that people are much more open to the documentary medium now. I don't quite know why that is. Maybe it's because it's been done successfully and people as a result are more comfortable with it as a device, as a storytelling device. And also it's sort of shed its sort of slightly woolly-jumper image.
>
> (Pathé, July 2006)

Contemporary documentary formats still seem to focus on ordinary people – and not only on the working class – but the focus seems to be about the hurdles they experience in life and how to overcome these hurdles. Although one can identify a focus on everyday experiences, this is not the case, for instance, in *Touching the Void* or *Deep Water*, unless one considers climbing mountains or sailing around the world as daily experiences. But there seems to be a focus on individuals, their emotional lives and their personal revelations and challenges, which produces knowledges, and which arguably instructs audiences on how to manage the self in challenging situations. In contemporary late capitalist cultures, such as Britain and the USA, cultural pluralism, lifestyle diversity and niche marketing have arguably produced fragmented and self-reflexive selves. It is within this context that documentaries such as *Touching the Void* and *Deep Water* should be placed. However, this means that the documentary project has increasingly shifted from a focus on the public sphere to the private sphere. It might be argued that this shift has made documentary more suitable for theatrical release, as these documentaries share a focus on the intimate, private world of individuals – a domain they share with their fictional counterparts.

I would argue that documentary is in a process of undoing its shackles from its utilitarian and pedagogic past, and has found new forms and voices, all of which illustrate and confirm documentary's hybrid history.

Documentary in the field of feature film production

The field of film production seems to be segregated from the field of television production. At the level of distribution, they meet, because films that are theatrically released also need a broadcast guarantee, but the funding structures, production methods and technologies are different. The UK Film Council, for instance, does not invest in television documentary. Budgets for documentaries which are theatrically released also tend to be much larger. If *Deep Water* had been produced for television, a budget of £1.2 million would not have been available. In fact, the BBC refused to take on this project for financial reasons. The size of the budget is caused mainly by the amount of archive material used and the technologies required in transferring archive material from a variety of sources to HD (High Definition) format:

> I think one of the good things about being in a fiction environment is that you can have much greater ambition for documentary, you can get into a

cinema and DVD distribution system, that's the same distribution system as the fiction distribution and people will seek out documentaries that they wouldn't otherwise see because of the way it's marketed and they think it's going to be a similar experience of going and seeing fiction and in a way it *is*.

(Director 1, April 2005)

The financiers of *Deep Water* were the UK Film Council, Film Four and Pathé, which would also distribute the film. This creates a field of power relations and unavoidable hierarchy. No financiers will offer to finance films without any conditions on how the production is to be realized. Certainly for a public body, such as the UK Film Council, both financial returns and 'quality' standards are of importance. But which conditions and how these conditions are implemented will influence the actual production, working relations and final text.

In the case of *Deep Water*, the UK Film Council, like the other financiers, used their standard contract (full contract available on website UK Film Council). In order to guarantee professional and high technical standards, the independent company has to work contractually with media professionals who need to be approved by the financiers. This means that the writer, director, director of photography, editor and other key media professionals need to be approved. Regular meetings will take place to discuss the progress of the project: scripts, working edits and the final cut need to be approved. At the level of production and financial planning, production schedules and auditors need to be approved. At a technical level, the firm which provides the technical facilities needs to be approved also. These working conditions are accepted and experienced as standard within the industry:

It's really a kind of mainstream financiers who made a lot of films and are putting up a lot of money and want to make sure that we're approaching it with intelligence, and legal safety and so they're challenging and asking questions and creatively they want to know that we're thinking through this and they want to challenge that creativeness. I wouldn't give someone, you know, a third of a million pounds without challenging what they are doing.

(Producer 1, May 2005)

In the case of *Deep Water*, the UK Film Council expressed a preference for most key professionals to have a fiction film background. In addition, a script of *Deep Water* was written in fiction format:

I've gone and looked at all the archive in much more detail and created a script, which is now 80 pages, which ... you know, it's written like a fiction script, with dialogue of interviews that we haven't recorded yet (laughs).

(Director 1, April 2005)

Still, *Deep Water* was selected for funding and has been presented by the filmmakers as a 'documentary' – which, considering it consists of 70 per cent archive materials, 30 per cent interviews and just a few reconstructed scenes, it seems to be. However, it seemed to have been approached by some of the financiers not only within the conventions of fiction production but also as a fictional text: 'Feature documentaries are feature films to us; so, they have the same conditions and funding as feature films' (UK Film Council, May 2006).

Communities of practice

Documentary filmmakers have developed working methods which are different from fiction production practices. Arthur describes documentary as a mode of production 'a network of funding, filming, post production and exhibition' (2005: 20). This description excludes, surprisingly, the text itself, but this point of view appreciates the characteristics of a specific field of production.

In the UK, there is no specific fund for documentaries, unlike the situation in the Netherlands, for instance where the 'Production Fund' offers specific funding and tailor-made contracts and production methods for documentary production. I have used Wenger's concept of 'communities of practice' (1999) to analyse and highlight the difference between different 'practices' such as documentary and fiction production processes, as Bourdieu's research mainly focused on individual artists and journalists as agents operating in a certain field of cultural production.

Characteristics of a community of practice (Wenger 1999) are described as:

- a joint enterprise;
- a shared repertoire;
- a mutual engagement.

'Joint enterprise' not only describes a stated goal, but also creates among participants relations of mutual accountability that become an integral part of practice' (1999: 78).

The experienced documentary filmmaker Michael Rabiger describes the 'joint enterprise' as follows: 'A documentary is the sum of relationships during a period of shared action and living, a composition made from the sparks generated during a meeting of hearts and minds' (2004: 33). There is a romantic element to this description of the production process of a documentary, but the emphasis on the 'sum of relationships' and the 'meeting' addresses a central feature of the documentary production process: the moment of recording. Whatever the preparation, whatever the agreements, unexpected events will take place; interviewees will formulate their replies differently from when the documentary was being researched. Silverstone (1985) notes that there is a 'certain arbitrariness, a serendipity' at the heart of documentary practice. One of the directors of *Deep Water* formulates the issue as follows:

> I think personally that the documentary process is fundamentally different from a fictional process and needs to be much more organic. There are things that you do which are inevitably an unknown. You are not going out and shooting a script, everything you shoot informs the things you do next.
>
> (Director 1, April 2005)

Pathé's representative emphasizes the fluidity between research and the shooting period in documentary production:

> It's very much an ongoing process of discussion, finessing and sort of finding your story, much more than you have with a shooting script that you lock off

before shooting on a feature film. But with a documentary film, you find your film in the process sometimes, I think, and what makes some of the most interesting documentaries, ones which are a little bit open really, and sometimes prizes are unearthed as you go along ... But I guess it's the research and sort of shooting period is more merged.

(Pathé, July 2006)

The commissioning editor from Channel 4 put the emphasis on the process of creation in the editing suite:

The unique chemistry of making a great documentary takes place in the edit ... however well you're prepared, it's there that you create this cocktail of the film, that you mix the ingredients, and you shape it. Whereas in fiction, it takes place with the writer. Because, once you get into the edit with drama, you can only change a small amount. Whereas in documentary, you can go, part five, let's bring that to the front. Let's reshape the story.

(Commissioning editor, Channel Four, June 2006)

It seems that the process of creation of a documentary is envisaged as a continuous process in which unexpected events can influence the direction of the production, while, on the other hand, the editing room is also seen as a place where creation of the film takes place. These characteristics may imply that control by financiers is more restricted than in fiction production.

The shared repertoire of a community of practice includes 'routines, words, tools, ways of doing, stories, gestures, genres, actions or concepts that the community has produced or adopted in the course of existence, which have become part of its practice' (Wenger 1999). The 'repertoire' also distinguishes the community of documentary practice from the community of fiction practice. The contemporary debate on the blurred boundaries between genres has been ubiquitous. On the other hand, it should be noted that a wide array of 'fictional' strategies and devices have been used in the history of documentary production.[2] However, to distinguish and claim a separate space for documentary production practice seems essential, without ending up at the other end of the continuum where one reduces documentary simply to a 'mode of production' or digs a postmodern hole in which all texts become fictional. Paget (1998: 135) provides us with a list of differences in the production methods between documentary and fiction, which is helpful (Table 10.1).

Table 10.1   Comparison between documentary and fiction

Documentary	Fiction
research/accuracy	invention/creativity
journalist/researcher	writer/creator
unrehearsed profilmic events	rehearsed profilmic events
real-world individual	character
behaviour	acting
commentary/statement	dialogue
montage	mise-en-scène
location/non-design	setting/design

(A more extensive list focusing on the text can be found in Paget (1998: 135).

I would like to add 'reconstruction' of events and interviews. Not that every documentary production entails these elements, but one could consider these elements as being part of the generic repertoire of this community of practice.

These issues can also be recognized in interactions within a documentary production environment, such as discussions about whether an interviewee is prepared to co-operate, the travelling to different parts of the world to interview certain people for the film, and concerns whether some important interviewee will withdraw or whether the interview will provide the information needed by the director. These considerations seem fundamental to a documentary production repertoire, but are absent from fiction production practice, and they create a very different relationship between director and interviewee than that between director and actor.

In the case of *Deep Water*, it was of crucial importance that the widow of Donald Crowhurst would co-operate with the film. To guarantee co-operation she was involved from the beginning. During the production process she was invited to see edited sequences to keep her involved and maintain good working relationships. These different relationships in the production process create moments of vulnerability in the documentary production process, which are not identifiable in the fiction production process.

Working with different financiers

Co-production and working with different financiers are more common than ever before. It is common for all financiers contractually to have full creative (final cut) and economic power over the film. A general increase in budgets makes it hardly feasible to realize a film with the support of only one financier. The complexity of involving several financiers has hardly been documented in academic literature but issues such as different interpretations of a film and practical issues such as bringing different people around the table at the same time are not difficult to conceive:

I mean, there's always a little bit of negotiation to be had and when you've got three financiers, they all have to approve it and they're all looking at these contracts and they've all got different issues that they want to address so they all come back with different things, so you have to get it sorted so everyone can agree on how to go back to whatever company we're dealing with and the whole process just takes a very long time. If you had one financier, it would be really easy but with three people you're dealing with three different sets of rights.

(Producer 2, June 2005)

During the production process, with still 12 weeks of editing left, a short edit of some archive material was shown to the financiers in August 2006 and in September 2006:

Basically, out of that meeting, I think what they picked up was that there is an issue about how likeable Donald Crowhurst is as a character on film, and how little we see him, how sympathetic he is, and how much the other sailors come across as much more attractive characters than him, and that's a problem.

(Director 1, September 2006)

McKee, in his standard work on fiction scriptwriting production (1999), argues that a fundamental aspect of the main character is 'likeability'. The issues of identification of the audience with the main character were raised. Although these issues are not completely uncommon in documentary production, they are not as emphasized as in drama production. Did Nick Broomfield ask if Aileen Wournos in *Aileen: Life and Death of a Serial Killer* (UK, 2004) was likeable enough to be the main character of a documentary? Did Molly Dineen ask herself if Geri was likeable enough to be the main character in a documentary? As the Fourdocs website (Channel Four) states 'A character does not have to be likeable, but compelling.'

There are lots of times in the story when you really want the story to be different. You really want the story to follow the laws of fiction story telling and it doesn't, and there's a terrible temptation to just go, well, we'll shuffle that around and it will work. But you can't. I think there's a lot to be said about the way in which the word 'story' goes completely unquestioned in filmmaking. Filmmakers always say 'I'm a story teller' and it's true, but stories are structures that carry a very particular way of seeing the world.

(Director 1, October 2005)

This point of view echoes Hayden White (1987) who maintains 'form is content'. Do real events offer this straightforward progression of beginning, middle and end? It could be considered to be a mould, which is used to structure events and make sense of our world. In itself, fictional story telling defies the incoherence of reality. The original approach to Donald Crowhurst had been to present him empathetically, as a man who, when confronted with certain pressures, made certain decisions which might be morally wrong but in the specific circumstances were understandable.

The lack of archive material of Crowhurst was also an issue. On the financiers' side, eight people were involved, only two of whom had significant documentary experience. The others had limited documentary production experience or none at all. In order to reconcile potentially different ideas about the focus of the film among the financiers and APT Films, the financiers decided to appoint a representative so that the financiers would speak with one voice. A well-known and experienced documentary producer, in fact the producer of *Touching the Void*, was appointed to take on this role. The disappointment of some of the financiers at this point in the production process revealed the disjunction between the two different 'communities of practice' of documentary and fiction films – as they are combined in the production process of feature documentaries.

Conclusion

In this chapter, I have argued that power relations in the field of film production are unavoidable, as financiers will place both creative and economic conditions on the way films are being produced. How conditions are formulated and shaped by the financiers has a significant effect on the interactions and relations in the field, both on other financiers and the production company concerned.

From a historical perspective, it seems that the boom in the popularity of documentary in the cinema in the years 2002–3 created a positive funding climate for *Deep Water* and the film was funded within a fiction production field. The financiers allowed a different production process to adapt to the demands of the film and the filmmakers, but in the end the different parties seem to have been operating from within different productional backgrounds. At a contractual level, this documentary had to follow the production methods of a feature film. Simple practical issues such as getting all financiers around the table played a role, and slightly different expectations for the film created a complex situation. Tensions appeared which could be seen as friction between different communities of practice. From the start, some of the financiers approached *Deep Water* as a fictional film text, as both the professionals involved, the script and, to a certain extent, the text were judged and approached by fiction criteria. In addition, the comparison to *Touching the Void* from the beginning onwards created a productional environment for *Deep Water* which appeared not to be conducive for the film.

As is often the case, a crisis brings ultimate differences to light. To a certain extent a theatrical release demands that a documentary operates in a fiction environment and at a certain level as a fictional text. For documentaries such as *Touching the Void*, of which more than half comprises dramatized scenes and therefore offers a form of identification comparable to a fictional experience, this might work, but for a more conventional documentary text such as *Deep Water* it proved to be a complicated route.

Acknowledgements

This chapter is based on interviews with key professionals involved in the production of *Deep Water* in the context of a research project funded by the AHRC entitled

'Contemporary Documentary Production Processes'. The arguments expressed in this chapter are the responsibility of the author and do not necessarily represent the opinions of the interviewees.

Notes

1 Stir-Fried Films is the film company which took on the development of *Deep Water* in the first instance.

2 *Nanook of the North* (US, 1922) often considered the first 'real' documentary, was a reconstruction of the life of Inuits.

11 Filmmakers and Their Subjects

Jerry Rothwell

> Every time a film is shot, privacy is violated.
>
> (Jean Rouch 1975, 2003: 88)

There is a moment in Werner Herzog's documentary *Grizzly Man* (US, 2005), when Timothy Treadwell, the film's central character, films himself candidly talking about his own motivations: 'I'm in love with my animal friends. I'm in love with my animal friends. I'm in love with my animal friends,' Treadwell repeats. Then frustrated at his own lack of words, he turns away as though giving up, before adding 'I'm very, very troubled ... It's very emotional. It's probably not even cool looking like this.' It's an odd combination of private confessional and public performance, typical of Treadwell's tone in much of the footage on which Herzog has built his documentary. What's remarkable about it is that Treadwell behaves as though someone is compelling him to talk, to transgress a private boundary, although in reality he is alone, the sole author and shooter of his footage in the Alaskan wilderness. He's talking to himself, but at the same time self-consciously concerned about how this comes across to an audience – a form of intimate performance to camera increasingly common in the age of the video diary and blog.

The use of self-shot footage of intimate moments is becoming part of documentary language and one of the ways that new technologies – digital video, internet distribution, home recording and editing – are transforming documentary practice. Of the recent successful long form documentaries, many have been substantially based on material shot by their subjects: the family's home videos in *Capturing the Friedmans* (US, 2002), soldiers' recordings in Iraq in *The War Tapes* (US, 2006), Treadwell's bear recordings in *Grizzly Man*, video and family photos in *51 Birch Street* (UK, 2005), and Donald Crowhurst's film and tape recordings at sea in *Deep Water* (UK, 2006).

For documentary filmmakers, the prevalence of recordings made by our subjects raises some difficult questions. Take almost any contemporary event and there is likely to be a vast resource of images and film taken by people who are participants in it, not just witnesses to it. The scale of this is quite new and it opens up different kinds of relationships between filmmakers and subjects, raising new questions about where the role of the filmmaker starts and ends.

Prior to the expansion of home video in the 1980s, it's hard to think of examples of film being used confessionally in this way. The costs of equipment and stock – and the commercial and public institutions through which they became available – on the whole prohibited diary-style self-shooting. Home movie-making was a pastime for the aristocracy, rarely included sound (which is fundamental to the confessional film diary) and tended to document family holidays, weddings and encounters with royalty, rather than emotional breakdowns.

In the early history of documentary, there was no role implied for subjects behind the camera as well as in front. Grierson's concept of documentary had observation at its heart. For him, cinema was 'an art based on photographs in which one factor is always, or nearly always, a thing observed'. No place yet for the thing observing itself, for people turning the lens on themselves. Which is not to say that Grierson wasn't interested in what his subjects had to say; reading his writings today it's striking that, at least in the early days, he believed that documentary is primarily a vehicle for people's experience. No sooner had sound finally reached the documentary (initially in the film *Housing Problems* (UK, 1935)) than there arose the remarkable idea of including actual speech in everyday life. Grierson's sister, Ruby, assistant director of *Housing Problems*, is famously said to have turned to her subjects and said, 'The camera is yours, the microphone is yours, now tell the bastards what it's like to live here.' But she didn't want them to start talking about their relationships or their preoccupations with their states of mind – their input was wanted about public matters, not about themselves, to illustrate an argument largely preconceived by the filmmaker rather than to lead us into their own subjectivity. The subject was there to illustrate subject matter. And, despite her comments, Ruby probably didn't leave them with the camera and the microphone at the end of the shoot.

With the benefit of hindsight, it seems the emergence of the domestic camcorder began a steady erosion of this dominant form of documentary. In the late 1980s, the BBC Community Programme Unit pioneered a new television format – video diaries – shot initially on Hi8 camcorders, self-authored, intimate, present-tense documentaries about people's lives from their own points of view. Since then, for better or worse, the video diary has become a standard tool in formatted television documentary: moments when the subjects give an intimate insight into what is happening to them, particularly at times when it would be difficult to shoot with a crew. Internet distribution such as MySpace and YouTube have created channels in which diary material, now stripped of any broader context, is the dominant form.

The attraction of the diary format is perhaps that it plays into our fantasy of seeing what really goes on when we aren't there, of getting closer to how life might be without the cameras present at all, the fulfilment of Vertov's impulse to 'show people without masks, without makeup, to catch them through the eye of the camera in a moment when they are not acting, to read their thoughts, laid bare by the camera' (Vertov 1984: 41). In today's television, self-shot material is seen as a guarantor of authenticity. When we see it we know we're supposed to be getting to the heart of things, spying through an open window into what the subject really thinks and feels. But what makes this material distinctively different from other material captured by the lens is precisely its mix of private and public, its ambiguous combination of intimacy and performance.

Perhaps the most direct example of this is the sequence close to the start of Andrew Jarecki's *Capturing the Friedmans* (US, 2002). David, one of the Friedman sons, speaks to a camera in his bedroom:

>Well, this is private, so if you don't, if you're not me, then you really
>shouldn't be watching this, because this is supposed to be a private situation.
>Between me and me. This is between me now and me in the future. So turn
>it off. Don't watch this. This is private. If you're the fucking, oh, God, the
>cops. And if you're the fucking cops, go fuck yourselves, because you're full
>of shit.

Recording a video diary, if you don't want it to become public, is a risk; perhaps more
so than a written diary, because the medium of video implies a mass audience. David
Friedman has three potential audiences in mind, even while making the recording.
One, himself, in the future, second, a public who 'shouldn't be watching this' but
somehow are, and third, the cops. Which makes you wonder what is compelling him
to record it, when he is so conscious of the possibility of others seeing it, even of
contributing to legal evidence against members of his family. Like an indiscreet office
email that ends up being forwarded to millions around the world, the video diary is
an experiment with the borders of public and private – and perhaps that's part of the
motivation. Secrets are a burden and recording them begins a process of exposure,
over which the subject's control is bound to be precarious. As filmmakers, we are
complicit in this experiment. We become the channel through which the fantasy/
nightmare of the private confession becoming public comes true.[1]

Using self-shot material demands a shift in thinking about the relationship
between documentary filmmaker and subject. Like Grierson, most filmmakers even
today perceive themselves as observers and interpreters. There is a strong resistance in
documentary culture to any meaningful editorial control being given to subjects. We
have a legal framework in which the signing of a release form usually hands over all
of the subject's rights, and an editorial framework in which they are largely excluded
from any decisions once the cut has started. Within this production model, responsibility for transgressions of privacy are placed firmly on the subject. If they feel a
boundary has been breached, the pat answer is that they should have thought about
that before getting involved.

The production practices surrounding diary material tend to undermine these
boundaries. At a legal level, self-shot diaries imply a different kind of consent; by
default the subject owns their own filmed material – and its inclusion in a film is
likely to involve a more complex negotiation than the signing of a release at the start
of shooting. Furthermore, because the filmmaker-director will usually be absent when
the material is shot, they are necessarily pushed to adopt a more distant role of
briefing, support, or selection. A good example of this shift in the role of the
documentary director is the feature documentary *The War Tapes* (US, 2006), a
gruelling portrayal of the lives of American soldiers in Iraq built from soldiers' own
camcorder recordings. Director Deborah Scranton was in regular email contact with
five soldiers of a single battalion for over a year. They sent her their tapes, and she
made suggestions about what to shoot, in a dialogue with them. At the same time,
she shot material with their families at home, which in the film gives the soldiers'
recordings a wider context. The final cut is hers, but the decisions she makes are
substantially shaped by her accountability to the soldiers themselves, and by their
trust in her handling of their material. The finished film, though made from material

shot by people who are broadly in support of America's war in Iraq, is in my view, one of the most devastating anti-war films ever made. But I imagine it is one in which the soldiers do not feel that their material has been taken out of context. In this example, and in our own experience with *Deep Water*, with Donald Crowhurst's family, the use of diary footage is a negotiation which continues throughout the production process, not just at the moment of shooting or acquisition (in the case of archive). As a result, the documentary becomes more of a process of joint exploration, in which decisions about what remains private are made in the context of an ongoing relationship between filmmaker and subject.

Key to the success of that relationship is that it demands a responsibility for the consequences of the filmmaking that go beyond the film itself. Documentaries have an impact off-screen as well as on. People can be made famous or notorious, become rich or be ruined, arrested or pardoned, fall out or be reunited as a result of documentary films. Because contemporary media feeds so voraciously off itself, any filmed material might have a much wider audience, in other contexts, than the filmmaker ever intended. Where film travels deeply into the private realm, this is particularly acute – it can and often does change the subject's world. It would be bizarre if the filmmaker – whose activities have set these events in motion — were seen as completely innocent of the consequences, and yet the conventional legal and practical parameters of television documentary do precisely that. By contrast, the ground rules for a 'joint exploration' model are an honesty about likely outcomes, about the context in which material will be used, and an accountability for the film's impact on the subject, all qualities which filmmakers are often criticized for lacking.

This begs the question as to whether this kind of relationship with subjects compromises the documentary filmmaker's other responsibilities, to their audience and to the truth of the story they are telling. One way of conceiving these shifts in documentary practice are as a continuous rise of the subject, towards a participatory utopia in which everyone is broadcasting their own 'unmediated' stories in their own words and images. But a characteristic of internet clip distribution sites like YouTube and MySpace – and increasingly of genres of 'compilation television' – is that footage is decontextualized, separated from wider meanings. The footage that rises to the surface is the footage that attracts instant attention. What space does this leave for a critical filmmaking in which material is taken at more than its surface value?

My own work has revolved around two kinds of practice: the first, participatory filmmaking in which my role as filmmaker is to enable someone to articulate their experience through a filmmaking process in which they have as much control as possible; the second, as a director of 'people-based' documentaries, in which the responsibility for the worldview of the film lies with me. When I started out, I often mistakenly blurred these roles, but there are clear distinctions between the two practices which tell us something about the relationship between subject and maker in documentary. For example, a recent participatory project, *DigiTales* (UK, 2007) involved me in working with Roma communities in Slovakia to create short one-minute films, based on their own photographs and voices. As a filmmaker on this project I am responsible for working with the subject/author to find the strongest way of telling their story, passing on technical and creative filmmaking skills, encouraging them to think about an audience, and supporting them to push themselves and their films as far as possible in quality and content. But crucially I don't on the whole question the validity of the story they are telling, and I don't juxtapose or recontextualize that story to change its meaning.

On the other hand, where I'm working as a documentary director (as opposed to a facilitator, or a workshop leader), that approach would be unsustainable; even – or perhaps especially – in a documentary which draws substantially on self-shot material. Bill Nichols (1997) has described documentary as occupying 'a complex zone of representation in which the art of observing, responding, and listening must be combined with the art of shaping, interpreting, or arguing'. The filmmaker is not just a collector of images. As a documentary maker you try to get underneath your subject's performance, which may include putting the material in a context different from that originally intended by the subject, as Herzog does with Treadwell's footage in *Grizzly Man*, or interpreting it in a way they disagree with. So an important ingredient of the relationship between maker and subject is an acknowledgement of that aspect of the journey – that in the end it may take the subject to places they would not have gone to on their own, and perhaps that they are uncomfortable with.

Treadwell and Herzog never met. And it's possible Treadwell would never have given permission to Herzog to use his Alaskan recordings in the way that he has. But like Scranton's *War Tapes*, Herzog, while disagreeing with his subject, manages to give Treadwell his autonomy and his self-shot material its integrity. I like to think that Treadwell would have recognized the end result and that perhaps *Grizzly Man* even says the things Treadwell himself was groping for when he stood alone in front of the camera and recorded his own confusion.

Note

1   Raymond Williams (1983: 242–3) points out that the meaning of the word 'private' underwent a shift from something undesirable (as in 'deprive' – withdrawn from the privileges of public life) in the Middle Ages to something desirable (seclusion and the protection from others) in early capitalism. In late capitalism, the promise of access to the private is a currency, the trade in which is central to all media forms, from YouTube to *Heat* magazine to docu-soap.

12 From Eight-Man Crew to One-Woman Band

My life in television documentary

Marilyn Gaunt

In 1970, I skipped out of the Royal College of Art in London, clutching my Master of Arts Degree in Film and Television. I'd had three fantastic years playing with the medium of film, had made a short fiction film and, in my graduating year, a 30-minute documentary which went on to win a coveted college Silver Medal. While at film school I'd assistant edited for a BBC series with Paul Watson. As a renowned documentary filmmaker and pioneer of the 'fly on the wall' style of documentary filmmaking, he'd given me a glowing reference and I thought the world was my oyster. In fact, it turned out, 'the world was my lobster'.

In those days there were only two places to go for an aspiring documentary filmmaker in search of a job: the BBC, or one of the new ITV Network companies.

ITV operated a Union 'Closed Shop', so to get a job you had to have an Association of Cinematographic and Television Technicians Union ticket, and to get that you had to have a job ... Catch 22. So the BBC was my first port of call. I was given very short shrift. They told this secondary school girl that they 'preferred Oxbridge graduates' and that they could teach them, in a few weeks, what I'd learnt at film school.

I shook the dust of the BBC off my feet and headed back to my native town of Leeds, where Yorkshire Television had set up only two years before. I took my graduating film into the canteen there and sought out an executive producer called Tony Essex. I just went up to his table as he was having his post-lunch coffee and asked if he'd look at my film. He did, and three weeks later I was offered a job as a trainee cutting room assistant. This got me the precious union ticket and my career in commercial TV became possible. Editing was my second choice of career and I really enjoyed it. With a strong union, once you were in, life and pay (£20 a week gross) were pretty good. I continued to make little films, and spent quite a lot of time in the studio bar, chatting up cameramen with clockwork Bolexs to spend a day with me for free, or rostrum cameramen and graphics people to do bits of animation and then editing the stuff at night, after work.

Through people I was filming I met David Geen, a freelance BBC cameraman, who was moving up to Leeds to supply a programme called *Nationwide*. We made a film together and he offered me a job as a sound recordist at £40 a week. So I left YTV after a year with an upgraded full union ticket and became Britain's first female location sound recordist. After three years with David I spent 6 months with cameraman Paul Berrif, before calling it a day. However exciting, it wasn't my career choice and I decided to move into research, which in those days was the accepted route to directing.

I ended up at Thames TV as freelance researcher on *This Is Your Life*. It was here, after almost eight years in the industry, that I got my break into directing, winning a place on their Trainee Directors' Boards. I began my directing career in the Schools and Children's Departments making half-hour films and studio inserts, and directing the live studio shows, *Magpie* and *Afternoon Plus*. In 1978, the ACTT was still a very powerful union. I had an eight-man crew: camera; asst. camera; sound; asst. sound; sparks; grips/driver; researcher; production assistant and me. If very large lights were used, you had to have a spark for each light.

A day's shooting schedule had to strictly adhere to union rules of working practice. As I recall, a shoot starting at 9am at a location 30 minutes from the studio would mean a minimum 7.30am crew call. Half an hour to load up, a minimum half an hour travel allowance, and half an hour to unload at location before shooting started. A tea break was required after three hours, at 10 30am. Lunch could be no more than 5 hours from call or it was a chargeable no-lunch break. Lunches usually took up two hours. You had to allow half an hour travel, one hour actually eating and half an hour back. So a 12-noon wrap for lunch would mean a 2pm re-start of shoot. Final wrap would be at 4pm to allow one and a half hours to load up, travel and unload before 5.30pm, and avoid a ten-hour break penalty incurring time-and-a-half next day. I once worked out that, under these rules, an exterior shoot during the winter gave you around two hours of useable shooting time.

It was restrictive, and often the bulk of the crew were in the crew-van while you and the cameraman and sound-man got on with it. The plus side of all this was that, as a director, if you knew how to deal with the numbers, you had enormous support and all you had to do was direct, and all those assistants learned their craft thoroughly before getting promoted, and were well paid while getting this training. So despite the restrictions, it was a very positive and exciting time for the then still reasonably young ITV Network.

ITV companies in the mid-1970s were still franchised under a watchdog with teeth, which insisted that they all include a quota of documentaries in their programming. Funding came from advertising and the Big Five – Granada, Central, YTV, London Weekend Television and Thames – took the largest slices of revenue. Thames, I think, had 12 one-hour slots a year that they had to fill with documentaries. I left Thames after two years and became a freelance director taking myself, and sometimes my ideas, around these companies and establishing relationships with different Heads of Documentary Departments. If one didn't like an idea, another might, and they had the slots to fill. Unlike today, a Yes from them was a Yes to the film being screened.

In this way, for more than 20 years, I managed to work an average of eight months a year making a whole range of films. The unions were still strong but, thanks to Thatcher, their power was weakening. By the late 1980s crews were getting smaller and rules less constricting, but still protective of over-working crew members. I considered this to be a good thing as a knackered cameraman never gives his best. Throughout this period I experienced enormous freedom to make my films in the way I wanted. Executive Producers and Heads of Departments, like John Willis and Catherine Freeman, never asked to see a film until I was ready and it was fine cut and perhaps a few minutes over-length. They had total trust in both me as a director, and their own judgement in choosing me to make a film in the first place. This, more than anything, has changed dramatically over the past few years.

From 1989 to 1993, I made six of 18 sixty-minute documentaries following ordinary people over a year, no sensationalist story lines, just films about the extraordinary within the ordinary. It was for Paul Watson's *Present Imperfect* series on BBC2. We filmed narratives over a year, not knowing if it would have a 'good' ending, or a real ending at all. They made compelling viewing but were of a kind that was to be commissioned less and less.

The writing had been on the wall for social documentary, since the new round of ITV franchise bids came in 1991. I remember seeing the franchise applications and only two, Border and Scottish, actually mentioned Documentary, the rest hid the genre under the heading factual programming. Over the past eight or so years changes in the industry seem to have accelerated.

When I skipped out of film school in 1970, there were only three television channels: BBC1, BBC2 and ITV. There were over 40 million viewers, and ITV had access to them all. Today there are around 50 million viewers but hundreds of channels vying for their attention. Advertisers, who paid extortionate rates to ITV in the good old monopoly days, now have the upper hand and call the tune. Bums on seats and thumbs off the change-channel button are what they expect and demand. This is not only true of commercial channels. When I returned to the BBC briefly in 1998 I found it to be far more viewing figure orientated for documentaries than Thames TV had ever been in the 1970s.

Budgets are getting tighter as revenue gets spread ever more thinly, with the resultant exploitation of young talent (made possible since the disempowerment of the unions) often working unrestricted hours for little or sometimes no pay, in order to 'break into' television. From this grows a different ethic and different working practices. Crews are becoming increasingly rare on social documentaries. My last four films were *Triplets*, *Kelly and Her Sisters*, *Living on the Edge* and *Lin and Ralph: A Love Story*, all for ITV. *Triplets* I shot with a three-man crew, plus a researcher. *Kelly*, 40 per cent shot by a two-man crew, 20 per cent by my Assistant Producer and 40 per cent by myself. *Living on the Edge* was 80 per cent me and 20 per cent my Assistant Producer. *Lin and Ralph*, 100 per cent me, as a one-woman band. Many might say this is a good thing because, on observational domestic documentaries, it helps to get intimacy you can't get with a crew. Although there is some truth in this, it is not universally the case and no-one can be a master of all trades. If you are a one-man band, your directing suffers.

So much of the pleasure of filmmaking for me came from the joint creative power that working with other talented people gave me. As director you could be the eyes in the back of the cameraperson's head, be assessing the wider picture while the crew were literally focusing on one detail. The crew were not rude mechanicals, but co-creatives who were often great sounding boards. I'm not saying that good films can't be made by one person, but doing it continuously, and with increasingly shorter time-frames, must lead to burn-out.

Television now follows the factory model, where programme making is becoming an homogenized process and all signs of true originality are being sacrificed in the interest of fast and cheap manufacture. An American academic once said that in the American TV industry the commercials were the product and the programmes the effluence. At the Sheffield International Documentary Festival in 2003, Channel 4 Head of Documentary Peter Dale admitted, 'I produce eye-candy for advertisers.' This from the channel that was set up initially to push the boundaries and open up the airwaves to minorities. This sea change led to concepts like formatted documentary series, where you make the viewer comfortable and loyal because they know what to expect, and Reality TV, where you can be certain of a good outcome before you start out, by choosing extreme characters and situations to provide confrontation and sensational incidents. No surprise, either, that the increased need for 'delivering' viewing figures has also led to increasing interventionism from commissioners and production executives. While on the one hand I hear pleas from documentary commissioners for passion and authorship from new filmmakers with great ideas, on the other I hear tales of commissioners wanting to select crew (if any), view rushes while shoots are still in progress, dictate style and content from music down to seeing and re-writing commentary and deciding which shots should be in the pre-title hooker, even re-editing and re-scoring films after the director has left the scene.

On one film I produced, the commissioner's philosophy was that serious documentary of the 'old-fashioned sort' is 'like muesli, we know it's good for us but it's not the cereal of choice. We have to re-package it in a Coco Pops packet to get people to watch.' The danger of course is that by doing this the muesli becomes Coco Pops. A good quick fix but ultimately shallow and unsatisfying fare, junk food for the mind. To me, this attitude illustrates a total lack of belief in the intelligence and sophistication of ordinary viewers, and a patronizing insistence that they have to be spoon-fed or they'll switch off.

It would be unfair to say all commissioners and production companies are this bad but it does seem to me that there is a growing orthodoxy that sees directors as mere suppliers of the raw material, rather than authors. They are the hunter–gatherers who go out and use their skills to bring back the goodies for their masters to cut up and serve as they wish. Trust and integrity are central to the special relationship that good observational documentary makers have with those they are filming. To lose all editorial control to people who have no personal or emotional commitment to participants presents the filmmaker with real ethical and moral dilemmas. Persuading people to take part in my films is becoming harder and harder, and experience has made me cautious about making editorial promises I may not be able to keep. People aren't stupid, and because of tabloid-style documentaries and Reality TV, they observe what can happen to people who open their lives and souls to the camera, and see no reason to believe my assurances that I have no hidden agendas.

When I made *Living on the Edge* in 2003/4, all the kids involved had diary cameras and were constantly talking on them about *Big Brother* and the antics of Jade. They loved it, but they knew she was being exploited. We overheard one 15-year-old lad asking a little girl we were filming, 'What are you having anything to do with them for? All television's interested in is viewing figures and money!'

I probably read like some old dinosaur, moaning on about the loss of a golden age, but it's not all bad news. Great documentaries are still being made and seen, in the cinema, on the festival circuits and even, if less frequently and often sidelined to minority channels, on television. Thankfully, unlike when I started out, television is no longer the only place for documentary filmmakers to go to fund their projects. The recent revival of cinema documentary has given the genre a huge boost.

In my early days the cost of film and equipment was prohibitive and the really positive side of new technology is that anyone with the talent can make a sophisticated documentary very cheaply, and the Internet may well ensure it gets seen. With the state it's in, the world needs documentary filmmakers with commitment, passion and a point of view, more than ever. The golden age of television documentary may be coming to an end, but it is my fervent hope that a new golden age, appropriate to the next generation of documentary makers, is dawning.

13 'You Want to Know That, This Is Real, This Is What Happened'
An interview with John Smithson

Wilma de Jong and Thomas Austin

John Smithson is Executive Chairman and Creative Director of DarlowSmithson Productions (DSP) in London. DSP employs about 180 staff and produces around 100 hours of factual programming per year for an international market. The company specializes in docu-drama, documentary and factual programming for both cinema and TV. Smithson is the producer of the award-winning documentary *Touching the Void* and co-producer of *Deep Water*.

What is your fascination with documentary?

I'm much more interested in telling true stories than I'm interested in telling fictional stories. And, by and large, contemporary stories. For me, the power of the true story is overwhelming. And that's why, on something like *Touching the Void*, for me, the power of that film was that the real people were talking ... I've done crime. I've done lots of great history stories, I've done science. We've always done disasters because they're powerful stories. Survival is a great genre because it's about the human condition. Documentaries are about people. People in extraordinary real-life events.

What makes a story suitable for theatrical release?

That's the billion dollar question ... what makes a project theatrical, compared to what makes a project just a very good TV documentary. And there's no hard and fast rules. There's lots of instinct I think that comes into it.

There's got to be something about that film that makes somebody want to spend seven or eight or nine pounds of their own money, to go out and see a documentary in the cinema. So I think, number one, it's got to be a fantastic story. Without a fantastic story, I mean, we looked at 300 stories last year, for that theatrical potential, and we short-listed maybe four or five, so let's say five out of 300. So, you're looking for a story that feels bigger than you might see on the TV screen. So, it's a story with a beginning and a middle and an end, which involves you, when you sit there in the cinema, and the story just washes over you.

A personal story?

Yes, I think you're right. Although the cinema is not necessarily as intimate as a TV screen, I think there's something about an intimate connection to a story. Even if it's about a major event. I don't think you'd want to see a big issue type, I think you'd want to see it through the point of view of the one individual. The cinema is at its best when you're seeing an intimate foreground, a very intimate, close-up story, in which the individuals are experiencing the big event, but it's from their point of view. *Super Size Me*, was very successful, it was a well-told story but it was about getting the timing right, it was out in cinemas just when it was an issue that was on the mind of the public. That's the other thing about theatrical documentary, you get the sort of *Zeitgeist* moment.

Some of the best novels are about that intimate experience of a major event. For example, a number of times we've looked at projects on the Tsunami, or we've looked at projects on Hurricane Katrina in New Orleans. Now these are very big events, but what we would be looking for is just one individual or one family's individual experience of the Tsunami, or one family's experience of Katrina. We just did a documentary for TV, a feature-length documentary for TV called *Falling Man*, which was a very different take on September 11th, because it was the story of the photograph of one of the jumpers from the World Trade Center. So, a very close-up approach to an enormous day, September 11th, one of the biggest days in our recent history, in terms of the scale of the event. In the end, it might go theatrical. I think (a) it's the power of the story; (b) I think it needs the intimacy of an individual story and preferably if that individual story has a universality about it.

The other area of theatrical documentary where you can break through is what you might call visual wow. A beautifully shot natural history documentary like *March of the Penguins*. Just using the photography, taking you into this different world, these cute animals and creating a story.

Touching the Void

Touching the Void was not about mountain climbing. They happened to be mountain climbers ... 99 per cent of the people who saw *Touching the Void* I would guess have not climbed mountains. But the themes were friendship, they were about your reaction to danger, your will to survive, these are universal things. In *Deep Water*, it's about one ordinary individual getting involved in something way over his head. And, again, that's a universal thing because people get into those sort of situations professionally and in their private lives. So I think those things are all vital. Obviously the quality of the filmmaking is important. It's important on television, and obviously it's important on the big screen as well ... more important because you're trying to involve people in a film, a cinema-going experience, of 90 minutes ... I'd say, you need a quality of filmmaking.

Dramatization, re-enactment and archive

Dramatization is not an essential, it's an option. In *Touching the Void* dramatization was a necessity because there was no other way, or we didn't think there was any other way to capture their story, because there was no archive film. How could you begin to understand what they did without re-enacting it? On *Deep Water*, there is no re-enactment, it wasn't appropriate to that film.

I love archive. It's one of the best things about documentaries. So when you have got a story of which archive material is available … in *Deep Water* we have fantastic archive, in *Falling Man* we have fantastic archive, never re-enact if you've got wonderful archive. I have no problem with re-enactment in documentary. Some of the purest school of documentary believe there's no room for re-enactment. I believe when you're telling a story, you should use whatever means at your disposal to best involve your audience in that story, and if that's re-enactment, then use it. But only if there's a justification for using it. In *Falling Man*, it would have been appalling. It was simply not an option to use dramatic re-enactment. Or to try to re-enact people inside the World Trade Center as it was about to collapse. It would have been appalling. It just wouldn't have been right.

Audiences and the cinema

Why is it that before *Touching the Void* there had never been a British theatrical documentary that had been both creatively acclaimed and commercially successful? There had been theatrical documentaries that had had creative acclaim, Kevin MacDonald's *One Day in September* won the Oscar for Best Documentary and was a very fine film, but had not been a commercial success. So there had never been that double whammy of creative critical acclaim and commercial success. And I think the UK market is really hard for theatrical documentary; (a) because there's not really a tradition of going to see documentaries in the cinema; (b) because most of the best documentary making is on TV. Whereas in some other countries – and you could argue why in the US is theatrical documentary more advanced that the UK – you could argue for two reasons: number one reason, you are less likely to see a good documentary on TV in the US than you are in the UK. Number two, if you're an independent filmmaker wanting to make documentaries, therefore the best outlet for your documentary may be theatrical rather than TV because you just can't get them on-air, whereas if you're a documentary maker [in the UK], chances are here, now with places like More4 and BBC 4, there are outlets for documentary makers. So, therefore I think the UK is a unique market.

So, with *Touching the Void*, when the decision was made to go theatrical, I had been sceptical about the UK theatrical documentary. I was sceptical because there had never been a documentary that had broken through. I'm passionate about story telling and about making quality documentaries, but I'm also passionate about people seeing them. I have a commercial edge. I don't think there's any point in making documentaries if people don't watch them. When I'm making a documentary for TV, I'm looking for a big audience. Hence, I'm sceptical about the UK theatrical documentary market.

Documentary on television

In the UK, any week you will find 10 or 20 really fascinating documentary projects on British TV, I don't believe in the death of documentary on TV. Or, I'm seeing fantastic documentary filmmaking done in a different way, for example, like in *The Apprentice*, it's a brilliantly made piece of modern television. Likewise *Jamie's School Dinners*. Not pure documentary … but as brilliant contemporary factual television. I just think they are fantastically well done.

But clearly something has changed in our times about documentary?

After doing documentaries for 20 years or something, I'm not sure personally that I buy the argument that there's greater interest now. I think we've always been interested in great true stories, I think we were 20 years ago and ten years ago. I think documentaries are made in a more modern way now, so the way I discussed the big intimate close-up story as a way of telling … I think we are telling true stories with more ambition than ever before. And there may be something that increases the appeal because of that. The creative thought that goes into a high end documentary now is as considerable in my view as the creative thought that goes into a feature film … We do a lot of co-production. *Touching the Void* had American money, American TV money, British TV money, Film Council money, Film Four money. A lot of productions we do here are co-productions with America, so we have US-UK money, sometimes we have US, UK, France, Germany, Australia, Italy, those are our main partners. And often they're co-production partners, so they're with you at the very beginning, or they do a pre-sale, so they buy in early into your film, or we sell them in the international market. Most of our programmes end up in Holland and Sweden or Denmark or Norway, but they are sold after, once they're made, to the key European territories.

But what about the issue documentaries?

They're good. I'm not knocking them, there is a real love for issue documentaries. You know, I watched an Arab-Israel documentary series on DVD the other day, which was fascinating. You know, one of those where you've got all the participants in the peace process from Clinton to Blair to the Israelis to all the Arabs, and, you know, I found that fascinating. So, you know, I'm not saying my approach is the only one.

Do you think that issue documentaries are suitable for theatrical release?

I think it would be very hard to do a theatrical documentary just on an issue. You would need a powerful story to illustrate the issue, so the Enron film, that I really liked, illustrated a powerful issue in American life, the behaviour of corporations.

Reality TV. Would you call that documentary?

I wouldn't call it documentary in the pure sense of the word, but it is dealing with real people. And by putting real people into a contrived situation, like putting them into a house, you are getting interesting human behaviour. So, yes, it is about the interaction of people. I would call that a construct. But most reality shows are constructs.

Like a pressure cooker.

Yes, a pressure cooker. But ultimately, it is about real people, and how real people react. So, I wouldn't knock them, I think they're a rather fascinating part of the television landscape, you know, I'm not saying that TV should only be for the documentaries. It's all part of the rich mixture of television. I have no problem ... You know, *I'm a Celebrity, Get Me Out of Here* was brilliantly well-made television. And as much thought goes into that, and as much goes into making *Big Brother*, as goes into making one of our feature documentaries. I don't like claiming the high ground for what we do.

Archive

I happen to believe that out there, there may be fantastic video material of ordinary people and ordinary lives that turn into extraordinary lives and extraordinary stories. That's one of the sort of fantasies of mine that out there, given the video camera revolution, how many millions of hours of video tape exist now of families' lives, that there must be some brilliant documentary material there.

You know, a family where it turns out somebody is a mass murderer, and they have all this video library. You know, it would be fascinating. There was one on the other night, *The Lost World of Mitchell and Kenyon*. You know, where people have captured real history from a generation that we're not used to seeing ... it's all part of the same thing, it's seeing the real. Somewhere, you know, there are fantastic documentaries, just sitting there.

On the shelf in the family room.

Exactly.

14 'The Idea That There's a "Truth" That You Discover Is Like Chasing the End of a Rainbow'

An interview with Ralph Lee

Wilma de Jong

Ralph Lee is Commissioning Editor, History, at Channel Four, UK.

Could you tell me what your role is at Channel 4?

I'm Commissioning Editor for History, so I'm responsible for most of the history that you see on Channel Four, which ranges from quite contemporary history, programmes about the 1980s, to living history experiments, like *That'll Teach Them*, *Escape to the Legion*, to big histories like *Monarchy* with David Starkey. I do all of Tony Robinson's programmes, *Time Team* and *The Real Da Vinci Code* and *The Worst Jobs in History*, and subject-driven history series. We do about 120 hours of history per year.

What kind of documentaries are you specifically looking for?

In a way, we thrive off innovation, and attacking either different subjects or subjects in different ways. There's a lot of history on television, and there's a lot of television for people to choose from, so we're kind of fighting for people's attention. I think the way we survive on Channel Four is by being distinctive. If you look at some of our approaches to history, whether it's using dramatization, using experiments, participatory programmes, using genealogy as kind of a driving mechanism, we're looking at different methods of engaging people with history.

When you get a proposal, what are the things you pay attention to?

I'm looking for people writing an idea for a programme rather than just writing a history essay. One of the problems is that people just send you pieces of history. 'Why now?' is the first question that I approach a proposal with. Why this? I think that's a really basic question that a lot of people writing proposals never ask themselves. They decide that it would be interesting to make a programme about the Poll Tax Riots. Or they decide that Oliver Cromwell is really interesting. But they don't say to themselves, 'Why would I put a programme like this on television? What would be the "X-Factor" if you like?' I look for new information, people speaking for the first time. I look for a sense of authorship in programmes, a particular person's particular view. Sometimes it's useful to use anniversaries, sometimes it's useful to use things that are current in the contemporary culture. For instance, last year we did a programme about *The Da Vinci Code*. Historians are probably horrified to hear this, but I think *The Da Vinci Code* is the biggest thing to happen in history in the last decade. Because most people reading that book are thinking, in one way or another, that they're engaging with history. And it's completely bogus, it's based on completely spurious history. So we made a sceptical programme looking at *The Da Vinci Code* as a book, it's quite a simple thing to do, but that's the right thing to do because it's answering a question that's out in the contemporary world. The programme was enormously successful.

So you're looking for history that can be related to issues in the contemporary cultural or social domain.

Absolutely. History is always most interesting where it's speaking to the present. I think we're enquiring into history in a really interesting way at the moment, trying to find intelligent ways of dealing with the world, and history is a useful place to inform yourself about that. If you look at Neil Ferguson's new series, *The War of the World*, it's a really fascinating warning about the dangers of basing your view of the world on ethnicity. What this series is really trying to ask is, why was the twentieth century so uniquely violent? It wasn't just about men having the ability to kill each other, it was having the desire to. What he points out is that most of the extreme ethnic conflicts took place in places which had the most extreme ethnic mixing. It is a really interesting analysis, because it's provocative in a way. Just because we live in a heterogeneous society, doesn't mean we can assure ourselves that we'll continue to accept one another.

When you think about production methods, what is different between documentary and fiction?

A documentary production, the unique chemistry of making a great documentary, takes place in the edit. It's there that you create this cocktail of the film that you mix the ingredients, and you shape it. Whereas in fiction, it takes place with the writer. Because, once you get into the edit with drama or with [fiction] film you can only change a small amount. There's lots of different ways that you can change what you're doing in the edit, substantially. You can throw it out and start again completely. You know you've got transcripts of all these interviews, you can just throw out some and use different bits, and make the film say a different thing, make the narrative work in a different way. Whereas with fiction you can't do that.

Yes, but also in the moment of recording a documentary there is an element of chance, and unexpectedness, because you aren't dealing with a character who has lines, you are dealing with a person talking about his or her life or experiences.

Yes, you don't know what they're going to say. You go into an interview, the people who are going to tell you the story. You're trying to take them somewhere, mentally, and you're hoping that they're going to have an experience, if you like, in telling you the story, and that that's going to translate to the camera. And you don't know what they're going to say or how they're going to say it, or whether they're going to cooperate, or whether what they say will come across well.

Even when you get into the edit, and after you've done all the interviews, and drawn together all these different sources, it's not possible to count the number of different ways you could tell the story, and each version of that story may be factually accurate and according to different people may be 'true'. But there's nothing definitive about it, so the idea that you create some definitive truth through documentary. The idea that there's a 'truth' that you discover is like chasing the end of a rainbow. I think the important distinction is between *a* true story and *the* true story.

Do you think that new technology has changed production?

Yes, because the new cameras are much more user-friendly, it's much easier to shoot additional materials without huge crews. The size of a documentary crew has become much more lightweight now. When I was a director, I would take a cameraman and a soundman, and the cameraman would be expected to do his own lighting, and carry his own bags, to be honest. The days where you'd each have an assistant and maybe a spark and a gaffer for documentary, are pretty uncommon. It's also not uncommon to find directors who shoot digital video, with basic lighting skills, you know it allows you to shoot stuff you couldn't do with a crew. If you look at how a documentary maker like Daisy Asquith works, she shoots everything on DV herself, and so she did a series called *Fifteen* where she worked with 15-year-olds, and you can't have that degree of intimacy with a couple of 45-year-old men and clunky equipment. It just doesn't work.

Do you think that the whole market of documentary has changed, that there is an audience out there that is more interested in documentary?

I don't think people are interested in documentary. Very few people are actually interested in the form of documentary. And I think the form of documentary is incredibly difficult to define. There are some purists who think that documentary is a particular thing. So, is *Jamie's School Dinners* documentary, is *Wife Swap* documentary, is *That'll Teach Them* a documentary, is *The Great Wall of China* or *The First Emperor* a documentary?

Would you call them documentaries?

I call them programmes. I think documentary sometimes comes with too many particular associations. I don't think people decide when they're watching television,

I think in their minds they know whether they're watching a factual or a non-factual programme, but I don't think they say, 'I must watch a documentary'. I don't think people particularly care about these definitions.

It's a hybrid form.

That's where all the innovation takes place, is at the edges, so at the moment there's a fashion for heavily interventionalist programmes, like *Wife Swap*, very heavily constructed, formatted documentaries. I think they're still documentaries, they're still dealing with a situation out in the real world, and they're still trying to reflect a situation in the real world. They're just doing it in a much more tightly controlled, restricted way.

Transformation is what drives a lot of those documentaries. From *Super Nanny* to *Faking It* to *That'll Teach 'Em*, to *Wife Swap*, they're about feeling that you've watched someone's life transformed. It's sort of powerful and empowering for the viewers that they feel that kind of privilege of seeing someone's life transform. Part of that is about seeing people having experiences imposed on them and how they react to it. And so you can learn everything you need to know about the Edwardian class system, by putting contemporary people in that situation. So there you have a programme which brilliantly reflects on both the past and the present.

But do you have good audiences for that kind of programme?

Very good, yes. Audiences like innovation. They want to see something new. Not every innovation works, but I think Channel Four is a broadcaster that is constantly trying to do something new. Sometimes really well, sometimes not.

There are two arguments there. Because there's a big audience out there that wants something familiar. They want *Antiques Road Show* and they want *CSI*. And what a lot of programmers discover is that, with a series like *CSI*, you play it once it does alright. You play it again, the same series, it does alright again. You play it a third time and it does better. Actually the regularity of knowing that *CSI* is on a Sunday night at 9 o'clock works, even if you have seen them before. So I think there's a big audience out there that want familiarity. But I think they're the audience that ITV and BBC 1 can do really well out of. Channel Four is always trying to connect with the smarter, brighter people who are looking forwards and changing and evolving and who have a slightly more adventurous outlook, and want more out of their TV, who want to see the world in different ways, they want to be provoked. And so it's that audience that we try and serve. So innovation is kind of written into our DNA.

Channel Four isn't driven by the bottom line. We're driven by a spirit of enquiry and we want to reflect the world in interesting ways and do interesting things and that sort of makes us commercially viable. We're not obsessed by – we're obviously always aware of ratings and commercial value in the things that we do – but that's not what leads. The interesting thing about bringing in Channel Four into the equation is that we back things for a different reason. We have a kind of ability to inject different things into the culture that aren't just driven by the bottom line.

The budgets for documentary have increased enormously.

We don't put all the money in, we co-produce. For instance, if you look at our film *The First Emperor* that probably cost about £800,000 or £900,000. The film about the *Battle of the Somme* was about £1.1 million. The one we did about the Blitz was £750,000. It's not uncommon at the moment for us to do feature-length or 90-minute documentaries for television that cost between £500,000 and £1.2 million. And we do that by co-producing, with National Geographic, with Discovery, with NDR, with ZDF, with France 2, and with various different European and American Broadcasters. There's more and more drive towards what people call 'superdocs' and it's a desire, because all of the broadcasters are clamouring for this territory. All the directors are in competition with one another, so where you can do *Super Volcano*, and you can get German, British and American broadcasters each to put kind of maximum money in, you can do something really big.

And you can sell it all over the world.

And then you can sell it all around the world.

So the audience has changed. They still want to be entertained, but not only that. They want more.

Why has it changed? People have always been curious. And television just serves them in a different way. None of these subjects are new. You can find documentaries that were on 30 years ago that were working in the idiom of their time. They might have been observational documentaries, they might have been *Tomorrow's World* programmes, you know, television has always done these subjects, there's no new subject under the sun.

... The traditional terrestrial broadcaster is haemorrhaging viewers. The market owned by those five terrestrials is getting smaller and smaller every year, but every year we see the share of multi-channels go up, it's now about 30 per cent. So we're looking at sharing 70 per cent instead of sharing 100 per cent. What we've got to make sure of, by launching new channels – E-4 and More Four, have been hugely successful – and by making sure that we're on all the other platforms ... is that when people fall off that, they fall into our laps rather than into someone else's.

15 Rice N Peas

Alternative, independent and provocative

Ishmahil Blagrove, Jr

I began my venture into serious documentary making, after spending three years unsuccessfully attempting to convince mainstream broadcasters to commission a documentary about the disproportionate level of violence within the black community of Britain. Determined to make this documentary, I undertook many freelance media jobs to raise the capital necessary, one of which was working as a reporter on *Gang Wars* (2003, Channel 4, UK). This documentary was supposedly geared towards exploring gang violence in Britain. While working on this documentary, I was privy to the most denigrating and prejudicial comments from other members of the production team. After eight weeks of a ten-week filming period, I had yet to interview a single white person or white gang in relation to the story. When I raised an objection and questioned the ethics behind such thinking, I was informed that white gangs did not really exist and that those that did exist were influenced by the black gangs. I was further informed that the issue of so-called 'black on black' violence was really a result of Caribbean youths deliberately targeting African youths because of their origin. These and many other such prejudiced opinions became frustrating obstacles towards telling a balanced and fair story as it appeared that the producers had already made their minds up as to what the story should be. In such cases, viewers are subjected to distorted forms of 'information'.

What was even more disturbing for me was that it was middle-class white liberal producers who were being commissioned by the mainstream to tell these stories. After being contracted as the reporter for *Gang Wars*, the identities of the unsuccessful candidates were revealed; they were all black. As a black male myself, I therefore question why was it relevant that the reporter of the story had to be black? Although being assured that this story was an authored report, I was continually harangued and goaded towards the direction they wanted me to take. This eventually led to me having to remind the producers that I was a reporter and not a model.

Greg Dyke, the Director General of the BBC, once famously commented that the 'BBC is overwhelmingly white and middle class.' It is my opinion that not much has changed and that this is clearly reflected in many of the notable minority programmes that have recently been commissioned which have raised concerns among the black community: *The Crouches* (BBC, 2003), *The Trouble with Black Men*

(2004), and more recently, *Shoot the Messenger* (BBC2, 2006), a drama that was originally commissioned under the title 'Fuck Black People'. Is there any wonder then why minority audiences still feel misrepresented within the mainstream media?

It was these experiences that led me to the idea for *Bang Bang! In Da Manor*, a film that sought to explore the realities of black-on-black violence. When I originally pitched the idea to a commissioning editor at C4, I was flatly told that the subject matter would not be appealing to 'Middle England'. This therefore raises some very serious questions: How influential is the desire to appeal to the broadest audience? And how does this shape terrestrial programming? Furthermore, with such attention given to viewing figures, what prospects are there for minority interest stories to get commissioned?

After spending three years unsuccessfully attempting to convince the mainstream broadcasters to commission the documentary, I was left with no other option but to finance and market the film myself. Free from the conformities of a commissioning brief, the production team found itself with much more creative freedom, enabling us to produce a final result that was more gritty than the sterile products saturating the mainstream. *Bang Bang! In Da Manor* was primarily aimed at the black British community with the intention of identifying some of the patterns of behaviour and sparking debate. However, because black British audiences do not constitute a significant number of viewers, the story was not commissioned, irrespective of the disproportionate level of violence and the fact that gun crime had become a serious problem within the black community.

Bang Bang! was eventually licensed by BBC4 and aired at 11:00 pm, to the complaints of many within the black community who said that it should have been aired on one of the terrestrial channels. The BBC only acquired the programme after lobbying from people who had seen the documentary; the film had been screened at over 100 cinemas and theatres across Britain and developed a market presence without any mainstream support. The programme was described by Detective Chief Superintendent John Coles, the head of Operation Trident, the taskforce responsible for dealing with black-on-black crime as, 'The most brilliant and interesting documentary' he had ever seen made about gun crime. A screening was hosted at the offices of the Mayor of London and a report was sent for Parliamentary recommendations. This made it very difficult for the mainstream to ignore and they were already under criticism by many within the black community for their recent airing of *The Trouble with Black Men*, a documentary presented by David Mathews which squarely placed the blame for the spiral of violence and underachievement at the feet of the black community.

Contrasting the formulae of the two similar documentaries, *Gang Wars* and *Bang Bang! In Da Manor*, the mainstream formula was to use the testimonies of the gang members as a backdrop and then have the expert testimonies of criminologists and senior police officers. What lent *Bang Bang!* credibility was that we refused to use text book academics as experts. The experts in *Bang Bang!* were a former LA gang member turned gang mediator and Dr Lez Henry, a Rastafarian and well-known dance hall DJ who embraced academia late in life. These experts had not only the academic credentials to accurately assess their findings, but also the life experience and street credibility to make young people sit up and pay attention. So even the selection of experts within *Bang Bang!* had an effect on the aesthetics of the programme.

As a result of my experiences with broadcasters, I have found it necessary to produce documentaries totally independent of mainstream funding. Reporting the stories we want from the angles we want has enabled us to create real, hard-hitting documentaries free from the biases of mainstream media moguls and corporate sponsors. After the success of *Bang Bang!*, Rice N Peas found even greater success with *Hasta Siempre* (2005), a documentary that explored the prospect of the Cuban revolution surviving post the demise of Fidel Castro. When screened in London at Canning House by the Institute of Latin American Studies, Rene Monzote, the press attaché for the Cuban Embassy in the UK, described the film as the most balanced documentary he had ever seen made about Cuba. The documentary is now used by the British Foreign Office in their training of overseas diplomats to Latin America.

While filming this documentary, it was important to continually remind some of the more left-leaning members of the production team of the need for objectivity and impartiality. 'Lose the romance' was the constant refrain used to remind the team to set aside our own biases. We were constantly thrust between finding the balance between pro- and anti-Castro opinion and between the various voices from socially diverse backgrounds and putting them on equally credible platforms. Therefore, commentators included a psychologist and a Marxist intellectual, as well as a prostitute, a dissident, a young man desperate to flee the island, and several hip hop artists who commented upon the racial discrimination in Cuba. At various stages of the filmmaking, it was determined that the production was too top heavy in either the pro-camp or the anti-camp, so we continually sought to ensure that each argument was balanced with a contrary opinion. Although the final result has been critically acclaimed as balanced, we still feel the story is slightly lop-sided, in that the pro-Castro camp had more articulate voices. We had tried to interview a prominent Cuban dissident, which would have secured the balance. However, having entered the country without the correct visa and with the dissident under constant surveillance, we decided not to pursue the interview, as it may have resulted in our arrest and jeopardized the production.

One of the most fundamental components of ensuring a quality product is establishing a relationship of trust and respect between the filmmaker and the subject. It is extremely difficult to tell an accurate story without the support and participation of one's main subjects. Much time is therefore spent by Rice N Peas in consultation with the subjects we wish to film. It is important to convince subjects of one's motives for telling a story and to be honest as to how their contribution shall be used. We therefore explained to the drug dealers and arms dealers in *Bang Bang!* prior to filming that we felt it was important that the public had some insight into their motivations and thoughts on the moral implications of their actions, and that we intended to air their opinions without prejudice or bias or attempting to demonize them for their actions. We wanted access to their lifestyle to gain insight and not to demonize them. As the subject was violence within the black community and most of the production team members were black and originated from the same socio-economic group as the subjects, the distance between subject and documenter was limited.

This was not the case when I was a reporter on *Gang Wars*. Many of the prospective hardcore contributors flatly refused to participate precisely because the programme was being produced for a mainstream broadcaster. It was their opinion that mainstream broadcasters were racist and prejudiced towards the black community and so they had no faith that such a story would be portrayed accurately or fairly. While making *Bang Bang! In Da Manor*, however, we interviewed the victims of violence and their families, drug abusers, the perpetrators of violence, and drug dealers. Convincing underground arms dealers, to display their wares was not an easy task, but without the daunting shackles of a corporate sponsor, we were able to explore areas where mainstream journalists have yet to go. Before starting *Bang Bang!*, we had established a checklist of interviewees whom we determined we had to have in order to make the film a more complete story than any other story previously told on the subject. The list included the victims of violence and their families, but also, for the first time, underground arms dealers, the inhabitants of an active crack house, and drug dealers. This was a tall order, but it was important to have each case represented. The most important issue surrounding the filming was to convince the arms dealer and drug dealers that their anonymity would be protected. By exposing their trades to us, they risked the possibility of many years in prison if identified. Many may consider retaining the anonymity of such unscrupulous individuals as unethical; however, as a documentary filmmaker, it is important to subjugate any personal opinions and ethics in certain situations and solely commit oneself to documenting the situation. I felt a sense of loyalty to the subjects, recognizing that they were assisting me in fulfilling my project by participating.

Similarly, when we made *Hasta Siempre*, some questioned why we had decided to film Yunnai, a naked prostitute getting dressed while explaining her life in Cuba. We felt this was an honest portrayal of who she was and what she did. Generally, when filming a subject, we attempt to portray what he or she does in order to give the viewer an idea of his or her lifestyle or responsibilities. It was therefore natural for us to film the subject when she had finished business with a client. The real issue for some viewers was not the representation of her trade, but the viewers' own social discomfort with nudity. In confronting these issues in the edit, we determined firstly whether the issue was a moral one or a contravention of social norms. Given the rise in prostitution in Cuba and that being one of the greatest points of controversy surrounding social implications of the revolution, we felt that a prostitute was the best expert to explain her trade and her thoughts on the revolution. The fact that her trade was illegal and that she could be quite severely punished if identified meant that she took a great risk: a risk which gave further credibility to her assessment of the achievements of the revolution. Were it not for the trust established between the production team and the subject, the magnitude of these implications would never have been captured on film. A central goal of our filmmaking at Rice N Peas is to remain true to our subjects. In previous organizations where I worked, I witnessed a lack of understanding and a lack of gratitude towards the subjects we filmed. An example encountered time and time again was the broken promise of sending footage of participants back to them once the final piece was edited. At Rice N Peas, honouring this agreement is standard practice. We recognize the fundamental role which the characters in our documentaries play, offering an insight into their world. Therefore, before releasing our documentaries to the general public, a preview copy of our documentary is always sent to our subjects for their perusal.

Another major obstacle for independents is the issue of distribution. In order to overcome this hurdle, Rice N Peas utilizes the internet as a means of distributing our films. The internet has created new opportunities; it has allowed us to bypass the established distributors and become independent distributors. In order to bring returning traffic to our site, we have developed an online magazine with articles and features with an editorial theme that is consistent with the Rice N Peas' mission statement. Our website offers a means to attract new customers, engage our loyal readers, increase our sales, and allows the constant exposure of our products. Rice N Peas is now an independent distributor and also issues international licences for our documentaries. With the advent of the internet, the US and Canada are now Rice N Peas' largest market; online sales coupled with licensing agreements now gives us the financial freedom to explore more diverse subjects. Due to the educational value of our programmes, we have begun issuing Public Screening Licences to Institutes of Higher Education, the National Health Service and other organizations that wish to screen our films.

A serious challenge to the mainstream media is currently underway, because with access to digital technology and the internet, the lines between alternative and mainstream are becoming blurred. New digital technology has made the production and distribution of documentary more accessible and affordable for the average person. This accessibility has loosened the shackles of many established documentarians and given birth to a new genre of freestyle filmmaking. No longer dependent upon commissioning budgets, studio equipment, or even a crew, a budding documentary filmmaker may now produce a high-end, broadcast-quality product with little more than a camera, a computer, and a good idea. *Bang Bang! In Da Manor*, for example, was made with a budget of £500, but grossed in the region of £70,000. *Bang Bang!* was eventually acquisitioned by the BBC for £27,000. After the film had been screened at over 100 cinemas and centres around the country, mostly to sold-out audiences, the reputation of Rice N Peas grew as producers of evocative, thought-provoking programmes. Subsequently, many cinemas and theatres opened their doors to future Rice N Peas productions.

The world wide web is now awash with films of both high and low end production value that otherwise could not have been distributed. The internet is as logistically important to these independent filmmakers as are the theatrical cinemas for the film distributor, because the internet allows the filmmaker to independently expose his product to a broad audience. After the success of *Bang Bang!* in cinemas, theatres and on BBC4, when we started our website and began selling the DVDs, it eventually came to our attention that the film was being pirated. Rather than oppose this 'illegal activity,' we welcomed the pirating and began distribution directly to the pirates at production cost value. This became a part of our marketing strategy, as the pirates were vital in distributing to areas around the country we found difficult to reach, and helped to create awareness about our product. These independent means of distribution allow filmmakers to connect directly to the market without a third party. Now with YouTube, MySpace, Google Video, and a whole host of other outlets, the internet allows filmmakers to host trailers of their films and links to their sites for direct purchases. Rice N Peas utilizes all of these outlets as well as targeted forums to expose its products. This type of easy access has brought, and will continue to bring, great success for the independent journalist for many years to come: with the advent and rise of digital technology, the revolution can now be televised.

16 'The Importance of Memory'
An interview with Ai Xiaoming

Sue Thornham

Ai Xiaoming (b. 1953) is a feminist, public intellectual, activist and academic. She is Professor and Director of the Comparative Literature and World Literatures Section in the Department of Chinese Language and Literature, Zhongshan University, Guangzhou, and programme leader of the university's Sex/Gender Education Forum. Since the 1990s she has been active in developing women's studies curricula and promoting women's and gay rights. More recently, her role as activist and public intellectual has led her to documentary filmmaking. In 2003, she was translator and director of the first Chinese production of *The Vagina Monologues*, staged by her students as one of the activities of the Stop Domestic Violence network in China. This led to collaboration with independent documentary filmmaker, Hu Jie,[1] in the making of *The Vagina Monologues: Stories Behind the Scenes* (2004), and her establishment of an independent digital video studio in 2004 which aims at empowering marginalized groups by providing media training workshops.

Since 2004, her films, produced in collaboration with Hu Jie, have been screened at festivals and universities in New York, Hong Kong, London, Malmö, and Beijing. They have included:

- *Garden in Heaven* (2005), which tracks the case of Huang Jing, a primary school teacher who was found raped and murdered in her home. The documentary follows the attempts of her mother to bring the case to court following a verdict of cardiac arrest by the local coroner.
- *Taishi Village* (2005). This film documents an event which became a test case both for China's claims to democracy and of its media reporting. Taishi village lies on the edge of the wealthy city of Guangzhou. Discovering that village land had been sold to developers by the elected local committee head, villagers petitioned for his recall and the holding of fresh elections. The film follows their efforts to secure justice, the imprisonment and beating of those who had led the petition, the arrest of the Beijing lawyers who sought to assist them, and the assaults on Ai herself.
- *The Epic of Central Plains* (2006). This film follows impoverished families in rural Henan province whose exploitation by the commercial 'blood economy' has resulted in wholesale AIDS infection. It traces both the efforts of villagers to secure recognition, medical care and compensation, and the

work of activists such as retired gynaecologist Dr Gao Yaojie, whose work in the prevention and treatment of AIDS among these rural communities has resulted in her house arrest.

- *Care and Love* (2007) again concerns AIDS infection in China. It follows the attempts to establish a 'Care House' in Hebei for young people infected with the HIV virus, again through community and civil rights action. It also tracks the developing relationship between members of the Care House community, and their fight for recognition and financial support.[2]

Like those of other Chinese independent documentary makers, then, Ai's films are part of a politicized 'art of record'.[3] In the face of an official media news and history that seeks to erase cultural memory, her use of local memories and voices offers both a 'counterhistory'[4] and an intervention into contemporary public discourse. Like other independent filmmakers, too, she faces problems of distribution. Her intended audience is that of mainland China, but censorship and state control mean that she must rely on vulnerable internet publication or distribution among activist and academic groups. Overseas exhibition may produce a sympathetic audience, for whom her images function as 'truths', but for an activist interested in making radical interventions into public discourse in China, such audiences are both unsatisfactory and potentially dangerous.[5]

Ai is also unusual among Chinese independent documentary makers in being a feminist academic and literary scholar before becoming a documentary maker. She is acutely aware of the politics of filmmaking, of the problematic nature of claims to 'make visible' or 'give voice to' marginalized 'others', and of the gendering of media coverage of 'public issues'. As Myra Macdonald writes, 'The personal and the political, access and exposition, do not inevitably exist on separate planes, or possess inherently different claims to legitimation' (1998: 120). Ai's attempt to share authorship with her usually female subjects gives weight to their own voiced interpretations, at the same time as her refusal to focus on a single 'personal interest' story insists that these are *public* issues.

In the following interview, conducted in March 2007, Ai talks about her reasons for becoming a documentary maker, her aims, and the difficulties she faces.

How did you get interested in making documentaries?

In 2003, we started to prepare the performance of *The Vagina Monologues*. Because the students would graduate in 2004, there would be no more performances, so I wanted to have a videotape … so that we could use it as support material for our teaching.

In the same year I saw Hu Jie's documentary, *In Search of Lin Zhao's Soul*. Lin Zhao was a woman, a college student. In 1957, like many intellectuals she responded to the call from Chairman Mao to comment on the policies of the Communist Party. Of course, she criticized many of the policies and the mistakes made by the Party. Several months later the whole situation changed, and she and many of that generation were classified as rightists, so she lost the chance to study, was sent away, and finally she was sent to prison. In prison, she wrote diaries with her blood, writing about many political ideas. She was sentenced to death in 1967, at the beginning of the Cultural Revolution … Hu Jie got copies of the letters and diaries from her friends and other survivors, interviewed them and made a documentary about it. I thought it was a ground-breaking film because no-one dared – dares – enter that taboo area, … and I invited him to show the documentary and give a lecture … At the same time, on International Woman's Day 2004, a woman graduate was murdered here on campus. There was an internet debate and many students thought it was the woman's fault. Perhaps she did something wrong and so caused her boyfriend's fury, so they blamed the woman. So we launched a campaign against violence against women and Hu Jie videotaped the event. And when I saw the programme he edited, I realized it was powerful to use video.

… Then I thought I could invite Hu Jie to videotape *The Vagina Monologues* … So we put it on stage again, just for the camera, and we started to make *The Vagina Monologues: Stories Behind the Scenes*, interviewing faculty and students … At that time I didn't know how to use a camera … From that programme, I learned two things. One was that a single camera was not enough to make the whole programme; we should have at least one more … And the other was that I was not satisfied with relying on Hu Jie's camera and his ideas because he was not familiar with feminist thought. We had lots of debates – whether to edit out this or edit in that. He thought something was not good from an artistic perspective; I thought it was very good, powerful. They were points students needed. So that was how I started to do camera and editing myself.

So then you learned to use a camera …

A little bit, a little bit, not a professional camera. Then we decided to make *Garden in Heaven* … At that stage, when the case was being investigated, the court simply refused to accept the evidence provided by the mother. They didn't accept that they'd done anything wrong. They insisted on their side, because all the investigation had been done by the police.

That was the young primary school teacher who was, you think, murdered by her boyfriend whose father was an important figure in local government. The police said she died of a heart attack but there was evidence of assault.

She had no heart disease. The second autopsy done by the independent experts from our university revealed that.

So why did you decide to make a film?

Because the police refused to accept the evidence, the conclusions from the independent experts. So I thought: what could we do, how could we continue our activism? I thought at least we should let more people know what happened. We should start to collect evidence and show the evidence to more people as a form of advocacy … And when the court's first session began, I went with Hu Jie … and I took a camera … And when we came back and I saw the tapes I'd done myself, suddenly I had the feeling that it was good, it was very good. It was good because it expressed what I felt, and it was good because I didn't have to say, 'You do this.' I could film whenever I wanted. And it was good because I could use the camera to say what *I* wanted to say. Sometimes it's hard for others to understand why you have a feeling about a particular scene ... I felt I was like a student: when you didn't know how to write you would ask someone to write a letter for you, but if you learnt some words you would think you could write the letter yourself ...

So from there you decided to make Taishi Village?

Taishi Village was not planned. 2005 was the tenth anniversary of the Beijing Women's Conference[6] so we applied to make a film about what women's NGOs had achieved in ten years ... But that plan fell through ... Then in September of that year I heard about the Taishi women's hunger strike and sit-in. It was close to the university where I teach, so I went to the village in the first week of September ...

And so you followed that through until the point where you were actually attacked ...

Yes, that's how it was made ... At first I went with some graduates ... But then I thought it wasn't safe for students to go with me, so I didn't invite any in the later stages because I couldn't afford for any of them to be hurt in the conflict. The police asked them to show their papers and then they informed the university. I thought it wasn't good for them, and they were too young.

And did you come under personal pressure as a result of that?

... Lots ... lots ...

And you were threatened.

I was threatened because of the issues. The last time we left Taishi village their counsel-at-law had already been arrested, and some village leaders were in prison. We were attacked but no-one followed up the issue even after we reported it to the police, and there were some documents that said I was behind the events. They pointed to three names: one was the counsel-at-law who was in prison, one was the young man who was beaten, and one was me. I thought it was totally ridiculous. I was actually just an observer. I felt so frustrated, I felt so angry, because how could a government document draw such a conclusion without any investigation, when actually it's a total lie? I shot all the scenes in front of the police camera, they videotaped what I was doing. They used their videotape as 'proof' that they had *not* done things, that they hadn't hurt any people, but what a ridiculous argument. From our video we showed the audience the old granny and the young boy who were hurt and hospitalized.

So did you feel frightened for your own safety, or for your career?

Yes, a little bit. Not for my career. I was warned by my friends to hide my tapes or maybe I would be taken in ... I think at that time I had friends, colleagues, who all thought I was a suspect in the event. I called a friend about something to do with teaching and the colleague said 'Oh, you've come back! Everyone said you were arrested!' I said, 'Arrested for what?' This means that in other universities in Guangzhou they had already heard that I would be taken in ...

I felt that I was isolated. No journalists would come, no colleagues would call me. They had heard rumours. They even believed the rumours. I called a senior professor ... and ... asked whether one of our powerful alumni would help me, because I had done nothing wrong. I didn't have a positive response. I felt disappointed. I thought: this didn't work, this won't work. Then a senior law professor in Beijing called me. She offered to help send the film to Central Government, to let them know what happened at the village level ...

When you were making it, were you trying to provide evidence to Central Government? Or were you making it to show to a wider audience?

Both ...

Did you get it to Central Government?

I think we sent it at the end of November. We thought it was OK, the film. We'd seen two hours – there were four episodes – and I sent it by express to my friend. She also suggested I send it to a law institute in the Chinese Academy of Social Sciences. I sent it there, and Hu Jie took it to Beijing, and friends in different circles and activists interested in the issue of free elections were all involved in distributing the documentary. Friends who have access to the State Council or the different departments of Central Government got back to us saying they had sent the film to high level leaders.

Has it had any effect?

Taishi still suffered injustice, but at the end of 2005 both the villagers and their counsel-at-law were released. We don't know whether the documentary helped. However, in Beijing many lawyers and NGO people, and the experts who worked on free election issues made copies and distributed them ...

From there you decided to make the documentary about AIDS in Henan Province?

Yes. In December, I got a call from a journalist in Beijing, who asked me to go to Hebei, because there was an outbreak of AIDS caused by blood transfusions. He had published a report, and he sent the report to us. Hu Jie and I had decided that we should make a documentary on human rights issues every year, and we were planning the film for the following year, and I thought that we hadn't done a documentary on health rights – on women's health issues. I thought it was a good opportunity, so we went to Hebei, about 300 kilometres from Beijing, to do some exploratory interviews. After eight days interviewing we decided to make the documentary ... We did that first trip together but we didn't have funding, so I went there and finished the shooting in about nine months ...

But when I was there I started to think about how the blood had become contaminated, and decided I should trace its origins. So I went to Henan to interview Professor Gao Yaojie, and she showed me the photos she had taken in the villages. I also interviewed the leaders in NGO circles dealing with HIV issues and met the committee for victims of AIDS caused by blood transfusion ... I was accepted as an independent observer on the committee and got information about what was going on ... They were from different provinces, but Henan was the province where AIDS was a serious problem, so I went to Henan. I went on the days when they had an event, so we caught the event, the protests ...

What was your aim for this documentary? Was it again to raise awareness with Government, or was it to raise awareness outside?

Both. We have sent out more than 200 copies and the NGO in Beijing made 500 copies and distributed them among AIDS NGOs and also among some foundations who fund AIDS activism in China. And we showed it to journalists, and those journalists showed it to their colleagues ...

You're now in a situation where people are trying to buy your footage. What issues does that raise for you?

That's true. I've had calls from friends who said a foreign company would like to buy footage, even pay £500 for a minute ... But it's very hard for me to say yes or no. We are always short of money, but I am afraid that I would be charged with selling information for profit, especially if it's to a foreign agency, and that would be a dangerous charge against me. It's a shame that we can't distribute all our films. I believe that if we could, we wouldn't need to apply for funding. But we can't, and no mainland station would currently accept our programmes ... I have been questioned about where I got the money to make these documentaries on so-called sensitive issues. There are rumours that I received money from foreign agencies, and that I make the documentaries for profit. It's designed to threaten people and marginalize my work.

You're making a documentary now about the Cultural Revolution and the issues that are still relevant today. Do you feel you have now become a documentary maker? Is that the most important thing for you to do now?

Yes. I don't think that in mainland China there is anyone else like me who has taken up a camera – someone with a strong academic background, and who has very clear ideas about feminism, women's interests, public interests, human rights, and memory. Documentaries are about memory – the importance of memory for individuals and for social change.

Who do you feel is the most important audience for these documentaries now?

All people ... but I think mainly for mainland China people. Audiences outside the totalitarian state have rich resources for discovering what happened in the past. They enjoy free speech, and they can say whatever they would like to say. But in China, especially for those who suffered, who lost their family members and who are still suffering from systematic social injustice, people need a way to understand others' pain. They have a right to information and to know what strategies others took to defend their rights. I think the ideal audience, who will understand their importance, are those activists like us: lawyers, freelance writers, journalists with ideas for change, and the people in NGOs. And I'd wish for officials in the Government to benefit from the critical thinking in our documentaries.

So you're very much part of an activist network?

Yes. And also the Taishi villagers said the documentary plays a part, is a part of the villagers' power. When the villagers negotiate with the government, the government knows they have a video programme, and if they distributed the video programme they would expose the mistakes, the responsibilities they should have taken ... In Hebei, ... when we did the documentary about the blood transfusions that caused AIDS they asked the villagers to stop us making the documentary and they refused. So then they asked them to stop us showing the documentary. And then they came here three times and said, 'Please don't show this documentary. We have worked very hard to deal with the issue. If you show the documentary and damage the image of the government, there will be no investment to support our local economy.' ...

So you're giving the villagers power. Can I ask how far when you're making the documentary you feel it's your voice and how far are you trying to give a voice to the villagers? Is there any conflict?

I think I benefit from my background in deciding which issue we should take, my training gives me the skills to do the research before we do the documentary, and it also gives me the experience to connect with different people at different levels of society: the academic level, the NGO level, among activist circles. And also to bring something to the local level – information needed for the issue, contacts with people who may help to resolve the problem ... I think documentary making very much relies on that: on people who are right at the centre of the issue and who are determined to use the camera to record it. So I can see the difference between the documentaries I have directed and the documentaries made by other independent documentary makers. Usually they will take one family, one story, but I do a campaign, the whole process of activism. I work with local people, local experts, and trace the different power struggles, confront pressure from above. Some documentary makers won't touch those issues. Sometimes they say that I'm privileged to take on those issues because I'm a scholar and can go places they couldn't go.

You see yours as having a politicized structure whereas they tend to follow an individualized, personalized structure?

You won't see any documentaries in mainland China like those made by us. I think if we continue to do this, in ten years that would constitute a historical heritage. We have documented, we are documenting the most important issues that China has been experiencing – so many conflicts in the change to a civil society. That's my ambition. I don't think anyone else has set this goal.

Is it a record, or advocacy, or both?

Both. But I think maybe it's more for the future because now distribution is very limited and many people are not allowed to watch these videos. One of my friends was taken in just because she made copies of *Taishi Village*. She was taken in for several hours and the police questioned her about why and from where she had the copies. And I always have the feeling that sometime when I come back to my apartment I will see that my computer has been removed or someone has searched my home, or all the videotapes are gone.

Can I return to the question of giving people a voice? Have you got a particular way that you want these people to come across? I was talking to you earlier about how the ordinary people don't just come across as victims ...

I think it's not that we have the privilege to give these people a voice. The voice is already, it's always there. It depends on how the documentary maker understands: whether you need to ask a question, which is always *your* question, or whether you just listen to their questions and their points. From my experiences I think that ordinary people are not like some stereotypes which say that they are illiterate, they have no voice, they should be given a voice. The voices are always already there. When I went to the villages, so many people would come to you, to tell you the story. And also I identified my camera as partly *their* camera. I would say to them, 'I'm a volunteer. I'm making a documentary. Just feel like you have a camera, you have a video studio. Tell me what kind of programme you would like me to make.' They would guide me to different places, to meet the vital people, to show me what happened. They know what are the most important things and the most important persons for the documentary.

So you see it as a collaborative effort?

Yes. When I went to Taishi village, I could see that they needed a camera, a professional camera, to record what was going on because they thought it was very important to document it, what happened there, what was going on, how they felt about it, because there were so many cameras from the authorities watching them. The police would even seize people, just telling them, 'You were on our videotape. That means you were at the scene.' So they feel that they just have to have a camera on their side to videotape from their perspective and to make their voice heard. You can see from our video that a woman shouted, 'Please come to our village. Please interview us. Please take the interviews, the clips, to the Central Government.' They believe that the camera is powerful, they just need such power. They also know that the authorities fear the camera; they fear its power to monitor, and they fear the distribution of information.

So the camera becomes a weapon.

A kind of weapon, yes.

What about the structure? Watching the documentaries you seem to structure them in a narrative way ... But in one you also use music from local opera as a counterpoint. What principles do you try to follow in structuring the documentary?

I still don't have any principles. In *Taishi Village* we edited it according to the timing: what was the most important event at this stage – and there were different stages and different events. In *Central Plains*, there is a timeline from the beginning of the year to the end. In *Care and Love* there is the process of revealing the problem and at the end there is some resolution.

I do pay attention to the music as a narrative part of the event, and I selected music from the local music, the traditional music. That started from the making of *Garden in Heaven*. Maybe I should say it started from the scene I shot in which ordinary people sing on the streets for money. They sang the traditional songs, traditional opera. I feel that traditional opera, traditional sounds, traditional drama are part of people's everyday lives ... Many of them have existed in local life for many years. I found that when we use that kind of music, the music already contains the sufferings or joys of ordinary people. The pain you suffer is not just from contemporary society; it already existed in ancient life many years ago. When you use that kind of expressive music, it is in harmony with the environment, with the content, with the local people.

Do you also think it's making a link between the current regime and past regimes?

In examples like the Henan operas we used, there are different operas. One opera concerns a woman warrior, so she's the counterpart of the activist, so that's the hymn for the activist. Many operas contain moral lessons about what kind of official is popular with ordinary people, so when people sing those kinds of operas it's like a criticism of today's officials, but it works as a metaphor – it's not that direct.

In Central Plains *you also cut back and forth between life in the village and what's happening with Professor Gao Yaojie …*

That's what I wanted to do, but I haven't had enough experience to achieve it, to make the programme as complicated as I'd like – not just a linear narrative, not just about what's going on, but to know more about their inner life, and to make the linkage between current reality and what happened in history.

You trace parallels between her experience in the Cultural Revolution and what's happening now …

When I worked with Hu Jie, he always said I tried to put too much information into one documentary. He said it's beyond the limits of documentary, it's not possible. So I edited that part after he left, and the next day I said, 'See, it's OK to include this.'

So do you think you are trying to stretch the documentary format to make it do things it hasn't done before?

Yes, but also we're producing a body of feminist documentaries. All the documentaries relate to women's issues: violence against women, women's health. And also women are the activists in our documentaries – not just the victims …

So where do you go from here? How do you see the future? You've now made four or five documentaries. Would you see yourself doing more?

Yes. But I feel overwhelmed by all this work. Sometimes I feel it's too overwhelming to keep going, because we need to finalize the programmes we have already made – to finalize, to refine, to make it shorter, to revise the subtitles. I have also started to shoot interviews for my project on memories of the Cultural Revolution, and I have my teaching. Hu Jie works here less than four months a year, back and forth, students have their own research, and colleagues have their own teaching load, so that many times I feel I am trying single-handedly to achieve such a tremendous goal. It's so important, but it's too much.

When I came to your apartment three years ago you had a dining room, but now … your home has become a studio. In asking where you go from here … I wonder whether there is a tension with your academic work … do you ever feel you want to write about documentary?

I think I would write if I couldn't go into the field, if my health wasn't good enough. As long as my health is good enough to take a camera, I should go into the field, to shoot, because there are so many things worth documenting. And when I reach people, I feel that I could not turn away from their pain and let it pass in silence ... A woman of 80 is the main character in my new project ... She said, 'I am 80. I'm going to die and there will be no-one who knows what happened, to preserve it.'

You were saying earlier that you wish you'd been to film school.

Yes, that made me cry. The Women's Film Festival took place in Taiwan, and I've also read some books about women directors. I feel empowered by those books. I feel that many women directors go through the same difficulties as me. I thought I should learn from them and that they are examples for me when I feel I'm in a very difficult situation, feeling isolated. You see, you are in a society where your works are not allowed to be published, it's difficult for you to get funding, and you have no team members – though you have students, you have colleagues, you have good friends ... Also when I saw the women's films I saw that many of the directors were from film school. They have had specialist training. That's what I envy ... I started to learn to make films – to use a camera, to edit – at the same time as making programmes. But I also think that at my age I have no time, I couldn't change my life to become a student at film school for four years. The reason is that there are so many serious problems happening in this society but there are only a few documentary makers who will touch the most controversial issues. Hu Jie continues to make historical documentaries about China from the 1950s to the 1970s ... but the programmes I have directed are all about current issues. That's the difference between us.

Tell me about your film about the Cultural Revolution.

I've started two – at first I thought it was one, but there's too much material. One is about a murder case, a murder case in the Cultural Revolution, and one is about a group of young people who were sent to prison for three to ten years, and I interviewed one about what happened, and how he spent his ten years in prison, how the situation is now for him and his friends. The murderer was a Red Guard. He killed two young students. He thought they were enemies, and he and his friends in the high school revolutionary committee had the right to sentence them to death. And then *he* was sentenced to 18 years. He is out now and has written a book ... I started to interview people about why they did this. They were all young students and they were encouraged to kill people in the name of the Revolution.

And you see that as having parallels with today?

One thing is to let people know what the Cultural Revolution means, what happened then. And also there are some issues related to society today, such as freedom of expression, freedom of association, and also issues of memory: issues about crime, about love, and about memory.

Do you feel there is a loss of historical memory?

It's not lost. It's the way in which ideology controls people's memory. You could construct a different picture, all the good things, and let the people believe it. But we can also collect people's memories and see how they experienced the turmoil of that time … I wish I could make the documentaries as good as I want to, but our programmes can be the raw footage for future documentary makers … It was very rare in the past for ordinary people to take photos. There were only documentaries made by the authorized documentary companies, and they have all the footage … When future documentary makers want to know what happened at the beginning of the new century, they can use our films as their footage. Things are changing rapidly. It's a form of rescue.

Notes

1   Hu Jie is an independent filmmaker who graduated from the Art College for the People's Liberation Army. His films include *Yuanmingyuan Artist Village* (1995), *Remote Mountains* (1995), *The Female Matchmaker* (1996), *On the Seaside* (1999–2003), *Mountain Songs in the Plain* (2001–3), *In Search of Lin Zhao's Soul* (1999–2004), *Bask in Sunshine* (2002) and *The Elected Village Chief* (2000–4). He also made a series of short films about migrant workers. His aim, he writes, is to challenge official historical narratives, using documentary to 'remember history'.

2   For more information about accessing these films on DVD, please email: films@cuhk.edu.hk or liyonggang@gmail.com.

3   The phrase is that of John Corner. For a survey of contemporary independent Chinese documentaries, see Yingchi Chu, 'The many voices of Chinese documentary', in Chu (2007: 183–211). Chu argues that they constitute a 'new critical discourse', although she is careful to refuse 'any narrow ideological reading of this widening documentary forum', preferring to read it as 'polyphony' (2007: 210–11). For a less optimistic view, see Lin Xu-dong (2005).

4   The phrase comes from Diane Waldman and Janet Walker, in their Introduction to *Feminism and Documentary* (1999: 19).

5   For discussion of this issue see Yingjin Zhang (2007).

6   The UN's Fourth World Conference on Women, held in Beijing in September 1995.

Part III

Contemporary Documentary: Borders, Neighbours and Disputed Territories

United 93 (Fr/UK/US, 2006) Universal Pictures. Source: The Kobal Collection.

17 Drama-documentary, Ethics and Notions of Performance
The 'Flight 93' Films

Paul Ward

Introduction: defining performance in (drama-)documentary

This chapter will examine what happens when two distinct ethical registers interact: the ethics of documentary filmmaking and the ethics of dramatic performance. In order to do so, I am going to discuss some films that have represented recent events using variations on the drama-documentary mode. There have been some interesting shifts in how documentary as a mode deals in topics, themes and imagery that traditionally are viewed as the preserve of fiction. Such films are often built on a speculative framework that for some commentators means that the films in question could in no way be called documentaries. The main examples to be discussed include the use of a semi-speculative dramatic frame for the exploration of real historical events, for example, films based on the events of United Airlines Flight 93 such as *United 93* (Fr/UK/US, 2006), *Flight 93: The Flight That Fought Back* (UK/US, 2005) or *Let's Roll: The Story of Flight 93* (UK, 2002). There shall also be a brief comparative discussion of the use of an *entirely* speculative frame to explore what *might* happen if certain events came to pass – as seen in the controversial television film *Death of a President* (UK, 2006). The main areas to be discussed are: the way in which such recent drama-documentaries address their audience and position them in relation to the depicted events; the point of documentarists using a speculative framework at all; issues relating to drama-documentary and performance (of real people and actors); and the ethical dilemmas raised by these issues.

The relationship between drama, documentary and performance at first seems seductively straightforward. Some films employ actors to play the roles of real people in various kinds of dramatic reconstruction of real events: such 'drama-documentaries'[1] therefore contain *performances* (where one person is playing another), they are constructed to capitalize on the intensity of *dramatic* scenarios, and these two elements qualify or modify the *documentary* impulse of the films in question. This raises questions about the ethics of representation, to which I shall return below. However, what are we to make of films where real people apparently 'play themselves' (or variations on themselves), or hybrids where a combination of actors and non-actors improvise in a documentary-like scenario?[2] Likewise, notions of performance and 'the performative' have become increasingly foregrounded as strategies for both the subjects and filmmakers involved in the documentary field. As Stella Bruzzi notes:

> When one discusses performance and the real event, this fusion has more usually been applied to documentary drama, where a masquerade of sponta-neity can be seen to function at an overt level ... within such a realist aesthetic [as that seen in documentary drama], the role of performance is, paradoxically, to draw the audience into the reality of the situations being dramatised, to *authenticate the fictionalisation.*
>
> ([2000] 2006: 153, emphasis added)

The performative is distinct from this in the sense that it 'uses performance within a non-fiction context to draw attention to the impossibilities of authentic documentary representation' ([2000] 2006: 153). In other words, a certain style of performance in drama-documentary (or, to use Bruzzi's term, documentary drama) is used to *authenticate,* whereas the 'performative' in other forms of documentary output is often used to *disrupt and distance* the viewer from the certainties of what they are watching.

Alongside these issues relating to the role of performance, it is also interesting to note that some films are taking up and using real archive footage not so much for rhetorical purposes (a commonplace feature of some traditions of documentary – for example, the films of Emile de Antonio) but for dramatic purposes within what is recognizably a documentary orientation. Of course, such usage can be dismissed as mere fakery, in the sense that real archive footage is made to 'perform' within a drama (or, more precisely, to perform *as* drama), but the relationship of the viewer to such material is often more complex than some commentators let on. In any case, what is important here, for the purposes of this chapter, is the way in which the use of real archive footage (or news broadcasts) not only *authenticates* a drama-documentary discourse, but also opens up a *performative* space within drama-documentary as a mode, where the recognizably real interacts with the dramatically 'irreal' (see Sobchack 2004). The 'irreal' does not simply refer to something that is 'not real' but is a distinction between objective reality on the one hand and outright fantasy on the other. The irreal is distinguished from both of these by virtue of being a *recognizable reality* that does not literally exist in the objective world 'out there', but might be said to be (hypothetically) derived from it. Many fictional films have as their foundation 'irreal' characters and settings, though the lines can become blurred when actual settings are used in a fictional context, real people are 'cast' in an irreal fiction, and so on. As we shall see, there are different ways in which something can be 'recognized as real' and this is further complicated by notions of re-presentation, re-enactment, re-construction, as well as understandings of performance.

Notions of performance in documentary are therefore potentially controversial – accusations of people 'not being themselves' or 'playacting' are rife, and are deemed to be a central problematic for a film's documentary status or credentials. As Nichols

(1994) has emphasized, however, such discourses about people 'performing' in documentaries need to be seen in relation to what he calls the 'virtual performance' – that is, the ways in which *any* of us can be said to be performing as social actors during interactions. Such performance is strongly allied to the 'canonic story form' or standardized narrative seen in many documentaries, where there is 'introduction to characters and setting, presentation of a disturbance or puzzle, a goal-oriented line of causally linked situations and events, followed by a resolution to the disturbance or solution to the puzzle' (Nichols 1994: 72). The 'virtual performance' is, according to Nichols,

> an unscripted and unrehearsed performance, which, like a scripted and rehearsed one, carries significant themes through bodily gesture, tone of voice and facial expression. Instead of an assumed identity performatively conveyed, it is the performance of a lifetime – the condensation of a lifetime into representative moments.
>
> (Nichols 1994: 72)

Thus, Nanook offers the 'performance of a lifetime' in Robert Flaherty's *Nanook of the North* (US/France, 1922) – the documentary offers up a more-or-less structured narrative, based around a performance by its central character. The key distinction to be made here is that documentaries such as *Nanook* offer a performance, but attempt to efface that it *is* a performance. As Nichols puts it: '[V]irtual performance presents the logic of actual performance without signs of conscious awareness that this presentation is an act' (1991: 122); documentaries therefore arguably represent 'the desire for performance that is not performance' (1991: 121).[3]

Ethics and performance in documentary

Such questions of performance and not knowing exactly when someone is 'being themselves' are commonplace in criticism of documentary films, at least in a common-sense way, but my feeling is that the issue of performance and drama-documentary needs rethinking in the light of the ethical issues raised. The extent to which something can be judged as 'right and proper' is an ethical question. In the documentary field, ethics commonly falls almost entirely onto the shoulders of the filmmaker and, more precisely, the filmmaker's probity and professionalism in ensuring that they do not mislead the viewers or misrepresent their subjects (see, for example, Winston 2000). As these comments imply, the notion of 'documentary ethics' is a negotiated, discursive category, rather than a set of inviolable rules: what is considered 'right and proper' may change or develop, legal restrictions on filmmakers may loosen (or tighten), a filmmaker may challenge what is acceptable. Documentarists exist in a broader social context, of course, and their rules and ethical dilemmas are played out in this arena. However, there is a gap between 'documentary practice' as a set of broadly accepted approaches to filming and representing reality and how documentary is perceived in general 'common-sense' terms. For example, it seems that there is often a conflation between the re-enactment or reconstruction of scenes, on the one hand, and being duplicitous *per se*, on the other; it is in the perception of the role of dramatic reconstruction and people 'performing' that much confusion over certain kinds of documentary resides. Documentaries 'tell the truth'; drama and performance is 'make believe': to combine the two is to be ethically suspect. Yet, documentary as a mode has always used varying degrees of drama and performance to tell its stories. The question of ethics in documentary – and especially drama-documentary – must therefore be seen as intimately related to questions of perform-ance, and not just 'read back' onto the intentions or professionalism of the filmmaker.

The ethical is especially emphasized in those texts that deliberately hybridize different modes of address, such as the ones under scrutiny here. Derek Paget and Jane Roscoe (2006) have discussed this in relation to the 'documusicals' of Brian Hill, e.g. *Feltham Sings* (UK, 2002), or *Pornography: The Musical* (UK, 2003), films that take real social issues and their 'actors' and construct a performed musical text around what are clearly 'documentary' situations. It is at the moments of song and overt performance that the 'documentariness' of the films is at its most precarious; paradoxically, according to Paget and Roscoe, this is what amplifies such texts' usefulness as commentary on real social issues and the ethical dimension that is central to this.

> In the vulnerability of their performances and in their amateurness, the ... Feltham inmates and porn stars are caught in a performative spotlight framed by documentary imperatives. With these films so clearly performed rather than observed at the *punctum* moment of the songs, the ethical is not just foregrounded as an issue, it is boldly asserted. The ethical is made complex in the song and verse sequences first by modalities of voice – there are significant differences between anyone's speaking and singing voices (the latter being far more vulnerable). But there are also visual modalities in which the aesthetics of music video collide with documentary and force comparison and contrast both with 'documentary proper' and with polished music video.
>
> (Paget and Roscoe 2006: n.p.)

It is this notion of a collision of visual (and sonic) modalities, leading to a highly charged form of documentary representation that I wish to examine here. In particular, it is the collision of the representation of real (and often recent and extremely emotionally resonant) events with an obviously constructed dramatic frame that underlines the ethical and performative questions we need to ask. Of course, for anyone other than actual eyewitnesses, the events of 9/11 were always 'already' mediated by broadcast news and other media institutions. However, the representation of the events themselves relied heavily on footage that was gathered from 'unofficial' sources such as tourist camcorders and mobile phones. The 'reality effect' of such footage is amplified; this in turn means that the ethical implications of reframing these events in a dramatic/performative arena are likewise amplified.

Alan Read (1993) has discussed the ethical dimension of performance in relation to theatre, but his commentary is potentially very useful for those thinking about the under-explored area of ethics and performance in documentary-related fields. He discusses the everyday/quotidian and the 'typical' as concepts relevant to theatre and filmmaking (especially documentary). What is interesting is how this notion of everydayness or typicality can be contrasted with the extraordinary events seen in some drama-documentaries. There is a discrepancy between the magnitude of the events depicted, and the drama that they inevitably entail, and the very authentic, quotidian, 'everydayness' that is meant to be the marker of drama-documentary.

In contrast to the magnitude of the events depicted, the notion of everydayness is accentuated in these films by the use of non-professional actors, or at least non-stars, to bolster authenticity. This ties in with an ethical debate about documentary filmmakers being 'honest' with the viewer – is it more honest to use unknown actors in dramatic reconstructions? If we do not recognize them as 'performers' in the usual sense – something that seems to be a prerequisite for guaranteeing authenticity – then there is also a chance that the status of what we are watching might become blurred – certainly more so than if we were watching a known star 'play a role'. Certainly, Read's points relate to everyday actuality and how theatre and performance might connect with this, but this relationship is a complex one:

> Regarding theatre then entails more than just looking at this theatre, it requires a poetics which will allow political and ethical judgements to be made. If judgement is to be possible it is no longer sufficient to say how one knows what is real, but how one knows what one is seeing and experiencing and its relation to reality. At a time when seeing has become believing it is worth reminding theatre that its responsibility is still to disrupt, not to acquiesce with this spectacle.
>
> (Read 1993: 59)

If we substitute 'drama-documentary' for 'theatre', I think the point that Read is making here is actually strengthened. We know that documentary films are representing to us some aspect of the real, social world; drama-documentaries are mediating actual events and people via dramatic conventions and performances. The key term here is *mediating* – by virtue of constructing a dramatic frame (for whatever reason) around very recent and traumatic events, a critical distance is placed between the actuality and its reconstruction. Central to this critical distance are the performances – and how they can both authenticate and undermine the verisimilitude of the events depicted. The performances (and issues such as casting of specific performers in particular roles) need to be interpreted in the broader context of how all films are received by their audience via what Noel Carroll (2003: 169–75) calls a system of 'indexing', where films arrive, as it were, 'already labelled'. We *know* we are watching a documentary (or drama-documentary) and therefore respond to it (and the people in it) in a particular way. It is this discursive context that provides the frame in which the original depicted events, their dramatic re-presentation, and the different modes of performance coalesce to form a peculiarly ethical debate.

Modes of performance in the tales of Flight 93

There have been a variety of filmed responses to the events of September 11th 2001, when the twin towers of the World Trade Center and other targets were attacked by terrorists. Among these are a number of films concerned with United Airlines Flight 93 – the so-called 'flight that fought back'.[4] One of the terrorists' targets was allegedly the Capitol Building in Washington, DC, and Flight 93 was hijacked on its way to San Francisco, shortly after it had left Newark, New Jersey, turning back to approach Washington. As it neared its target, the surviving cabin crew (both pilots had apparently been killed) and passengers stormed the cockpit and the plane crashed in a field in Shanksville, Pennsylvania, short of its target, killing everyone on board.

One of the main differences between *United 93* and the other two films I have seen is that *Flight 93: The Flight That Fought Back* and *Let's Roll: The Story of Flight 93* use straight-to-camera interviews interspersed between the dramatically reconstructed scenes. These interviews are with the partners and family of the dead passengers and crew, and people who were involved on the ground that day, such as Lisa Jefferson, a supervisor at the Verizon Airfone company who spoke with passenger Todd Beamer, overhearing him utter the now-famous phrase 'Let's roll'. Of course, this offers an intriguing shift in register throughout these films – between dramatically performed scenes re-enacting known or partially known events and interviews with actual protagonists in these real-life events. Ultimately, this reduces the dramatic power that the acted scenes have – or, more precisely, it reduces any *documentary* power that they might have. The viewer is asked to believe (or at the very least, suspend disbelief) in the dramatic reconstructions, but there is a constant reminder of the 'more real' in the shape of the bereaved interviewees. *Let's Roll*, in particular, tends to cross-cut between reconstruction and interview in a way that sometimes seems to be trying a little too hard to authenticate what are, after all, semi-speculative representations of events. For example, in one sequence, Lisa Jefferson describes what certain people said, and we then see the same lines re-enacted in the dramatic reconstruction. Similarly, there is an attempt to dramatically cross-cut between interview and reconstruction when Deena Burnett, the widow of passenger Tom Burnett, reports what she said to her husband during a phone call and then 'Tom Burnett' (played by Antony Edridge) appears to respond to her from within the dramatic reconstruction.

This is of course a commonplace strategy, a mixing of talking head interviews about a specific topic or set of events, cross-cut with dramatic reconstructions of those events. The examples noted above are clear attempts to 'suture' across the drama and documentary modalities; as noted, this potentially helps to authenticate the drama, but at the same time could be said to undermine the drama, make it appear stilted. This is something that *United 93* avoids in favour of a more dramatically intense approach: a real-time reconstruction of the events, showing what happened in the air and on the ground. Again, the events are scrupulously based on flight recorders and telephone conversations – apart from some elements that we might call 'informed speculation', such as the shots that open the film, showing the four terrorists preparing and then departing for Newark airport. This results in what is, on one level, a more dramatically coherent film – quite simply because the drama is allowed to build in intensity without the cutaways to interviews. At the same time, of course, this could be argued to lessen the documentary power of what is on screen: as well as resting on a large measure of speculation about exactly how certain events came to pass, there is a trajectory to the drama that tends to evacuate the connections to the broader real world context. The explanatory power that any documentary should arguably have is significantly reduced in films like this, as the debates about 'authenticity' and 'believability' are conducted (if they are conducted at all) at the level of minutiae: did Mark Bingham really look like that? Did Todd Beamer really say 'Let's roll' in quite that way?[5] We can of course argue about what is the 'point' of such films – to commemorate the heroic actions of the passengers and crew? To try and explain what happened and, more to the point, why? If it is the latter, then connections to a broader context are entirely necessary, though they may not be entirely welcomed by some of the audience.

There appears to be a common-sense notion that for anything to be labelled as 'drama' (or 'dramatic') requires that it has an intensity, a caught-up-in-the-moment element that by its very nature militates against wider reflection, contextualization or thought. Put simply, drama and dramatic performance appeal to our emotions, documentary, by contrast, appeals to our intellect. Of course, such a dichotomy glosses over the complexities of drama, documentary and their hybrid forms. This is precisely why watching the Flight 93 films is an uncomfortable experience on so many levels: there is no doubting the combination of fear and bravery the people involved must have felt, but it is perhaps debatable whether we as viewers more fully understand what occurred that day after viewing any of these films. Certainly, *Flight 93: The Flight That Fought Back*, with its use of split screen and a voice-over delivered by Kiefer Sutherland, could be said to be cynical in its aping of *24*-style dramatic tropes. As noted above, *United 93* has a more 'unified' dramatic structure in that it unfolds as if the events are happening before our eyes, with none of the retrospective viewpoints of interviewees, nor voice-over to make connections between scenes. How do these different dramatic approaches to the same source material, the same highly traumatic events, impact upon the ethical dimension of these films?

Ethical space, death and performance

Vivian Sobchack has written about how ethical space is inscribed within fictional and non-fictional worlds and, in particular, how certain events and characters can effectively disrupt the diegesis of a fiction film. Sobchack's main example is that of the death of a rabbit in the hunting scene in *La Règle de Jeu* (France, 1939), a death which 'exceeds the narrative codes that communicate it' (Sobchack 2004: 247). It is a real death of an existent rabbit: as Sobchack puts it, the representation of the death therefore has a 'ferocious reality' that is lacking in the depicted death of a fictional character in the same film (2004: 247).[6] What Sobchack is pointing to here is the fundamental difference between representations (or performances) of death in terms of their non-fictional or fictional status; it is especially striking when two types of death appear in the same ostensibly fictional space.

I would like to take Sobchack's observations as a starting point to think about the modes of performance we see in the films that are the focus of this chapter. We are witnessing actors performing the events leading up to the deaths of their characters. In the Flight 93 films (aside from *United 93*), the pro-filmic/extratextual existence of the real people represented by the actors on the screen is underlined by the use of the authenticating interviews with loved ones and family members, who talk about their lives outside of the events that day. The films therefore take on a commemorative role that emphasizes the honourable and brave deaths. But what status do the deaths and their performance have in documentary terms? They are somewhere in between a fictionalized re-presentation and something recognizable as the real world of a documentary. Of course, this is a common feature of based-on-a-true-story films that take and adapt real people's lives, casting actors to play them. There is something similar going on to the amplification seen in the docu-musicals Paget and Roscoe discuss, in the way that real events and people are clearly and obviously *dramatically performed* by actors – even to the death. As Sobchack argues:

> In fictional cinema, the representation of death, however graphic, is experi-enced as abstract – that is, hypothetical or 'irreal'; it is a character who dies and not the actor who plays him. The nonfictional representation of death in the documentary, however, is experienced as real – even when it is not as graphically displayed as it often is in the fiction film.
>
> (2004: 241)

There is some considerable blurring between the highly charged representations of the deaths seen in the Flight 93 films, and the events on which they are based, something we can ascribe to the magnitude and proximity of those events, as well as the use of what Steven Lipkin (2002) calls 'warranting' devices and the use of actual locations and the casting of some real people who went through the events on the day itself.[7] Lipkin's point about warranting refers to the ways in which a drama-documentary (though he uses the preferred US term, 'docudrama') validates its assertions and actually makes an argument by locating its drama in relation to real indexical footage and other 'data': this material acts as an anchor, that 'warrants' that what we are watching is (to some degree) true.

An instructive comparison can be drawn with a 'warranting' moment from the fiction film *Contact* (US, 1997), wherein real documentary footage of then-US President Bill Clinton is co-opted by the fictional frame of the film in order to bolster the authenticity of the film's science fiction premise. In *Contact*, the footage of Clinton is taken from an actual news conference where the President reacts to an announcement by NASA concerning possible signs of life on a Martian meteorite. As Sobchack points out in her discussion of this moment (2004), there is an ethical issue here with the use of the footage and its commingling with the fictional narrative starring Jodie Foster; however, the chief problem raised by this particular instance was the fact that it *drew attention to itself*, thereby having an opposite effect to the one intended (to use Lipkin's terminology – the warranting does not work). As Sobchack observes of this moment, from the time she went to the cinema to see *Contact*, the audience 'who had been intent on the screen and immersed in the narrative seemed suddenly to remove themselves to their seats, where they rustled and murmured at being so abruptly cast back into the immediate historical present' (2004: 259). This was due to the fact that the Clinton footage was in the very recent memory of the film's audience – the co-opting therefore did not work, simply because the non-fictional status of the footage had not 'worn off', and this blocked its successful recontextualization within a fiction. There is, of course, an ethical issue in such instances, one firmly based on the probity of the filmmakers, and the potential for them to seamlessly commingle 'real' and 'irreal' imagery, thereby duping the viewer. As this instance demonstrates (and there are countless others), the relationship of the viewer to the viewed is hardly ever as straightforward as them being simply 'duped' in this way.

A case in point is the controversial film *Death of a President*, first broadcast in the UK on 9 October 2006, on the digital channel More4. This film shows the events leading up to the assassination of George W. Bush on 19 October 2007 and what happened afterwards. Produced by Simon Finch and directed by Gabriel Range, the film follows the conventions of their earlier film *The Day Britain Stopped* (UK, 2003) by constructing in forensic detail something that has *yet to happen*, as if looked back on by a filmmaker in the diegetic future.[8] Fictional (yet strikingly convincing) irreal characters such as Larry Stafford ('Former Head, Presidential Protection Detail' – played by Brian Boland) and Eleanor Drake ('Former Special Advisor to President Bush' – played by Becky Ann Baker) reflect back on the events of that day via straight to camera interviews, while we see footage from that evening, leading up to the assassination. This footage is cleverly doctored, and digitally manipulated to seamlessly commingle the real Bush (speaking at a similar event to the one posited in the film, as well as gladhanding well-wishers outside the building afterwards) with his fictional advisors. What concerns me here is the way that *Death of a President* uses these techniques and how this opens up an ethical space for us to consider the fictional death of a real person in what is a kind of drama-documentary. This links directly back to the issues noted above in my discussion of the Flight 93 films – of performance and drama and how they are mobilized in certain documentary modes. *Death of a President* is of course a fiction in that the events depicted have not happened, but the furore around the film raised a number of questions about what could or could not legitimately be shown in a film that uses 'documentary' conventions.

One thing worth emphasizing in this discussion is the representations of death in the Flight 93 films and *Death of a President*. In the former set of films we know that the deaths actually happened, but we do not get to see them in the filmic representations. In the case of the latter film, the 'death' of the title did *not* actually happen – it is a fictional construct – and yet we *do* see it (however fleetingly) represented onscreen. This raises questions about the 'creation' of performance from archive fragments and/or digitally manipulated imagery – an ethical dilemma for filmmakers if ever there was one. The representation of death is always ethically charged, but such a charge is attenuated by the ontological status of the imagery. In the case of a fiction film, where we *know* (via extracinematic knowledge and, it has to be said, common sense) that a represented death has not really happened before our eyes, the death 'matters' less, quite simply because we know that it has been served up for us as part of a narrative. What is happening in the dramatized documentary format of *United 93* is interesting in relation to representations of death: we know that the deaths *actually* happened, that the filmic imagery refers to a set of events and a number of deaths that really *did* occur. At the same time, though, we recognize that the events on the screen are being performed for us by actors. There is an interesting 'code switching' that goes on therefore, in terms of simultaneously knowing the real-world events to which the onscreen action refers, while also knowing that we are watching a performance (or set of performances that constitute a drama). In the case of *Death of a President*, on the other hand, we know that Bush has not in reality been assassinated, that the act has been dramatized or performed using digital effects and other cinematic trickery, and the aftermath authenticated using recontextualized real footage (of Cheney et al., akin to the usage of the Clinton footage in *Contact*) as well as recognizably 'documentary' talking head interviews where the interviewees are played by actors. And yet, the film has a considerable 'charge' in Sobchack's meaning of the term (as well as, it has to be said, a *dramatic* charge): the film's central focus is arguably an examination of why this particular President's death might 'matter' so much.

Something else worth noting about these particular dramatized deaths is the ways they are structured for us as viewers within a specifically (drama-) documentary gaze. The deaths of the passengers in *United 93*, while deferred to an offscreen space, have a grim inevitability – we know they are going to happen and it is the causal chain unfolding and leading up to the deaths that forms the narrative arc of the film. It is as if the film memorializes the dead and then averts its eyes at the last moment: the final sequence of *United 93*, where the passengers charge the terrorists and we see them breaking into the cockpit and attempting to wrest control of the plane, ends with a subjective/point of view shot as if from the cockpit, as the plane plummets to the ground.[9] At the point of impact (or, rather, just prior to it) the screen cuts rapidly to black. There is no sound. After a more or less naturalistic, *cinéma verité* style up to that point, such 'excess' is remarkable – it paradoxically shies away from and yet draws attention to the moment of death. *Death of a President*, on the other hand, offers up the moment of Bush's 'death' in a classic 'accidental' way, as if the camera just happened to be there and stumbled across the assassination. As Bush is shaking hands with people, two shots ring out and Bush lurches forward, clearly hit. Mayhem ensues, as Bush is bundled into his waiting car by Secret Service agents, and the crowd scatter. The representations of death in *United 93* and *Death of a President* are dramatic, but in very different ways, suggesting very different kinds of onlooker.

One of the major problems with representations of death in documentary, as Sobchack has suggested, is that they are inscribed within a space that implies a certain kind of gaze. The horrified onlooker, who *accidentally* sees something, for example, or the gaze of someone observing from a 'professional' distance. In *Death of a President*, the dramatized (which is to say, fictionalized) moment of Bush's death is captured using all of the conventions of a certain kind of gaze – the 'accidental' in Sobchack's typology:

> Inscribed as the least ethically suspect in its encounter with the event of death, the accidental gaze is cinematically coded in markers of technical and physical *unpreparedness*. The film gives us visual evidence that death was *not* the filmmaker's initial object of scrutiny, that it happened in front of the

camera suddenly, randomly, and unexpectedly, surprising the filmmaker's vision and disallowing any possibility of the filmmaker's intervention or complicity.

(2004: 249; original emphasis)

It is no surprise to find that one of Sobchack's examples of this gaze is that which structures the looking in the Zapruder footage of the assassination of JFK. Of course, using such conventions to imply a non-fictional viewing position in a fictional film – that is, to authenticate certain footage – is a mainstay of the drama-documentary form. Events appear to spill uninvited into the (wholly constructed) diegesis. The important phrase here is 'appear to' – in drama-documentary generally, things are conceived and presented in such a way as to give the appearance of being accidental, of the filmmakers being unprepared for them, but this is of course part of the authentically presented drama. In *Death of a President*, the dramatic force of course revolves around the depiction of Bush's assassination and much of the negative criticism of the film concerned itself with whether it was right and proper to ever show the fictionalized death of a living person, whoever they are and for whatever reason. (This does of course beg the question: which is worse – a fictional death, or a real one? From the reaction of some critics and viewers, one would think that the filmmakers had *actually* assassinated Bush.) Central to the film is an ethical problem, but it is one that is linked to documentary performativity and the way that such a film asks questions of its audience, questions relating to what they have witnessed. Bill Nichols notes that, as documentaries have moved to become more performative, there has been a shift of emphasis, that

> reconfigures questions of validation. The process of identifying a problem and proposing a solution no longer has operative force. Our assessment and engagement, then, is 'less in terms of [the message's] clarity or its truth value with respect to its referent than in terms of its performative force – a purely pragmatic consideration' [White, 1987: 39]. Questions of pragmatics shift the dominant from the work's referential relation, its indexical binding to fragments of the historical world, to its relation to its viewers. *We* are what such films refer to.

(Nichols 1994: 99–100; original emphasis)

One can think of the oft-quoted film by Errol Morris, *The Thin Blue Line* (US, 1988) which uses all manner of stylistic tropes and 'performative' tricks to construct a documentary which not so much 'tells the truth' about the murder of a Dallas police officer, than it does demand that its viewers weigh up the relative truthfulness of different accounts that they hear. Likewise – and as I have argued elsewhere (Ward 2005: 40–8) – we can see the Nick Broomfield films about killer Aileen Wuornos as ultimately having little interest in finding out 'the truth' of what happened; rather, they are an examination of the ways in which Wuornos was mediated and sold to the public. In other words, each film can be said to be directly about 'its relation to its viewers', and ask the audience to make ethical judgements, something that the Flight 93 films and *Death of a President* also explicitly do. While watching these films, the viewer is simultaneously expected to weigh up three 'levels' of conduct: that of the actual, existent social actors represented in the drama-documentary (the real people who die on Flight 93, or Bush, Cheney et al.); that of the performers/actors in the films; and that of the filmmakers. Such a complex network of interpenetrating ethical judgements emphasizes how effective a forum drama-documentary can actually be for interrogating historical events and actions.

The films examined in this chapter offer up different attempts to engage the drama-documentary form in what is a profoundly ethical debate about the represent-ability and performativity of certain traumatic events. The fictional, 'mock-documentary' format of *Death of a President* should not detract from the fact that it raises serious questions about the scope and ability of both drama and documentary (and, indeed, their fusion: drama-documentary) to represent death, especially a death that 'matters' so much. The Flight 93 films, while offering the dramatically recon-structed lead-up to the actual deaths, do not show them, demonstrating what Sobchack refers to as 'death's unspeakability and the limits of representation' (2004: 256). If anything can be described as 'unspeakable' or somehow 'beyond' (or at the limits of) representation, then it is clearly a moral/ethical issue. It is in their fusion of dramatic and documentary conventions, however, that such films explicitly ask us as viewers to interrogate the very process of performing or re-enacting real, historical events – with the hope being that we come to a greater understanding of both the (real) events and their (drama-documentary) re-presentation.

Notes

1   'Drama-documentary' is but one term to describe a range of tendencies in film and television production. As Paget (1998) has made clear, there are distinct usages and nuances in how 'drama' and 'documentary' are com-bined, with different traditions emerging on either side of the Atlantic, for example. For the purposes of this chapter, I have deliberately chosen the term 'drama-documentary' to describe all of the films under discussion, even though, technically speaking, they may fall into different categories in that they deploy 'drama' and 'documentary' conventions in different ways. (And, of course, *Death of a President* is, strictly speaking, a fiction film, albeit one that engages with and critiques certain documentary conventions.)

2   Some intriguing examples here are Penny Woolcock's television films *Tina Goes Shopping* and *Tina Takes a Break* (UK, 1999 and 2001 respectively) and Pawel Pawlikowski and Ian Duncan's *Twockers* (UK, 1998). For brief discus-sions of the *Tina* films, see Ward (2005: 34–40); for brief discussion of *Twockers*, see Ward (2007). Other key examples are to be found in recent Iranian cinema, such as the works of Kiarostami, for a discussion of which see Rapfogel (2001).

3   A documentary that inflects the notion of performance in a much more overt and knowing manner is Jonathan Caouette's *Tarnation* (US, 2003), where the life of the central character (Caouette himself) is performed via highly-mediated snippets – photographs, home movies, voice recordings. This film is clearly approaching documentary notions of performance in a

very different manner to a film like *Nanook*; the 'performance of a lifetime' we see in *Tarnation* is upfront and emphatic rather than effaced.

4 As well as those films noted in the introduction to this chapter, there is a 2006 US television film simply entitled *Flight 93* (directed by Peter Markle), but I have not seen it.

5 The iconic phrase 'Let's roll' was uttered by Todd Beamer just prior to the passengers moving to try and break into the cockpit and overpower the terrorists. Beamer had been in a telephone conversation with Lisa Jefferson and the phone line was still open as he said this. Transcripts of telephone and air traffic control transmissions have been released, and the families of those involved have heard the recordings, as part of the 9/11 Commission investigation, but the recordings have never been made generally available. The phrase lends itself to a gung-ho pronunciation – indeed, George W. Bush has co-opted the phrase to such effect in some speeches – but the way Beamer says it in *Let's Roll* (Beamer played by Noah Margetts) and *United 93* (David Alan Basche) is actually very low-key, almost whispered – a desperate exhortation to get it over with, rather than some ultra-patriotic exclamation.

6 'Ferocious reality' is a term coined by critic Amos Vogel.

7 For example, in *United 93*, which is an entirely reconstructed version of the events, some people play themselves in the unfolding drama – e.g. Ben Sliney, Thomas Roberts and Tobin Miller, who are all real air traffic control personnel who were on duty that day. An additional layer of authenticity is added by some of the deceased crew being played by real-life airline crew (e.g. deceased Flight 93 pilot Captain Jason Dahl is played in *United 93* by another United Airlines pilot, Captain J.J. Johnson).

8 I have written elsewhere about *The Day Britain Stopped* and its 'conditional tense' strategies, and the way it mixes fictional and nonfictional material to address viewers in a specific way (see Ward 2006). In the same essay, I also make a case as to why films like *The Day Britain Stopped* (and *Death of a President* can be included here) should be viewed as part of the 'mock-documentary' category.

9 A similar shot features as the 'climax' to the dramatic sequences in some of the other Flight 93 films.

18 Mockumentary
A call to play

Craig Hight

Mockumentary is now a staple of contemporary fictional narrative. From archetypal film texts such as *David Holzman's Diary* (US, 1967), *This is Spinal Tap* (US, 1984) and *C'est arrivé près de chez vous* (*Man Bites Dog*) (Belgium, 1992) through to the television series *The Office* (UK, 2001–3), the form has demonstrated a popularity and, on occasions, a sophistication that suggest that it deserves to be acknowledged as one of the more robust and certainly more interesting documentary hybrids.[1]

An initial definition of mockumentary might focus largely on the text itself, defining the form as consisting of those fictional texts which employ a sustained appropriation of documentary codes and conventions. In these terms, mockumentary is little more than a 'parasitic' form. At another level the form appears to offer an inherent reflexivity towards documentary (and by extension all non-fiction forms) through demonstrating how easy it is to fake documentary modes of representation. And yet most examples of mockumentary do not develop a clear critique or commentary of documentary forms, and for many audiences mockumentary is more easily labelled as 'playful' rather than subversive.

The discussion below provides a more comprehensive definition of mockumentary before moving to consider cross-platform mockumentary, that is those texts which operate simultaneously across a number of media platforms. The emergence of cross-platform mockumentary is a feature associated particularly with the increasing dominance of digital media platforms such as the world wide web and DVD. These mockumentaries suggest both a continuity of mockumentary into digital media, and the increasingly complex nature of mockumentary discourse within the contemporary mediascape.

Defining mockumentary discourse[2]

A useful starting point for defining mockumentary is Nichols' three-part definition of documentary (Nichols 1991: 12–31). There is not the space here to do full justice to his arguments, but Nichols has proposed that documentary constitutes a genre that needs to be defined, first, through reference to an institutional practice developed and maintained by a 'community of practitioners', a practice that claims to represent reality to audiences in as accurate, objective and unbiased a manner as possible.

Second, documentary can be defined through reference to a specific 'corpus of texts' which collectively demonstrate a familiar set of codes and conventions. These codes and conventions are typically grouped as documentary modes of representation (with the key modes being expository, observational, and interactive or participatory). Each of these modes is centred on specific forms of representing the social-historical world, and are couched within wider discourses which support their presentation of various forms of 'evidence' of reality. The interactive mode, for example, focuses particularly on forms of testimony from social actors and expert knowledge from representatives of institutional discourses, while the observational mode relies on the common-sensical belief in a camera's ability to capture footage which bears an indexical link to reality itself. Third, Nichols argues that documentary necessarily involves a 'constituency of viewers' who bring specific expectations and assumptions to their reading of documentary forms. Here audiences typically engage with these texts through a documentary mode of reading which is based on a familiarity with and acceptance of the validity and integrity of these generic modes of representation.

Nichols recognized the need for this three-part definition of documentary because of the slippage which occurs between the levels of production, transmission and reception within media practice. For example, a given text can entail forms of representation outside of the conventional modes of documentary but still be identified and accepted by audience as 'documentary', if it is recognized as the application of the institutionalized code of practice of documentary filmmakers. This three-part definition also explains the damage done to the genre by fake documentaries. A fake documentary entails a pretence of documentary practice beginning with the fraudulent intentions of the filmmakers. It represents a deliberate lapse in standards for documentary proper, and is judged on those terms by audiences and other documentary practitioners. Fake documentaries are by definition a very different order of text from mockumentary.

Adapting Nichols' definition of the documentary genre, mockumentary can be defined as a *discourse*, one identified through reference to three levels of media practice:

1. Mockumentary arises from a variety of agendas on the part of fictional media producers. It draws in particular on parodic and satiric traditions, but is not reducible to these.
2. At the textual level, mockumentary appropriates styles not only from the codes and conventions of documentary proper but from the full spectrum of non-fiction media, including hybrid forms. And mockumentary discourse operates within a range of generic traditions (including, surprisingly, non-fiction itself) and potentially intersects with all forms of media.
3. And mockumentary is capable of providing a complexity of forms of audience engagement, often (but not necessarily) involving different senses of reflexivity towards the non-fiction and hybrid forms which it appropriates.

It is at the interaction between these three levels of practice that mockumentary is located.

The agendas of mockumentary

Any mockumentary text can be partly defined through the intentions of the filmmakers or media producers who have created that text. To date, the form has exhibited the broad patterns discussed below, although it is important to recognize that these are by no means mutually exclusive. Rather than suggesting a taxonomy, they should be viewed as common, overlapping tendencies within the production of mockumentary, tendencies which both govern the nature of the appropriation of non-fiction forms within a given text and suggest the manner in which audiences are encouraged to engage with that text.

Novelty

These are one-off mockumentary texts within an existing media practice. If we were to take a broad definition of mockumentary, this agenda could include all forms of April Fool's Day jokes initiated by various news media.[3] The infamous 1938 *War of the Worlds* radio broadcast commonly attributed to Orson Welles could also be seen to fall into this category, together with television skit shows which might employ the mockumentary style as a one-off interruption to their usual practice, and those television series, both dramatic and comedic, which have used the mockumentary form simply for one episode. Perhaps the most famous of this latter group is the live premiere of the 1997 series of *ER*,[4] but there are similar one-off mockumentary episodes from series as diverse as *The X-Files*, *The Simpsons*, *M.A.S.H.* and *The West Wing*.

Promotion

The *ER* episode can also be seen to fall into this tendency, where the appropriation of non-fiction codes and conventions is employed largely for promotional purposes. More typical of this agenda is a long history of the use of mockumentary within electronic forms of advertising. There are any number of examples consisting of mock-interviews, or a serious voice-over for absurd content, or simply the intertextual use of fact-fiction forms. These references are not always intended to parody those forms but are more typically intended to tap into what is assumed to be a series of common frames of reference for audiences. A wider examination of this agenda would also need to include the use of mockumentaries to promote films, television programmes and computer games, such as the increasing tendency to use short, trailer-length segments on promotional websites.

Dramatic style

This tendency covers the range of non-comedic mockumentaries, those which employ the mockumentary form for dramatic purposes. As with the other agendas listed here, this could be further differentiated according to the specific mode of documentary representation or non-fiction form which a text references, which in turn often suggest a specific production practice employed by filmmakers or producers. For example, there are a number of mockumentaries which mimic observational documentaries, in order to provide a sense of immediacy or apparent spontaneity to a dramatic production. In many cases this involves filmmakers adopting a largely improvisational style of filmmaking (such as Woody Allen with *Husbands and Wives*, US, 1992), and at times this serves to disguise a low production budget (one reason why mockumentary is often favoured by student filmmakers). A dramatic mockumentary might use the observational form in order to justify a limited set of narrative information being provided to an audience, through replicating the partial access available to a documentary film crew (*Interview with the Assassin* (US, 2002)), or even the limited frame of a camera itself. This tendency has been used to particular effect with science fiction and horror narratives such as in *The Last Broadcast* (US, 1998), *The Blair Witch Project* (US, 1999, discussed below) or *The Wicksboro Incident* (US, 2003).[5]

Parody and satire

Despite the number of examples which could be listed for the tendencies discussed above, the bulk of mockumentary practice has clearly emerged from within parodic and satiric traditions, although the complexity of parodic discourse itself is also suggestive of the variety of mockumentaries which fall into this broad label.[6] Parody typically exhibits an ambivalence towards its target, offering both a mocking of the text that it references and an effective reinforcement of its authority; what Hutcheon refers to as the 'paradox' of parody (Hutcheon 2000: 68). This, however, does not necessarily suggest that parody is only ever parasitic, nor that it does not have the potential to be subversive or transgressive. As Harries notes, parody essentially involves 'the process of recontextualizing a target or source text through the transformation of its textual (and contextual) elements, thus creating a *new* text' (Harries 2000: 6).

A parodic text's relationship to the text(s) that it parodies is also partly determined through audience interaction. The ambivalence of parodic discourse towards its target operates to provide a complexity of forms of engagement for audiences, and, in a sense, that ambivalence is also ultimately decided by the viewer. Whether a text is truly transgressive, and to what extent, depends very much on factors such as the levels of extra-textual knowledge which audiences bring to this encounter (as discussed below).

The most complex and interesting examples of mockumentary practice are those texts with a deliberately satirical agenda. Satire establishes a more political stance towards its target, intending to replace it with something better (Harries defines parody as a more muted or weaker form of satire because of its ambivalence about its target). Plantinga's excellent piece on the seminal mockumentary film *This is Spinal Tap* offers a useful illustration of the complexities of the ways in which satire and parody can operate within a given text (Plantinga 1998). He argues that while the film is gently mocking of 'classic' rockumentaries such as D. A. Pennebaker's *Don't*

Look Back (US, 1967) and Martin Scorsese's *The Last Waltz* (US, 1978), it ultimately follows the pattern of parody in paying these films a degree of respect and even reverence. At the same time, however, *Spinal Tap* provides a much more aggressive and devastating satirical deconstruction of heavy metal masculine posturing.

As can be seen from just this initial schematic of agendas, mockumentary discourse has involved a variety of often conflicting strategies and intentions. Mockumentary texts can range from the trivial use of non-fiction forms to densely layered and innovative textual constructions looking to engage with audiences in a multitude of ways. They have reinvigorated genres, taking a distinct textual strategy which goes beyond aesthetics to provide a fresh perspective on a conventional form (*The Blair Witch Project* in horror, *The Office* within sitcom). In fact, the best examples of mockumentary typically construct a complex set of forms of engagement for audiences, drawing upon a range of intertextual references and seeking to engage with viewers' knowledge of wider visual culture and key social-political discourses. They establish characters with which the audience can identify, and develop narratives which do not depend purely upon knowledge of other texts in order to be successful. The specific types of engagement constructed by a text can suggest the overall agendas followed by a producer or filmmaker, and they provide for audiences a number of specific forms of *play*, in particular, encouraging viewers to engage with their own detailed expectations of a continuum of non-fiction and hybrid forms.

The mockumentary text: modes of appropriation

Mockumentary discourse involves the sustained appropriation of non-fiction codes and conventions, particularly those which constitute the documentary genre. The difficulty of identifying mockumentary discourse purely through the nature of its intertextual referencing, however, is derived from the increasingly problematic nature of any textual definition of documentary itself. To some extent, Nichols' definition of documentary has always involved constructing somewhat artificial boundaries around the genre, despite his explicit intention to avoid any strict taxonomy (Nichols 1991: 32–4). The existence of hybrid forms such as drama-documentary (Paget 1998; Lipkin 2002) and nature documentary (Bousé 2000) has always suggested more of a continuum of fact-fiction forms that cross over generic boundaries. A dilemma for documentary culture as a whole is that it increasingly incorporates a variety of textual strategies and aesthetic styles derived from fictional traditions.

The most prominent of these styles are exhibited by the well-researched proliferation of television hybrid formats. These are typically grouped into labels such as reality gameshow, docu-soap but could also include a variety of lifestyle programming and gameshows proper which incorporate a great deal of reality material. Corner's useful phrase for much of these trends is 'documentary as diversion' (Corner 2002) and it is still an open issue whether these constitute a significant (and permanent) transformation of mainstream documentary practice itself. There are paradoxical trends here, with hybrid formats both replacing documentary as a staple of television programming, but also apparently helping to generate a rise in audience interest and participation in more conventional factual forms.

Such trends within documentary culture also need to be couched within an acknowledgement of wider social and cultural patterns of engagement with mediations of the 'real'. There are too many trends to properly survey here, but these include a quite dynamic interaction between the discourses of surveillance, autobiography and creative expression. In part, documentary culture is increasingly integrated with a wider and disquieting rise in the use of surveillance systems within modern societies, marked in particular by an associated increase in the acceptance of surveillance footage within television programming. Together with the emergence of an amateur surveillance culture centred on camcorders and more recently webcams, videologs and phonecams, such trends suggest (among other things) a collapse of distinctions between public and private space and an increased realm for personalized forms of confession and expression. Although clearly intersecting with more established traditions of personal media production such as amateur photography (Hight 2001), it is the aesthetic of amateur video – grainy, hand-held, accidental and partial perspectives on typically trivial events – which is increasingly reinforced as the marker of authenticity. This naturalization of non-professional footage is itself a natural consequence of increased access by audiences to technologies which effectively allow them to play the role of producers, publishing content directly online and outside of the practices which define professional journalism. Documentary aesthetics, then, are increasingly appropriated and transformed as modes of practice within online, emergent models of broadcasting.

All of these concurrent, overlapping and at times competing patterns within wider documentary culture share a preoccupation with fundamental aspects of documentary modes of representation. However, this continuity with conventional (analogue) audio-visual documentary is paired with a fracturing of any broader social-political consensus on what constitutes a documentary agenda and how it should be positioned and valued within contemporary society. Mockumentary plays within this terrain, drawing strength from the instability of documentary culture as a whole, and more recently from the ways in which aspects of documentary aesthetics are refashioned through digital media practices. Mockumentary discourse, in one sense, is simply adding to the complexity of exchange between analogue and digital forms of mediated reality. It offers a sense of play within an expanded fact–fiction continuum, emphasizing the complex and contradictory forms of engagement which are already present within non-fiction culture.

One key aspect within this broader documentary culture is the significance of *reflexivity* as a feature both of individual texts and the wider climate of reception for non-fiction forms. Nichols provides useful pointers to how reflexivity operates within documentary proper:

> The reflexive mode of representation gives emphasis to the encounter between filmmaker and viewer rather than filmmaker and subject. This mode arrives last on the scene since it is itself the least naïve and the most doubtful about the possibilities of communication and expression that the other modes take for granted. Realist access to the world, and the ability to provide

persuasive evidence, the possibility of indisputable argument, the unbreak-
able bond between an indexical image and that which it represents – all
these notions prove suspect.

(1991: 60)

Nichols outlines a number of forms of reflexivity, which can easily be grouped as a
continuum between 'formal reflexivity' and 'political reflexivity'. Formal or stylistic
reflexivity involves employing documentary aesthetics for an ambivalent commentary on the form, creating an awareness of the constructed nature of documentary
filmmaking, including the significance of the mediating role of the filmmaker herself.
Political reflexivity entails a more explicit attack on the underlying premises of the
genre and its associated 'sober discourses' (Nichols 1991: 5), calling into question the
integrity of the image itself or at least our common-sensical belief in the ability of the
camera to accurately and objectively document the social-historical world. In more
detailed and sustained attacks, this can involve the 'revealing' of documentary as
simply another constructed fiction. The distinctions between formal and political
reflexivity rest partly on their differing ways of inflecting documentary modes, and
partly in their interpretation by *audiences*. An instance of formal reflexivity may in
certain circumstances also be politically reflexive. (In fact, it is possible for there to be
unintentional reflexivity; for a reflexive moment to be associated with a text whether
or not that has been the intention of the filmmakers themselves.) Nichols speculates
that the arrival of the reflexive mode in documentary entails a 'maturation of the
genre', with the incorporation of traditions of satire, parody and irony from fiction.
The overlap with mockumentary here is obvious.[7]

Audiences: modes of reading mockumentary

The third part of a definition of mockumentary discourse centres on the encounter
between audience and text. Harries argues, in relation to the reception of parodic
texts, that:

Not only do parodies create 'something' (new textual configurations as well
as modifications to pre-existing canons), they also foster 'ways' to view texts,
developing and nurturing *critical* spectatorial strategies. While parody does
indeed rely on and cannibalize other texts, its reworkings affect not only the
viewing of previous textual systems but also the construction and viewing of
future related canonical texts.

(2000: 7)

The range of viewer readings of a parodic text can include: those who do not
recognize the target and therefore do not realize a text is a parody; viewers who
realize a text is parody but do not recognize the exact references which are made;
those who recognize the intent and the target but do not appreciate the nature of the
irony which is created; and the group of viewers who are able to fully enjoy the ironic
position which is created in relation to the targeted text (citing Rose, Harries 2000:
108). Mockumentary complicates these positions still further by playing with a

documentary mode of reading, drawing in particular on what Sobchack calls the 'charge of the real', or those core assumptions viewers have of footage which is assumed to be indexical to reality:

> The charge of the real is always an *ethical charge*: one that calls forth not only response but responsibility – not only aesthetic valuation but also ethical judgement. It engages our awareness not only of the existential consequences *of* representation but also of our own ethical implication *in* representation. It remands us reflexively to ourselves as embodied, culturally knowledgeable, and social invested viewers.
>
> (Sobchack 2004: 284)

Mockumentary discourse deliberately engages with documentary's rhetorical address to its audience, incorporating this within particularly the novelty, promotional, dramatic and comedic agendas outlined above. In effect, the most crucial transformation of documentary practice performed by mockumentary is to change documentary's call to action into a *call to play*.

Such texts necessarily entail a number of challenges to audiences. More political reflexive examples (*David Holzman's Diary* or *C'est arrivé près de chez vous* (*Man Bites Dog*)) invite viewers to call their fundamental socio-political assumptions and expectations about factual discourses into play.[8] In more general terms, mockumentaries involve greater work on the part of viewers in identifying the ontological status of a given text, and hence the modes of reading which should be adopted in approaching it. Students, for example, often ask whether a documentary such as *American Movie: The Making of Northwestern* (US, 1999) is in fact a mockumentary. It takes a parodic perspective on its subject, and seems to move beyond the rational, empathetic perspective typically adopted by filmmakers towards participants in a documentary. Other documentary examples such as *Cane Toads* (Australia, 1988) and *The Natural History of the Chicken* (US, 2000), which feature comedic sequences, challenge any boundaries that we might establish between reflexive documentary and mockumentary, precisely because they complicate the task for audiences in identifying the status and intent of their constructions.

On the other hand, this also suggests something of the pleasures to be had with engaging with mockumentary discourse. Audiences can enjoy the references to documentary and associated forms; the specific nature of the parodic or satiric stance towards a targeted textual form or cultural discourse, and the sociopolitical commentary which may result; or audiences can choose to simply engage with a mockumentary at a narrative level. As noted above, the best mockumentaries (such as *This is Spinal Tap*) allow for a variety of forms of engagement, effectively encouraging audiences to make repeated viewings in order to add layers of appreciation to their reading of a text.

The degree to which such a text is reflexive towards its intended targets and/or non-fiction forms as a whole is clearly dependent upon both immediate and wider contextual factors shaping an audience's encounter with that text. The New Zealand television mockumentary *Forgotten Silver* (1995), for example, was intended to be recognized as a mockumentary by audiences while they were actually viewing its initial broadcast. A combination of the sophistication of its extra-textual framing and textual constructions, including its appeal to New Zealand national identities and historical narratives, meant that many local audiences only realized it was fictional some time after their viewing. The sense of surprise and even outrage of some viewers at being tricked triggered for many a heightened sense of reflexivity towards the factual forms which the programme mimicked so effectively (Hight and Roscoe 2006).

A key issue here is whether or not a text clearly 'flags' its status as a fictional text, and the extent to which audiences are able to recognize these cues and begin to engage in a mockumentary frame of reading. As suggested above, this form of text perhaps demands a greater sense of critical and contextual awareness and engagement on the part of audiences. A consequent issue is whether the increasing popularity of mockumentary discourse suggests that it might be perfectly suited to wider trends towards such textual complexity within contemporary culture (Johnson 2005). Certainly the complexity of modes of reading mockumentary is enhanced by the layered forms of experience provided by many digital media, and by the fractured experience of reading a text across different media platforms. Cross-platform mockumentary allows a text to appear in different forms across a number of media, complicating audiences, engagement with a single fictional premise, but also effectively increasing the possibilities for these audiences to engage with a mockumentary's call to play at a number of levels.

The cross-platform template can be partly traced, once again, to the archetypal mockumentary feature film, *This is Spinal Tap*. The film's producers have exploited new platforms to allow audiences to continue to engage in the film's fiction, and in particular more actively participate in the musical career of the (fictional) band Spinal Tap. A promotional website[9] allowed for the distribution of CDs of the fictional band's music, included a fictional discography created for the band by the film's distribution company and the band's real-life touring schedule – allowing audiences to adopt the ontologically playful role of real fans who attend actual concerts by the fake band. The special edition version of the film's DVD release also provides a model for other filmmakers; the audio commentary for the film includes the main actors in character, discussing the making of the text as if it actually was a documentary. A much more consistent and deliberate example of a cross-platform mockumentary text, however, can be seen in *The Blair Witch Project*.

The Blair Witch Project

The feature film itself [10] needs little introduction. It famously begins with a full-screen caption stating:

> In October of 1994, three student filmmakers disappeared in the woods near Burkittsville, Maryland, while shooting a documentary called '*The Blair Witch Project*'. A year later their footage was found.

The remainder of the film consists of what appears to be an edited narrative combining 16mm film footage from the unfinished documentary by the three filmmakers, and video footage for an intended 'making of' documentary on the process of their filmmaking. The ending of the film appears to suggest (without actually showing) the murder of the three by supernatural forces. As with many mockumentaries, the film was produced using an improvisational production technique with the cast taken out into the woods and apparently subjected to a horror version of improvisation where they did not know what the producers were going to frighten them with next (McDowell 2001).

As is well documented elsewhere, the film benefited from one of the more successful publicity campaigns conducted by an American studio, and included such novel details as 'missing' posters for the three filmmakers and the original Internet Movie Database listing which suggested that the lead actors (Heather Donahue, Joshua Leonard and Michael Williams) were dead (Rickard 1999: 37). Another mockumentary, *Curse of the Blair Witch*, aired on the Sci Fi Channel two days before the film opened (12 July 1999) providing a detailed history of the Blair Witch and including footage from the film. Effectively an extended trailer for the film's release, it used an expositional format (the original format intended for the film itself) combining excerpts from the students' 'lost' reels of film, interviews with their family and friends and with folklore experts.

A key part of the promotional campaign was a website set up in June 1998 (Roscoe 2000: 4), which included sections offering a timeline of historical events in the Blair Witch mythology and biographical details on 'the filmmakers'. On April Fool's Day, 1998, the website was relaunched to include additional documents of their disappearance including photos, audio from the DAT tapes used by the students, images and quotes from Heather's journal, and segments of the film supposedly shot by them (Castonguay 2004: 74). There were also a number of apparent fan sites praising the film, and there is some uncertainty over whether Haxan studios crafted these as part of its campaign, or whether directors Daniel Myrick and Eduardo Sánchez recognized very early on the promotional possibilities that these online 'word of mouth' testimonials offered (Roscoe 2000).

The television mockumentary and apparent wealth of online discussion helped to generate audiences' initial expectations that the film was an actual documentary. In reference to the website, Telotte argues that it worked to 'frame the film narrative within a context designed to condition our viewing or "reading" of it, even to determine the sort of pleasures we might derive from it' (Telotte 2004: 38). Schreier has conducted research into the variety of newsgroup discussion which were generated by the film's audience, and offers a familiar taxonomy of audience responses:

> First of all, there are those who know perfectly well that the film is fiction; they watch it as a horror film and evaluate it according to the standards of the genre. A second group of viewers also realizes that the film is a fiction; yet they appreciate the film's special status as a hybrid and enjoy the oscillation between fact and fiction that it provides. And a third group of viewers, while eventually coming to realize the film's fictionality, are nevertheless temporarily confused as to its ontology.
>
> (Schreier 2004: 331)

Although *Blair Witch* is primarily couched within the conventional narrative of horror films, it is saturated in the contrasting aesthetics of both film documentary and television documentary hybrids. (If the film was in fact a documentary, it would be classified as a highly reflexive example of the genre; the students' footage runs like a training film on how to make a documentary.) The contrast between the attempted rationality and distance of a 'professional' filmmaking stance, and the more intimate, informal and confessional nature of the hand-held video sequences is paralleled by the increasing tensions between the characters themselves. These tensions are suggestive of wider contestations between systems of knowledge, with the students' attempts to maintain a sober and 'objective' stance towards their subject eventually giving way to a more desperately emotional attempt to make sense of events and forces which appear to be outside of scientific knowledge.

Both the film and the wider fiction which is offered in much greater detail in the television mockumentary, website and various print materials which closely followed offered a variety of forms of evidence for audiences to explore. A key aspect of all of these texts is their withholding of a definitive conclusion about the disappearance of the three students, a denial of closure to their collective narrative. The film itself partly offers the pleasures of a detective story, but one in which a final revelation is deferred, while the other texts provide a wealth of further evidence to explore. This collective of *Blair Witch* texts encourages audiences to explore this evidence through the various pathways provided by the website, and the narratives of the film and television texts. The DVD, in fact, provides for more pathways through this material by both grouping these texts together (including providing links to online material) and allowing easy access to the chapters of the two audio-visual texts.

Walker refers to the variety of *Blair Witch* texts, including the series of wider associated texts (such as fan sites, discussion groups and the wealth of short film parodies inspired by the film[11]), as a 'metatext'. In Walker's terms, these should be viewed as collectively offering:

> a complex interweaving of at least three levels of narrative 'reality' (the film itself, the auxiliary fictional texts, the production and reception history of the film), each furthered fragmented by multiple perspectives, none of which can claim authority or primacy. There is no center and no predetermined point of entry. It is a heteroglossic space, a multimedia version of collaborative hypertext.
>
> (Walker 2004: 166)

The Blair Witch Project, in other words, is a cross-platform mockumentary allowing for multiple senses of the word 'play'. Audiences are encouraged to engage with the various forms of evidence offered about the disappearance of the three student filmmakers, to participate in the playful speculations concerning the status of this evidence and 'what it all means', and to even contribute to the wider metatext initiated by the film by demonstrating their appreciation of the original fiction through their own filmmaking practice.

None of this is to deny the limited nature of the manner in which audiences are positioned within this metatext. The forms of interaction allowed by Haxan and the film's directors are essentially engagement with a closed system (Brooker and Jermyn 2003: 326). The pathways through this system are tightly prescribed, and, in fact, in order to actively participate (through discussion and creative practice), audiences need to go outside the closed world which is provided. There were no links, for example, from the official website to the variety of parody websites, or newsgroups which offered detailed assessment of the *Blair Witch* evidence. Telotte argues that ultimately the website in fact did little more than construct an ongoing relationship for audiences within the marketing agenda of Haxan studio.

Currently the overwhelming tendency for mockumentaries is to have an audio-visual text as the primary text, with any online presence clearly intended to be a secondary or supporting text. Many mockumentaries have promotional sites which to varying degrees 'flag' the status of the film or television programme as fictional texts. Others serve different agendas in different parts of a site, just as mockumentaries will include cast listings in the credits, so websites will both continue the fiction while also including biographical details of the key actors. *The Office*'s BBC website, for example, provides background information on key production members and actors, but also has materials that are 'in-character' for the series (such as interviews with 'David Brent').[12] The possibilities for 'play' here are quite limited, and the sense is of an effort to simply archive memorabilia for a mockumentary text in the same manner as DVDs, or to continue the largely passive forms of interaction allowed through television broadcasting (a pattern followed by the webisodes which accompany the US version of the series).

The potential for cross-platform mockumentary, however, is perhaps much greater than that suggested by *The Blair Witch Project* or similar metatexts.[13] Telotte acknowledges the possibilities here, employing Janet Murray's terms of immersion, agency and transformation (Murray 2000) in discussing the potential the film suggests for digital forms of narrative (Telotte 2004). (Immersion refers to a form of engagement where the viewer is taken out of their immediate context and brought into the realm of a digital fiction, agency refers to the ability to feel as if we are participating in the fiction, and transformation the potential to 'role-play' characters within that fiction.) The template for narrative interaction provided by key genres within games media offers a useful comparison here: 'For the purposes of talking about videogames, the "back-story" is the diachronic story, and the story that happens in the fictional present is the synchronic story – an ongoing narrative constituted by the player's actions and decisions in real-time' (Poole 2000: 106). The closeness of this description to the metatext of *Blair Witch* suggest the possible development of linkages between the forms of (reflexive) play generated by mockumentary discourse and wider gaming cultures. The website, television mockumentary and print materials can be seen to offer the 'back-story' of the *Blair Witch* narrative, while the film itself offers the immediacy of a verité journey through one part of this wider narrative. The levels of 'interaction' with this fiction are obviously considerably more limited than those possible within games media. A more games-oriented version of *Blair Witch*, for example, might have featured direct participation by allowing users to role-play an investigative team looking to solve the mystery of the students' disappearance.

There is enough in *Blair Witch* and other more incomplete and tentative experiments in cross-platform texts to suggest the potential of mockumentary discourse to inspire new forms of cyberdrama. While none of these examples currently provide a detailed digital archive of the sort suggested by Murray's definition of a hyperserial (2000: 253–8), as cinematic, televisual, online and mobile forms converge across digital platforms, there is an increasing means to generate further mockumentary 'metatexts', offering audiences multiple forms of play with the institutional forms and discourses of the fact–fiction continuum.

Notes

1 'Documentary hybrids' is a term that has been applied within academia to fact–fiction forms associated with the documentary genre.
2 The discussions in this chapter are part of ideas developed in Hight (forthcoming), which is a revision and extension of ideas presented in Roscoe and Hight (2001).
3 These are invariably flagged to audiences, either through the absurdity of content, the placement of such stories within a news bulletin, or simply by news announcers reminding their audiences of the date.
4 See Roscoe and Hight (2001: 134–8).
5 There is also a clear overlap here with some forms of drama-documentary which appropriate documentary codes and conventions. (Note that this is in contrast to this author's earlier definition of mockumentary which insisted upon a strict distinction between these two hybrids, see Roscoe and Hight (2001: Chapter 3).)
6 See Roscoe and Hight (2001), especially Chapters 6 and 7.
7 In fact, Nichols, and other writers such as Ruby (1977), tend to conflate the distinction between fictional and non-fictional reflexive texts. What this suggests is the potential for mockumentary discourse to range across both fact and fiction. This contrasts with this author's earlier argument (see Roscoe and Hight 2001: 32–5) that reflexive documentary is the (factual) counterpart to (fictional) mockumentary.
8 See Juhasz and Lerner (2006) for detailed discussions of the subversive uses of mockumentary by avant-garde and experimental filmmakers.
9 The original site has evolved to a fan site: http://www.spinaltapfan.com/.
10 For a detailed history of the film and its reception, see the introduction to Higley and Weinstock (2004), and Roscoe (2000).
11 See Castonguay (2004: 69).
12 See http://www.bbc.co.uk/comedy/theoffice/
13 Such as for the film *Nothing So Strange* (2002). See http://www.macarthurpark.com and its links page.

19 Documentary Modes of Engagement

Annette Hill

One of the most distinctive aspects of documentary studies has been the attention given to documentary modes of representation. In his analysis of such modes Bill Nichols refers to a 'constituency of viewers', asking the question: 'what are the assumptions and expectations that characterise the viewing of a documentary?' (1991: 24). He argues that just as there are documentary modes of representation, there is also a 'documentary mode of engagement for the viewer' (1991: 25). Modes of representation and engagement are connected as audience responses to documentary form part of the socio-cultural contexts of production. Rather than focus on representation, I want to address the under-explored issue of documentary modes of engagement. By using quantitative and qualitative research, we can see what viewers have to say about their various documentary experiences. In this article, the focus is on British television audiences and their responses to contemporary television documentary.

In contemporary television documentary has become increasingly stylized, drawing on hybrid formats, popularizing documentary for peak-time schedules, mixing fact and fiction in a variety of documentary modes. The large range of documentaries, including investigative journalism, specialist documentaries on history or science, observational documentary, and docudrama, makes it difficult for viewers to adopt a single mode of engagement. The various stylistic techniques used within different types of documentary, such as the interview, eye witness testimony, caught-on-camera footage, and reconstructions, also add to the ambiguity associated with documentary. Viewers' experiences of documentaries are drawn from their broad understanding and critical engagement with the changes taking place in factuality. It is in this fast-paced factual environment that modes of engagement take shape. Audience research highlights multiple modes of engagement with an ever expanding range of documentaries. Indeed, not only do audiences respond to various documentary modes in different ways, but they respond to the mix of styles within one documentary in multiple ways. Viewers have to be fast on their feet if they are to respond to the changing nature of documentary.

Documentary in Britain

As Jason Mittell has argued, television genres are constructed through production and reception processes (2004). Programme makers draw on production traditions, referring to previous practices to construct a documentary similar to, or a variation on, another type of documentary; and audiences draw on their knowledge of previous documentaries to recognize it as a distinctive genre. Thus, it is within the context of documentary television in Britain that culturally specific responses can be understood. Indeed, what is understood as documentary in one country can be quite different to the classification of documentary in another country with different production contexts and traditions. For example, in Sweden, there are two general types of documentary, those made in Sweden and those imported from abroad. Imported documentaries are mainly shown on commercial channels and audiences perceive them as 'tabloid'. Thus, a documentary such as *The Boy Whose Skin Fell Off* (Channel 4, UK) which won awards in Britain was perceived in very different ways in Sweden within the context of imported documentaries on commercial channels. The first thing we can say about documentary audiences is therefore that there is no one type of viewer, but many types of viewers who have culturally specific responses to particular kinds of documentaries.

Briefly, the general production context of documentary television in Britain is grounded in the long-established and dominant role of public service broadcasting. The BBC has been the most significant broadcasting institution in Britain since the beginning of radio and television. It has a remit to inform, educate and entertain the public, and is the largest provider of documentary. The other major player is the commercial channel ITV. Although it has an entertainment focus, British regulation ensures that ITV produces news and factual programming in peaktime schedules. Channel 4, first broadcast in the 1980s, is a public/private hybrid with a remit that ensures some documentary provision. The newest main channel Five has an entertainment focus, but also devotes peaktime hours to documentary. The key point is that British viewers have for a long time associated the main television channels, both public service and commercial, with homegrown documentary production. They have also come to expect a variety of documentaries in peaktime schedules.

The five main channels in Britain are no longer alone in their competition for audiences. Multichannel television has grown significantly since the 1990s. In 2006, 70 per cent of the British population had access to multi-channel television, and during a weekday profile of 23 million viewers the market share for multi-channel television rivalled that of the main five channels (Ofcom 2006). Rather than wither on the vine, factual programming as a whole has survived well in this competitive environment. The impact of increased commercialization in British factual production has been that news has remained consistent in the schedules, but there has been a growth in other kinds of factual, in particular popular factual. News can briefly be defined as flagship productions, providing the main source of public information, current affairs encompasses long form journalism, political debate, consumer-based stories, and investigative journalism. Popular factual, also known as factual entertainment or reality TV, is a broad category for a variety of one-off programmes, series and formats that follow real people and their everyday or out-of-the-ordinary experiences. A survey by Dover and Barnett showed a consistently strong news output for the main channels, with the number of hours of news maintained across a 50-year period (approx 15 per cent in peaktime). The same survey indicated an increase in documentaries and popular factual, and a decrease in current affairs on the main channels over the past decade (Dover and Barnett 2004). In a report by the regulatory body the Office of Communications on British television in 2005, general factual (meaning all factual content that was not news or current affairs) was the largest growth genre. Across all five channels there were more hours devoted to general factual content in peaktime than drama.

The documentary audience is one that can choose from a range of factual programming from 6.30 to 10.30pm. However, a quick look at the top ten factual programmes in 2006 showed that certain kinds of documentary attracted large audience shares (*Broadcast*, figures compiled from BARB). The big budget David Attenborough natural history documentary series *Planet Earth* on BBC was number one with 9.4 million viewers (33 per cent share). The next highest rated documentary was the BBC programme *9/11: The Twin Towers* at number seven on the list (6.44 million viewers and a 30 per cent share). Outside the top ten, other channels did well with popular documentaries such as *Ladette to Lady* (5.4 million, ITV), *Half Ton Man* (5.1 million, Channel 4), and Five's highest rated documentary *The Seven Year Old Surgeon* (2.9 million). The fact that these documentaries are at the populist end of the scale – *Ladette to Lady* could equally be called formatted factual entertainment – highlights the trend in what one viewer called 'shockumentaries'. To reinforce the impact of reality TV on factual trends as a whole, number two in the top ten was the reality gameshow *Big Brother* with 7.73 million viewers (39 per cent share).

The audience research is based on surveys and focus groups. The survey used programme categories in order to gather information on viewing preferences and attitudes. As a result of selective genre, scheduling and ratings analysis for documentary, the following categories were chosen to represent the broadest range available to viewers. There are specialist documentaries in history or science, and natural history documentaries. General documentaries can either be a strand, or stand-alone documentaries on any number of topics. There are observational documentaries, either as singles, or as series, some of which are called docusoaps. There are investigative documentaries, which share common ground with current affairs. Similarly, reconstruction programmes may be part of documentary; these involve the use of closed circuit television or home-video footage and/or the dramatic reconstruction of recent events – typically accidents and crime-related incidents 'caught on camera'. There are other types of documentary missing from this group, and this was addressed by opening up the range of programme titles in the qualitative research. For example, arts documentary was not part of the survey but was discussed by a minority of participants. Similarly documentary films such as *Super Size Me* (US, 2004) had been shown on television and were discussed in the qualitative research.

Based on a representative sample of British viewers (4,516 people aged 16–65+), the viewing preferences for documentary show that a large proportion of the population watch this kind of television on a regular or occasional basis. Table 19.1 shows two-thirds of the sample watched documentaries at least sometimes (65 per cent). If we break down documentary into selected modes of representation, then natural history stands out as a type of documentary that appeals to general audiences, also reinforced by its number one position in the top factual programmes of 2006. The other specialist documentaries for history and science attract quite a different viewing profile. More males, in an older age group, and a higher socio-economic status watched history/science documentaries. For example, 51 per cent of 16–24-year-olds watched these documentaries compared to 71 per cent of people aged 55–64. The highest numbers of people who never watched history/science documentaries were younger people from a lower socio-economic status – 44 per cent of 16–24-year-olds, and 37 per cent of lower working-class groups never watched these documentaries. If we compare specialist with observational documentaries, then there is a slightly more female, lower socio-economic profile for this type. General documentaries, undercover investigations and CCTV/reconstructions are less popular than the other more traditional documentaries and attract a mixed audience overall.

There are several points to be drawn from the viewing profiles for documentaries. The comment by Brian Winston that documentary has traditionally been for elite audiences holds true for history and science documentaries (2000). The typical viewer is older, male, and well educated. Interestingly, the people who never watch reality TV are also from a similar group of viewers. For example 64, per cent of people aged 55–64 were reality refusniks. As Winston foretold, the popularity of docusoaps would have a significant impact on documentary. This impact can be seen in the different types of viewers watching, not only documentary, but other kinds of factual and reality programming as a whole. The impact is also visible in the distinction made between different kinds of documentaries, where the long-standing popularity of natural history documentary makes it an all-round entertainer, whereas history and science are the domain of elite audiences. There is another element to the impact of popular factual programming on documentary and that is the use of different stylistic techniques within all documentaries. An awareness of stylistic changes within documentary and factual programming is something that all viewers share, regardless of their age or socio-economic status. These general attitudes towards documentary highlight how viewers may watch different types of programming but they share a general understanding of trends in television.

Table 19.1 Regular/occasional viewers of documentaries (per cent watch at least sometimes)

Type	Total sample	Males	Females	16–24	55–64	Upper middle class	Lower working class
Natural history	70	73	65	60	73	73	64
History/science	64	73	57	51	71	77	56
General documentaries	59	57	62	56	58	64	62
Observational documentaries	64	59	67	65	65	58	66
Undercover investigations	44	48	44	48	43	38	49
CCTV/ Reconstructions	53	52	56	58	53	44	56

Note: Unweighted sample 4,516.

Documentary styles

The public service broadcasting remit includes programming that is informative, educational and entertaining. Much discussion in media studies has focused on the public knowledge project of public service broadcasting, especially around the provision of factual programming that can inform and educate the audience (see Corner 1999). There has also been debate about popular culture, and the role of television as an entertainer (see Hartley 1999). These two apparently simple terms of information and entertainment are loaded with ideological baggage. From the viewer's perspective, to classify a documentary as informative, or entertaining, or both, also carries further meaning in terms of their broader understanding of public service and commercial broadcasting in Britain, and current trends in factual and reality television.

Table 19.2 outlines the classification of selected documentaries according to the categories of information and entertainment. When audiences define factual television, they tend to use the term information to sum up the knowledge-providing role of genres such as documentary. As we shall see later in this chapter, the terms information and entertainment are deceptively simple as they carry a range of value judgements. Comparing the data with that outlined in Table 19.1, we can see that the separation of history/science is also apparent in the way these respondents classify documentary according to how informative it is perceived to be. These specialist documentaries are the most informative of all the types listed. The high number of people who thought natural history was a mixture of information and entertainment suggests an awareness of the popularity of this genre, and also the spectacular styles so common to blockbuster series such as *Planet Earth* (BBC1, 5/03/06–10/12/06). Similarly, the classification of observational documentary as mainly informative and entertaining, or entertaining, shows awareness of the hybridization of this genre and the success of docusoaps, which draw on an observational style of documentary while also using narrative techniques from soap opera. Many viewers referred to long-running docusoaps such as *Airport* (BBC1) as a form of popular documentary which contained 'characters' who would 'act up' for the cameras. The close association of this form of documentary with the more popular factual style of CCTV/ reconstruction programmes further emphasizes the entertainment frame for these kinds of documentary.

Corner calls docusoaps and reconstruction-style programming 'documentary as diversion' (2002). This is all too apparent to audiences who are critically engaged with the stylistic changes taking place within documentary. In the focus group discussions, many viewers discussed their awareness of documentary as a changing, highly stylized genre. For example, this viewer criticized the formatting of documentary: 'We've got mass market documentary formats, *Life of Mammals, Walking with Cavemen, What the Victorians Did for Us,* and that is basically dumbed-down documentary, so it sort of treats you as if you're a bit of a muppet' (34-year-old male mobile phone consultant). The popularity of documentary is detrimental to its knowledge-providing role; it has 'dumbed down' to appeal to the lowest common denominator. Another viewer provided a more nuanced description of documentary. They too were critically aware of different representations within documentary, but they used the very same programmes criticized in the above quote as examples of 'heavyweight' documentaries:

> Documentary news programmes, the ones that go behind the scenes and they are said to be less biased, *Newsnight, Panorama, Horizon*. Then the sort of, what I'd call serious documentaries, *Mammals, Walking With Cavemen*, all of them are heavyweight documentaries. Then I've got a category of what I'd call special interest documentaries. You know, which I think people with a special interest watch, *Jamie's School Dinners, Gardeners World, Antiques Road Show*. And I put that one on the edge, you know, *Cosmetic Surgery Live*, that might be a serious documentary to some people, but it also to me is voyeurism.
>
> (34-year-old female teacher)

Table 19.2 Classification of documentary as informative and entertaining (%)

Type	Informative	Informative and entertaining	Entertaining
Natural history	24	59	4
History/science	33	50	3
General documentaries	27	37	14
Observational documentaries	8	44	31
Undercover investigations	26	29	13
CCTV/ Reconstructions	19	38	24

Note: Unweighted sample 4,516.

There are a wide range of representational modes that include news, serious documentaries, and special interest documentaries, which are defined not by the specialism of the documentary itself but by the interests of this viewer. Popular factual programming is also at the limits of the documentary genre, but included in this list because the viewer recognizes that her critical take on *Cosmetic Surgery Live* (Five, May 2004–) may differ from someone who will perceive it as something else. In fact, in all the discussions of *Cosmetic Surgery Live*, everyone agreed it was on the edge of factuality, signifying their uneasiness with such an extreme experiment in television.

These two examples emphasize the high degree of audiences' critical engagement with trends in documentary television. The connections between documentary and reality formats are explicitly made in order to underscore the degree to which documentary is changing. Another viewer commented: 'I wouldn't say, "Oh, that's a documentary I would like to see", probably because I would never guess so from the title. It's difficult to spot a classic documentary. It could easily be a reality show' (40-year-old female property developer). Here, reality TV masquerades as documentary, highlighting the cross-pollination of genres. The notion of masquerade is useful in that the term sums up a general understanding among viewers that documentary is made up of many parts, all of which involve some element of performance. Elsewhere I have commented on the relationship between authenticity and performance in reality television (Hill 2005). In more recent work, I analysed audience responses to the restyling of factuality, and one of the key points to emerge from the research was the performative turn in factual television as a whole (Hill 2007). Corner has addressed this in his discussion of the fictionality of factual television and the factuality of fictional television, pointing out that documentary sits at the borders between fact and fiction (Corner 2006). Corner's point is that documentary has reached a new level of stylization and that we should acknowledge this by addressing the cross-fertilization of documentary and drama, information and entertainment in factuality.

Table 19.3 Attitudes to truth claims and performance in documentary (mean, 100 = agree strongly, 0 = disagree strongly)

Type	Perception of documentary as true-to-life	Perception of performance in documentary
Natural history	77	34
History/science	74	37
General documentaries	64	56
Observational documentaries	62	65
Undercover investigations	63	52
CCTV/ Reconstructions	65	50

Note: Unweighted sample 4,516.

Table 19.3 outlines audience attitudes towards the truth claims made within selected documentaries. Respondents were asked how much they agreed with the statement that specific programme categories were 'true-to-life'. Table 19.3 also outlines audience attitudes towards levels of performance of people in selected documentaries. Respondents were asked how much they agreed with the statement that 'people acted up' in specific programme categories. The results provide more evidence of audience awareness of documentary styles. There is a clear difference between natural history and history/science documentaries and other kinds of documentary. The first point to make is that although natural history may be classified as a mixture of information and entertainment, it is still perceived as true-to-life. The entertaining elements within documentary do not necessarily mean viewers lose their trust in its truth claims. The viewer who classified series such as *Walking with Cavemen* as 'serious documentary' represents a general perception of these specialist documentaries.

The second point to make is that while the stylization of these documentaries does not get in the way of 'claiming the real', other trends in documentary do not fare so well. Observational documentaries are perceived by audiences as performative. Two-thirds of the sample thought observational documentaries were both true-to-life and contained high levels of performance. This apparent contradiction is symptomatic of the hybridization within observational documentaries, where audiences associate docusoaps with this type of television. There are thus at least two distinctive modes within audience understanding of observational documentary, that of its fly-on-the-wall camera style and also its use of larger-than-life characters. Kilborn's analysis of docusoaps in *Staging the Real* nicely encapsulates the representational modes within this hybrid genre (Kilborn 2003). He argues that docusoaps are a result of the cross-pollination of observational documentary and soap opera, thus mixing styles so that a docusoap follows people going about their everyday lives and at the same time dramatizes stories and characters. The data in Table 19.3 back up his point that both elements of fact and fiction are at work in this hybrid genre.

Comparison with CCTV/reconstruction shows indicate that there are subtle distinctions made between the use of dramatic techniques in specialist documentaries like *Walking with Cavemen*, or emergency services series like *999*, and those used in observational documentaries such as *Airport*. In the case of *999*, it uses actors in dramatized reconstructions of accidents. For viewers, this is different to the editing of ordinary people as larger-than-life characters in docusoaps. Once again, the apparent contradiction serves to highlight how the context within which documentary is watched is essential to the development of documentary experiences. *999* may use actors, but these actors are essentially re-telling a true story. Whereas long-running docusoaps are well known for their characters, some of whom have gone on to have media careers. What is more, high profile fakery scandals surrounding docusoaps such as *Driving School* also impact on viewers' evaluations. The obvious dramatization of stories in *Walking With …* or *999* actually work in their favour, as Ellis has suggested in his analysis of the impact of fakery scandals on documentary (Ellis 2000). The obvious artificiality of these dramatizations is easy for viewers to evaluate, whereas the perceived trickery of observational documentary is not obvious to see. Perhaps one of the most important points to make about documentary viewers is that they change their mode of enagement depending on their expectations about the documentary they are watching and the contexts of documentary production and reception practices. In this sense, there are multiple modes of engagement with documentaries, a topic explored further in the final section.

Multiple modes of engagement

Corner argues that a documentary aesthetics takes its bearings from 'inside the documentary experience, with its distinctive mix of objective and subjective dynamics' (2005: 56). The value of documentary aesthetics, and analysis of the pictorial, aural and narratological aspects of documentary, lies in a 'reflexive commentary on some of the most important things to be explained' (2005: 56).

The mix of objective and subjective dynamics is described as 'looking at' and 'looking through' (2005: 54). Corner draws on research in visual arts to differentiate between first-order observation (looking at something), and second-order observation (looking through something). Looking through involves a reflexive mode of engagement. It is observation of ourselves experiencing something; through second-order observation we can transform the experience, taking it to an 'imaginary space' without losing touch with what is real about the experience to begin with (2005: 52). For Corner, documentary is concerned with the dialectics of 'referential integrity' and 'aesthetic value'. This creates a documentary experience 'at once sensual and intellectual, referentially committed yet often possessed of a dream-like quality for the indirectly suggestive and associative' (2005: 53). The 'intermittent aesthetics' of production design can have a 'cueing function', and so the different ways of looking at documentary as real and associative respond to the different aesthetics common to documentary production (2005: 54).

In order to trust documentary's truth claims, most viewers have to suspend disbelief and foreground its referential integrity. For example, this viewer explained, 'Documentaries are an illusion, but ... you don't notice it too much' (30-year-old male gardener). Or, as this 25-year-old female student commented: 'I think if you watch documentary, you kind of put yourself in a kind of ignorant point of view, you know, you kind of believe in the documentary.' She takes an 'ignorant point of view' in order to immerse herself in the referential integrity of the genre. Ellis suggests there is a soft boundary between fact and fiction, where documentary invites 'two distinct regimes of response: those of the factual "our world" and those of fiction "a parallel world"'(2005: 351). Viewers 'understand they fiddle a bit to make a good documentary' but what is vital is that 'it still feels like a real situation' (26-year-old male student).

These two perspectives on documentary underscore a double mode of engagement, drawing on objective and subjective responses. The idea that 'documentaries are an illusion, but you don't notice it too much' encapsulates the sense of the documentary experience as sensual and intellectual. It also highlights the idea of two worlds, the one we know and the one that is represented for us in documentary. If we consider one of the fundamental aspects of documentary which is that it tells us something about the world, then the double mode of engagement acts as a two-stage process in the documentary experience. For Nichols (2001: 40), 'documentaries invoke a desire-to-know' (epistephilia). When we watch documentary 'we bring an assumption that the texts, sounds, and images have their origin in the historical world we share', we expect documentaries to have an 'indexical relationship to the events they represent' (2001: 35). But at the same time, we understand that the evidence used in a documentary has been re-presented to us, 'that the film as a whole will stand back from being a pure document or transcription of these events to make a comment on them, or to offer a perspective on them' (2001: 38). This viewer comments on the 'desire to know' function of documentary. The interviewer asks what he can learn from documentary and he replies: 'How ants fuck [laughter] ... I mean, you wouldn't know that, would you? I mean, it's just great' (30-year-old male gardener). The playful way he responds to the comment shows his awareness that documentaries can tell us about the most unusual things, and he takes delight in knowing documentaries have this encyclopedic function. This viewer is the same person who said that 'documentaries are an illusion'. He perfectly illustrates the two-stage process where viewers draw on the referential integrity and the aesthetic value of documentary at the same time.

When we consider the referential integrity of a documentary alongside our response to the aesthetic values, there are also other responses to take into account, such as emotional responses, or psychodynamic responses. In *Being a Character* (1993), Christopher Bollas considers the relationship between psychoanalysis and self-experience. He argues that the psychodynamic process involves a double mode of engagement: 'The simple experiencing self and the complex reflecting self enable the person to process life according to different and yet interdependent modes of engagement: one immersive, the other reflective' (1993: 15). Bollas argues that these modes of engagement can happen during our conscious and unconscious experiences. Referring to the psychologist Winnicott, Bollas calls this 'intermediate space': 'the place where subject meets thing, to confer significance in the very moment that being is transformed by the object' (1993: 18). For example, when we encounter objects, some mean more to us than others; they might evoke previous experiences, connect with friends or family, or even become part of our dreams, so that the next time we see such an object it carries psychological baggage. The moment of transformation when the object is no longer just another object but is psychically connected to us is a moment when we enter intermediate space, both experiencing the moment and reflecting on what it means to us.

We can apply the idea of immersive and reflective modes of engagement to watching documentary. Prior to the experience of watching documentary, we have already collected generic material that will become part of how we experience a particular programme. After the viewing experience, we will consciously and unconsciously store generic content and experiences in a holding area, ready to be drawn on at certain moments in our lives.

Factual programmes are particularly rich areas of analysis for the more psychodynamic aspects of viewers' experiences because they occupy an intermediate space between fact and fiction. We can experience watching real events in a documentary and at the same time reflect on the authenticity of what we are watching. This is where the viewer participates in the constructed real world of the programme and also reflects on the nature of this real world and how it has been staged for us to watch. Being a factual viewer means taking on multiple roles, as witness and interpreter, and occupying multiple spaces, between fact and fiction.

What the psychodynamic approach offers is another level of interpretation of audience responses. Birgitta Höijer (1998: 176) explores how viewers identify genres, position themselves as an audience, and at the same time experience conflict or inconsistency in their responses. She argues that viewers live with these contradictions and that they 'are natural parts of our understanding of ourselves and the world' (1998: 179). A psychodynamic perspective provides a 'frame of reference for understanding basic dilemmatic aspects of audience reception and for understanding the different functions that different genres have for the audience' (1998: 174). The ambiguity and contradictions that have been so much a part of the empirical data here highlight how responses to documentary are part of our conscious and unconscious experiences. That people change their minds, and are not always sure what documentary is, or how to describe their experience of it, is a natural part of understanding documentary. The psychodynamic aspect of documentary experiences is only one part of the picture overall, and not necessarily the most important part, depending on the specific responses of viewers, but it is part of the complex picture that emerges from the audience research.

The idea of immersive and reflective modes of engagement as outlined by Bollas is similar to the two-stage process of the documentary experience as described above. We can look at this from an arts aesthetics perspective, a documentary theory perspective, or a psychodynamic perspective, all of which highlight the double role of the viewer in the documentary experience. Consider how viewers respond to *Jamie's School Dinners* (Channel 4, 2005). This was a four-part series where celebrity chef Jamie Oliver attempted to improve healthy eating in schools. This series was described by viewers as 'almost documentary', 'documentary-style reality TV', or as one memorably put it: 'a new style of documentary, kind of like *Big Brother* meets *Panorama*' (23-year-old male shop assistant). The following quotes are from a focus group discussion:

> I very easily put it into the documentary category. It's certainly not news, although it became news. It generated news, from results of the show, so that was actually interesting. It sort of fell upon itself. I would say, it's a documentary, and because we know Jamie Oliver, I'd give it a little bit of reality show on top of it.
>
> (31-year-old female assistant curator)

> I think it was really good, quite ground-breaking in some respects.
>
> (36-year-old female personal assistant)

> It did seem like one guy on a crusade to quite literally change the world, as it were, and certainly to change these children's worlds ... you know TV crossing over to real life and making a difference.
>
> (34-year-old female teacher)

> I don't know if he cares about what he did but he really has to prove that, you know this man is just chitty-chatty, not cockney, that got on people's nerves, that thing and then he did that programme about 15 [Oliver's restaurant] ... which kind of raised my eyebrows a bit and I thought there is more to this guy. So, when he did that, he really did blow me away, actually. You could see the real him and I think that we did, because, you know, to have that much passion for something that is such a good cause and feel so strongly about other people's children and about the development of our young people and the future of the country, I think, you know, you have to be a really firmly genuine decent person and that's what came across.
>
> (36-year-old female personal assistant)

> And how the politicians have actually taken note of the cause. I think it's an interesting thing. I hope it actually works.
>
> (39-year-old female library worker)

> It is working, because there are now various schemes across the country ...
> Politicians should be doing what he did and I think it really shows what
> politicians are.
>
> (34-year-old female teacher)

> It wasn't really reality TV as in, climb-the-wall kind of thing, it was more ... I
> found it was more a documentary.
>
> (33-year-old female business development executive)

> Yeah, I would say it was more of a documentary.
>
> (36-year-old female personal assistant)

These quotes highlight several significant aspects of the documentary experience.
First, there is the cultural specificity of this type of programming. The series is
addressing a particular problem in British education, the privatization of children's
school meals and the impact of this government policy on the health and well-being
of young children. Responses are therefore bound up with the reception of the series
in the wider public arena, both in terms of other people talking about it at work, or
with family and friends, and also the press and political responses to the series. The
culmination of these responses is the changes to government policy on children's
school meals.

Second, Oliver's drive to make a difference to something so important to many
viewers shows how the series had a powerful impact on the audience, transforming it
into something that goes beyond television – 'TV crossing over to real life and making
a difference'. This is television as part of the public knowledge project, not 'just
entertainment', but television for the public good. Thus, the broader context of
documentary as part of public service broadcasting in Britain becomes a framing
device for understanding the impact of this series. The fact that *Jamie's School Dinners*
attempted to make a difference to a critical issue in society makes it a 'groundbreaking' documentary. This series doesn't fit neatly into a recognizable documentary
mode. It has some connection with news as it was a topic of news stories; it has some
connection with current affairs as it was dealing with a topical social issue; it has
connections with reality TV in the focus on a celebrity, and the constructed nature of
the experiment to introduce healthy menus in schools. Nevertheless it is 'more of a
documentary' than any other category because of the perceived elements of *Jamie's
School Dinners* as television for the public good. These viewers situate the series within
a broader understanding of the changes taking place in factual television – it is a
hybrid of different styles, crossing boundaries between fact and fiction. And yet, at
the same time they also situate the series within their understanding of public service
broadcasting – a contemporary documentary for popular audiences. This apparent
contradiction is part of the multilayered responses to the series.

Third, the series is experienced as true-to-life. This is a contradictory response to
the mixture of performance and authenticity in the series. There is Jamie Oliver,
someone who these viewers are aware of from previous television series, his popular
cookbooks, advertising, and general appearances in the media. He is a celebrity chef,
and viewers are critically engaged with the construction of his celebrity status
through this kind of programme. Oliver's own production company makes *Jamie's*

School Dinners; these viewers may not know this detail but they are instinctively suspicious of his persona, 'chitty chatty', and the dangers of over-exposure, 'getting on people's nerves'. Thus, Oliver has to overcome the suspicions of viewers that this series is a star vehicle. He has to persuade them that he really cares about the state of children's school meals. Phrases like 'change the world', or 'he really did blow me away', emphasize his transformation from celebrity chef to crusading father. The comparison of Oliver, who is perceived as a 'genuine' and 'decent' person, with politicians, further underscores this transformation. In the series, politicians are shown to be artificial, more caring of their public image rather than the issue of healthy meals. Politicians and celebrities share a public stage, and Oliver could be accused of mixing both of these public personas in his agenda to use his celebrity status to change educational policies. It is partly because the series is perceived as 'more of a documentary', as part of the public knowledge project, that these viewers believe in the integrity of his actions, and the referential integrity of the documentary itself.

Overall, these quotes highlight the complexity and ambiguity that are part of documentary experiences. Viewers respond to documentary in objective and subjective ways. They are aware of the artificiality of documentary, that it is an 'illusion', but at the same time they expect it to document the world, to provide information on a variety of matters. Viewers are aware that documentary is part of wider changes taking place in the production of television, that there are new styles, hybrid genres, commercial pressures, that impact on their experience of documentary. And yet they hold onto an idealized notion that documentary can be informative, part of television as a public good. Viewers are both immersed in documentary and reflective of it, ensuring multiple modes of engagement with documentary and its wider role in society and culture.

Conclusion

There is a need to explore what audiences think about documentary and the various modes of representation that are part of this broad genre. Through looking at viewers' responses several issues emerge to open up our understanding of documentary experiences. Documentary modes of engagement are part of particular production ecologies. Genre expectations are dependent on production contexts, and what is commonly understood to be documentary in one country will not necessarily be the same in another. This means that there is a need to explore documentary audiences in different countries and cultures. The notion of a documentary audience does not capture the diversity of responses to different kinds of documentary around the world. The research analysed in this article captures a British documentary audience, and even here, there is a need to qualify this by taking into account the variation among the kinds of viewers who watch history documentaries and those who watch observational documentary. That the majority of viewers share general attitudes towards the changes taking place within factual television highlights how documentary is part of a shared, public understanding of public service and commercial television in Britain. Some of these attitudes may be similar to other viewers in other cultures, but some will inevitably be different, and it is this distinction that needs to be made in order for audience research to contribute to documentary studies.

Another issue to emerge is viewers' critical engagement with the impact of popular factual programming on documentary. The way viewers understand the relationship between different modes of representation within documentary, and more generally across factual television, highlights the degree to which documentary is changing. For viewers, there is no doubt documentary has become stylized, and that in considering their responses to documentary viewers have to also reflect on the cross-fertilization of documentary and drama, information and entertainment in factuality. In order to respond to the wide range of documentary and popular factual programming in television, viewers have to be flexible. Rather than one mode of engagement, there are multiple modes of engagement with documentaries.

There are various approaches to understanding these multiple modes. One approach is to use documentary theory to outline the double mode of engagement that encapsulates a common experience when watching documentary. This emphasizes the constructed nature of documentary and its 'claims to the real' at the same time as acknowledging that documentary is based on facts. Thus we have a fictional and real world sitting side by side, hence the often-used expression 'blurred boundaries' to capture the documentary experience. Another approach is to use arts criticism, where 'looking at' and 'looking through' are objective and subjective experiences for arts, and also documentary. Paintings may be two-dimensional objects but they can imply so much more in the aesthetics of the paintwork and emotions conveyed via the artwork as a whole. Although we experience documentary television by looking at it on a flat screen, we also look through it and around it, that is to say we experience documentary at a multidimensional level. The reference to objective and subjective experiences suggests another psychodynamic approach to documentary. The idea of a double mode of engagement extends to conscious and unconscious levels, where the viewer can be immersed in a documentary, and at times step back and reflect on this. This approach also highlights the inherent contradictions, ambiguities, and often unsaid or unacknowledged aspects of documentary experiences. All three approaches offer useful insights into understanding documentary audiences. The necessity of using ideas from different disciplines suggests that documentary is a rich site for analysis and that documentary audiences have much to offer in furthering knowledge of this changing genre.

A note on methods

The data referred to in this article are taken from a larger project on factual television audiences in Britain and Sweden (see Hill 2007). The data here are from the British study only. The research methods included an analysis of media content of a range of factual and reality programmes over a six-month period in 2003, and a scheduling and ratings analysis of a range of programmes during the same timeframe. This background analysis formed the basis for qualitative and quantitative audience research. A quantitative survey was conducted with a representative sample of 4,516 people. The sample included people aged 16–65+ living in Britain. There were 12 focus groups, with respondents aged 18–60. The recruitment method used was quota sampling and snowball sampling. The sample was based on the criteria of age (roughly split into two groups of 20–30-year-olds, and 40–60-year-olds), gender (even mix of male and female), socio-economic status (working and middle class, and educational levels from school to university). Occupations included unemployed, students, administrators, teachers, sales assistants, technicians, office workers, carers, artists, and retired people. Participants were from White British, British Asian, Black, and European (German, Greek, Norwegian, Polish) ethnic groups. This was not a feature of the focus group sample, but a result of the diversity of London where the groups took place. Questions were related to four themes concerning genre evaluation, truth claims, information, and ethics. This research received funding from the former regulatory bodies the Broadcasting Standards Commission and Independent Television Commission, now Ofcom.

20 'Ask the Fastidious Woman from Surbiton to Hand-wash the Underpants of the Aging Oldham Skinhead ...'
Why not *Wife Swap*?

Su Holmes and Deborah Jermyn

A foul-mouthed mum lets fly with a tirade of four-letter abuse in a furious bust-up in the new series of *Wife Swap*. Jobless Lucy Compton, 28, loses it on a boozy night with her 'new partner'. She tells prison officer Spike Cresswell, 47: 'You're boring, f*** off home'. . . . Lucy feels the heat in Spike's neat semi in Nottingham where the two children have early bedtimes and are punished regularly. She lets her own nit-infested kids swear at the neighbours.

(Nathan 2004)

The most subversive television for years.

(Aaronovitch 2003)

In the light of Sara Nathan's preview of the then forthcoming series of *Wife Swap*, published in *The Sun* newspaper in the summer of 2004, David Aaronovitch's assessment in *The Observer* seems surprising and arguably hard to defend. RDF Media's internationally successful format swaps two wives from different homes and families for two weeks, in order for them to experience one another's lifestyles and reflect on their own. With its attention to contrived conflict, the latest *Wife Swap*, according to Nathan, promises another cheaply-produced, sensationalist and voyeuristic look at the most vulgar and mundane aspects of 'ordinary' (and clearly working-class) lives. Yet Aaronovitch's (2003) review invokes *Wife Swap* as an example of how, 'sometimes television has the power to be really subversive and change our notions of who we are'. Such critical ebullience has often historically been associated with documentary, but seems conspicuously out of place when used in relation to its 'poor' contemporary cousin, popular factual programming. Is it possible that a reality TV series, a programme plucked from that most condemned and vilified of recent televisual forms (see Holmes and Jermyn 2004: 8–9), and so enticingly trailed by a tabloid newspaper, could lay claim to making a socially significant and potentially radical intervention in its participants' and viewers' lives?

In this chapter, we explore how *Wife Swap* lends itself to oppositional and ambivalent readings, offering up the promise of a thoughtful and provocative insight into contemporary gender roles and class identities in the context of what appears to be a cynical and deliberately incendiary manipulation of its participants. In doing so, we do not seek to mount an unqualified defence of reality TV (nor *Wife Swap*), but instead aim to extend the existing critical work which interrogates the innovation of the form, and its cultural, political and aesthetic implications. Indeed, in a discussion that is far from unequivocally enthusiastic about the political possibilities of the programme (and which largely maps out its *departure* from the documentary form), John Corner nevertheless ends with the brief qualification that 'by using real domestic settings and routines [*Wife Swap*] exposes some of the rhythms, tensions and contradictions of everyday living and indeed the structures of wealth, class and culture in ways not open to more conventional [documentary] treatments' (2006: 73). Drawing on episodes from the UK series 1, 2 and 3 (tx 2003–4),[1] it is precisely this potential we wish to explore.[2]

In 2001, Corner influentially theorized the emergence of a 'post-documentary culture' – less a context in which documentary was 'now finished', but one which was witnessing its 'relocation as a set of practices, forms and functions' (Corner 2001). As part of this context, Corner observed how documentary was often invoked as an idealized generic referent. If genres are constituted discursively, then generic labels are *always* to some extent evaluative (Mittell 2004) – something clearly suggested by the fact that while 'one industry source [says *Wife Swap*] ... is "Reality – salacious tabloid crap"', '*The New Statesman* described *Wife Swap* as "the most important documentary series of the decade"' (Robinson 2004: 18). Interestingly, in seeking to recruit families for the programme via a notice on the British Chess Federation's website, one *Wife Swap* researcher sought to bring gravitas to the programme (in a markedly middle-class space) by drawing on exactly the referent of documentary, describing it as '[looking] at family life in contemporary Britain *in a way no other documentary has done before* [our emphasis]' (Firouazabadi 2004). The malleable nature of generic categories here is evidently also functional for academics. Corner says that *Wife Swap* might be seen as involving 'game show competitors in a real-life setting' (2006: 72), while Helen Piper, in aiming to *challenge* the tendency to equate apparent fictionalization with trivialization, argues that we might better approach it as a form of 'improvised drama' (2004: 274). The implicit hierarchy of generic references here, improvised drama being 'above' the game show, is then reflected in the extent to which each author is willing to see *Wife Swap* as a valuable contribution to television factuality. Piper aims to suggest that assessing the programme through documentary criteria is inappropriate, not because it fails to provide material which might withstand such scrutiny, but because it 'obscur[es] the narrative innovations and potential use values of an entire new generation of television' (2004: 274).

It is not simply discourses of genre which are relevant here, however, but their intertwining with discourses of gender. In the debate surrounding the perceived relationship between popular factual programming and documentary, the terms of discussion have often been gendered – as mapped across the binaries of hard/soft, public/private, social/personal and objective/subjective. The positioning of documentary as a 'masculine' genre, especially in terms of its relations with the public sphere, is evident here, and this clearly builds on a longer history of the relationship between gender and genre. For example, even in 1999, in the Introduction to the collection *Feminism and Documentary,* Diane Waldman and Janet Walker described the relationship between feminism and documentary film as a 'mostly uncharted universe' (1999: 3), an absence which is considerably more evident where television documentary is concerned. In the UK context, work on television documentary has primarily, although not exclusively, (e.g. Bruzzi 2006), been undertaken by male authors. While this does not of course preclude a consideration of feminist concerns, studies of gender politics (at the level of production or representation) have hardly been prominent. At the same time, and despite the gendered contours of the debate, feminist work has not had an explicitly salient presence in the growth of work on reality TV[3] – although it has had some (van Zoonen 2001; Moorti and Ross 2004). Liesbet van Zoonen, for example, argues that reality TV has in part been both derided and controversial *because* of its flagrant disregard for the historical, gendered division of private/public realms. Its success proves (with a 'wider popularity' than feminism'):

> [T]hat the Bourgeois division between the public domain ... and the private with its own code of conduct is not widely appreciated, and has moreover lost its social functionality ... Television in general has contributed in a great many ways to disclosing the private realm hidden by Bourgeois mores. We discover on television what has been ever more invisible in the world around us, the private lives of ordinary people: initially mostly in the enacted fantasies of sitcom and soaps but currently in a variety of formats in which real life is shown.
>
> (2001: 671)

This seems especially resonant where *Wife Swap* is concerned: this is a programme which explicitly delights in peeping behind a once closed door, and positively revels in opening up a version of domestic life to public view. Series Producer Jenny Crowther recognizes this when she remarks that the programme satisfies a fundamental human nosiness:

> You know what happens in your own home, and how you run your own family, and how you treat your own kids and what your husband says to you and what you say to your husband, but you're never quite sure how it happens in other families.
>
> (Channel 4 DVD, *Wife Swap* Extra, 2004)

Tellingly, Crowther's imagined viewer here is evidently female. In fact, her comments suggest that the programme-makers may, however unconsciously, work with a primarily female audience in mind (and also indicate how 'nosiness' about the neighbours is enduringly believed to be a particularly 'female' preoccupation). Nevertheless, embedded in the curiosity she describes, and its fascination with the everyday, there lies the potential for a revealing and instructive reconsideration of the ramifications of the dichotomy between the public ('quality'/serious factual programming) vs private (tabloid and reality TV) spheres; one which doesn't situate the alleged 'feminization' of factual television or its shift of focus towards the 'private' as evidence of 'dumbing down', but rather as an *'opening up'*.

Keeping it in the family: Opening up the home in the 'formatted documentary'

There is clearly a long-standing relationship between the institution of television and the institution of the family (see Stratton and Ang 1994). At the level of representation, outside of advertising, 'the family', with its domestic, and thus gendered, associations, has predominantly been most visible on television in soaps, sitcoms and game shows. As already discussed, these genres have been invoked to position the generic status of reality TV (or to separate it from documentary) precisely because they are all seen as 'light', and are generally held in low critical esteem. Equally, the concerns of domesticity and family have also had a significant presence in popular factual programming.

In fact, *Wife Swap* can also be situated within a recent and wider turn of interest across television and the media towards the figure of 'the housewife'. This preoccupation can be seen as one of the consequences of the fallout of third-wave feminism and the media's effort to make sense of contemporary women's problematic 'choices' regarding marriage, motherhood and the workplace. For example, in discussing the hugely successful US drama *Desperate Housewives*, Anna Marie Bautista contextualizes its popularity by pointing to two similarly themed and highly successful reality TV shows from this period. She notes that in recent years:

> The popular media has been saturated with images of the housewife, most of them 'desperate' in some way or another: these include the housewives being compared and contrasted on the reality show *Wife Swap* as well as the trials of domesticity encountered by the hapless Jessica Simpson on *Newlyweds*.
>
> (2006: 156)

Similarly, Sharon Sharp notes the proliferation of programmes offering a 'feminine perspective on the domestic sphere and the contradictions of lived female experience' (2006: 119), again situating *Desperate Housewives* alongside reality programmes such as *How Clean is Your House?* (C4, 2003–) and *SuperNanny* (C4, 2004–), as evidence of 'the new fixation on the housewife and domesticity in televisual discourse' (2006: 119). In addition, in the UK one could point to programmes such as *Mum's on Strike* (ITV1, 2005–); *The House of Tiny Tearaways* (BBC3, 2005–) and *Anthea Turner: Perfect Housewife* (BBC3, 2006–) or history-hybrid shows such as *The 1900 House* (Channel 4, 1999), while the US has seen *A Wedding Story* and *A Baby Story* on TLC constitute 'the most successful cable programming line-up on American daytime television' (Stephens 2004: 191; see also Maher 2004).

Sharp's suggestion of a 'feminine perspective' is not unproblematic, however, as explored in relation to *Wife Swap's* ambivalent mediation of gender and class identities. But the domesticity of television has certainly encouraged a 'desire for intimacy' at the level of documentary subject matter (Kilborn and Izod 1997: 65), including particular adaptations of observational filmmaking which offer the sense of getting close to people's lives. It seems revealing that one of the clearest precursors to aspects of *Wife Swap* from a documentary heritage is the fly-on-the-wall series *The Family* (BBC1, 1974), which followed the lives of the working-class Wilkins family from Reading. Offering a degree of access or 'intimacy' which was unsurpassed on British television at that time, it is now regularly positioned – much to the chagrin of producer Paul Watson – as a precursor to the docusoap and the wider explosion of popular factuality. The interweaving and interlocking stories of the family, and particularly the focus on a series of different couples within it, offered recurrent glimpses into the organization of gender relations and domestic responsibilities in the domestic sphere.

The Family retained, however, a more deliberate desire to extrapolate the 'typical' from the particularistic base of the Wilkins family (and it was the suggestion of typicality which often prompted the moral outrage directed at the programme). In other words, *The Family*'s intentions as a social (documentary) project are constantly apparent. This has of course been foregrounded as a key marker of difference between popular factual programming and the heritage of documentary: the idea that the former has little to 'say' because of its pursuit of the personal, as well as the framing influence of the format, means that its discourse becomes 'literally self-sufficient, an action and a space ... detached from social project' (Corner 2006: 95). This de-valuing of the personal is itself a product of the historical dominance of patriarchal, bourgeois sensibilities. But even without this critique, it seems problematic to suggest that *Wife Swap* doesn't position itself as a 'social' project, or that this can only be signalled through a narrow range of textual strategies.

Wife Swap might be seen as offering a unique textual space by virtue *of*, rather than 'despite', its generic hybridity. Soap opera has been studied in terms of its blurring of public and private space, and appeal to a female audience 'whose own experience of the concepts of work and leisure are in a constant state of compromise' (Thumim 2002: 218). But soap operas, or other fictional forms for that matter, have arguably not trained such sustained attention on the politics of gender relations in the domestic sphere – nor could they. As Piper rightly observes: '[A] treatment that took seriously the domestic everyday conflicts of two nuclear families, would [n]ever make it further than a commissioning executive's wastepaper bin' (2004: 285). The fact that audiences are only too willing to watch this narrative indicates its different epistemological basis, and its investment in, and appeal to, the 'real'. At the same time, it also speaks to a television culture in which drama must be guaranteed in factuality as much as fiction. The 'dramatic moment' which emerged unexpectedly in the documentary is no longer enough – it has become an expectation – and the format emerges to meet this demand (Corner 2006: 91).

Wife Swap draws from observational documentary and the docusoap the claim to offer an often entertaining look into lives 'lived', while it also draws its premise from the formatted arenas of later reality programmes. These place the self under pressure in situations which have no existence outside of the staging of the pro-filmic event. Shoring up and manipulating his own terms of generic distinction, RDF Media's Stephen Lambert, executive producer of *Wife Swap*, rejects the label of 'reality

TV', and instead prefers the term 'formatted documentary' (Bruzzi 2006: 137). Lambert openly discusses *Wife Swap* (along with *Faking It*) as a response to the fact that in observational documentary:

> There was a difficulty in finding real life situations that have a beginning, middle and an end. The great attraction of a formatted documentary is that you can still use all those documentary skills to reveal character and bring out emotion, but you're guaranteed this structure.
>
> (cited in Hoggard 2003: 23)

The rather tautological term of the 'formatted documentary' is of course in itself an example of the idealization of documentary (is formatting only a more explicit dramatization of convention and construction?), although it is true that exactly what Lambert means by 'those documentary skills', and how they relate, apparently seamlessly, to the formatted framework, remains ambiguous here. The framing influence of the format is often equated with entertainment values, perhaps because its most immediate economic and cultural currency is to be found in the game show, while it is also associated with a loss of agency for both filmmakers and participants. But to equate the concept of the format with only trivialization and constraint is to efface what we want to suggest here are its *productive* possibilities.

'What will they learn about their own lives?': Constructing 'the swap' in *Wife Swap*

The voice-over to each edition explains how 'the two wives have agreed to swap homes and families for two weeks to see what they can learn about their own lives', posing various narrative enigmas along the way: for example, 'What's it like living with a traditional man?' (Deirdre and Margaret, series 3). In this regard it notably de-activates the game show referent, and sets itself up, as Piper also observes, as a 'collective process of "working through"' (2004: 275). From this point, the programme follows a set format in which the wives swap homes, and then live for one week under the rules of their 'new' family – as guided by the 'household manual' left by the absent wife. In week two, and on 'rule change' day, they get to intervene in the existing family routines, often making changes which better reflect their own family routines and ideals back home.

While the couples involved are overwhelmingly heterosexual, the programme-makers evidently seek to bring together contrasting couples in order to heighten tension and the dramatic nature of the swap. Their juxtaposition need not be embedded in class e.g. the Dee and Sonia episode, series one, where white (and avowedly racist) Dee swaps with black (and progressively-minded) Sonia. However, class *is* frequently the crux of the contrast. When the new wives and the viewers are invited into the homes, the *mise-en-scène* is loaded with clues about the lifestyle of the host family (Piper 2004: 276), and whether the camera is examining frozen beef burgers or apparently pretentious chandeliers, we are invited to judge these clues as markers of (class) taste. Of course, gender and class are often demonstrated to be deeply intertwined, as perhaps most clearly played out in the series two edition where the now notorious 'benefits scrounger' Lizzie Bardsley swapped with aspirational working mum Emma. Lizzie's aggressive manner and unwieldy, obese, body connote both working-class disorder and an unregulated femininity, especially when contrasted with Emma's petite, neat, prettiness. In this regard, Stephen Lambert's suggestion (see Gies forthcoming, 2007) that the programme is not about 'judging' the families which take part, and is *solely* about learning from the transformation, is clearly problematic.

Furthermore, the emphasis on a 'collective process of working through', or 'opening up', should not distract us from the traditional gender imbalance which underpins the format. Although the programme is fascinated by the politics of the domestic gender contract rather than the participants' sexual identities, its title pivots on women's historical status as object of exchange (Gies forthcoming). Furthermore, while soap opera has valued the importance of friendships *between* women (Geraghty 1991), the premise of *Wife Swap* is based on the notion of women swapping roles to *judge* each other's gendered work of domestic efficiency and personal intimacy in the domestic sphere (Sharp 2006). The dynamics of the swap can also be interpreted as placing the women at a structural disadvantage where power is concerned: they are uprooted and dropped into hostile and unfamiliar territory, invariably meeting resistance and coming under attack (Gies forthcoming). As Natasha Forrest observes in her review of the programme on *The F Word*, a website dedicated to 'contemporary UK feminism':

> On the surface *Wife Swap* could be seen as a positive programme for women in that it exposes the ways that women still have to struggle and make impossible compromises … Instead *Wife Swap* managed to pitch the women against each other so successfully that each episode ended with the poor confused husbands looking on in wide-eyed innocence as their wives laid into each other.
>
> (Forrest 2003)

But while the format certainly offers a known, familiar and repeatable structure, Forrest's description arguably homogenizes its narrative *content*; witness, for example, how the Nicola and Jayne edition, in which the two wives are married to estranged brothers, ends not with the women '[laying] into each other', but in an ultimatum between one of the couples. Having observed her brother-in-law's dedication to his children, the episode finishes with the materially privileged, but emotionally neglected, Nicola telling her aloof husband he must engage more with family life from herein or their marriage is over. Furthermore, not all editions pit a 'career' woman against a 'down-trodden' housewife, and even when this is apparent, this does not automatically foster a structure in which the narrative places the *women* on trial (see the discussion of Deirdre and Margaret below). It is certainly true, however, that the programme does not unproblematically or securely offer the sense (as Geraghty (1991) describes with respect to soap opera) of being 'down among the women'. Yet this is not simply the product of a structure which often pits wives at war: it also emerges from the contradictory nature of its gender ideologies, the variations between episodes, and the space which is afforded to the male subject.

'If I hadn't had this experience ...': Deirdre and Margaret

If there is an ideological consistency or 'metanarrative' at work across *Wife Swap*, it is to loosely endorse a position of compromise between the two family set-ups. Extremes are revealed to be flawed, one-sided and suspicious, and following an ideological struggle (in which each family – in Gramscian terms – must engage in 'negotiations with opposing groups, classes and values' (Turner 1996: 178)), the middle-ground of the battlefield is often preferred. The episode featuring Deirdre and Margaret illustrates this well. Margaret, 'a stay-at-home mum for more than 20 years' from Wolverhampton with eight children, swaps places in Leeds with 'self-made businesswoman' Deirdre who has one child (3-year-old Frankie) and who runs her own multi-million travel business. At an economic level, an emphasis on class difference is less pronounced here, with both families enjoying relative wealth, although Margaret's large family is presented as working-class 'made good', and new wife Deirdre casts a distinctly disapproving middle-class eye over her 'new' husband's 'cheap' Coca-cola, half-eaten frozen kebab, and busy floral wallpaper.

Here, the more 'middle-class' household is presented as more egalitarian ('modern') in its division of gender roles although, contrary to some discussions of the show (cf. Springer 2004), it would be misleading to suggest that this is always the case. In terms of gender, the women clearly represent (stereo) 'types'; workaholic Deirdre whose son is in full-time nursery care professes, 'I constantly think about my business ... I think motherhood can be boring' while über-housewife Margaret reflects, 'right from a very young age I wanted to have a large family'. So too are their husbands constructed and selected as deliberately contrasting types; the 'soft' Brian – who is an employee in his wife Deirdre's company, whose son manages to 'wrap me round his finger' and who later admits in the programme to being scared of his wife – juxtaposed with the beer-swigging, 'tight-wad', 'traditional man' Phil, who declares 'I've never been under the thumb.'

But, in part through its very careful editing, the programme facilitates a movement between distance from, and identification with, the individuals involved in the swap. Indeed, Piper argues that the programme deliberately sets up types (regarding class and gender) only to subsequently take pleasure in problematizing and undermining them (2004: 277, 299). This is facilitated by, the way the format sets up a number of perspectives on, and subject positions for, the participants, ranging across the more detached voice-over, the musical soundtrack, to the more 'intimate' confessionals to camera. While the voice-over initially sets up the pairs in typically broad strokes, and the pop soundtrack aims to literalize the sentiment of particular scenes (as Deirdre scrubs away we are treated to the strains of 'Working in a coal mine ...'), it is the confessional to-camera moments which often facilitate identification and insight – for both participants and viewers. Each of the participants get 'confessional' time alone on camera, and even the insufferably bullish Phil is allowed an empathetic moment when he fights back tears following new wife Deirdre's removal of his family photos in her bid to 'de-clutter' his home. ('Photographs of my *parents* have been removed ... It wouldn't be as bad if we had been *burgled*'.) By the end, quite predictably it could be said given the series' emphasis on reaching concession and self-discovery, Margaret is seen tentatively seeking other kinds of fulfilment in part-time work outside the home, having 'managed' Deirdre's business in her absence and Deirdre has committed herself to working less hours in order to spend more time with her son.

Yet along the road to this change of heart and despite their very different lifestyles, both women nevertheless powerfully voice their dissatisfaction with the lot of traditional motherhood. In one sequence a montage illustrates the women 'settling into their new roles', with Deirdre accompanying the kids to the paddling pool while Margaret, who admits 'I can't remember the last time I ever wore tights', tries on a new business outfit in a changing room,[4] and reads a book on business etiquette. As we see Margaret growing in confidence in the workplace, she exposes the lack of recognition that accompanies the work of motherhood, despite her championing of the role. She observes sadly, 'You really are somebody here, whereas at home, I've always felt a bit forgotten.' Later, having taken centre-stage to successfully deliver a presentation to a packed conference room in London, she is quite clearly over-whelmed by the sense of personal satisfaction it brings and how this contrasts with her usual life as an (invisible) full-time mum. This dichotomy is underlined by the image of her plumpish, 'motherly' body squeezed into the professional working attire of a pencil skirt, a style which is far more 'suited', of course, to Deirdre's neat frame. After her presentation Margaret enthuses to the camera, 'I would love to have the chance to do something like this I really would. But it wouldn't be full time.' Ideally, she explains, she'd want a balance 'between a lot of contact with my children and still having something that fitted me'. We then return to the scenes of appreciative applause that met her presentation, as she says in voice-over, 'I need Phil's support for me to do anything like that [at this juncture we cut back to her, now fighting tears] and I haven't got that.'[5] Here, Margaret painfully reveals the sense of isolation and loss of selfhood she experiences at home, while her call for a compromise situation between work and home ('a balance') illustrates the sense of the programme dramatizing a Gramscian-style struggle towards a negotiated middle-ground.

From her initial perspective as career woman, Deirdre too exposes the alienation motherhood holds for her. In a strikingly frank moment, Deirdre admits, 'I play with Frankie infrequently, because if I'm brutally honest, I find it boring … I don't really know what to do with [children].' In part, the episode must trace Deirdre's bid to acquire and learn these 'maternal' skills, a process which is seen at certain points through an idyllic lens. Significantly, Deirdre's account, above, of how motherhood is 'boring' is preceded by a to-camera confessional from her husband Brian where he supports the choices made by his absent working wife, insisting that 'I don't think that stay-at-home Mums are the be-all-and-end-all.' But we then cut to an image of Deirdre with her 'new' family, happily galloping around the sun-drenched garden in Wolverhampton to the tune of 'Teddy Bear's Picnic' while the voice-over explicitly qualifies Brian's comments (and might also be said to undermine Deirdre's disclo-sures) by observing, 'But sometimes, being a stay-at-home Mum can be fun …'.

Deirdre clearly undergoes a process of self-discovery in the course of the programme and subsequently embraces aspects of Margaret's parenting style, being evidently moved by the 'strange mirror image' of her home life she finds in Margaret's home. Crucially though, and *contra* the emphasis on warring wives, it is not Margaret but *Phil*, Margaret's emotionally detached, tetchy and often physically absent husband, who holds the symbolic mirror up to Deirdre's own workaholic lifestyle. As she concedes shortly before the end of the swap:

> You see, Phil, I'm similar to you ... and I'm just seeing here how important it is to spend quality time with children, which I never did in Leeds. Because there was always an excuse. I've been thinking while I'm here I must and I will spend more time each day with Frankie.

For Deirdre, the swap is represented as having brought about life-changing revelations; 'If I hadn't had this experience being at the receiving end of Phil Clarke, I could be talking to myself 15 years down the line. And I don't want that to be true.' But if this is the perspective taken by Deirdre by the end of the swap, it is worth noting the long heritage of debate as to whether narrative 'closure' recuperates, or invalidates, the ideological perspectives which have preceded it (Maltby 1995: 337). Indeed, the moment when Deirdre describes playing with her only child as 'boring' remains remarkable for the manner in which it features a young, accomplished and highly articulate mother *on television* blankly debunking the myths of motherhood. Not only does it question that such skills are innately present in women, but it also questions whether the role is innately rewarding, a position that is interrogated too – albeit in a different manner – by Margaret's simultaneous 'journey'. Furthermore, it is important to recognize that even though the women are typically more central (as the series title suggests), it is not merely the wives/mothers who are under scrutiny. Deirdre, as part of her own journey of self-discovery, continually comments on, questions and interrogates Phil's role in his family, for example ('Why don't you eat food here?'... 'Do you feel you could spend more time with [the children]?') and a recurrent, highly politicized strand of the programme is its rendering of a challenge to the traditionally socially acceptable vision of the distant/preoccupied breadwinner father, or 'the stranger in our home'.

Indeed, more so than the career woman, this 'character type' is arguably the most pathologized by the programme. Men who have this kind of role in their home are recurrently constructed as insensitive, odd, or even cruel, though they too can acquire a greater sense of self-awareness in the course of the swap. In the Nicola and Jayne episode, we open by learning how Nicola runs the house single-handedly while her wealthy 'financial services manager' husband Jason spends four hours a night alone in his games-room ('I have no involvement in the rest of the house ... everything I want is in here really'), playing with his computer games rather than his two children, who apparently barely see or know him. His 7-year-old son Louis shows more apparent maturity than his father when he comments blithely, 'Sometimes he locks himself in. I just find that weird, 'cos if you was in a family, you wouldn't really lock yourself in to go on the Play-Station.' The subsequent epiphany Jason undergoes, when he realizes the pleasure that is to be had simply from taking Louis to a karate lesson for the first time; when he understands the sheer volume of his wife's labour at last; and when he recognizes he could well lose his wife if he doesn't change, is every bit as narratively central and revelatory as the epiphanies of his wife and sister-in-law. 'I apologize for the last 10 years', he tells her at the end when the couples meet up after the swap; 'I just want to put things right ... I've been wrong on 80 per cent of issues that are the problem in our house. I've treated you in the past like an employee and not a partner and that will change.' The programme and its participants cumulatively suggest, as Jason himself eventually comes to realize, that his distance from his family is absolutely something that must be 'corrected'. The political implications of this structure are undeniably different when the career-oriented spouse is a woman (in that the programme can return her to a 'weaker' position, agreeing to do more 'traditional' womanly tasks) (Gies forthcoming). But this is precisely an example of the programme's ambivalent relationship with conservative/ progressive discourses, while we have also drawn attention to the range of insights and positions which are explored prior to the final resolution.

Staging and 'observing' the swap

But the fact that these insights are *produced by* the format, a structure into which different participants are slotted, can simultaneously make for an uneasy viewing experience. As acknowledged earlier, on the one hand, *Wife Swap* belongs to the era of *staged reality* formats in which we are asked to 'search' for the real in a formatted environment, with the key site of 'truth' being located in the self. Yet the fact that each original family *does* exist in some form outside of the pro-filmic event maintains a link with the epistemological roots of observational documentary and – to some degree – the docusoap. Corner, however, describes the *Wife Swap* participants as evincing a 'self-consciousness' in performance which exceeds both conventional observational documentary and 'even docusoap observation' (2006: 72). This implies that it is best placed alongside later reality formats which are entered into as a performative opportunity in their own right (e.g. *Big Brother*) (Corner 2001). But while the *Wife Swap* participants all seem fully cognisant of the demands of an era in which 'the real person who cannot rustle up a heightened TV persona is asked to step aside' (Parker 1998, cited in Piper 2004: 282), the programme is not as self-consciously performative as *Big Brother*. There is little or no discussion between the participants about who is 'playing up' to the camera, and who is 'being themselves'. This is not to suggest that these conversations don't take place, and this is precisely the point: as with the 'observational' claims of the docusoap, we are told very little about the relationship between subjects, camera crew and production team. There are to-camera interviews (in which the subject usually looks off-camera left) which obviously acknowledge the presence of the crew. We also occasionally hear a quiet question being asked as a prompt ('And why does that upset you?'), while the participants themselves, usually in moments of desperation or humour, will direct a question to the person behind the camera ('God, how *many* kids live here? There *never* are eight kids!'). But the crew are rarely seen, despite their acute proximity to the events which unfold.

However, the DVD '*Wife Swap* Extra' chapter raises, perhaps inadvertently, some intriguing questions about the relative agency of the programme-makers and partici-pants in the programme. This DVD feature includes the programme-makers being interviewed about the overall series' accomplishments, as well as their experiences of particular episodes. In relation to the Nicola and Jayne edition, we learn that there was particular friction going on behind the scenes (though not outlined in the broadcast programme itself) between Nicola's husband Jason and the episode's producer/director, Vicky Hamburger. In this episode, after the 'rule-change' Jayne had insisted that a new lock be fitted on Jason's games-room to prevent him absconding there away from his family every night. Rather than him subsequently confronting Jayne as a result, we learn from Hamburger in interview that 'He was basically quite unhappy with *me* about it.' We then have access to previously 'unseen footage' which features the following exchange between Jason and Hamburger (off-camera) following the arrival of the locksmith:

J: You've obviously got that one planned as well, haven't you?

VH: What? I haven't got anything planned.

J: Well, you asked me if there was a key for the office.

VH: Who did?

J: No, you asked me, ages ago.

VH: I never asked you that question.

J: You did, you said …

VH: It must have been someone else.

Their difference of opinion is not resolved but the exchange clearly suggests a genuine tension regarding who instigates the details of the rule-change; the producers or the wives. We then cut back to Hamburger in interview where she explains what happened next; 'Because we had had this little bit of tension between us, I sat down with him and said, you know, are we OK now, *and we turned on the video diary camera*' (emphasis added). Hamburger's use of '*we*' here is particular telling and is followed by a return to more 'unseen footage' where Jason is seen in the bedroom talking directly to the 'video diary' camera. But this is now revealed not to be the personal, private space we have arguably presumed it to be, given that it is presented and constructed in a manner which suggests that the subject themselves directs it (it is in these moments only that the participants speak to the camera rather than to the crew or other participants, who are never seen or heard in these scenes). Here the DVD Extra reveals, first, that the producer/director appears to have prompted Jason's video diary, rather than him having turned to it purely on his own volition. Second, and even more disconcertingly in terms of keeping faith with the viewer, it becomes apparent that Hamburger is *present* and *asking questions*, i.e. 'directing' the reflections that Jason makes in the 'private' space of the video diary, as we clearly hear her asking him off-camera, 'What happened this morning?'

All of this raises significant questions about the involvement of the programme-makers and the relationship between the production team and the framing influence of the format. To be sure, the 'household manual' functions not merely as a source of information and instruction for the 'new' wife, but also the foundations of her basic 'script' for rule change week. While the wife is presented (quite literally when using a wall or flipchart) as the sole *author* of the changes, the 'script' has already provided the dramatic framework: if the man of the house hates pets, a rabbit will be introduced to live indoors; if the children are subject to an army-like regime of discipline, daily chores will be ousted and sleep-over parties planned. But even taking this into account, there are further questions about how autonomously and spontaneously these changes are implemented and effected. Beyond the 'unseen footage' on the DVD for example, in a telling moment in the Margaret and Deirdre edition, Margaret turns Deirdre's home office into a bedroom for their young son (whose original bedroom was smaller). While Brian expresses his concern at the change, Margaret reassures him, 'It's OK, we measured the desk, it will fit [in here].' The reference again to 'we' is an unsettling reminder of the collective 'labour' involved in staging these scenes, and concurrently, how little we are told of the participants' actual agency here. Indeed, while we have emphasized the potentially productive value of the process which is dramatized here, if *Wife Swap* belongs to a group of programming in which 'realities are staged because it allows programme-makers and participants to tease out a truth which could not be *articulated without an intense process of surveillance*' (Gies forthcoming, 2007); our emphasis), this is not without implications at the level of agency and ethics.

Surveying the swap

To cast the complex framework outlined above as an ideological 'compromise' between the potential social value of the content and the 'constraints' or demands of the ('entertainment') format, however, is to reify the duality between popular factual and 'serious' documentary interrogated earlier. The gravitation toward 'domestic banality' (Piper 2004: 274) is certainly made watchable, and thus commercially viable, within the context of the format, and the dramatic certainties this provides. But to equate this with a loss of seriousness or social import is problematic. There may be some truth to the argument that *Wife Swap's* micro-focus on 'extreme' family examples leads to a collapsing of gender and class inequalities onto the individual criteria of 'lifestyle' choice and taste (Piper 2004: 278), but this is not entirely satisfactory. There is certainly no longer any modernist belief in, or desire to represent, a/the unified concept of *The Family* (1974) (see also Stratton and Ang 1994), and a *Wife Swap* family is as likely to be chosen for its perceived 'atypicality' and 'aberrant' potential. If *Wife Swap* is constructed to present a flawed vision of the twenty-first century family (Sharp 2006), delivering a series of 'isolated' snapshots that lead us to question and reflect on conventional gender roles, then David Aaronovitch's provocative appraisal (2003) (cited at the start of this article) may be an incisive one after all. But even taking this into account, the line between typicality/particularity is undoubtedly blurred in reality TV. *Wife Swap* participants are positioned as both individuals *and* social types, and it is the play-off between these concepts which becomes so compelling. Furthermore, we do not need to be told (to ape Paul Watson's commentary in *The Family*), that there are 'many [people] like Margaret' (or Deirdre) for her representation to resonate with struggles surrounding the contemporary construction of gender. The programme *stages* 'reality' to play out questions that ultimately affect everyday life. In fact, if the docusoap has been seen as presenting a closed world which simply says 'this is life as it is' (Dovey 2000), then *Wife Swap* at least wants to ask: 'how might it be different?'.

Notes

1   Selected episodes from the first two series are available on the Channel 4 DVD, *Wife Swap: The Best of Series 1 and 2*, 2004.

2   While opinions have clearly varied, the series has also attracted, 'cautious critical appreciation', unlike many other reality programmes, (Corner 2006: 71). In fact, alongside impressive viewing figures (6 million tuned into the UK's Channel 4 broadcasts in 2003), the programme has also won numerous industry accolades. These include the Broadcasting Press Guild's Best Documentary Series award in 2003; a BAFTA for Best Features Programme and an EMMY nomination for Best Non-Scripted Entertainment Programme in 2004 (www.rdftelevision.com/reality/WifeSwap, accessed 12 Sept. 2006).

3   This is particularly so when compared to work on the television talk show.

4   This sequence is interesting for the way in which the images of Deirdre trying on new clothes draw on the convention/connotations of both the Hollywood's woman's film and the 'makeover' strand of lifestyle reality TV. In both genres, the changing-room montage sequence is utilized as a marker of the transformation of the self.

5   Note, too, how close attention to editing here also reveals a minor 'continuity error'; Margaret's apparently continuous speech is evidently taken from at least two junctures and edited together with the applause acting as a bridge; at the start of the sequence she is wearing a jacket, but when we cut back to her she isn't.

21 Simulating the Public Sphere

Jon Dovey

In this chapter I want to argue that formatted reality television game shows (RTV Games) like *Big Brother* (Channel 4, 2000–) and popular TV documentary formats like *Wife Swap* (Channel Four, 2002–) and *Faking It* (Channel 4, 1999–) might be best understood as simulations. In these programmes we see the dominant observational traditions of documentary being redeployed as part of a different system of representation based on simulation. This proposition does *not* rest upon Baudrillard's seductive rhetoric of the simulacra. By simulation I refer to that process in which dynamic models are observed in order to generate understanding of complex processes. This definition is derived from, among others, the research methods of natural science, social science, military planning and financial forecasting, all of which depend increasingly on building models to understand complex systems.

While TV producers and commissioning editors are not setting out to deliberately adopt or mimic these methodologies, the impulse to simulate has embedded itself at every level of the production process. The attempt to record social reality has been completely swallowed by the impulse to simulate social reality in performative models. Factual television practices have by and large abandoned empirical observation that rested upon the lack of relationship between observer and observed and replaced it with the observation of simulated situations that only exist because of the intervention of the TV production. Factual TV has moved from direct empirical observation to the observation of simulated social situations. This chapter will argue that simulation is a useful framework that helps us to understand popular factual TV in a way that goes beyond the well-rehearsed positions of 'media panic' (Biltereyst 2004). Moreover, thinking about popular factual TV through this framework helps us to understand a programme like *Big Brother* as a prototypical new media product. Although disseminated primarily through traditional television, *Big Brother* is in many respects a typical new media object in so far as it is an international brand that exists as a multi-platform hybrid of traditional and new media. A programme like *Big Brother* not only delivers audiences to advertisers but also to phone lines, cable subscription and internet use as the viewer is drawn into a simulated game world. As such, this chapter applies some of the work that I have been doing in thinking about what a 'New Media Studies' might be – that is to say a discipline that looks at 'New Media' but which also therefore represents a methodological renewal of 'Media Studies'. This renewal does seem to me to involve interdisciplinary cross-pollination with various aspects of computer science and 'cyberculture studies', such as the study of Human Computer Interaction, Artificial Intelligence, software theory and study of networked systems (see, e.g., Lister et al. 2003).

The identity simulator

The specific work of understanding *Big Brother* through new media analytic frameworks was inspired for me by the work of Bernadette Flynn who has written comparisons of *Big Brother* and *The Sims* computer game (2002, 2005). RTV Games can be thought of as story-producing mechanisms, producing narratives of identity, affiliation and exclusion for players and for audiences. At the heart of this text machine is a simulation, a dynamic rule-based game system that changes over time. In classical play theory (e.g., Huizinga 1949; Caillois 1979), the 'game' is understood as happening in a special demarcated physical and cultural zone, the 'magic circle' of play where the players all agree that reality is subject to commonly accepted rules. The reality game show is such a closed system, like the experimental computer simulation, or the psychology lab. The *Big Brother* house, the *Fame Academy* building, the *Survivor* jungle location or *Temptation Island*, are all closed environments, fiercely policed by security guards and surveillance. Into this closed system with its own perimeters the system managers – the producers – introduce characters who have been cast on the basis of what we might call their character algorithms.

In *The Sims* computer game, characters are developed according to a set of algorithmically controlled possibilities, e.g., 'Neat', 'Outgoing', 'Active', 'Playful', or 'Nice'. The producers of RTV gameshows cast housemates according to sets of characteristics which they hope will create drama and narrative, i.e., the belligerent character, the flirt, the mother figure, the quiet but deep one, the eccentric, and so on. For the producers these characteristics constitute the algorithms that they hope will make the simulation run in an interesting way, i.e., stimulus from X applied to character Y might well have outcome Z. Of course, the real fun is when the unexpected happens, just as in computer games based on *The Sims* part of the pleasure occurs when the AI does something you hadn't predicted as a result of its interactions with other AIs. Jane Roscoe has described these moments as 'flickers of authenticity – the moment where the simulation appears to break down and the viewer affect of the "authentic" is created' (Roscoe 2001). Part of this affect is due to the possibilities for unpredictable emergent behaviour to arise from the simulation. Another way of putting this would be to talk about the process of improvisation in music or drama, set keys or rhythms might be established at the start of a jazz piece but no one quite knows where it will go nor will one performance repeat the music of the last.

The 'character algorithms' are then set in dynamic motion through the experimental framework of the many challenges and tasks that constitute the daily life in the identity simulator. This daily diet of 'challenges' and games is consistent with many other types of factual entertainment which have a commonly ludic content. This game playing is also reminiscent of role play situations, especially those associated with team-building efforts in the contemporary workplace where we are encouraged to bond through play.

Big Brother is a simulation in so far as it is a closed system, bound by rules, into which characters are introduced who are set up in dynamic role play. The *Big Brother* environment is a model just as a computer simulation or a psychology experiment is a model.

Watching, talking and doing

A privileged relationship to social reality is one of the leading 'claims' of the traditional discourse of documentary. Work like Barnouw's classic *Documentary: A History of the Non Fiction Film* (1974) is redolent with the passionate social engagement of twentieth-century filmmakers. Documentary film in the heroic period of modernism and in the incendiary late 1960s was as much about changing the world as it was observing it. Nichols sums up this tradition in his well-known position that documentary presents us with arguments about our shared world, propositions about the world that are made as part of a process of social praxis. Documentaries are akin to other 'discourses of sobriety', science, the law, education, that shape social reality (Nichols 1991: 3–4).

Brian Winston has a similar sense of documentary history, when he writes about documentary finding its place on the 'battlefields of epistemology' he captures some of the ways in which documentary filmmakers and critics argue about the world we share when they argue about its documentary representation (Winston 1995: 242). Documentary history has taken its role in the mediated public sphere for granted – it has been a given of documentary practice and documentary studies.

One of the drivers of media panic occasioned by popular factual TV over the past 15 years has been precisely an anxiety that the moral seriousness of the documentary tradition was being driven off the airwaves by vulgar factual entertainments – 'documentary diversions' as John Corner has called them (2002). I have analysed these debates extensively elsewhere (Dovey 2000). Like all debates about popular culture, the terrain is rarely susceptible to binary reasoning, however, the evidence does not suggest that popular factual has driven serious documentary from broadcasting. Schedule analysis shows that the majority of popular factual has replaced talk and quiz shows in the TV schedules not 'serious' public sphere documentary. The demise of the 'traditional' documentary has more to do with the economics of broadcasting under conditions of intensifying competition and wider cultural changes in the development of a newly demotic public sphere (Dovey 2000). This shift is typically observed in the 1991 decision of the Discovery Channel to rebrand 'The Learning Channel' as 'TLC' in order to broadcast not worthy educational films but lifestyle documentaries – subsequently TLC has become a highly successful cable brand on the back of everyday life reality documentaries such as *A Wedding Story* (1995–) and *A Baby Story* (1998–) (see Stephens 2004).

In this context of concerns about the loss of documentary's public sphere role, I briefly want to think about the relative 'impacts' of observational and simulated documentary work – taking at 'face value' for a moment the documentary call to social praxis. There is a reasonably well-trodden path that we can use to retrace 'documentary impacts': *Cathy Come Home* (Ken Loach, 1966) is alleged to have formed part of the debate that established the housing charity Shelter; Roger Graef's (1982) series *Police* led to a change in the handling of rape cases by UK police; investigative 'miscarriage of justice' stories have led to individual verdicts being overturned, notably in the case of Errol Morris' The *Thin Blue Line* (1988) which brilliantly managed to deconstruct the whole notion of truth at the same time as getting Randal Adams off death row. But beyond the notable examples, the evidence for documentary making an instrumental impact on the world in the way of the sober discourses of law or medicine is pretty thin. There are probably more examples of documentary creating 'media panic', furore occasioned by the form and ethics of the work itself, e.g., the films of UK director Paul Watson, *The Family* (1974), *Sylvania Waters* (1992), observational films that provoked widespread public discussion about ethics, manipulation and documentary truthfulness. When traditional documentary theorists or practitioners claim privileged access to social reality, it is surely to a more diffuse sense of the documentary mission within the mediated public sphere – to a common-sense understanding of communicative action, that there is a relationship between seeing, talking and doing in the world. If we accept this role for factual film and TV, then it seems to me we must accept that popular factual is doing, albeit systemically rather than intentionally, all kinds of 'work' in the public sphere.

For instance, the debate triggered by allegations of racism on UK *Celebrity Big Brother* in January 2007 facilitated a more thorough 'working through' (Ellis) of race in UK culture than any previous TV programme. By 17 January 2007 the UK media regulator Ofcom had received over 19,000 complaints alleging racism on *Celebrity Big Brother* over the previous three days. The broadcaster Channel Four had received a further 3,000 complaints, the Asian newspaper *Eastern Eye* had gathered 20,000 signatures of protest in two days. This level of complaint was record-breaking, Ofcom had generally experienced 'controversiality' in terms of hundreds of complaints rather than thousands. These complaints were part of a wave of discussion of racism that dominated the UK and Indian public sphere for several days, the UK Chancellor of the Exchequer Gordon Brown was forced to make placatory remarks in the face of street demonstrations in India while visiting there. The furore was the result of disparaging and critical behaviour by three white women housemates against the first Asian to appear on UK *Celebrity Big Brother* the Bollywood actress Shilpa Shetty. Without going into a detailed textual analysis of the events shown, three young white working-class 'celebrity' women appeared to form an alliance based on their common dislike of Shetty; these kind of emergent groupings are typical of the narratives of affiliation and exclusion that structure the *Big Brother* text. So what made these events different to the extent that they provoked the biggest wave of public protest in UK television history? The protests were led by the Asian UK community incensed at a display of the kind of 'everyday racism' with which they are all too familiar. The racism was not blatant insult or abuse, which would not be tolerated even as part of an RTV game show, it was the far more common insidious racism of people who are polite enough in face-to-face dealings with people of colour but then go back and make jokes to other white people about that person's food, accent, or hygiene. Overhearing the way white people talked about them in private was more than just a 'flicker of authenticity' (Roscoe 2001) for the thousands of Asians who protested, it was a powerfully accurate portrayal of their social reality. The race and gender politics of these events were further complicated by the perennial British issues of class and empire. Shilpa Shetty is a very middle-class Indian – carefully and beautifully spoken, reserved, confident. The two Essex girls and one Scouser who set themselves up as Shetty's nemeses are all products of completely different working-class communica- tive cultures in which confrontation and combat are nearer the norm. It could be argued that the interactions between these two different codes tapped into all kinds of British cultural fault lines generated by white working-class discomfort at the growing power of an Asian bourgeoisie in the UK. This short account of a case study in *Big Brother* controversy is intended to illustrate the ways in which behaviours and patterns of relationship that emerge from *Big Brother* turn out to make a significant contribution to talk in the public sphere. The talk in this case is significant not because it concerns who is being 'real' or 'authentic' but because it generated a greater volume of discussion about racism in UK society than any previous TV programme.

The Shetty controversy is not an isolated case. The *Big Brother* literature is full of examples where the programme provoked significant public sphere discussions on important topics that are – despite the globalized format – very culturally specific. Writing about *Big Brother Africa* (2003) Biltereyst observes:

> the programme was praised by an unexpectedly large variety of people ... intellectuals and scholars claimed that *Big Brother Africa* successfully brought under attention issues such as AIDS, and openly questioned national stereotypes.
>
> (Mathijs and Jones 2004: 10)

Pitout argues that the first series of *Big Brother* in South Africa was structured by post-apartheid hegemonies:

> With South Africa's history of apartheid the blend of people belonging to different cultural, racial and religious groups contributed to the excitement and media hype. Having black and white people living in the same house in South Africa would have been illegal ten years ago.
>
> (Mathijs and Jones 2004: 173)

Kilicbay and Minark (in Mathijs and Jones 2004: 140–50) argue that *Biri Bizi Gozetliyor* (Turkish *Big Brother*) provoked public sphere 'topics of discussion' reflecting the specific context's modernity and secularism:

> Surprisingly we have found that each season had its own theme such as political correctness, hegemonic masculinity, gender roles, being a dutiful citizen, being respectful of dominant moral codes and so on.
>
> (Mathijs and Jones 2004: 149)

The place of RTV game shows in the popular public sphere is tacitly acknowledged by the appearance of the Columbian Prime Minister in the *Big Brother* house in 2003, using his appearance to explain to housemates and viewers a forthcoming referendum on economic austerity measures (Denhart 2003).

In all the cases above, the formatted reality TV gameshow has a particularly productive effect on public sphere discussion, raising issues, airing concerns, exploring anxieties that are all already part of the cultural context for the production. However, this is clearly not the intention of the programme producers. *Big Brother* is a massively successful global media franchise, turning Endemol, the rights holder, into one of the most successful independent media companies in the world. Nevertheless the public sphere discussion seems to be a characteristic emergent quality of the *Big*

Brother system. The simulation model that is at the core of the reality TV game is producing 'real-world' outcomes in the shared public communicative space of the mediated public sphere.

Simulation as model

The definition of simulation I want to use is derived from computer applications within the social sciences. Gilbert and Doran argue that first of all simulation is a process of modelling:

> We wish to acquire knowledge about a target entity T. But T is not easy to study directly. So we proceed indirectly. Instead of T we study another entity M, the 'model', which is sufficiently similar to T that we are confident that some of what we learn about M will also be true of T.
>
> (1994: 4)

Typically, the phenomena under consideration are dynamic, a model therefore consists in 'structure plus behaviour'. Simulation happens when we observe the behaviour of the model, when it is 'set running'. In Gilbert and Conte, this approach is summarized thus:

> [Computer] simulation is an appropriate methodology whenever a social phenomenon is not directly accessible, either because it no longer exists ... or because its structure or the effects of its structure, i.e., its behaviour, are so complex that the observer cannot directly attain a clear picture of what is going on.
>
> (Gilbert and Conte 1995: 2)

This justification for the use of simulation is interesting because it lays emphasis on complex structures and behaviours which are not directly observable, such as identity and sociality, the content of the RTV game which here are seen as complex and dynamic processes subject to multiple networked determinations rather than linear cause and effect. Simulations made by social scientists using computer programs are being used to address fundamental problems of societal organization and evolution in ways that are explicitly designed to take account of highly complex interactive systems whose characteristics are always permanently emergent rather than fixed or predictable by any linear cause and effect mechanical method.

In a less arcane field, simulation is also of course widely used by the military; this has been growing for many years. In 1996, the US Department of Defense Modelling and Simulation Office asked the National Research Council to convene a conference in which military trainers and members of the entertainment industries could share information. It was attended by game developers, film studio representatives, theme park industries , military trainers and universities (Prensky 2001: 315). Marc Prensky, in his book *Digital Game Based Learning* (2001) claims that the US military are the biggest spenders in the world on simulation games for training. It is clear that warfare is now conducted on the basis of knowledge produced through simulation. This highly rule-based mediated version of war of course produces its own counter-image in the form of terror – a viral resistance to the systemic totality of the computerized war machine.

Real-world uses of simulation to produce knowledge are not confined to social science or military planning. There are numerous other examples. Currency markets use simulations every day in order to calculate the best market advantage for speculation. In science, simulations are used increasingly in recognition of the fact that understanding emergent behaviour is an important aspect of understanding many natural processes, e.g., in immunology to predict micro-biological behaviours.

Simulation is used then to represent complex processes with multiple agents and causalities at work – in this way it seems to answer a theoretical need for ways of producing knowledge that take account of the levels of interaction between micro-level agents and macro-level forces as well as addressing a need articulated by postmodern theorists for a method of representation that takes account of rapid change. In all the cases cited above, real-world knowledges are being produced that have real-world effects – embodied, direct and material. The simulation has become a significant way of producing knowledge, modifying behaviour and entertaining ourselves.

Big Brother as gameplay

In the case of *Big Brother*, the mimetic content produced by the system is centred upon another and different kind of simulation, that of the game in which the players are called upon to perform certain roles in accordance with a set of rules. Here the simulation in question is not a computer program but of a kind of play more akin to 'let's pretend'. There are two levels of play in operation here. First, to use Caillois' (1979) definitions of play, the whole event is staged within a space characterized by mimicry in which participants are called upon to play a part in an imaginative construct, here the housemates are playing a version of themselves which engages audiences in endless speculation around whether or not this performance of self is a true 'authentic' self or calculated performance. At the second level, the day-to-day action of the house is structured by games of 'agon', competition in which house-mates compete against one another or against *Big Brother* to win food supplies and treats, etc.

Moreover, this game play takes place within the overarching context of social psychology experiment which uses 'role play' and observation as its method (see Palmer 2002). The entire apparatus of *Big Brother* resembles a social psychology experiment redesigned for mass entertainment consumption. The isolation, surveillance, comments from psychologists who explain behaviour and the confessional diary room all mark the programme as a psychology laboratory. As such, it is a deliberately designed 'model' of human interaction in exactly the same way that a computer simulation is a model designed to investigate other natural and social processes. The experimental or behaviour modification techniques of psychology are here adapted to entertainment TV.

I want to establish that these forms of 'play' are also simulations that are concomitant with computer simulations in the way that they are models of 'behaviour plus structure' which exist outside of the day-to-day experience but which are designed to model it. Many of us are familiar with this process through the experience of role play – how many of us have been on any sort of training in the last ten years when we were not at some point asked to go into role to simulate professional conditions? Here we encounter simulation as an embedded form of social learning. Although the object of role play was originally behaviour modification and training, it has some similarities with simulation insofar as it also sets up a model situation outside everyday perimeters in which the participants are encouraged 'to see what happens if'. This social role play also has much in common with play theories, deriving in psychology from the work of Joseph Moreno who invented psychodrama as a therapeutic technique which effected personal change through direct embodiment of improvised role play. Moreno's development of the technique encompasses children's play and story telling as well as the use of theatre, founding the 'Theatre of Spontaneity' in Vienna in 1923.

Factual TV playtime

Factual TV entertainment formats are now brand leaders in the ratings war between channels. Simulation is now the driving force of a great deal of factual TV programming: the impulse here is 'What if?' – 'What would happen if we got a burger cook to pretend to be a cordon bleu chef?' (*Faking It*, Channel 4, 1999–2003), 'What would happen if we persuaded wives to swap families for two weeks?' (*Wife Swap*, Channel 4, 2002), 'What would it be like to live in a Victorian house?' (*1900 House*, Channel 4, 1999). The majority of popular factual programmes are now based on events that have been set up and constructed by the producers themselves. 'Factual' TV has, more or less, abandoned any notion it ever had of observational documentary practice in which the attempt was made to capture reality as it actually happened without intervening in any way. Instead there is only intervention – only recording and editing of simulated conditions.

On television the constructed documentary form has become dominant, its factual quality guaranteed only by the casting of non-actors in the producers' scenarios. The camera only captures events that are happening because the camera is there. In the docusoap – the forerunner of the reality game show – dramatic narrative structure and casting techniques together with a self-conscious performance of subjects for camera all ensure that we are looking at experiences constructed and modified for the series itself. Without the camera's fame-conferring gaze, there is no event worth filming, the camera constitutes the reality.

Verité to simulation

At one level its possible to see these developments as being the ultimate popular triumph of the Rouchian tradition that the camera creates and catalyses social reality more than documents it (see Winston 1995: 148–69). This is a persuasive argument but I'd want to put it into a wider cultural context and ask Why here? Why now? It is not because filmmakers or commissioning editors have been suddenly rediscovering the French creator of *cinéma verité*, Jean Rouch.

Both observational (direct cinema) and reflexive (*cinéma verité*) modes of factual representation were achieved during the exact same period (late 1950s/early 1960s) as the first realizations of the meanings of an image-saturated and stage-managed society – the period in fact of the publication of Daniel Boorstin's *The Image* (1963) which offered one of the first analyses of image-based public life and the mass effects of the PR industry. I would argue that the direct observational mode of documentary practice emerged in response to this moment as a way of seeming to 'get behind the scenes' of a foregrounded stage-managed reality. Hence films like *Primary* (Ricky Leacock, 1960), *Meet Marlon Brando* (Maysles Brothers, 1965), observational rock performance films, e.g., *Don't Look Back* (Leacock and Pennebaker, 1966), all of which are attempts to show reality by direct observational techniques of the backstage process of stage-managed performative events. The observational mode clearly emerged as the dominant TV documentary tradition in response to and as part of these cultural circumstances.

However, by the end of the century, this kind of observationalism can be seen to be played out for a number of reasons. First, and most significantly for the purposes of my argument, observational documentary operated as part of the philosophical belief system of empiricism. However, this foundation has clearly suffered multiple philosophical and pragmatic shocks over the last hundred years. Philosophically for instance, through relativity, and new ideas about the ways in which observers effect what they observe. Pragmatically, in so far as science now more often that not concerns itself with processes that are in fact not observable, sub-atomic processes or astronomical cosmology, for instance. Here empiricism can be seen to have outstripped its own project, to have as it were reached the edge of the observable world before moving on into ways of representation that depend upon simulating natural phenomena. Simulation helps us to understand a world that no longer seems susceptible to cause and effect logic but more and more to non-linear causality and network logics. By network logics I mean the understanding that all events or behaviours may have multiple determinants and variable outcomes, that any given node in a network has numerous in and out points. Planning or predicting outcomes in a network therefore becomes a cybernetic problem, a matter of feedback estimation, of probability management and of risk calculation.

The 'problem' of the observational can also be seen in operation in the great faking scandals that engulfed documentary practice in the late 1990s. It is possible to read these events as the new modes of performativity, mimicry and simulation, challenging observationalism. 'Faking' controversies dominated factual TV reception in a three-year period starting in 1996 when German TV producer Michael Born was prosecuted and jailed for four years as a result of selling more than 20 faked documentaries and culminating in the UK in 1998–99 when the press 'exposed' a number of documentaries as 'fake'. These campaigns led to the regional commercial franchise Carlton TV being fined £2 million by the commercial regulator the ITC for 'faking' a documentary, *The Connection* transmitted in October 1996 (see Winston 2000: 9–39). Factual television and documentary practice was under severe epistemological pressure. What emerges from this feverish bout of self-questioning and doubt? *Big Brother* – conceived during precisely the same period that these scandals were circulating among the mediacrats of Europe. The perfect beauty of the reality game show and the performative factual mode in this context is that because everything is set up, no one can be held accountable for fakery. Since the whole event is a game, any quasi-legal obligations that producers may previously have had to meet are displaced. The whole terrain of debate has been shifted from the legal to the ludic. Problem solved.

Reality TV and reflexive modernity

The question that remains is: If programmes like *Big Brother* are a simulation, what are they a simulation of? In *Freakshow* (2000), I argued that some elements of contemporary factual media, especially its emphasis on First Person Media and intimacy should be attributed not merely to greater commercialization and marketization of television but also to attempts to represent identity and sociality after the end of tradition. I used one of Anthony Giddens' formulations of the consequences of reflexive modernity: 'Life politics is about how we live after the end of tradition and nature – more and more political decisions will belong to the sphere of life politics in the future' (Giddens and Pierson 1998: 149).

The Reflexive Modernity argument is that in contemporary social life, identity and ethics are under constant re-evaluation for all kinds of reasons. Essentially the description of contemporary society in the West as a condition of 'reflexive modernity' argues that the project or trajectory of modernity has been radically transformed by its own success. (This is rather like the argument about empiricism above – itself constitutive of modernity – that it has through its own success reached the limits of its own aims.) The social structures of modernity have been transformed by their own fulfilment. Formations of class, labour, gender and technology that underpinned the formation of modernism have all been radically challenged. Neo-liberal employment practices including short-term and freelance employment in the context of a highly aspirational culture deny the subject the possibility of long-term security or personal development (Sennett 1999). Increasingly flexible family structures which break out of nuclear family models as a result of changes in sexual and gender politics leave many of us with neither ethical map nor moral compass. Changes in gender roles also cut across our experiences of work, parenting, and identity. Similarly our relationship with nature, which, as Giddens explains, was previously a 'given', is now under scrutiny, reproductive politics are now opened to a degree of choice, genetics opens up whole new areas of ambiguity which we are trying to learn to deal with. Moreover, these scientific developments occur within a context of widespread mistrust of scientific technical systems, described by Ulrich Beck as part of 'risk culture'. This instability of identity and social structure is all experienced within the context of a consumerism marked by aspiration to a high degree of social mobility – where lifestyle choice replaces class, education or gender as determining social identity.

It is hardly surprising then that these questions of 'life politics' are reflected in the mediated discourses of everyday life that have become the staple fare of factual TV. This focus on identity work should not be misinterpreted as a merely individualistic concern, for identity in this context is deeply wedded to belonging, to group consciousness. The narrative action of *Big Brother* is constituted as on ongoing improvised drama of affiliation and exclusion, driven by the weekly eviction process which is deliberately designed to undermine group identity while at the same time the daily action of challenges and tests is designed to reinforce it.

Subsequently other commentators have made the same set of connections, notably Ib Bondebjerg in his article 'The Mediation of Everyday Life: Genre Discourse and Spectacle in Reality TV':

> This reflexive modernity and the new awareness of the self in public and private life as well as of the mediation of the self in a network society moving from a nation state to global frames ... [are] the fuel of the new reality genres ... It is also a reflection of the deep mediation of everyday life in a network society which creates a strong need for audiences to mirror and play with identities and the uncertainties of everyday life, thus intensifying our innate social curiosity.
>
> (Bondebjerg 2002: 162)

In the context of this pervasive 'make-over culture', it should therefore come as no surprise that factual programming looks increasingly like part identity lab, part intimacy simulator in programmes like the recent *Wife Swap* (Channel 4, 2002–), in which husbands and wives swap for 4 weeks, *Trading Races* (BBC2, 2001), in which participants swapped skin colour and lifestyle, or the very successful *Faking It* (Channel 4, 1999–), in which subjects are asked to try to learn a new professional identity in just four weeks. *Wife Swap* is a particularly interesting text in this regard. The title is of course designed to suggest some kind of salacious content but in fact the programme turns out to be exactly the blend of sociology and voyeurism that a producer might dream up thinking about the questions of reflexive modernity. Each programme brings up questions about who does what kind of domestic work, how work outside the home is gendered, how this new status of women in the workforce affects parenting and attitudes to parenting. Equally the men, the husbands who don't swap, are also called into question, the traditional man, the new man, and everything in between, has been portrayed and more often than not found wanting in yet another example of the contemporary 'crisis of masculinity'.

The reality game show can also be seen as having a productive role in this processing of the themes of reflexive modernity. At a primary level its clear that the talk about *Big Brother* or *Survivor* or *Fame Academy* is as much about ourselves as it is about the participants – our water cooler conversations are the site for viewers to do our own identity work, when I express a preference for an Irish, lesbian ex-nun as *Big Brother* contestant, I am saying more about myself and what kind of man I am than about anything else. While the primary goal of the reality game show is profit through entertainment and participation, these programmes also actively produce the conflicts and problems of reflexive modernity as a by-product of their discursive effects. We have seen above how *Big Brother* has generated public sphere discussions in different national contexts on a wide variety of topics arising out of modernity, tradition, morality, health and sexuality. Although the RTV game show does not set out to do public service work, its simulations are nevertheless productive of emergent debates that raise questions about the way we live now, in terms of identity, relationships, gender and ethics.

22   The Work of Work

Reality TV and the negotiation of neo-liberal labour in *The Apprentice*

Nick Couldry and Jo Littler

This is a battle between the individuals now, and it's going to be an incredible second half of the series.

(Mark Frith, editor of Heat[1])

Introduction

It has been argued that we face a crisis of 'the society of formal work' characterized by endemic instability in the work domain (Beck 2000: 21); and that, at the same time, powerful neo-liberal discourses are seeking to eliminate social and collective opposition to that crisis's consequences (Bourdieu 1998: 95–6). In this chapter we are concerned with the shift in work-focused practices, norms and values that are inscribed within neo-liberalism; more specifically, we look at how lived practices of work are reproduced in the high-profile 'reality game' of *The Apprentice*, in particular in its UK version, and in the politics of its use of a documentary format.

There has been a shift in the forms of power and the social bonds which hold the workplace together (Sennett 2006). Organizations at all levels, from boards to sales forces, are required to respond ever more quickly to short-term demands (whether of stock market investors or powerful customers) (cf. Bunting 2004: 36). This tends to undermine older models of bureaucratic power and foreground charismatic leaders who can front change at the apex of one-way command structures (enhanced by instant electronic communications) that rely primarily on a surveillance-based centralization of functions and self-governance rather than the social bonds that previously sustained corporate loyalty (Sennett 2006: 47). While new forms of networking, sociality and affective forms of labour have emerged, trust between employees is overwhelmingly reduced, and the successful employee must constantly adapt to new structures (Hardt and Negri 2005: 110–11; Sennett 2006: 49). As a result, power and the norms of employee performance are transformed, and 'success' becomes redefined in terms of 'the magic of "being discovered", which involves luck, self-presentation, image and finding oneself in the right place at the right time' (Yiannis Gabriel, quoted in Bunting 2004: 154). The power-'play' of *The*

Apprentice's reality game offers a useful entry-point for understanding how norms of 'playful' performance at work are constructed and naturalized in contemporary British society.

At the time of writing, there have been 17 different international versions of *The Apprentice*, which have garnered various degrees of popularity: in Finland and Germany, for example, it was cancelled after one series. By contrast, in the US, it reached the ranking of 7th most popular primetime programme, and in the UK *The Apprentice* has been so popular that the current series is being moved to the main BBC channel, BBC 1, from BBC2.[2] It is surely significant that the programme has gained particular popularity in two countries where working hours are so high: they continue to rise in the USA, and the UK remains the only country in the EU with an opt-out from the European Working Time Directive stipulating a maximum 48-hour working week. The issue here, however, is not so much levels of working hours, but the contradictory norms and values on which such an 'overwork culture' (Schor 1992; Bunting 2004) depends. The media ritual (Couldry 2003) of 'reality TV' is an important social form in this context. By presenting the 'reality' of work and business in the form of theatrical entertainment, *The Apprentice* transforms the norms of the neo-liberal workplace into taken-for-granted 'common sense'.

Some background

Our article focuses on the UK version of *The Apprentice*. The rules of the format are well known: the initial contestants compete, first in groups and in later episodes directly against each other, for the prize of a job with the corporate mogul (in the UK, Sir Alan Sugar) who is also their chief interlocutor in the game's confrontations. When a group of contestants is on the losing side in a programme's task, one of them is fired at the end of that programme: the one to be fired is either the losing team leader or one of those who the losing team leader has nominated, the decision being Sir Alan's.

The US version, while identical in format, offers a different inflection of neo-liberal norms, as we will note in detail below. Indeed, it can be argued that the US version displays a neo-liberal 'contract' more securely embedded in norms of sociability as well as long-established entertainment values. In the US version the potential employer (Donald Trump) is presented, unambiguously, as a celebrity of fabulous wealth, access to whom is always touched by awe and mutual, if unequal, respect. By contrast, Sir Alan Sugar in the UK version rejects any idea of his celebrity as 'natural', emphasizing throughout his hard-won triumph over his working-class upbringing. The UK version of *The Apprentice* thus shows more obviously the *tensions* behind neo-liberalism's impoverishment of the social, just as does New Labour's political translation of international neo-liberal doctrine (Hall 2003: 10–24).

Not surprisingly perhaps, given these tensions, the broadcasting objective of the UK *The Apprentice* was shamelessly ideological: 'to bring business to those who might not have thought it was for them' (Jane Lush, BBC Controller of Entertainment Commissioning, quoted BBC 2005). While the programme is a game, its 'point' – in this, it is similar to most reality TV – depends on a claim to 'reality': '[it is] the first entertainment show to have a real point – to show what it really takes to get ahead in business' (Daisy Goodwin, editorial director, Talkback Productions, quoted BBC 2005). Hence, the emphasis in the opening credits: 'this is the ultimate job interview'. At the end of Series 2, the BBC2 controller, Roly Keating praised the programme's 'blend of documentary skills' (quoted *Guardian*, 11 May 2006). The historical roots of this particular claim to documentary reality are interesting: the inventor of *The Apprentice* and its overall producer is Mark Burnett, a UK-born ex-paratrooper, well known previously for developing the *Survivor* format, which also claims to present reality – in that case, 'human nature' – under game conditions. This is also the Mark Burnett who translates the lessons of his reality games into motivational speeches at IBM and other corporate settings.[3]

Jane Lush's comment also indicates how *The Apprentice* provides a popular education in what it means to be a contemporary entrepreneurial worker. Indeed, the BBC explicitly promotes the programme as part of its educational remit (BBC 2006/7).[4] This is one of the more subtle ways in which the programme is imbricated within a specific historical conjuncture within which the values of the public sector and public education are being melded with those of private business. The programme fits snugly into a Blairite landscape in which a variety of state schools are, in a variety of ways, being turned over to private corporate interests, whether through the Private Finance Initiative (PFI), City Academies, the channelling of business and enterprise specialist schools, or the more general encouragement of enterprise as a core educational value (Monbiot 2000; Whitfield 2001). That *The Apprentice* participates in the normalization of this formation was particularly apparent in a feature in *The Independent*'s educational supplement detailing the UK government's decision to provide £180 million for all 14–16-year-olds to undergo five days' worth of 'enterprise training'. The cover image featured a glowering Sugar, and the headline read, 'You're hired: Why Gordon Brown wants children to be more like Sir Alan'. (Notably, that article did not even remotely question the ethics of the government's policy, focusing solely on the technocratic issues surrounding its implementation (Wice 2006).)

As a format, *The Apprentice* occupies a distinctive place in the universe of reality-based entertainment. In one direction, it can be related to the rise of business-related computer games such as ZooTycoon™ (Microsoft) and OilTycoon (Global Star Software).[5] But in its performance format, and with its narratives of self-transformation, it is closer to 'democratic' games shows such as *American Idol* and *Pop Idol*. But while those shows, through their use of popular music and audience voting, offer a narrative of collective 'dealienation' (Stahl 2006: Chapter 4), *The Apprentice* offers a narrative of unfettered individual competition regulated not by 'the people' but by a single powerful businessman.

Sir Alan's arbitrariness and aggressiveness as the programme's celebrity have excited critical commentary in the UK from business leaders. But this apparent conflict with everyday banal reality, no doubt accentuated for dramatic purposes, does not undermine the programme's *normalization*, more generally, of a particular type of power – individualized and charismatic – that fits well with contemporary corporate transformations. Whatever its theatre, *The Apprentice* must be seen as part of a wider process whereby television seeks increasingly to govern the norms of everyday life (Ouellette and Hay, forthcoming; cf. generally Rose 1996).

Let us now examine how this works in detail. Our commentary in what follows is based on a detailed analysis of Series 2 of the UK programme (BBC2, February–May 2006) and its follow-up programmes, *The Apprentice – You're Fired* (BBC3), drawing in places on comparisons with Series 1 and 2 of the US programme (2004). All references to UK episodes are to Series 2, unless otherwise noted.

Governing work in chaotic capitalism

The Apprentice is framed as both an entertaining spectacle and popular education concerning what it means to be a successful entrepreneurial worker in contemporary culture. The British version, in particular, with its more pronounced orientation towards the mode of aesthetically polished documentary, makes the subject very available to be viewed safely at one remove. The shots are long, letting the action unravel before us, distanciated from us. As viewers we are guided into the programme from far away, up high over the London skyline, before we pan in close to observe these trainee entrepreneurs in their newly-natural habitat. A subtle distinction is created between the smoothness of the visual and narrative frame (with its urbane, *film-noir* photography, slick electronica soundtrack and calmly modulated voice-over) and the foregrounded brashness of its subject (the working-class, rough and ready abruptness of Sir Alan and his exposed, sweating and vulnerable proto-employees). The programme therefore readily lends the scene to be read as a quasi-ironic spectacle as well as an educational product which informs and instructs on contemporary business values. Such a built-in distance works to short-circuit criticism to some extent: it already appears to have slightly removed itself from what's being portrayed. There is an additional cultural resonance here too. While Britain, unlike the USA, is short on 'natural resources' (Lawson 2006), it attempts to make up for this through marketing itself as a knowledge-economy hub for the creative industries. It is from this context that we might understand the *aestheticization* of the UK *Apprentice* as opposed to the more 'straightforward', fast reportage style of the US version, with its lack of any very pronounced distance from Trump's own particular pre-ironic brand of gaudy wealth. It is also in relation to this context that we might understand the emphasis in the UK version on a tougher, more aggressive variant of 'meritocracy'. More widely, this aestheticized narrative framing also works effectively to naturalize and endorse certain themes in contemporary business discourse, which it is worth considering in a little more detail.

The neo-liberal imperative of rolling back state provision and increasing corporate power is a process that is globally uneven and not uniform in its nature. The specific contemporary Anglo-American formation of neo-liberal corporate capitalism is simultaneously marked by polish and chaotic extremity, combining both brutal forms of primitive accumulation and a tendency to 'activate germs of talent' in increasingly sophisticated ways (Thrift 2006). It is also characterized by 'a cancellation of the promises made to employees', as Robin Blackburn puts it, combined with 'a surge in upscale real-estate prices and the turnover of the luxury goods sector'

(Blackburn 2006: 69–70). This somewhat chaotic combination of the rough and the smooth is easy enough to spot in *The Apprentice*. Luxury goods are emphasized as highly desirable, as the just deserts and the rewards of each challenge. The availability of the high-end treats such as 'pole position seats on the catwalk' at London fashion week (Series 1: Episode 5) or 'a champagne bar at Vertigo 42, one of the highest buildings in London' (Series 1: Episode 1) as the reward for the winning team at the end of every episode indicates their simultaneous status of hard-to-gain treat and ever-ready possibility. The contestants and viewers are invited to admire objects, property and land owned by Sugar; we are, for example, reminded in Episode 1 that 'He's got his own fleet of executive jets and a Mayfair property portfolio' (and it is notable that Trump – his US opposite number – has made most of his money through real estate). The fact that there are no safety nets for contestants on the programme is constantly emphasized; indeed, the risk of being cast aside is turned into a source of dramatic excitement and tension ('You're fired!'). (In the Finnish one-off version of *The Apprentice*, by contrast, the slogan was the polite phrase 'You're free to leave' which doesn't have quite the same brutally dramatic edge.)[6]

Even more fundamentally, the chaotic nature of contemporary capitalism is reflected in the cultures of work incarnated in the programme which encourage people to 'govern themselves out of' precariousness (*or* out of the status of social loser) and into successful working agents by, as Thrift would put it, 'activat[ing their] germs of talent'. The UK *Apprentice* enshrines the individualized atomized self as the privileged or meaningful site of work. In this way, the contemporary formations of chaotic capitalism are governed not simply by top-down regulation and governance, but by the active participation of individuals, by their psychological engagement with such structures: what Foucault termed 'governmentality'. As Nikolas Rose puts it, applying this term to the individualization of post-Fordist working cultures, 'the government of work now passes through the psychological strivings of each and every individual for fulfillment' (Rose 1999: 118).

The theatrics of *The Apprentice* provides an education in these social techniques through heightened, close-up focus on individual responses to a pressurized context. In Episode 6, for instance, after Sir Alan has told the contestants they will be selling used cars, the voice-over tells us 'there's only a few hours to learn about it ... So it's straight into the classroom to learn how to catch a customer.' Through such techniques, viewers are therefore presented with a mixture of psychological intrigue (in the form of how the contenders relate to their context); social drama (in terms of the interrelation between the characters); and assessment (in that they are both encouraged to participate in assessing the contestants' performance and to imbibe these lessons – whether directly or indirectly – to aid their own personal self-management). The programme therefore invites various modes of spectatorship, from the explicitly codified form of viewing as direct business education – the motivated viewer can also buy the tie-in book published alongside the series, guiding the reader to learn 'how to be an apprentice' (Sugar 2005) – to a less overtly educational form of watching in which neo-liberal governance is absorbed through narrative pleasure. Yet through *The Apprentices's* complex 'realist' construction as documentary, a highly particular view of contemporary capitalism is naturalized. *The Apprentice*, in other words, is documentary realism with a price attached.

How *The Apprentice* presents 'the social'

So far we have reviewed how the UK version of *The Apprentice* depicts the general business landscape, and how this translates into certain values which individuals must display if they are to succeed within the domain of the programme. In this section, we look at how the programme presents the social world of work. In these terms, the contrast with the US programme is here quite striking, as the norms of interpersonal aggression are presented with so little disguise in the UK programme. The correlations and distinctions between these different versions can partly be understood in terms of their relation to broader social and cultural contexts, as the USA and the UK share a number of key features but also diverge from each other.

The degree of verbal aggression in the UK version of *The Apprentice* is high, whether between contestants or Sir Alan's one-way assaults on contestants in 'the Boardroom'. This aggression takes more than one form. Whereas Sir Alan appears to relish extreme directness and harshness, the multiple job interviews that make up the contest of Episode 11 intensify the mental aggression, even if the interviewers are sometimes softly spoken: as Nick Hewer, Sir Alan's adviser throughout the series, commented in the follow-up programme to Episode 11 (*The Apprentice: You're Fired*, BBC3), Sir Alan's team of interviewers acted more like 'interrogators' than interviewers. This continuous aggression, whose detailed implications we will consider shortly, incidentally contrasts sharply with how interpersonal relations are conducted in the US show. While competitive pressures are, of course intense in the US version also, there is little shouting, either among the contestants or by Donald Trump in 'the Boardroom'. Within the US contestant teams, we are shown more discussion and deliberation, and fewer obvious attempts to dominate others purely by verbal aggression. Within the social world of the US show there is therefore at least some *prima facie* basis for interpersonal trust. By contrast, in perhaps the 'money-shot' of UK Series 2, Syed shouts down Sharon's complaints at others' duplicity: 'Everyone's knifing every other fucker in the back, so what's the fucking problem?'

It is worth looking more specifically at how verbal aggression is used and made sense of in the UK show. The UK contestants are assumed – at least this is nowhere contested on camera – to accept that the price of being on the show is to face Sir Alan's verbal aggression in all its unpredictable forms. Indeed, being able to withstand verbal aggression emerges as one of the core character strengths measured and, as it were, tempered, in the UK show. In one typical incident (Episode 6), Sam is asked: 'Can I ask you a direct question?' 'Of course Sir Alan.' 'Do you think if you weren't there it would have made any difference?' Syed's outstanding ability to endure and even occasionally deflect such aggression is praised by Sir Alan (*The Apprentice: You're Fired*, following Episode 10). The ability to cope with aggression is linked, as in so many other reality TV shows, to the 'learning' experience which participating provides: Ansell, who came third overall, comments (*The Apprentice: You're Fired*, following Episode 11) on how much he learned from having Sir Alan 'carving into' him. This reference to 'learning' implies a claim about the 'reality' for which you are being educated, which was made explicit in the same discussion by a contestant from the first UK series (Saira Khan) when she justified the hyper-aggressive interviews just shown as representing 'the culture you'll be working in'. In these ways we can see the programme working to naturalize two norms: the norm of domination by verbal aggression, and the norm of *willing submission to* aggression.

Ruth, the show's runner-up, who of all the contestants appeared to have the most intense identification with Sir Alan's persona, lets slip in Episode 12 that 'that bloody man has had me on my knees'. There is surely anger here, but it cannot be acknowledged within the show's discourse. Why this anger cannot be acknowledged becomes clearer when we look at how Sir Alan's aggression works within the UK programme's 'documentary reality'. Sir Alan's right to *exercise* aggression without restraint is shown to trump any other assessment norms. At the end of Episode 11 (in effect the series' semi-final), Sir Alan confronts Paul who was distinguished for having never been on the losing team in any of the previous programmes' tasks; as a result, Paul had never appeared until this point before Sir Alan in 'the Boardroom'. From the perspective of team success, this record would seem to be evidence in Paul's favour but Sir Alan turns the tables on Paul in an interesting confrontation:

> the fact that you've won all the tasks doesn't mean jack shit to me because *I* haven't talked with you yet. So you speak to me now, you speak to me now, because, I'm telling you, it's getting close to that door [pointing at the exit door].

As elsewhere (see above), team dynamics are seen to be inconsequential; all that matters is individual combat, and there is only one combat that ultimately counts, combat with Sir Alan.

This exclusively charismatic model of power[7] is integrated with the editorializing of the show which emphasizes the moments when fear is generated. Such editorializing places the viewers in the position of voyeurs of fear. In these terms, it is similar to how *Big Brother* encourages the pleasure of watching contestants' self-presentation crack under strain to reveal 'emotional truth', as Annette Hill (2002) has argued. In *The Apprentice*, at the end of Episode 11 when Ruth's survival is in the balance, following a severe reprimand, Sir Alan keeps her waiting for a few seconds as we watch her face blush, before he tells her she's through to the final. Once again, the programme's documentary values – its implied claim to psychological 'realism' – is enmeshed with a very particular version of the norms for how power operates, through aggression and fear, in the contemporary business world.

Business as entertainment

We want briefly to explore now how media's own authority within the domain of the programme is naturalized. We will leave to one side the larger question of how reality TV works to sustain its claim to reality (Couldry 2003: Chapter 6) and concentrate on how in the UK show the imagined world of business is presented as in some respects *continuous with* the world of media and entertainment. In some ways this is hardly surprising and has already been noted: so the prize of winning the series is always associated with fabulous wealth, suggested by the house in which the contestants live throughout the series: 'I've found you a house in the best street in the country', says Sir Alan in Episode 1, pointing out to gasps from the contestants that a neighbouring house has just sold for £45 million. The rewards each week for the successful team have been discussed earlier, as have the occasional glimpses of Sir Alan's lifestyle (for example, the fleet of luxury cars at his London house) ('now *that's* a house' comments one of the contestants – Episode 7). More interesting is the overlap between the model of business success presented in the series and the world of entertainment: the final challenge that decides the show's winner (Episode 12) is not a conventional business task but 'putting on a show' in the Tower of London at a few days' notice.

Perhaps more surprising is the overlap between the programme's values and those of tabloid journalism which emerges particularly in the follow-up programmes shown on BBC3. On the face of it we might not expect to see the editor of the celebrity magazine *Heat* turn up as an 'expert' commentator on the show – as he did on more than one occasion – since there is little similarity between most business tasks and running a celebrity magazine. Nor would a *Sun* lifestyle journalist be an obvious choice as a business expert, but one such (Jane Moore) appeared in the follow-up to Episode 10 opposite the *Heat* editor. Her comment about Syed who had just been eliminated was striking: 'He'd make a fantastic tabloid journalist', she noted, because of his plausible charm in getting stories out of people. Given that Syed's apparent duplicity has been a running theme of the second series, this might be seen as ironic, but if so, the irony is undeveloped. At work here is the programme's construction of its own authority within the entertainment world of 'celebrity culture' that overlaps with the programme's quite particular presentation of the world of business. This foregrounds both how business culture is increasingly drawing on tabloid discourse to construct an image of itself as cool, contemporary and 'democratic' (Littler 2007; McGuigan 2006) and the sheer range of techniques *The Apprentice* draws on to stake its claim to documentary 'realism': in this case, a documentary realism which is in turn used to naturalize neo-liberal working cultures.

Conclusion: 'realism' and the need for ethics

Mark Andrejevic has persuasively argued that reality TV in general is a sphere in which 'the participation of consumers in the rationalization of their own consumption is sold as empowerment' (Andrejevic 2004: 15). In *The Apprentice*, as we have shown, this focus is re-tooled towards labour – it becomes a site where the participation of *workers* in the rationalization of their own work is sold as empowerment (for both viewer and contestant). The programme educates its viewers (in dramatized form) in how to become 'empowered' by struggling within and reproducing the norms of a harsh, unpredictable, precarious, increasingly competitive working climate. As a result, the highly distinctive *performance* norms of contemporary business culture are themselves naturalized and presented as part of the 'real world out there'.

We could stop our argument here perhaps, but to do so would be to omit one key point: the *ethics* of the documentary format we have analysed. For we believe that important ethical questions are raised by supposedly 'documentary' formats such as *The Apprentice* which are at the heart also of the potential – but surprisingly underdeveloped – debate about the ethics of reality TV generally. In fact, two rather different types of ethical question intersect here. First, there is an ethical question about whether we are happy to live in societies where reality TV formats – with their reliance on surveillance, interpersonal aggression, ritualized humiliations – have themselves become normalized, indeed legitimated as an apparent source of knowledge about today's social 'realities'. This is an important question (see Couldry 2006) but one not specific to *The Apprentice* and so we leave it to one side. Second, there is an ethical question about *The Apprentice* itself as a particular documentary format; it is this second question on which we would like to focus in concluding.

As we saw earlier, BBC's claims for *The Apprentice* as a programme turn, in large part, on claims about its status as a presentation of reality: both its educational value for contemporary living and, necessarily intertwined with that, its status as, in some sense, 'realistic' and 'truthful'. *The Apprentice* is, on the other hand, also a form of entertainment which should give it, *prima facie*, some licence to dramatize and accentuate its presentations for the sake of being good entertainment. This ambiguity, far from being unusual, is precisely the ambiguity on which reality TV, as a form of media ritual, depends (Couldry 2002, 2003). It follows, however, that, where the factual claims involved in a reality TV game are *themselves questionable*, or in some other way require to be opened up for debate (for example, because they embed *norms which are themselves highly questionable*), there are some ethical issues to be discussed. And, as we have seen, *The Apprentice* makes quite particular 'realist' claims about contemporary capitalism, and the appropriate norms for the exercise of corporate power over employees in the workplace. There is nothing 'factually neutral' about the show of isolated quasi-employees (that is, stand-ins for the role of employee within the fiction of *The Apprentice* game) being humiliated by their 'employer' in front of their rival 'employees'. There is nothing neutral either about the way that any values of group cooperation or even basic social respect in the workplace are, as we have argued, consistently devalued in the programme's presentation of what is 'really' at stake in today's world of work. *The Apprentice*'s presentation of 'dog eats dog' capitalism has, as we saw, been contested by business leaders as an inaccurate presentation of today's workplace, but the social *norms* on which *The Apprentice* is based are protected by the programme's status as 'just a game': this, after all, is the ideological power of 'games', that their premises become difficult to criticize, while being conversely easy to absorb, because they can always claim to operate within the domain of the 'as if'.

When games, including reality TV games such as *The Apprentice*, rely for their premises on highly contestable factual claims about social reality or, just as problematic, highly contestable norms chosen from among the range of norms which *might* govern social reality, then those claims and those norms should, we suggest, themselves be opened up to debate in a way that the ambiguous documentary/game status of reality TV *precisely prevents*. Unless this is done, we are entitled to level against reality TV producers a challenge analogous to that Onora O'Neill posed in her 2002 Reith Lectures to news producers:

> If powerful institutions are allowed to publish, circulate and promote material without indicating what is standard analysis and what is speculation, which sources may be knowledgeable and which are probably not, they damage our public culture and all our lives. Good public debate must not only be *accessible to* but also *assessable by* its audiences.
>
> (O'Neill 2002: 95)

The alternative for media producers is of course equally simple: to stop claiming that programmes such as *The Apprentice* exhibit 'documentary' qualities, and to acknowledge instead that they are games based on premises, and norms, that there is no reason for us as viewers to necessarily accept.

Notes

1 Speaking on *The Apprentice: You're Fired*, following Episode 7 of *The Apprentice* (UK series 1).
2 See http://en.wikipedia.org/wiki/The_Apprentice#_note-0. Accessed February 2007.
3 See Prose (2004: 61). Thanks to Carole Stabile for alerting us to this reference.
4 The BBC's 2006/7 Statement of Programme Policy explicitly states that it will, as one of its future priorities, 'Continue to strengthen the range of popular factual that appeals to younger audiences, for example with factual formats in subject areas such as business (such as *The Apprentice*).' http://www.bbc.co.uk/info/statements2006/tv/bbctwo.shtml. Accessed February 2007.
5 For discussion, see Opel and Smith (2004).
6 See http://en.wikipedia.org/wiki/The_Apprentice#_note-0. Accessed February 2007.
7 Compare Weber's (1991) well-known division between traditional, rational and charismatic authority.

Part IV

Digital and Online Documentaries: Opportunities and Limitations

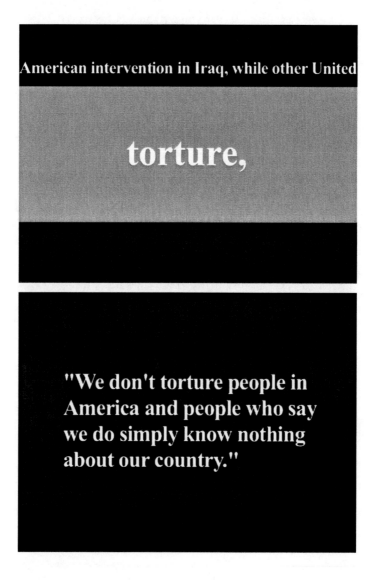

Stills from Tony Cokes' *Evil.8: Unseen* (2004 – Video 8 min).
Source: Scott Pagano. Courtesy Tony Cokes.

23 Documentary Viewing Platforms

Ana Vicente

The relatively uncommercial aspect of documentary throughout its history has forced the genre to the continuous search for its ideal platform. Television became the ideal window for documentaries when the high cost involved in a theatrical exposure could not justify the presence of low box office earners in cinemas. This would have a major effect on the way documentaries were funded, produced, distributed and viewed. While fiction would follow the exploitation of the film's rights via the traditional exhibition chain across all platforms (theatrical, video, television), documentaries went on to be funded largely by broadcasters and mainly aimed at television audiences.

Up to the late 1990s, only the odd music or celebrity-related documentary was considered for mainstream theatrical distribution. It was almost inconceivable to think that non-fiction and fiction film genres would one day compete not only in the major international film festivals but also in terms of box office figures. The surge of documentary hits that occurred from 2002 in the United States, Europe, Australasia and to certain extent also in South America and Asia raised the big question ... Was this documentary boom a mere fad or were we witnessing the birth of a new trend in the film industry?

The reasons put forward to explain the boom in theatrical documentaries at the beginning of the millennium are varied. Digital technology cut the costs of production and post-production processes enormously, enabling low budget filmmaking; the multiplication of media channels gave birth to a more 'sophisticated' audience that sought to be challenged by films, not merely entertained. Some documentaries also adopted a 'cinematic look', away from the traditional wobbly camera work of observational and *'cinéma verité'* styles. Other arguments point to the limited space granted for 'creative documentary forms' on prime time television slots, first in the USA and later on in Europe. Whatever the reasons, (some) documentaries' commercial viability in theatrical windows is for now undeniable. As Table 23.1 shows, eight of the ten all-time top grossing documentaries were released from 2002 to 2006.

Table 23.1 Top 10 feature documentaries, 1994–2004

Title	Year	WW Gross Millions (US$)
Fahrenheit 9/11	2004	$222.4
March of the Penguins	2005	$127.0
Bowling for Columbine	2002	$58.0
An Inconvenient Truth	2006	$49.0
Winged Migration	2001	$32.3
Modonna: Truth or Dare	1991	$29.0
Super Size Me	2004	$28.6
Touching the Void	2004	$13.8
Aliens of the Deep	2005	$12.7
Hoop Dreams	1994	$11.8

Source: Screen International (July 2007). Figures not adjusted for inflation.

This chapter explores the viewing platforms and distribution channels that documentary films may use in the immediate future. Advances in technology first changed the way in which films were produced; now, technological advances are transforming the ways in which those films reach their audiences. New inexpensive and convenient platforms – DVD and Video on Demand (VoD)[1] – have varied the viewing patterns of the consumer and are shifting distribution channels and long-established business models for documentaries.

The documentary genre has now positioned itself on a par with 'independent' fiction film and is borrowing similar marketing methods and approaches to reach its audiences. For instance, some documentaries are using the filmmaker's celebrity status as a marketing tool to help advertise and sell the film. Works by Morgan Spurlock, Michael Moore, Nick Broomfield, Spike Lee, Sydney Pollack and Kevin Macdonald capitalize on the director's popularity to draw in viewers.

The main buzz in the 2007 Berlin European Film Market (EFM) centred around the pre-sales of deals, often involving several hundred thousand Euros as an advance minimum guarantee on documentary films still in pre-production or production stages. Spurlock's documentary on the search for Bin Laden in Afghanistan was sold to at least ten main territories at Berlin (Macnab 2007; Tartaglione Vialette 2007). Martin Scorsese's documentary on the Rolling Stones, Shine a Light, was sold to 15 countries during the EFM and the American Film (Noh 2007), and the BBC's feature-length wildlife film Earth was licensed in nine main territories[2] (Mitchell 2007). This trend is probably set to continue in the coming years, when we expect to witness the wide-scale release of high-profile documentaries as well as surprise festival hits.[3] Nonetheless, the high-profile documentary is but the tip of the iceberg, constituting just a tiny percentage of the total of documentaries produced. Hence, the question we should be asking ourselves is, which platforms or media will all the other 'theatrical' documentaries use in order to reach their audiences?

The main bulk of documentary film production is constituted by critically acclaimed films and by independent projects.[4] As with 'art-house' and 'independent' fiction film marketing, the festival circuit, award ceremonies, word of mouth, press coverage and reviews are the main channels for the marketing of documentaries. A major difference, however, is that documentary films have a far more limited reach when using traditional distribution methods. First, despite the critical acclaim a documentary may enjoy, its sale or licensing to all main territories is rare. Second, even when a film is sold for widespread theatrical distribution, profits and revenues are not guaranteed. For instance, the award-winning film *Working Man's Death* (Austria, 2005) has not secured UK distribution and some of the companies releasing the film did not recoup costs or make a profit. This is due to the high prints and advertising[5] costs involved in the film's marketing in the build-up to release.

Traditional distribution systems simply do not work for the main bulk of feature film documentaries produced. Documentary audiences are growing around the world and there is little doubt of the existence of many untapped audiences that occur due to a lack of exposure or access to the product. Even though the quality, directing style and subject matter of these films may deserve a theatrical exposure or what this entails – press coverage, publicity – the high marketing costs involved make the use of traditional distribution channels economically unviable. Moreover, the producer and/or filmmaker is usually the last on the revenue chain, leaving little or no chance to recoup costs, let alone enjoy significant revenues.

In recent years we have seen the appearance of alternative distribution channels that have broken the traditional distribution pattern. Peter Broderick, President of Paradigm Consulting, touched upon the new models of distribution at the International Documentary Festival, Amsterdam, in 2006. Broderick listed some of the inconveniences of the traditional 'all rights deals' for documentary production teams, including the loss of control over the picture, drop in the distributor's motivation after a weak opening, loss of video window opportunities, loss of potential revenues due to cross-collateralized deals and, finally, loss of the project's independence. He argues in favour of alternative models that include the splitting of rights and that take advantage of new distribution opportunities flourishing thanks to advances in digital technology from digital theatrical exhibition to DVD sales, to VoD online.

Digital technology has kept the costs of theatrical exhibition low for those documentaries that adopt a low-key release through festivals or specialized screenings. As we have observed, only a few of the documentary films released gain box office success. What is more important, however, is the significant increase in the number of documentary films that are exhibited in cinemas. In 2001, the Netherlands pioneered *Docuzone*, funding ten digital projectors in cinemas that had committed to screening documentaries on a weekly basis. In 2004, the project was extended to a pan-European circuit of cinemas in eight countries. *CinemaNet Europe* releases 12 documentaries a year in more than 100 theatres across Europe on a fixed day every month. In the UK, the Digital Screen Network scheme funded by the UK Film Council is equipped with digital projectors in around 200 cinemas. Robert Kenny, operations manager of the London cinema chain Curzon, states that half of the 20 documentary films they exhibit yearly would not have been screened without the accessibility of digital film projectors.

However, it is revenues derived from video/DVD and VoD rights that can be most profitable, if well exploited. Specialist video distributors enjoy a network of outlets to reach general audiences, but increasingly, the largest revenue-generating potential lies in reaching documentary's core audiences. For instance, Robert Green-wald's documentaries *Outfoxed: Rupert Murdoch's War on Journalism* (US, 2004), *Uncovered: The War on Iraq* (US, 2004) and *Wal-Mart: The High Cost of Low Price* (US, 2005), secured theatrical distribution after an independent DVD release. The produc-ers associated with www.moveon.org, the organization that produced and distributed *Outfoxed*, initially sold thousands of DVDs to groups for private screenings. This was followed by word of mouth and online reviews. Within two months of the DVD release, more than 200,000 DVDs units had been sold. Most recently, UK director Phil Grabsky drew on this distribution model from the conception of his documentary title *In Search of Mozart*. The production of the six-language DVD version added £16,000 to the film's overall costs but DVD sales reached over 10,000 units with a retail price of £20 per unit (Jacobsen 2007).

As for television, it is difficult to predict the effects that the digital switch-over will have for the feature-length documentary. Bo Stehmeier, head of sales and co-productions for Dutch documentary distributor Off the Fence, predicts that viewers will not be dependent on documentary slots on television, but rather will become more pro-active in the search for the titles they want to see on other VoD platforms. Broadcasters are already following this path: in France Arte, Canal +, FR2 and FR3 have VoD services for documentaries as does the Documentary Channel in Canada.

The emerging trend of the current decade is the rise of VoD delivered over online platforms. At present, discussions on potential pitfalls or shortcomings of online documentary and fiction film distribution are ongoing. Some of the main concerns are the limited availability of the technology required for the mass consumer market, the need to generate awareness about a film and/or its content providers, the lack of industry consensus to accept deals granting non-exclusive online rights, security hazards concerning rights protection (Digital Rights Manage-ment),[6] as well as questions about revenue-splitting and the application of different business models. Nevertheless, the general consensus among media organizations pioneering this movement, distributors and content providers, is that these issues will be resolved by the end of the decade and a viable, contextualized framework will be in place. A report by David Graham Associates, written for the European Parliament, predicts that, by 2012, large numbers of people in Europe will be ordering films from multi-language film portals, in the subtitled or dubbed version of their choice.[7]

A documentary community and a framework for discussion of the development of documentary form and medium of outreach are already in place. Formed by filmmakers and media practitioners in the international documentary context, www.DocAgora.org was launched in 2006 to promote the discussion of new models of documentary production and distribution. One of its goals

> is to bring awareness, knowledge of the new platforms and alternative ways of outreach, seeking for valid business models and to create a dialogue

between potential funding bodies, supporters and partners in society and media who care about socially engaging docs as a tool for expression and change.

(Breuer 2006)

Discussions on these topics have been in progress since 2006 at major international documentary film festivals and forums such as IDFA, Hotdocs, Thessaloniki, Silverdocs, as well as in online documentary specialist forums like www.D-word.com. The online distribution of documentaries has three main benefits, critical for the success of this new platform in offering what the traditional distribution system is failing to achieve: (1) a wider availability of the product; (2) a viable economic model for the rights owner; and (3) as noted by Broderick, complete control of the picture retained by the filmmaker/producer.

Increasingly, documentary audiences want to watch and keep up with the winning films at international film festivals or with the nominees in the major competitive runs for the Academy Awards or European Documentary Awards. Distribution through the 'all rights deal' and individual licensing territory means a film like *Working Man's Death* can be released in six European countries and never in the UK, for instance. Rising availability through the distribution of documentary-on-demand will boost documentary viewing not only for new films, but also classic titles that become available to stream or download at any time. For instance, Dizga Vertov's *Man with a Movie Camera* (USSR, 1929) is available for free viewing from www.archive.org.

The second main advantage of the online distribution of documentaries is the application of a new business model that benefits first and foremost the makers or rights owners of the project and not just the intermediaries. Since most online documentary platforms are emerging at the time of writing, we cannot ascertain the revenues that online distribution will bring. www.Nomadsland.com, a VoD platform for the distribution of 'quality' documentaries, has announced a total of 22,000 downloads for the documentary *From Dust* (UAE, 2005) and around 15,000 for *The Art of Flight* (US, Sudan, 2005) in the first two months since they were made available.[8] Currently, a wide array of business models are being launched, tested and scrutinized. The main topics for discussion revolve around ways to provide content to viewers and protection to the rights' holder. Should providers make content available for viewers for a fee or should content be free to view, leaving sponsors and advertising companies to foot the bill? Is the investment in DRM cost-effective for content providers?

Additionally, a number of films that for legal issues are censored in cinemas or on television can reach their audiences when distributed online. In the UK, Ken Fero's *Injustice* (2001) identified several police officers believed to be involved in deaths in police custody. Just one of the central London cinemas decided to go ahead with the screening in spite of warnings from the Police Federation, the rest of the screenings were pulled. Equally, the first version of the documentary *McLibel – Two Worlds Collide* was released at the end in 1997, sold to TV around the world, was seen by 26 million people (as 'streaming video' on the internet, on home video, and on cable television in the US, as well as at festivals and specialized screenings) and yet was never broadcast in the UK due to broadcasters' fears of being sued by McDonald's

(Armstrong 1998). Following the release of *Super Size Me* and in view of McDonald's 50th Birthday, a new feature-length version *McLibel* was broadcast in April 2005 on the BBC. One of the most downloaded documentaries of all time (unseen at that time on television) was *Loose Change* (US, 2005), a documentary about 9/11 conspiracy theories. The film was first available on the web in April 2005 and by May 2006 had received 10 million viewings (Tringale 2006).

In this new vast array of content and viewing platforms, the challenge is for the viewer in selecting not only the films he/she wishes to watch but also the content provider they use. Building up a general international awareness on a film will still be a key factor in the recipe for success. In this respect, film festivals and award ceremonies will continue to play an essential role. In fact, a growing number of online content providers are associating with documentary film festivals to increase awareness of their platform and films. www.Docutube.com was born from the Sheffield international documentary festival and www.doc-air.com from Jihlava IDFF in the Czech Republic. These websites' aim is to provide an online platform to showcase the films presented at their festivals, addressing the audience in order to further promote the films after the event.

The ideal scenario for the marketing of a feature documentary in VoD platforms is to first make best use of the documentary film festival run, then maximize press coverage and reviews to generate as much awareness as possible, and finally, to make the film available via traditional platforms as well as on the new VoD medium. Since online communities are not driven by traditional marketing strategies but rather by sharing a common interest, grass roots marketing targeted to specialist communities' websites is becoming the most effective promotional method for documentaries appealing to a specific core audience. For instance, while several successfully crossed over to larger audiences, *Etre et Avoir* (France, 2002) attracted the teaching community, *Touching the Void* (UK, 2003) appealed to mountaineering enthusiasts, *The Corporation* (Canada, 2003) to activist groups, economics professionals and students or those involved in large corporations, *The March of the Penguins* (France, 2005) to animal lovers, *An Inconvenient Truth* (US, 2006), to environmentalists or the ever-growing community concerned about the threat of global warming, and *A Lion in the House* (US, 2006) to those affected by cancer and their families.

The future of documentary distribution is now more promising than ever. New technologies have opened new avenues for documentary production and delivery to audiences. Digital technologies and the spread of VoD platforms, both online and in television are changing the way in which most documentaries are distributed and viewed, transforming the interaction between the filmmaker and the audience: the filmmaker increasingly needs to define, know and find his film's audience, while viewers are more actively searching for the content they wish to view on a growing multiplicity of platforms.

Web resources

VoD, stream or download (to rent or own)
http://www.onlinefilm.org
http://www.doc-air.com
http://www.docsonline.tv
http://www.lovefilm.com
http://www.artevod.com
http://www.documen.tv
http://www.nomadsland.com
http://www.nfb.ca

VoDby subscription
http://www.canalplusactive.com
http://www.joiningthedots.tv

Free non-profit educational
http://creativearchive.bbc.co.uk
http://www.archive.org

Notes

1 VoD is usually run by broadcasters, Telcos and distributors, and might be Pay-per-View or subscription-based.
2 *Earth* had already been licensed to Germany, Japan, France, Spain, Switzerland, and Greece.
3 Some of the festival hits we have seen over last years are: *Capturing the Friedmans* (US, 2003), *Spellbound* (US, 2002) and *Into Great Silence* (Germany, Switzerland, 2005).
4 Independent project: namely films financed with private or public funds and outside the traditional broadcast commissioning system. Typically feature-length docs that have a presence in the international film festival circuit but depend on DVD/TV sales to reach their main audiences and/or generate revenues.
5 A small release of just four prints in cinemas usually involves a cost of €50000 – 60000.
6 Digital Rights Management (DRM) refers to a system for protecting the copyright of data circulated via the Internet or any other digital platform, designed to enable the secure distribution of data and prevent its piracy.
7 http://europarl.europa.eu/downloaddigitaldelivery
8 The price for download (to own) or stream (1–30 day rental) ranges from $1–20 and is fixed by the rights holder. All revenues are split on a 50/50 basis every month while the film remains on the site. Films are uploaded on a non-exclusive basis.

24 Online Documentary

Danny Birchall

In the 1990s, exponents of the theory of media convergence predicted that in the coming together of telecommunications and broadcast networks there would soon cease to be a distinction between such things as 'television' and 'the internet'. They were correct about the physical infrastructure of networks: many homes now rely on only one connection to deliver telephone, internet and television, and use online services like Skype for telephony. Content is following suit more slowly: television is becoming detached from schedules with hard disc recorders and TiVO-type services, and online video websites proliferate. The internet is a medium increasingly characterized by moving images, but these moving images themselves carry the character of the internet.

The rise of YouTube and Google Video in 2005, and the acquisition of the former by the latter in 2006 did not themselves create a boom in online video, but these sites did increase the ease of distribution, taking the burden of hosting away from the content provider and providing near-universal embedded Flash video players in a marketplace riven by competing codecs and players. YouTube, with its 10-minute limit on uploads, tagging and blog-friendliness initially embraced the popular and amateur end of the market, while Google Video sought to establish relationships with distributors and studios.

In the context of this burgeoning world of online video, documentary has a place, but it has to be considered in a wider sense than in film and on television: limits on length, amateur production values and emergent aesthetic forms mean many things are found online that would never make their way to a television or cinema screen, and some forms of non-fictional moving image flourish only on the web. The questions for makers, consumers and scholars of moving images are what distinguishes documentary online from documentary made for other channels, and whether the internet has any distinct, useful or unique characteristics that offer documentary anything more than just another means of distribution.

Four such sets of characteristics are outlined below. First, in organizing geographically diverse individuals around a common interest in watching or making documentaries, there are new forms of community; second, new means of creation and distribution are given to political and campaigning documentaries that seek to either change people's minds or reinforce a viewpoint; third, we have increased access to 'dirty reality' in the form of footage of current events and violent conflict; and, fourth, video diaries and other moving images give us an increased range of intimate access to the lives of other people.

Community

While the phrase 'Web 2.0' is used in many contexts, at its core is the idea that a new generation of web technology enables people to share more easily what they make and think, and moves the power to shape definitions and links between content from the hands of professionals into our own. Through these links and sharing, communities are built. While linear video itself isn't an inherently Web 2.0 form, websites built around video frequently contain these new tools of community.

YouTube is a community for the world at large, but for UK-based documentary makers the most notable online community is FourDocs. The site works as a starting-point for budding documentary-makers, offering tutorials on the entire filmmaking process from cameras to compression, interviews with leading documentarists, and even open source stock clips. This more focused community brings a more sophisticated level of feedback and discussion about individual pieces of work in the forums devoted to them.

With a trademark 4-minute length limit, films tend towards the intimate and reflective: moments in life, simple themes elaborated, and thumbnail sketches of individuals. FourDocs has pushed the envelope inwards with an additional strand of 59-second films (with a televisual precedent in the early 1990s' BBC2/Arts Council 'One minute TV' scheme), which pare observation and reflection to their bones. As with short film funding schemes in the early 2000s, which replaced grants for making 35mm films with a larger number of smaller budgets for digitally-shot work, there is a danger, however, that sites like FourDocs may become the only, rather than a complementary, outlet for new documentary work, and that either the overall quality of the field or the quality of individual work may suffer as a consequence.

Campaigning documentaries

The success of big-screen documentaries with a political angle like *Fahrenheit 9/11* (2004), *Super Size Me* (2004) and *The Corporation* (2003) has inspired others to make political or campaigning films that will never acquire theatrical distribution. The internet is the most obvious alternative means of distribution for those inspired by Michael Moore but who lack his reach or recognition. Two successful documentaries seen only on the internet exemplify the issues of production and distribution for such filmmakers.

Dylan Avery's *Loose Change* is an independently-produced documentary which asserts that a large and rather improbable US government conspiracy was responsible for the events of September 11th 2001. The film uses news footage, talking heads and an insistent, provocative voice-over inviting viewers to question the 'official' version of events. Built on shaky foundations, it has been attacked from both left and right, but its call for the 'truth' in response to its unanswered questions has a certain amount of pull to an audience already aware that it has been lied to about the war in Iraq. The controversy that surrounds it would almost certainly deny it mainstream distribution of any sort, but on the internet it can claim an audience in the millions.

'We' The Unauthorised Arundhati Roy Musical Documentary is a very different kind of documentary. It uses footage of a speech Roy made in 2002, a year after the attack on the World Trade Center, in which she takes issue with the US military domination of the world, the polarization of the War on Terror and the disregard paid to the world's poor. The film mixes sound and image of her talk with footage of world events and the wars in Iraq and Afghanistan, blending them together in a form somewhere between a music video and *Koyaanisqatsi* (US, 1982). Where *Loose Change* appeals to the curious intellect, *We* appeals to the emotion and conscience.

Earlier political and campaigning documentaries embodying similar issues were much harder to disseminate. Peter Watkins' *The War Game* (UK, 1965), made for but not shown by the BBC, was a tremendously influential propaganda tool for the Campaign for Nuclear Disarmament, but its distribution was tortuous: 16mm prints from the British Film Institute were physically ferried around the country by individuals and shown in community and church halls, laboriously building the kind of political and affinitive network that is instantaneously available today.

The internet makes low-budget documentaries like *Loose Change* and *We* easier to make, as well as distribute. Both operate on the edge of intellectual property legislation in using a large amount of archive footage. Documentaries that rely heavily on such footage usually have that footage cleared for broadcast only, making redistribution and reissue difficult: none of Adam Curtis' television work (*The Century of the Self* (2002), *The Power of Nightmares* (2004), *The Trap* (2007)) is commercially available on DVD, for example. By contrast, the easy availability of material to work with online is matched by the ease of remixing and redistributing it.

YouTube and Google Video are also used to publish short works which campaign or agitate. YouTube carries a 'news and politics' channel in which users post television clips, their own footage, or talk to camera in support of their political position or activism. However, the immediacy and 'everydayness' of postings on YouTube, combined with the relative anonymity of posters make it fertile ground for a phenomenon known as 'astroturfing': the fabrication of fake grassroots activity. *Al Gore's Penguin Army*, a short animated attack on Al Gore's *An Inconvenient Truth* (US, 2006), portraying the former US Vice-President as the Batman villain boring even his own army of tuxedo'd penguins to sleep turned out to be the work not of a passionate lone activist but of a PR agency whose clients included oil giant Exxon.

Dirty reality

Documentary often offers us unpalatable and unpleasant facts and experiences, uncovering tales of war, abuse and torture. Usually, these are given a political or moral context by narrative, which frequently strives for reconciliation and justice either within the film or as a call to action. Even the sensationalist 'Mondo' series begun with *Mondo Cane* (Italy, 1962) which juxtaposed barely thematically linked 'outrageous' anthropological footage, had a coherence in their very promise to shock or amaze. The internet makes it possible to encounter images of atrocity directly, without such comforting frameworks.

The video of the execution of American journalist Daniel Pearl in Pakistan is available on www.LiveLeak.com. The footage of his execution itself is over in seconds; the majority of the video consists of Pearl talking under duress about his Jewishness, intercut with images of American aggression, and a list of his captors' demands. Its immediacy is shocking, but it is nevertheless a highly-mediated representation of the act and a very deliberate piece of propaganda. The form is effectively mocked by Amir Jamal's Hanif Kureishi-scripted *Weddings and Beheadings* (UK, 2007), which likens the hackwork of filmmakers forced to capture beheadings to ubiquitous wedding videos.

In Iraq, the documentary output of American soldiers equipped with video cameras and internet connections has become quite prolific. In ifilm's 'warzone' channel, soldiers' oral testimony about significant events in their service ('Watching my Company Commander Die', 'Short Order Body Retrieval', etc.) are brought together by the site under the banner 'Back From Iraq'. Alongside these are 'Soldier Music Videos' in which servicemen edit video footage of assaults and conflict to music. Parts of the war, such as Fallujah and Ramadi become at once intensely personalized as testimony and turned into spectacle, as explosions, attacks and even moving acts of solidarity and friendship are cut to a soundtrack. In some cases soldiers' videos are part of a larger project, such as Deborah Scranton's *The War Tapes* (US, 2006), (which, while a feature film and winner of a Tribeca Best Documentary award, has eschewed established distribution models in releasing a 'preview' DVD before a theatrical debut), that knit together several stories into a more traditional narrative whole.

Neither jihadi nor soldiers' videos are naïve or unconstructed (an instinctive Eisensteinian grasp of montage now seems commonplace) nor unmediated (almost all the war videos carry an implicitly political point of view), but they do share a quality of immediacy unique to online video in their accessibility and lack of wider balance or framework.

The lives of others

Almost as soon as the world wide web and its graphical interface, the web browser, appeared, so did the 'personal home page'. People made information about themselves available on the internet in such a way that theoretically anyone could see it, but in practice few did. In this fashion, the web has always offered one of the fundamental aspects of documentary: a way to see into the ordinary lives of other people, but added its equalizing correlative: anyone can give as much of their own lives as they wish to the world in general.

In 1996, Jennifer Ringley, an American college student, began living her life under the gaze of a webcam. Her website provided a sequence of still images rather than moving image, but the relentless subjection of every moment of her life to surveillance, from sexual activity to hours spent watching the television, gathered her a large following for the next five years. Unusually for an internet phenomenon, her project prefigured the popular use of the webcam by commercial pornographers. Online pornography, with a large and guaranteed customer base, has usually been the first of the internet's business sectors to marketize new technologies. The webcam in particular offers the ideal combination of the illusion of intimacy and exhibitionism to customers who are flattered to see themselves as voyeurs rather than mass audiences.

In the late 1990s, blogging became an everyday activity for millions. The technical bar to entry was lowered, and the dimension of seriality was added, turning personal revelation into a diary, with a subscription facility and the incentive to return for constant updates. Though the 'blogosphere' has generally come to refer to amateur political punditry, personal journals remain a significant phenomenon, and with the further lowering of the bar to entry on moving image, some bloggers have become video bloggers, or vloggers, talking about themselves or their lives on camera.

The vlogging style is quite formulaic: vloggers talk straight to camera in a piece that usually lasts less than five minutes; it is often scripted, and follows an argument, a story or a point to be made. YouTube allows users to post a video as a 'response' to another video, and many of the personal posts are in the form of answers to others' personal posts, though the tone often descends into either abuse or merely expressing respect to the original vlogger for having 'made it' (achieved a large audience) on YouTube.

One personal diarist, Peter Oakley, using the name 'geriatric1927' began vlogging on YouTube in his eightieth year, self-consciously drawing attention to the difference between his age and YouTube's youthful demographic. Sitting in his living room, wearing headphones and beginning each episode with 'Good evening YouTubers', he recounts the story of his life, misspent youth and career in weekly episodes entitled 'Telling it all'. He rapidly gained star status, despite being initially reluctant to forego his anonymity or take his fame any further than YouTube itself.

Vlogging's episodic form also holds some of the same attractions as serial drama. Lonelygirl15 was another YouTube phenomenon, the bedroom diary of a 15-year-old girl, covering friends, family, emotional anxieties and her parents' involvement in a strange religious cult, which proved to be a work of fiction. A predictable brouhaha followed, but the series successfully continues as overt drama: the aim of the hoax was not so much to deceive as to gain an audience, and in a crowded moving image marketplace, apparent authenticity was the factor that made it stand out.

Conclusion

As new forms of moving image and audiences for it flourish online, documentary in its widest sense has acquired unique and captivating aspects. The elements that we are used to seeing in documentary films as a mode of representation: talking heads, archive footage and verité are being reconfigured into new, often fractured and fragmentary forms, mostly by amateurs. The kinds of documentary we find on the internet follow forms that the internet has established such as brevity, community, seriality and personal connectedness as much as they follow forms established in the field of documentary filmmaking itself.

The immediacy of new online forms should not be mistaken for a lack of mediation: they are as deliberately constructed as any existing documentary forms, if not more, because of technical constraints. By contrast, authenticity is highly prized by audiences: the feeling that what one is watching is 'real' is valuable enough to be faked for either political or commercial ends.

Some of this material pushes the boundaries of what we might be used to calling 'documentary'. Forms considered surpassed in the linear 'evolution' of documentary such as propaganda documentaries and uncomplicated 'truthful' verité have re-emerged, or reminded us of their continued presence as a modes of documentary making. Certainly, few strive for the kind of anthropological objectivity that characterizes many contemporary feature-length documentaries. This is not to say, however, that scholars of documentary should discard or ignore what falls beyond the traditional boundaries of their study. When we look for how soldiers fighting the war in Iraq have understood and apprehended their experience using moving images, for example, it would be unwise to privilege recorded first person testimony over edited music videos, not least for the realization of the subjective perspective inherent in the editing.

Indeed, the definition of 'documentary' as a whole might usefully be stretched in the direction of this new kind of material. The combination of intimacy and dirty reality in particular feeds the appetites that popular audiences have always turned to documentary in order to satisfy. Conversely, the fragmentation of forms and 'naïve' production of moving image is best studied by those who have a knowledge and understanding of the forms being adapted.

To return to our starting-point, platform convergence may be followed by true content convergence: the launch of Al Gore's youth-oriented Current TV, an 'interactive' television channel where viewers create news and factual stories might be either the YouTube principle reaching the mainstream or merely the old model of public-access cable television on a global scale. In either case, new forms and modes of documentary production established online may outlast their specific medium.

Websites

Google Video: video.google.com
YouTube: www.youtube.com
FourDocs www.channel4.com/fourdocs
Loose Change: www.loosechange911.com
We www.weroy.org
Al Gore's Penguin Army www.youtube.com/watch?v=IZSqXUSwHRI
LiveLeak www.liveleak.com
iFilm's Warzone www.ifilm.com/warzone
Peter Oakley: geriatric1927 www.youtube.com/user/geriatric1927
Lonelygirl15 www.lonelygirl15.com
Current TV uk.current.com

25 Public domains

Engaging Iraq through experimental documentary digitalities

Patricia R. Zimmermann

Public domains

Public domain, or PD, crosses through the new media ecologies of documentary – works for which copyright has either expired or never existed. An archive with no doors and no rules, public domain presents the open text that can commingle with other texts. Public domain means works exempt from proprietary interests that form our common aesthetic, cultural and intellectual landscape.[1] This category is not stable, of course: works change their passport status and migrate from proprietary to public domain continually, rapidly, and fluidly. Nor is this category universal, as public domain often implies countries of the global north that comply with the Berne Conventions.

The word domain connotes the internet, a virtual and often imaginary space where cyberactivity coagulates, convenes, coalesces. However, in this quest for free culture unfettered by capitalist exchange and intellectual property, lawyers, documentary hackers, remixers, copyright pirates, mash-uppers, clubbers, found footage artists – often white male cybercowboys hacking and whacking on their iMacs and iPods – focus on the image, fetishizing and eroticizing its acquisition and capture as though it were an illicit drug like crystal meth that can get you high and keep you high.[2]

In this time of war and empire, however, the term public domain needs a new definition, one that is more plural and beyond an exclusive focus on the fixity of the image and the artifact. It needs a definition that moves into transitional zones and provisional places that are created, interrupted and rewired by documentary interventions. A new conception of public *domains* must consider a new kind of documentary politics within this new media ecology: it must create places where publics can emerge. Public domains materialize new publics and actualize new spaces and domains. Some new forms which stretch the traditional expectations of documentary have circumvented the theatrical setting and instead adopted a strategy of infiltration into consumer grade technologies to produce critiques of the war on terror and how it wedges into everyday life. For example, an online satirical game called *Airport Insecurity*, a wordplay on the more common term airport security, asks the player to inspect airline passengers and luggage for forbidden items like toothpaste and hair gels, but the list changes each moment, making it difficult to detect contraband. Some of the items on the prohibited list include pants and hummus. The game developed in response to the Fall 2006 US security agency change in policies regarding what could be brought on to flights. The game is downloadable for cellphones (www.persuasivegames.com/games/game.aspx?game=airportinsecurity).

Public domains activate new ways of thinking, acting, connecting with others across difference, and expand the construct of documentary through diversity of form and content.[3] In response to the expansion of economic empire, the consolidation of channels of distribution and exhibition by transnational media giants, and the persistence of war, documentary practice has moved from a single analog film exhibited in theaters or on television to a diversity of forms and content, indicating a plurality of strategies, interfaces, and public intersections.

Empire and war no longer exert power solely through force or embedded reporters or press restrictions. They enact and inscribe power through the production of panic: they replace the freedom of messy interaction implied in the inventive ideas and concrete practices of public domains with a systematic incarceration of imagination and mobility. Surveillance, border patrols, passports, data mining, packet sniffing, learning objectives, teaching outcomes, pay-for-view, news blackouts, silence.

Empire and war no longer just provide a field of operations to achieve national objectives. They are now in the manufacturing business. They produce endless product lines of panic, amnesia, and anaesthesia.[4] Empire and war have migrated into the business of the mass production of chaos and incomprehensibility. As a result, the classical construct of the public sphere – a place for the open discussion of ideas among equals to create and sustain civil society – has become a fantasy, a chimera, a collective hallucination concocted by theory to enforce the science fiction of democracy. In our current era of expanding empire and endless war, the public sphere does not exist *a priori* in some essentialized, dormant state. The current political economy of massive media mergers is heavily invested in the production of blindness with regards to the war in Iraq. The American mass media continually render the war invisible despite the endless visibility of soldiers and IEDs. As a consequence, we must move from the abstraction of public sphere towards a concept of provisional materializations of transitory public spaces. We must consider how to mobilize a new conception of documentary interfaces to materialize and produce public domains.

A conception of documentary public domains means plural pasts, collaborative histories and practices, and a refusal to separate the past, present and future (Berkhofer, Jr. 1995: 170–201). It means decentering the white male unities of empire and mobilizing the polyvocalities of multiple others that can dismantle it. It means reverse engineering our ideas about independent and oppositional media into a concept of public media (Zimmermann 2005). It means we no longer can adopt a media model of push back – make and they will come and they will learn the truth. It means adopting a quite different documentary rhetorical and political strategy and tactic of pulling in – create a space with, by, together, side by side.

Panic

Panic. That's the operating system of the war on terror. Panic is produced and mobilized. The Pope's comments about Islam coincide with the E.coli bacteria spinach outbreak. Both create a phantasmatic of panic, with fear of the unknown shutting down borders everywhere, from countries to people to difference to ideas.

The current problematic outbreak of Islamophobia has distinct visual markers in the commercial mass media, visually shaping panic. In September 2006, Pope Benedict XVI delivered a speech at a university in Germany, a country with 1.9 million Muslim Turkish guest workers and Turks born in Germany. Pope Benedict said, 'Show me just what Mohammed brought that was new, and there will you find things only evil and inhuman, such as his command to spread by the sword the faith he preached.' [5]

On CNN, a white male news anchor in a business suit occupied the center of the frame, flatly describing the reaction around the globe to the Pope's speech. Behind him, digitally composited images formed four quadrants from Indonesia, Gaza, Sudan and Pakistan. These images showed large groups of angry people with picket signs in different – but untranslated – languages. It was an image of chaos, undifferentiation, nameless crowds.

Translation: white male anchor equals calm rational discourse, swarming masses of Muslims equals incomprehensibility, violence, and untranslatability. This image erased the significant cultural, political and religious differences of these countries, promoting a visual geography that equates Islam and Muslims with panic. And then, by extension, justifies the US exporting war, its cyberwarfare tactics clean, direct, immutable in comparison to the messiness of others, erupting in hysterics.

CNN and Fox News represented the response in the so-called 'Muslim world' as a visual iconography of racialized panic lacking specificity, location or history. Pakistan is Indonesia, Indonesia is Morocco, Morocco is Malaysia, Malaysia is Saudi Arabia in this orientalized cartography. Panic here functions as a projection of all that is unspoken about the war, all that cannot be said but erupts in these endless repetitions: that which we refuse to understand but which erupts to threaten us, kill us, maim us, destroy us.

However, if you can unplug yourself from cable news for a day or so, a very different kind of public media documentary practice charting the Iraq War, the War on Terror and the politics of Muslim identity emerges. For example, you might want to leave CNN and journey into the blogosphere to read Muslim intellectuals and journalists from all over the globe analyse everything from the Pope, to Zidane's headbutt, to racial profiling on airline flights. www.Altmuslim.com features some of the most penetrating writing and news coverage from a quite different vantage point.

www.Shobak.org, a blog and listserv, features the snappy, gutsy analysis of post-conceptual artist Naeem Mohaeimen. Mohaeimen is a member of the Visible Collective, whose website, performances, and installations called www.disappeared inamerica.org track the politics of detained migrants. Independent public media from around the globe have resisted this production of panic, amnesia and anaesthesia. They operate in what theorist Arjun Appadurai has called cellular convergences. He writes,

It is also the organizational style of the most interesting progressive movements in global society, those movements which seek to construct a third
space of circulation, independent of the spaces of state and market, and
which we may call movements for grassroots globalization.

(Appadurai 2006: 131)

These new forms of documentary collaborations across difference and nations
mobilize larger transnational goals and solidarities, and very frequently combine
analog, digital, and embodied practices that are multiplatformed and migratory.

New media ecologies for new public domains

Public media – especially the myriad of documentary practices of the current moment
– looks different now than it did in the 1970s, 1980s and 1990s. We must remember
these significant structural, political economy and aesthetic changes as we analyze
works that engage Iraq, and as we think through our strategies of resistance to war
and empire. The oppositional media environment where we will make it, we will
reveal it, we will speak the unspeakable and show the unshown – and they will come
and gain consciousness – is over. The flows have been reversed, the formats have
multiplied, the participating producers have increased, authorship is dispersed,
multiple and horizontal. The binary oppositions between commercial and non-profit,
between amateur and professional, between performance and documentary have
dissolved in exciting, problematic, confusing ways.

Thus, public domains are not only to be entered, but are transitional, provisional, pluralized, fluid zones that are constantly created and mobilized through
documentary inventions and interactions among many, rather than being created by
one producer or one media object. As elaborated in the *Deep Focus* report produced by
the National Association of Media Arts and Culture (NAMAC), the new media ecology
differs dramatically from the old media formations which pitted independent media
against commercial/for profit media. As *Deep Focus* argues, the new media ecology is
layered, multiplatformed, swiftly changing, and reconfiguring audiences and outreach. It is altering the relationships between production, distribution and exhibition
with long tail marketing, niche markets, blurrings between professional and amateur,
new economic models, and new emerging sectors of public media such as music,
clubs, the internet, iPods, RFID (radio frequency identification), mobile media, viral
media, flash, remix, installation, and beyond (National Association of Media Arts and
Culture 2004). Beyond the market, we can deploy this model to consider that public
media conceptualizations of documentary must be oriented to the creation and
mobilization of public domains rather than to the production of singular static
objects.

The public domain is not one entity, but many: public domains. And open
source is not one strategy of open access to code, but rather an active process of
opening multiple sources.[6] Open source is not so simple a way to access code
democratically and in a transparent, collective way, but open sourcing can
be marshaled as a metaphor and a model to navigate the new complex media

environment which requires thinking through new documentary strategies for opening up ideas, access, distribution, platforms. Public domains are activating rather than activist, moving from content to process, from what is on the screen to thinking of the screen as simply one nodal point around which communities can be formed. In other words, deploying concepts such as open sourcing and public domains in new documentary iterations entails moving away from one screen to multiple screens and platforms that facilitate communities: the production of publics and the opening of sources.

This strategy suggests a participatory model of public media that shifts from making documentary works for communities and instead proposes making works with communities which form around practices, contradictions, openings. This collaborative documentary work is often invisible in the commercial, feature film, 'independent' media sector that infuses major international film festivals like Sundance and Tribeca. It entails being invited into someone else's space for a shared exploration of ideas and practices, rather than maintaining a differential in experience with media tools and representations. Instead, this new conceptualization of documentary means embracing and submerging in the heterogeneous array of practices and technologies that are reshaping the media landscape. It also suggests movement away from an auteurist model of documentary media production as artisanal self-expression towards a redefined model of documentary media activating participation in the production of new collaborative knowledges.[7]

Collaborative knowledges to say no to war

A wide, diverse range of groundbreaking documentary works that engage this concept of public media counter the CNN view of Muslims, Islam and the occupation of Iraq by expanding the kinds of voices heard and specifying place and history. These documentaries create and open up public domains.

The *Shocking and Awful* series, executive-produced by Deep Dish Television, involved over 100 independent media producers around the globe to chart the war in Iraq from the ground up. Deep Dish is a pathbreaking public media collective marshalling satellite distribution for public media. A large-scale documentary series, *Shocking and Awful* features the voices of Iraqis, international anti-war activists and US military personnel speaking off the record to non-imbedded, independent journalists. The series features 12 half-hour episodes ranging from occupation, women, cultural destruction, economics, oil, and resistance.

Code Pink, the feminist anti war group, partnered with the Iraqi indy media collective to produce *Fallujah*, a searing exposé of the destruction of that city by US troops in November 2004 in a major offensive that went largely unreported in the US commercial media. Over 2,000 Iraqis died; 250,000 people lost their homes. Displaced Iraqis describe the military assault and their current living conditions in refugee camps. Comparing the siege of Fallujah to Guernica, the documentary was screened in this year's prestigious Whitney Biennial. That screening spurred over 1,000 university and public library purchases.

In contrast to the mass-mediated panics the commercial media propagates and promotes, independent public media can deactivate this dangerous and volatile manufacture of panic, fury and fear. Public media documentary on Islam, Muslims and the occupation in Iraq opens up a transnational public space for a larger, more expansive, and more complicated conversation. And as borders close and panic accelerates like a virus, maintaining a vigorous, analytical and resistant public domain is a necessary inoculation and antidote.

How to think about history and public domains

Heterogeneity is a central feature of this notion of documentary public domains that are constructed, reactivated, mobilized, as this modality can loosen up the unities of discourse and practice that produce panic, amnesia and anaesthesia. This vast, untapped domain of imagining and creative public domains requires many approaches and tactics to move beyond the artefact into historical understanding of the significance of these works, a critical engagement with the forms of knowledge they yield, and an enactment of an anti-war epistemology. Robert F. Berkhofer, Jr., in his *Beyond the Great Story: History as Text and Discourse*, has argued that advances in the philosophy of history have moved history away from a single, metanarrative and omniscient viewpoint based on referentiality, realism and facts that represses heterogeneity towards a more particularized, multicultural, construct of plural pasts. Berkhofer (1995: 263–83) terms the structure of these plural pasts 'polyvocalities', where more than one viewpoint is present and contradictions and disjunctures abound, opening up historical analysis to different explanatory models.

Ranajit Guha, in his *History and the Limit of World-History* (2002), argues that the complicity between history and imperialism should not be viewed as only an 'expropriation of the pasts of the colonized by the colonizers', but, instead, as a necessary component of globalization that installs Europeanized development on the rest of the world by disconnecting stories and histories from the everyday. The state and history become intertwined, redefining temporality as a linear narrative progressing from the storyteller down, rather than emerging from interaction with the listeners gathered together to hear a story again, and again, and again (Guha 2002: 48–75). Listeners gathering, and storytellers telling, of course, show us a concrete example of the public domain, different from the public sphere because it is enacted and embodied. As a consequence, Guha (2002: 22) observes that 'the noise of world history and its statist concerns has made historiography insensitive to the sighs and whispers of everyday life'.

Guha suggests that history requires regrounding in the specifics of everyday life through a creative engagement with the human condition: 'no continent, no culture, no mark or condition of social being would be considered too small or too simple for its prose' (2002: 22). For Guha, the elite histories of Indian nationalism narrated history from the point of view of the colonizer and were thus incomplete, ignoring the subaltern, defined as the people and the everyday. Subaltern history is not unified, but expressed in 'living contradictions' that must be charted by looking at the overlaps, contacts, struggles, and accommodations between elites and subalterns.

Partha Chatterjee (2000: 18) has also elaborated on subaltern history as a more 'intricately differentiated and layered' process of restoring active agency to the everyday that involves not unities, but a 'constant process of interrogation and contestation, modifying, transforming and enriching'. Guha advocates an opening up of all the pasts, not simply one, to retrieve retellings, re-perceptions, and re-makings of our narratives, which are always, and ultimately, acts of invention of possible futures.

Guha's critique of historiography and his vision for a historical practice that is renewed and revitalized through a grounding in life rather than maintenance of state power are instructive for thinking through how we can think about oppositional, independent, documentary within this new media ecology surrounded by war and empire. In Guha's terms, public domain documentary practices are stories from the listeners, not the storytellers.

Evil and panic

Postconceptual artist Tony Cokes has produced a series of shorts called *The Evil Series*. Rejecting the image as the focal point of the war on terror, Cokes animates text from Bush's speeches, news stories on bombings and Abu Ghraib, anti-terrorism websites and *New York Times* Op Ed pieces against changing red, white and blue backgrounds to unpack the semiotics of the war on terror. Post-rock soundtracks generate disjunctions between the horrific discourse of war and the pleasures and latent erotics of rock consumption. *The Evil Series* challenges the idea of documentary as a realist form based in images, and instead proposes to return documentary to its roots in an epistemological practice of documents and evidence.

Cokes's documentary intervention opens up new territories in not only artistic practice and conceptual design that challenge previous configurations of video art but in exhibition itself. *The Evil Series* rethinks and rewires production, collaboration, distribution and exhibition to create and generate new forms of public space for critical engagement. Cokes's documentary works are migratory works that create public domains, moving and morphing and adapting, sometimes single channel, sometimes shorts before features, on plasma screens in environments, as installations, as curated groupings.

Rather than a representation *of* the world, Cokes situates the video image as a space of conjecture *about* the epistemological structures of the world, a constructed provisional zone where realism is jettisoned for the production of a conceptual zone of possibilities and unsettlings. For Cokes, the production of space for contemplation and metacommunication is paramount. *The Evil Series* insists on creating a liminal zone between fine art practice, post-conceptual art, advertising, popular music, remix culture, club culture, and critical theory. These documentaries, as part of the lineage of the essay documentary form, produce a public domain where ideas and exploring new vectors and relationships replace panic, amnesia and anaesthesia.

Rather than a postmodern pastiche or a more twenty-first-century-style contemporary remix or mash-up of cultural forms, Cokes's work builds his arguments about pop music, the post-9/11 world, George Bush, or Abu Ghraib by plugging these different cultural modalities into each other to facilitate new structures and new collaborative knowledges. Cokes's documentary practice seeks to unsettle unexamined, normative thinking, unravel commonsensical assumptions, and unmake assumptions about cultural production and consumption. This task is extremely difficult both conceptually and artistically. It also has a long tradition in conceptual art, art derived from an idea rather than from the internalized state of the artist's subjectivity or the artist's interaction with the materiality of the object. Cokes interrogates the dry, remote approach of much conceptual art by linking concepts with the more sensuous and embodied pop cultural modes of spectatorial positioning, thereby expanding and problematizing traditional documentary forms from both the high art and popular culture fronts. For example, he employs post-rock soundtracks (rock music without the typical verse/chorus structure and 4/4 beat, operating as popular culture renditions of minimalism), graphic design from advertising (a pared-down minimalist aesthetic that rejects the congestion of much postmodernist art and montage), and an emphasis on text embedded within the works.

The Evil Series functions as a set of interventions into the transparency of the image, ideology and narratives of nations and their fantasized others. Most importantly, Cokes's documentary practice itself functions as a theoretical exercise in reorganizing expectations about how to read media texts (many of the works in *The Evil Series*, for example, challenge and confuse the very notion of a 'readable' text through the multiple layers of scrolling text), and therefore represent a blurring of the borders between theory, mass culture, art culture, and popular culture.

The Evil Series questions the very nature of the image and representation by disposing of images of war and destruction almost entirely, focusing instead on discursive structures and visual design as public domains for plugging ideas into different sockets and new vectors. In these pieces, documentary is redefined as design of public domains. The various pieces in this series all involve post-rock soundtracks which sustain disjunctions in reading the text, juxtaposing discussions of Abu Ghraib with the accessible, easy-to-digest beats of popular music that loops.

US military and activist actions in the United States or Europe dominate independent documentaries chronicling the war in Iraq. These works often default into realist representational tropes and giving voice to the voiceless or images to the image-less (strategies of 1980s and 1990s political media). Cokes's work focuses on the latent epistemological structures of the post-9/11 environment and the ensuing War on Terror. *The Evil Series* proposes a public domain of unsettled mediation and contemplation.

Transformative history

Hayden White has argued that history is an imaginative and transformative act, one where fiction and fact are endlessly flowing in and out of each other. He sees the historian's work as a process of active engagement, of transforming archival materials rather than the delivery of facts and evidence. He argues that historiographic practice needs to be re-imagined: 'I think the problem now, at the end of the twentieth century, is how we re-imagine history outside of the categories that we inherited from the nineteenth century.'[8]

Developing this line of thought about the political function of history, Tzvetan Todorov has advanced that

> Totalitarian regimes of the twentieth century have revealed the existence of a danger never before imagined: the blotting out of memory. These twentieth century tyrannies have understood that the conquest of men and territories could be accomplished through information and communication and have created a systematic and complete takeover of memory, hoping to control it even in its most hidden excesses.
>
> (Todorov 2001: 11)

F. K. Ankersmit has similarly argued that 'the time has come that we should think about the past, rather than investigate it' (Ankersmit, in Domanska 1998: 73). Similar to Guha and White, Ankersmit argues for a reconceptualization of history as an interrogation of the incongruities between the past and the present and the invention of new languages for speaking about their juxtaposition. For Hayden White, the idea of an inert, immobile past that is evidentiary and empirical is a fallacy. He claims, 'It is impossible to legislate the way people are going to relate to the past because, above all the past is a place of fantasy. It does not exist anymore. You can't replicate, by definition, historical events.'[9] If we use a notion of public domains, it is possible to develop a new media language for thinking about the documentary production and physicalization of White's historical 'place of fantasy'.

New environments, different histories

The materiality of the archive – texts, artefacts and documents – drives film and media history, evidentiary traces of the past quilted together to form patterns, connections, explanations. For professional academic historians, archival records are never complete nor totalized. Archival absences – not enough early cinema saved or amateur films waiting to be recovered – often loom larger than the subject of study itself. Lost films, deteriorating images, abandoned records, silences, mark our media arts histories. The political urgency of the archive can be mapped in these gaps and fissures: the structuring out of the marginal and the inchoate, the chaotic and the untameable, documentary practices which refuse the rules and therefore reveal the most about the disruptions of historical processes.

Over the past 20 years, film and media history (often referred to as the 'new film history') has moved from the analysis of existing evidence to the recovery of lost archival objects and categories which expand the archive and rethink what it privileges and marginalizes. The past is never inert nor nostalgic, but always interacts with the present and the future, looking backwards and forwards simultaneously in endless recombinations and endless mutations. The questions we ask of history should not be reduced to what happened when; rather, the past demands questions of how and why: questions of significance, not linear progression and causality. Contemporary historiographic theory rejects the idea of the causal chain and instead has adopted the notion of the collage, where different temporalities and categories of evidence are remixed into new combinations to provoke new explanatory models and new connections.[10]

The image centers all of this historical work, defining the contours and scope of media histories. Live multimedia performance, in this context, presents a complex historiographic problem for documentary because it is not located solely in the realm of the image. First, it is virtually absent from most film and media histories, most likely because it is ephemeral, fleeting, rarely documented – an archival impossibility. Second, its multiple artistic and political practices are dispersed across and then folded into histories defined by somewhat more unified fields, such as fine art, theater, performance art, avant garde cinema, video art, contemporary experimental music, hip hop, digital media, documentary studies. Third, it presents a spatialized and environmental rather than a time-based documentary practice, a different set of historiographic locations and concerns defined more by participant ethnographies and oral histories rather than archival documents, artefacts, and texts.

In some ways, these historiographic conundrums and unified categories have perhaps contributed to the absence of live multimedia performance from our histories of documentary. Or maybe our histories of media have focused too much on fixed textual practices and documents, thereby overlooking a range of performative political interventions that figure documentary mediations as fluid, moving, malleable interactions with audiences and performers. But a preliminary excavation into live multimedia performance has the potential to shift the ground of documentary history from the image to constructed, interactive environments and infiltration of different spaces that emphasize not individual artistry but collaboration.

In a period where people feel isolated from each other and where media become both miniaturized and domesticated in the home, the hidden history of live multimedia performance provides a way to rethink documentary tactics. As an immersive experience based on conceptual ideas and pleasure, the multiplication of formats, images, music, and interfaces to create new social spaces moves our thinking about documentary away from the image alone. As the dominant commercialized practices of digitality disembody, isolate, disconnect and desensitize, the layered histories of live multimedia performance suggest that gatherings of people are still important, that total immersive experiences predate the internet, and that embodied, sensual interaction is part of politics. It is a history that repositions media history from documents and images to spaces and environments. It is a history of iterative media making and forming and reforming public domains.

Dismantling war

In 1994, a woman who owned a hip hop label asked media artist Art Jones, a former member of the Not Channel Zero collective of African American and Latino political media activists, to do a live remix at The Knitting Factory in New York City. Jones had been hanging out at the NuyoRican Poets Café, seeing the power of improvisational performance for political discourse. Armed with two VCRs, two monitors, and a Radio Shack AB Switcher, Jones did his first remix with videotapes while a spoken word performer used a mike. The performance combined media, hip hop music and spoken word. From there, Jones started mixing in bars and clubs with video decks, and then, later, mini-DV decks. He moved into computers for live remixing in 2001.

Inspired by site-specific happenings in the 1960s and 1970s, Jones saw that remixing held the possibility of breaking radical documentary practices out to a different audience through combining music, visual artists, video projectors. In the past ten years, according to Jones, for a collective of African American and Latino political media activists, live remixes constitute 'perhaps one of the only areas not coopted by the commercial media'.[11]

Live remix performances tap into a general cultural malaise of isolation which fuels a craving for fun and direct, pleasurable social interaction. 'Live remixes are deployed in the service of topical ideas like the war in Iraq and the presidential election, delivering politics to larger social activities and gatherings,' according to Jones. Live performance inverts how the field conceptualizes political documentary media: rather than making a topical film and then working to attract an audience to receive the message, artists and collectives instead are taking work to the audiences and responding to them – live.

Robert Whitman's expanded cinema with multiple projectors and sound, Ken Jacob's projections, Warhol's Velvet Underground, psychedelia, served as predecessors to today's laptop remixers in clubs. At Woodstock 94, kids with laptops, who Jones affectionately heralds as 'the lost tribe of MacIntosh' (a rather contradictory concept linking anti-corporate activists with a large computer manufacturer) talked to each other with their laptops, generating a communal spirit that Jones sees as the radical potential of live multimedia performance.

Live remixes, now with sophisticated software running on paper-thin laptops, constitute a resolutely anti-corporate ephemeral documentary environment designed to intervene in the colonization of consciousness by commercial mass media and even the more subterranean subcultures of the participatory internet. Compared to traditional film schools and art schools, which often emphasize a somewhat romanticized view of individual artistry, live remixing requires collaborative engagement as well as a 'different way of engaging the spectator'.

Live multimedia remixes intervene in the quiet contemplation of the object and the construct of documentary as a fixed image. The central theoretical problem posed by live remixes revolves around the question of whether the spectator can be engaged in a more compelling, immersive, and embodied way. Jones has done remixes on the war in Iraq, cyberwarfare, and empire, either alone or in collaborative teams. However, some VJs simply generate video wallpaper without political content for clubs, creating screen after screen of abstract, beautiful images with no connection to political or social relations, a practice that Jones sees as ignoring dialogue with the audience/participants. With computers, images and sounds can be subdivided, live cameras can be added, more improvisation can erupt, and VJ/DJs can be more responsive, creating a more encompassing environment.

At the 2007 Sundance Film Festival, documentary filmmaker Travis Wilkerson premiered a new anti-war live performance work entitled *Proving Ground*. This multimedia piece included Travis doing a live performance of a script about the relationships between imperialism, war, bombing, and Brecht, a live rock band, and a central movie screen flanked on each side by four high end plasma screens repeating the central images. The performance featured archival documentary film of wars throughout the twentieth and twenty-first century digitally composited with an endless streaming of bombs falling from planes. Within the commercial feeding frenzy which is Sundance, Wilkerson and team managed to carve out an embodied public domain, to widen and complicate the media iterations and media ecology and complement the more conventional realist, deductive documentaries on the war screened there, such as Rory Kennedy's masterful *Ghosts of Abu Ghraib* and Charles Ferguson's penetrating muckraking expose, *No End in Sight*.

Collaborative histories

Anthropologist and filmmaker David MacDougall has proposed moving ethnographic film away from making a film 'about' towards making a film 'with'. Rather than a documentary strategy that is an omniscient monologue, he proposes the act of cinema is a contemplative and participatory act which is always a relation and an encounter, an act of collaboration and dialogue between the subject and the person filming. MacDougall argues for interconnection rather than separation to produce a compound documentary work and an elaborative, embodied knowledge (MacDougall 1998: 75). In elaborating his ideas about a collaborative ethnography, he explains, 'The goal is not simply to present "the indigenous view" nor to invade voyeuristically the consciousness of other individuals, but to see social behavior and indeed culture, as a continual process of interpretation and invention' (1998: 131).

Contemporary theory in both ethnography and historiography has grappled with this problem of how to construct historical models based on heterogeneity, plurality and polyvocality, from one set of evidentiary groups to many different registers and kinds of evidence. Commenting on the need for a transcultural ethnography that takes into account multiple interstices and disjunctions, David MacDougall has observed that 'the transcultural makes possible an overlapping of experiential horizons, where certain indirect and interpretive leaps of understanding can take place' (1998: 141). Arguing that the politics of including minorities in the history of India goes beyond the embrace of a new set of archives and instead raises questions of explanatory models, Dipesh Chakrabarty claims that the past is disjoined in nature and always plural: 'thus the writing of history must implicitly assume a plurality of times existing together, a disjuncture of the present with itself. Making visible this disjuncture is what subaltern pasts allow us to do' (2000: 109).

Robert Berkhofer (1995: 171–91) has pointed out that historiography's engagement with Foucault and postmodernism has pushed aside coherency, continuity, and univocality for fragmentation, differentiality and polyvocality to demonstrate how the local and the contingent can become more salient. He shows how traditional notions of historical continuity are displaced by heterogeneity and discontinuity. And in cinema studies, Phil Rosen (2001: 107–44) has advocated a model of temporal hybridity that is counterposed to the linear coherences of historiography and the pursuit of an authentic, transcendent 'pastness'. In history, the process of explaining an event by collecting what seems to be isolated facts under a general hypothesis is called colligation. In the arts, the connection of different kinds of materials and forms to create collisions to create new ideas is called collage. Newly emergent forms of documentary practice, then, are interested less in documenting what is not seen than in engaging colligation to generate epistemological questioning.

Locative media

WiFi, mobile phone cameras, and RFID are ubiquitous, invisible, and often – at least for the average cable TV-surfing, iPod-listening person – incomprehensible. WiFi refers to wireless fidelity, the technology that enables you to connect to a local area network at an access point to check your email while on the road. RFID is an acronym for radio frequency identification, tags that track everything from library books, to Wal Mart shipments of goods, to your car passing through toll booths without plopping in quarters. The Preemptive Media Collective (PM) reengineers your thinking about mobile digital technologies imbedded in our everyday environment. PM's art practice works not only to help spectators see these invisible technologies that track our lives and our data, but also to demystify them through a new form of documentary intervention in documents and interfaces themselves. The war on terror is not out there, but in here, in our walls, our iPods, RFID tags.

Locative media represents a newly emerging zone in performative multimedia. Locative media constitutes a new global independent media movement interested in the convergence between digital domains and geographic spaces. It anchors the digital, often viewed as ambling around in a place-less realm, in geographic space. Artists marshall portable, networked computing devices like GPS, mobile phones, RFID as well as wearable technologies to map space and intervene into data streams. Locative media practices focus on horizontal, user-led and collaborative projects to interrupt and interrogate a powerful system of observation and control (Tuters and Varnelis n.d.).

In live performances and real-time actions, the PM art, technology and activist collective disturbs, dislodges, and redesigns new media technologies that we often ignore, like the bar codes on driver's licenses or radio frequency information devices used for EZ pass on highways. At the forefront of the 'locative media movement', Preemptive Media repositions highly specialized technologies within the democratic discourse of amateurism, which refutes technology as inaccessible, remote and too complicated and instead argues it should be accessible to everyone. The emerging locative media movement has gathered steam and attention since 9/11 and the 2001 Patriot Act, which authorizes unprecedented data mining, invasions of privacy, wiretapping, and internet surveillance. Locative media resituates documentary as a meta-critique of emerging technologies in process.

Preemptive Media Collective's *ZAPPED!* (2005) foregrounds radio frequency identification tags (RFID), first used by the British military during World War II and then to track wild animals in the 1960s. In the past 20 years, RFID has been utilized for electronic tolls like EZ Pass, pets, prisoners, dance clubs, kids, the Department of

Defense and Wal Mart, the largest profit-making enterprise in the world. The Spring Independent School district in the Houston area uses RFID tags on elementary students to track their school bus rides.

The *ZAPPED!* Project features workshops for kids and adults on altering the remote wireless detection chips. Phrases like 'Help me! I'm a consumer!' 'This is GOD. You have sinned. Be prepared for eternal damnation!' and 'Don't hire me – I'm a felon' are inserted on the chips to pop up on scanners in stores. Instead of prices, these phrases appear. The RFID School Kit consists of a lunchbox and a keychain detector to locate RFID hotspots. Roaches with clandestine RFID tags taped to their backs are hidden in the lunchbox and then released in Wal Mart storage areas by activists sporting the blue Wal Mart vests, bought on E-Bay.

Some academics have questioned whether locative media is actually just another name for sabotage, civil disobedience and illegal hacking, charges locative media artists like Preemptive Media might find a bit old-fashioned and tidy for the reverse engineering strategies of altering technologies like RFID to make visible these imbedded, invisible technologies as a form of public education and political consciousness raising.

The end of empire and war: a fantasy

Our era of empire, infinite war and massive media consolidation poses enormous obstacles to imagination, freedom and collectivity. The public spaces for an interventionist, argumentative public media and radical documentary practice shrink daily. Public domains seem elusive, theoretical, phantasmatic, lost. These variegated, diffuse practices map an engaged and interventionist digitality. Experimental digital documentary works – like *Fallujah, Shocking and Awful, The Evil Series,* Disappeared in America.com, Shobak.org, *Airport Insecurity* gaming, *Dismantling War, Dismantling Empire, Proving Ground,* installation, gaming, live multimedia performance, preemptive media, locative media – may offer a way to reclaim and reinvent exhilarating, if transient, documentary public domains beyond the strangleholds of corporate media.

These multimedia documentary environments are malleable, musical, contingent, and collaborative. They are situated in real spaces. They resolutely intervene in power relations and consciousness. And they are fun. These engaged documentary digitalities that can be endlessly reassembled can, perhaps, mobilize that most elusive, but necessary, ingredient of any radical media practice and any new conceptions about public domains: a hopeful, raucous convergence of like-minded people that dismantles convention, disassembles power and disturbs the universe.

Notes

1 For useful discussions of the concept of public domain, see special issue of the Sarai Reader, *The Public Domain* 01, Amsterdam: The Society for Old and New Media, 2001.

2 For a substantive and thorough discussion of the battles between intellectual property and anti-copyright artists and activists, see McLeod (2005).

3 For a discussion of tactical media as a way to generate connections across difference, see Thompson (2004).

4 For an analysis of how panic blurs the borders between the political, the institutional, the psychic and the pharmaceutical, see Orr (2006). For an analysis of how panic is always racialized, see Morris and de Bary (2001).

5 'Pope Benedict XVI and Islam' http://news.bbc.co.uk/2/hi/europe/5349808.stm, 16 September 2006.

6 For a cogent analysis of open source culture and its relationship to old media forms of licensing, patenting and copyright, see Lessig (2004), and Poster (2006).

7 Critical ethnography has been interested in countering the orientalism of representation by offering a model of collaborative ethnographies where both the maker and the subject enter into the practice of media to produce new knowledge. For a discussion of collaborative knowledge production, see MacDougall (1998).

8 Interview with Hayden White, in Domanska (1998: 16).

9 White in Domanska (1998: 24).

10 For discussions of how strategies of historical collage can remedy the epistemological and political problems of linear causality in historiography, see Berkhofer (1995: 245–70). See also Chakrabarty (2000: 97–113).

11 Interview with Art Jones, 16 September 2005.

26 Documentary on YouTube
The failure of the direct cinema of the slogan

Alexandra Juhasz

YouTube is the realization of many of my dearest held aspirations. I share these highly anticipated, if perhaps idealistic dreams of universal access to a democratic media with a host of scholars and makers whose rich body of radical media work I highlight in my upcoming digital 'publication', *MEDIA PRAXIS: A Radical Website Integrating Theory, Politics, and Practice. MEDIA PRAXIS* is an enduring, mutual, and building tradition that theorizes and creates the necessary conditions for media to play an integral role in cultural and individual transformation. I am a student, teacher and participant within this distinguished tradition, one that travels from the Soviets of the 1920s, through American beatniks of the 1950s, and African and Latin-American anti-colonialists of the sixties, to today's digital frontier.[1] Across the hundred-year history of the moving recorded arts, radical media theorists and makers have predicted a soon-to-come utopia where expanded access to the production, distribution and exhibition of media might reign, a magnificent future where media consumers would become producers because they could at last afford the means of production and distribution; where they could document the look, feel and meat of their daily lives; then add these records of their everyday experiences to the public sphere; and participate in the production of culture without the expertise bought at film schools. Might we all simply have been foretelling YouTube, a media environment that makes the most of the best of new media, at least as those assets are delineated by Henry Jenkins and David Thorbun (2004: 3): 'access, participation, reciprocity, and many-to-many rather than one-to-many communication'? There are many among us, like internet scholar, Douglas Schuler, who assert that the digital delivers what we've long been awaiting: 'for the first time in human history, the possibility exists to establish a communication network that spans the globe, is affordable, and is open to all comers and points of view: in short, a democratic communication infrastructure' (2004: 70).

But why, then, when I visit this marvelous place, is the stuff I see there so thoroughly unsatisfying? Every few months, I will follow through on a link, generously forwarded to me by a friend or net-acquaintance, and it inevitably takes me to some humorous confection mocking a piece of mainstream culture I never saw in the first place; a silly man dancing out the history of American music; two otters holding hands; some kid coming out in his bedroom; two voluptuous long-haired fake-breasted babes making out in a hotel room. Wanting better, I'll travel down the page only to find more of the same. Still hoping for something just a little more interesting, I'll try a key-word of some value to me, say 'queer realism'. But there are no videos to be found under such a bookish term. 'Queer' works, but what emerges feels of little more use than the blond honeys I got on the first pass. I am assaulted, primarily, by parodies of, clips from, or interviews with cast members of mainstream fare like *Queer as Folk*, *Queer Eye for the Straight Guy*, *The L Word*, or music videos from a band called Garbage with a *song* called Queer accompanied by posts that say: 'I love this video and song', and 'I want Shirley Manson to rape me'. The banality of this revolution is far more notable than its populism. Its failures utterly profound given its radical promise.

What YouTube gains in access, it lacks in knowledge. But perhaps I'm simply a snob, found out to be embarrassingly disdainful of what real folks actually make and like, especially given the Marxist leanings of the tradition I study. Or maybe this is merely a matter of refining my search tools and processes. For I have determined that if I devote the time necessary, there is an astounding range of documentary to be found on YouTube. But by looking more closely in this chapter at the loads and loads of documentaries on YouTube, I hope to establish that my problems are much more than personal. My method will be academic: I will first hold YouTube to the distinguished tradition of *MEDIA PRAXIS*; and I will then look closely at one small thread on YouTube – queer documentaries – through the theories and shared assumptions from the specific tradition that anticipated it, New Queer Cinema (and in particular writing by and about the works of lesbians, queers of color, and AIDS activists). My model is academic because it assumes that we make better media when we are serious students of what has come before. So, my process performs the work, and the troubles of expertise. In 'That withered paradigm: the web, the expert, and the information hegemony', Peter Walsh explains how knowledge hegemonies of the past, like that of media praxis, are easily toppled by the World Wide Web as the internet opens up closed bodies of knowledge by shattering the layperson/expert dichotomy based on rules and rituals that once regulated access (2004: 366–7).

And let's face it: the beauty of YouTube is that it's for neither experts nor academics. Like cinema in its pre-history, there's a gee-willickers enthusiasm for the *fact* of production, in and of itself. It seems that YouTube's staple docs – the overly-sincere or glibly-ironic talking-head clips about popular culture or personal satisfaction that populate its pages – are auto-generous, unrelated to a history of images before them, springing forth, virgin-borne from this newly accessible technology. But, I subscribe to a world-view oft-discussed in *MEDIA PRAXIS*, founded on the belief that regular people who make media to participate in and change their world should also speak to history and make theory giving context to their work. By this I do not mean high-fallutin' obscure opaque writing by continental philosophers and their acolytes, but rather, simple but systematic claims about the culture people produce and consume and its relations to the past and past work. From these regularized claims more powerful production, as well as community and politics, ensues. 'I love this video and song', allows for no further conversation; it isn't conversation. 'I want Shirley Manson to rape me' threatens any possible association.

The failures of YouTube, even as its technology succeeds in creating the possibilities for (near) universal access, are due to its inattentiveness, or inability to unite. But on *MEDIA PRAXIS*, as in these pages, I am committed to connections: linking past theories of radical media with contemporary political practices, interrelating living communities of committed mediamakers with histories from which they can learn. I will suggest that this kind of slow, structural work – the method of experts; the labor of scholars; all tried-and-true practices available to any who will make the effort – allows a critical learning hard to establish from the rapid, solo work of linking across surfaces. For instance, *MEDIA PRAXIS* may be 'published' by MediaCommons, a digital academic press in-development that plans to use this most contemporary of media to 'create a network in which scholars, students, and other interested members of the public can help to shift the focus of scholarship back to the circulation of discourse'.[2] Scholarly circulation is committed, connected, and complex; YouTube is fast, furious, and direct. YouTube's decided disinclination towards ongoing bonds is made manifest through a corporate, postmodern architecture founded on the transitory and evocative link. Meanwhile, the tradition of *MEDIA PRAXIS* demands not merely numbers, access, and reciprocity but also, at the same time, a connected and lasting base of knowledge, an associated community, and a will to action. 'The sphere of the new film language will, as it happens, not be the sphere of the presentations of phenomena', explains Soviet filmmaker/theorist Sergei Eisenstein (1988: 77), 'nor even that of social interpretation, but the opportunity for *abstract social evaluation*'.

Writing in 1928, when he was participating in and anticipating the maturation of the new medium of his age, Eisentein theorized the transition from cinema to 'pure cinema', from the technology's childhood to adulthood. He thinks from the 'tragic faults' of his own recent film, *October,* one that he explains spans 'two epochs in cinema' (1988: 74). Eisenstein predicts a dialectical overturning of cinema's previous stages to a new period that 'will come *under the aegis of a concept – under the aegis of a slogan.* The period of the "free market" in cinema is coming to an end' (1988: 77). He anticipates that which is beyond the limits of narrative and documentary, and past profits and consumerism: a new epoch of pure cinematic perception and epistemology. In our time, Alexander Galloway (2006: 60) enumerates similar claims made by the digital's most fervent boosters of our new epoch:

> They write that advances such as new media, new technologies, new and faster methods of transferring information, democratization of technological luxuries, diversification of access to digital networks, the standardization of data formats, and the proliferation of networked relations will help usher in a new era marked by greater personal freedom. Heightened interpersonal communication, ease from the burden of representation, new perspectives on the problem of the body, greater choice in consumer society, unprecedented opportunities for free expression, and, above all, speed.

Galloway's claims – high on expanded freedom, communication, and consumption – never make Eisenstein's bold declaration for (universal) radical knowledge. Following

Eisenstein's distant lead, and in the face of a contemporary celebration of digital media's 'unprecedented opportunities', I will establish that access without theory, history, community, and politics, and access enabled by (post) capitalism, is not yet all we might demand the future of the cinema to be.

The cinema of the slogan

> It will be the art of the direct cinema of a slogan. Of communication that is just as unobstructed and immediate as the communication of an idea through a qualified word.
>
> (Sergei Eisenstein, *Soviet Cinema*, 1920s)

Could the eminent revolutionary filmmaker/theorist, Sergei Eisenstein, again quoted from his 1928 article, 'Our *October*. Beyond the played and the non-played', be prophesying the internal contradictions and 'tragic flaws' of documentary on YouTube today? It seems both prescient, and also naïve of this distinguished communist to call forth the *slogan* for his own developing medium, cinema. The slogan seems so much more apt for the technological developments now displayed on YouTube. For the slogan links activism and commerce – the simplistic selling of ideas so as to move people to fight or buy, no matter – in a manner perfected by and definitive of our era, and its definitive medium, the internet. Certainly the slogan – a pithy, precise, rousing call to action or consumption, or action as consumption – astutely describes the form of YouTube documentaries, especially in terms of their brevity and clarity. Given that the cinema consolidated itself at 90-minutes, and then television did so at 30, it has been quite a relief, really, especially given our high levels of distraction, to minimize our viewing to a reasonable three minutes: 'communication that is just as unobstructed and immediate as the communication of an idea through a qualified word'; bite-sized, word-sized, postage-sized cinema; strong, intense, interchangeable, and forgettable films; the stuff of YouTube.

Certainly, this particularly appetizing format had already been conventionalized by the television advertisement and later its music video, but those things sold products, whereas most YouTube documentaries do not (unless we understand that the ironic mimicking of mainstream media, or even the heart-felt response to one's favorite daytime drama, are cheap but effective advertisements, in this case made by consumers and not the ad-men of yore). But slogans simplify in the name of selling or striving. And, given that nothing of documentary form or content, outside of duration, is yet standardized on YouTube but perhaps only standardizing, and that its pages hold or could hold every possible style of documentary ever made, what we currently see is the many possible forms of documentary simply shoved into a shorter, simpler format. Certainly direct-to-camera talking-head confessional realism is the documentary format of choice, given its sheer ease of production. And the straightforward documentation of important public/private events (marches, speeches, interviews, community meetings) are also highly evident. But, on any one page of YouTube you'll actually find a dizzyingly eclectic array of documentary styles, from sources as varied as art-videos, music videos, and mainstream television. And of course, there are advertisements, some even by ad-men.

The slogan prevails on YouTube. Most of the site's diverse producers cram their eclectic content and miscellaneous formal devices into the length, strength, and function of a music video: selling something through artisnal and forceful condensation. That is, unless one posts a precariously un-sloganlike documentary onto the site, accepting the standardized viewing practices of modern-day viewers who scan along one's carefully produced 20-minutes of abstraction or 50-minutes of rhetoric, reducing its depth to surface because that's all this screen, and the viewing practices it conventionalizes, can hold. Once posted on YouTube, one's best cinematic slogan, in all its stirring surface fanfare, could get a lot of hits, but it will rarely be seen with the level of care and commitment that engenders connection. The viewing context of YouTube serves to quiet the radical potential of even the most repeatable and rousing of phrases. No matter how hard you shout, no matter how well crafted is your slogan, no matter how deeply you feel it and how precise its summary of the unjust, your cry, potentially heard by many, is only one such call in a sea of noise. This quieting function of the sloganlike structure of YouTube is described by David Sholle (2004: 347) as he delineates the disparities between 'information' and 'knowledge' technologies, the former defined by the piecemeal and fragmented, the transitory, and through rapid flow while the latter is known through structure, endurance, and situatedness. Information moves fast, and reaches many; knowledge comes slowly and waits to be found by the trained.

Certainly political filmmakers have always wanted larger and more diverse audiences; they have sought to be heard and understood by many. However, radical filmmakers have never been able to isolate this demand from a commitment to activist exhibition (that creates possibility for conversation and then action), and radical form (that creates new ways of seeing and knowing). 'I would like to add that a militant film has to reach further', writes Joris Ivens about his 1937 Spanish Civil War film, *The Spanish Earth,* made to raise money for ambulances. 'After informing and moving audiences, it should agitate-mobilize them to become active in connection with the problems shown in the film' (1969: 137). Ivens' claims for connection are structurally untenable given the architecture, ownership, and advertisements on YouTube. It is not that such goals couldn't be reached on the internet, but that given the corporate ownership of YouTube, they will never be realized on this dominant site.

When Eisenstein set forth the slogan as a model for pure cinema, this was in dialectical relation to the tired-out cinema of the free-market, and the first stages of Soviet film. However, as we know too well, films continued to consolidate within the capitalist model of narrative Hollywood film. We are currently seeing how the promise of the epoch of the slogan, still possible on YouTube, is held short by the closing down of critical possibilities of conversation, community, and complexity. In its short history, YouTube has allowed individuals to speak and even be heard in unprecedented numbers about an awesome range of topics including the implicit critique of capitalism expressed through the volume of documentaries on its pages that are dedicated to individuals' isolation and pain.[3] In the following brief demonstration, after celebrating this significant accomplishment – Access – I will then sketch two ways that YouTube's corporate architecture forecloses the next critical steps by disenabling what I will call Knowledge/Theory/Context and Ethics/ Community/Politics. I will conclude by looking more closely at the failures of the direct cinema of the slogan by holding queer documentaries on YouTube to the tradition of queer media criticism, and will demonstrate how the linking of postmodern and postcapitalism on these pages forecloses the knowledge and activism that are definitive of *MEDIA PRAXIS*.

Access

> I will give you my definition of art: art is making.
>
> (Jean Renoir, *Popular Front Cinema, France and the globe, 1930s* (1974: 99))

Renoir states a premise dear to radical filmmakers: art production has been elitist, kept distant from people due to hard-to-get machines and training. Radical cinema will be made by the many when media is structured so that consumers become producers. YouTube does model to the many the possibilities of making. It provides a platform for the easy distribution of non-professional, democratic media production. Open the floodgates, and see, Jean, it's true, everyone can be an artist, people are making in numbers unprecedented in cinema's history. Radical film theorists also assume that once more people can speak, knowledge itself will transform to the shape of regular peoples' experiences and needs. Feminist documentary filmmaker, Barbara Halpern Martineau (1984: 263), articulates a position commonly held by committed media theorists. The 'simple' or 'naïve' form of the talking-head – certainly the most normative realist mode on YouTube because it is now, and has always been, the easiest form for non-specialists to learn while also allowing for new voices to be heard – is of political use: 'by empowering ordinary people to speak as experts, they question a basic assumption of dominant ideology, that only those already in power, those who have a stake in defending the status quo, are entitled to speak as if they know something'.

YouTube allows everyone and anyone (with access to the technologies) to speak about everything and anything they please. I speak, you watch. But without context or community, who cares, and more critically, then what? Under the key-word 'queer documentary', I find a clip from a longer documentary, *Queercore*, posted to the site by its maker, Bret Berg, who is creating web-based documentary content for and about LGBT youth. The 4:39 minute excerpt allows us to meet, in standard talking-head style, the organizers of an all-age, lesbian-focused, queer dance club in Los Angeles. Yes: these young women are rarely afforded expertise. But, left hanging from the documentary that surrounds them, and boxed in by two other trailers for random, if queer, documentaries – one on lesbian femmes and the other on Queer Dragon Boat Racing – their specialist knowledge about organizing queer community events is deflated, dispersed, and thus, de-valued.

Knowledge/Theory/Context

> Q: How do you explain the camera as a gun? A: Well, ideas are guns. A lot of people are dying from ideas and dying for ideas. A gun is a practical idea. An idea is a theoretical gun.
>
> (Jean Luc Godard, *Post-68 France*)

Within the tradition of *MEDIA PRAXIS*, the construction and dissemination of ideas, even 'theory', are understood as critical to the project of cultural transformation. Beyond regular people making media, in numbers, they need to do so in conversation with past and developing thoughts. While art starts with making, it culminates with comprehending, according to 1960s Third Cinema filmmaker/theorist, Tomas Guitterez Alea:

> Art's function is to contribute to the best enjoyment of life, at the aesthetic level, and it does this not by offering a ludicrous parenthesis in the middle of everyday reality but by enriching that very reality. At the cognitive level, it contributes to a more profound comprehension of the world.
>
> (1997: 116)

While the ease of posting media on YouTube allows enjoyment of life, and its comments function opens access to the sharing of words, the site's architecture limits the gun-potential of theory through downsizing and dumbing-down: 'hahahahaha' or ' ☺ '. Here we find ideas far from theoretical guns, and closer to ludicrous puns. Like this response to the trailer for *All Natural*, a documentary about transgender queers. 'I'll bet you are worried you're gay because you can't get a girlfriend. But you can't get a girlfriend because you have an ugly mind. Gay people don't want to hang with creeps like you, so don't worry about that. Just worry about your ugly mindset.' In a second post, this author's thoughts are elaborated upon: 'p.s. I'd tell you my IQ, but I know you can't count that high.'

YouTube, like the internet more generally, according to Wendy Chun (2006: 2), works to 'free the flow of information, reinvigorating free speech', but this occurs in an anarchic and privately motivated environment that disallows the unification of these oddly assorted, if free, demands, images, styles, or viewers. Space limitations, as well as a rapidly conventionalizing culture built upon comments, phrases, or at best slogans – ☺ – rather than sentences or paragraphs, limit participants' abilities to communicate with complexity. It seems rather hard, with such words, to gain collective intellectual or filmic momentum, the 'abstract social evaluation' or 'profound comprehension of the world' our tradition seeks. For, without a linked body of theory as their guide, newly liberated artists must rely upon popular culture. Octavio Getino and Fernando Solanas, also writing about and making Third Cinema, in Latin America in the 1960s explain:

> The cinema of revolution is at the same time one of destruction and construction: destruction of the image that neo-colonialization has created of itself and us, and construction of a throbbing, living reality which recaptures truth in its expression.

In our epoch, documentaries made for YouTube primarily replay, de-construct and re-construct mainstream media, or other distractions or parentheses from daily life: kittens, comedians, clips-already-aired. YouTube registers a media, post-capital and post-colonial, where the majority of technology's newest makers aren't thinking past the mainstream culture's quieting confections. 'Just as they are not masters of the land upon which they walk, the neo-colonized people are not masters of the ideas that envelop them' (Solanas and Getino 1997: 37).

Thus, theorists of media praxis have often proposed that radical media should promote critical reading practices. In their writing about the Trans-Atlantic Black Cinema of the 1980s, Isaac Julien and Kobena Mercer discuss a cinema organized to make the critical connections between popular culture and its internal contradictions:

> What is in question is not the expression of some lost origin or some uncontaminated essence in black film-language but the adoption of a critical voice that promotes consciousness of the collision of cultures and histories that constitute our very conditions of existence.
>
> (1988: 4)

While any discrete video on YouTube might perform the function heralded by Julien and Mercer – for Julien's very own videos could be posted there – the total YouTube experience, where Julien's video would be randomly sandwiched between clips from *Queer as Folk* and clips from documentaries about *Queer as Folk*, undermines both the adoption of a critical voice and its associated growing of consciousness. YouTube is defined by empty and endless collisions of discrete documentaries aligned by an apolitical search engine, itself organized around broad and often banal user-generated keywords. Thus, YouTube manufactures collision without consciousness: each lone documentary unmoored from the critique, culture, history, or intention – the context – that produced it.

Pratibha Parmar, also a participant within the New Queer and Black-Atlantic Cinema movements of this time expresses a commonly held interest in scattering authority. 'The more we assert our own identities as historically marginalized groups, the more we expose the tyranny of a so-called center' (1993: 4). YouTube serves well the de-centering mandate of post-identity politics by creating a logic of dispersal and network. However, while there is unquestionably both freedom, and otherwise unavailable critical possibilities, offered by such fragmentations, YouTube limits our possibilities for radical comprehension by denying opportunities to re-link these peripherals in any rational or sustaining way. Collective knowledge is difficult to produce without a map, a structure, and an ethics.

Ethics/community/politics

> The real crime of representation is representation itself.
>
> (David MacDougall, participatory ethnographic cinema, 1970s)

A significant strain of media praxis is dedicated to considering the power at play in acts of representation. Communal production and engaged reception have been two strategies modeled by this tradition to counter the power imbalance inherent in the cinematic act.[4] The re-thinking of human relationships through cinema can be understood as a media ethics, an intellectual and practical attention to how media-tion affects individuals and communities. From this tradition, Jonas Mekas writes about the New American Cinema in 1962:

> The new independent cinema movement – like the other arts in American today – is primarily an existential movement, or if you want, an ethical

movement, a human act; it is only secondarily an aesthetic one ... One could say that there is a morality in the new.

(1978: 104)

On YouTube there is amorality in the new. Since there is no place for ideas or interaction about production to surface, communal authoring, while possible, is rarely taken advantage of. Communal consumption is almost definitively absent. As for engaged reception: individual viewers may be creating useful maps across and between material, but these are hard to share. It is virtually impossible for two or more viewers to go down any YouTube road together.

Because people consume media in isolation on YouTube, even if a documentary presents radical content, the viewing architecture maintains that viewers must keep this to themselves. In this way, even as the self may be changing because of the conditions of new media, the self is also consolidated. 'The boundaries between the subject, if not the body, and the "rest of the world" are undergoing a radical refiguration, brought about in part through the mediation of technology,' writes cyber and trans cultural media activist, Allucquere Rosanne Stone (2000: 517). Like much new media, YouTube disturbs the public/private binary, opening up new possibilities for combinations inconceivable without the technology. Yet YouTube forecloses the construction of coherent communities and returns production, consumption, and meaning-making to the individual, re-establishing the reign of the self. Alexander Galloway (2004) explains that the end result is fragmentation, and while this may be continually exciting to postmodern cowboys endlessly anticipating the demise of the self, it has never served well people who are political, people who need to stand strong together in the name of something that must not be in the here and now. Thus, *MEDIA PRAXIS* has also defined and long debated utility. 'Intentionality is commonly a discredited concept in media criticism,' writes AIDS activist videomaker, John Greyson, about this 1980s media movement. 'Yet for any video artist making social change media (and certainly for the majority of these AIDS producers), it is a central issue.' YouTube strips intentionality from any documentary production found on it pages by unmooring it from its context and community.

In 1969, Julio Garcia Espinosa wrote his manifesto about filmmaking, neo-colonialism, and socialism, 'For an Imperfect Cinema'. Here he included a lengthy if utopian description of a world to come that seems surprisingly familiar. The world he anticipates might almost be our own: one where there is surplus time and material resources, expanded education and cheaper technologies, simply put, a world where *everyone makes films*.

Quoted below, but not like a slogan, is a paragraph or two by Espinosa, left intact so that the richness and depth, the knowledge that he builds through lengthy listing, can be surveyed in full. Espinosa forecasts that changing conditions will result in the revolutionary outcome of universal art production. We will see that almost all that he anticipated has come to pass here in the United States, but perhaps not in Cuba from where he wrote. But because of YouTube's postmodern and post-capitalist wedding of technology and commerce to access and communication, sadly we end not with social justice, as he wished, but fragmentation, as he feared.

When we ask ourselves who it is we who are the film directors and not the others, that is to say, the spectators, the question does not stem from an exclusively ethical concern. We know that we are filmmakers because we have been part of a minority which has had the time and circumstances need to develop, within itself, an artistic culture; and because the material resources of film technology are limited and therefore available to some, not to all. But what happens if the future holds the universalization of college level instruction, if economic and social development reduce the hours in the work day, if the evolution of film technology (there are already signs in evidence) makes it possible that this technology ceases being the privilege of a small few? What happens if the development of video-tape solves the problem of inextricably limited laboratory capacity, if television systems with their potential for 'projecting' independently of the central studio render the ad infinitum construction of movie theaters suddenly superfluous?

What happens then is not only an act of social justice – the possibility for everyone to make films – but also a fact of extreme importance for artistic culture: the possibility of recovering, without any complexes or guilt feelings, the true meaning of artistic activity. Then we will be able to understand that art is one of mankind's impartial or uncommitted activities. That art is not work, and that the artist is not in the strict sense a worker ... For us then the revolution is the highest expression of culture because it will abolish artistic culture as a fragmentary human activity.

(1997: 72)

Espinosa's final wish for humanity will not be realized in our time, at least not through documentaries on YouTube.

YouTube through New Queer Cinema

Any political movement with a media component needs self-aware writing that creates a social, political, intellectual and aesthetic context and structure for under-standing new media work, for connecting it to other work, present and past, and then, most critically, for relating the work on display to contemporary claims and acts bent upon changing the world. While this might sound like too much, I have learned that the integration of a theoretical practice with a media practice is definitive of and integral to media praxis: that is, media that is made in connection to an articulated project of world and self-changing. For instance, in *Queer Cinema: The Film Reader*, the first paragraph of the general introduction explains that queer film cannot be understood outside of queer theory, an approach to rethinking human sexuality that sustains the film work produced, the critical writing about it, and the community served and hailed by this integrated body of cultural production. Activist rants, bits and pieces of queer television, hot guys kissing on a gay pride float, each of these stand-alone snatches of queer documentary practice, each of these isolated and solo fragments found on YouTube, are not the stuff of a political or film movement until someone, or better yet, some group unifies them, by linking their claims, strategies, and goals.

This was the function of B. Ruby Rich's seminal 1992 article, 'New queer cinema'. While the movies came first, the article theorized their style, function, and context. Rich explains how many of these films from the early 1990s share a postmodern vocabulary, both aesthetic and political, while also making sure to note the critical differences between the media practices of the girls and those of the boys (Rich 2004: 15–22). Then, Andrea Weiss (2005) builds upon Rich's taxonomy in her article 'Transgressive cinema: lesbian independent film', to note that lesbian cinema can be defined by its 'attempts to construct alternative visual codes' deriving from 'lesbian self-definition' and the '1970s lesbian/feminist movement'. Note how form and politics are linked to and through theory in both of these written works. This explains why the politics of AIDS is key to understanding what New Queer Cinema was and queer video on YouTube is not. Monica Pearl suggests that 'New queer cinema is AIDS cinema' (2004: 23) because a great many of these films and videos were created in the name of, or in response to this devastating crisis that needed answers ... immediately. While all the films and videos were certainly not *about* AIDS, they shared what Julianne Pidduck calls 'an ethical ground' (2004: 86). I understand Pidduck to mean something quite simple and definitive for effective media praxis: New Queer Cinema was made when producers were fighting for something, and in the name of that goal, particular and linked media forms, practices and strategies were developed, in dialogue with other work and producers. Michele Aaron, in her Introduction to *New Queer Cinema: A Critical Reader*, describes a mutual style and politics organized around defiance: of what it meant to be gay, the sanctity of the past, cinematic conventions, and the meaning of death, precisely because of the place of AIDS. Because YouTube cannot generate an ethics – a shared sensibility and belief system – between its video or its viewers, it also forecloses the possibility for media politics.

Furthermore, as these few examples from the critical writing connected to New Queer Cinema demonstrate, when people theorize a political cinema while and after it is being made, a critical conversation about the imperatives and commonalities of form, as well as content, emerges. Since there is no formal unity and consistency across the works found on YouTube, this theoretical prerequisite is also belied. Without such theoretical bedrock – that is, theory about form – queer documentaries on YouTube cannot take what is the most common second step for political film movements. Namely, as representation increases, those studying a movement quickly realize that expanded visibility is only the most preliminary of radical ambitions. For while it is certainly true that YouTube opens up access and visibility so that, for instance, young, isolated queer youth can see images of people like themselves in ways unimaginable without the technology,[5] this isolated practice is a preliminary and solo step. What happens next according to Anat Pick is the realization that 'screening lesbianism is not simply a matter of making the invisible visible, but of negotiating different regimes of visibility', thus using cinema to herald 'new ways of thinking, being, and screening lesbian and queer' (2004: 115). New ways of seeing, like the delivery platform that is YouTube, are only the first move in a more radical and multifaceted project that commits to innovative thinking and novel ways of being. Here we must return to Eisenstein's demands for 'abstract social evaluation'. It is this, most fundamentally, where YouTube fails, not because radical queer thinking and being, epistemology and ontology, are not modeled in the content and even form of some of the videos on display, but because this is neither coherently nor consistently patterened across the work and across the pages that surround the work.

Given YouTube's aimless structure, there's no way to build. For instance, the term 'Lesbian Community' delivers to me first, seemingly erroneously, a TV news clip about Prince William, of the UK, splitting up with his girlfriend, then a short clip featuring the popular but ubiquitous dykes-on-bikes from an un-named gay pride parade, something from a Rosie fan club, a clip from the seminal lesbian documentary *Forbidden Love*, a few clips from lectures and shows at various gay and lesbian community centers (these, however, primarily featuring gay men). Meanwhile the vast majority of clips (remember from 'Lesbian Community') are titillating glimpses of gay male sex including videos called Bears and Leather Guys, Hot Speedo Guys, Gay Leather Guys, and Gay Guardian Angel.

(Lesbian) community is defined by interactivity, strong affective bonds, a shared moral culture, and deliberation, according to Amitai Etzoni (2004: 87) who answers the title of the essay, 'Are virtual and democratic communities feasible?' with a relatively resounding no. At odds for lesbians, and others, seeking community on the internet is the interplay between commodity and community, a sloganlike predicament that defines the structure and limits of YouTube. In their introduction to *Queer Online*, Kate O'Riordan and David Phillips document how 'through the 1990s, ownership and control of the infrastructure of the internet, including the backbone carriers, ISPs, and Web Portals, became increasingly the domain of fewer, larger, and more integrated media corporations' so that a gay and lesbian internet that was once answerable to 'geographic and political communities' began answering 'primarily to advertisers and investors' (2007: 5). YouTube's edifice, which reduces media production and consumption to the discrete and unlinked output or viewing practices of random queer individuals, also functions to disallow the establishment of community, which was perhaps the foremost goal of New Queer Cinema. The liberated mediamakers creating and viewing queer content in unheralded numbers, do so with no plan or possibility beyond their private production and consumption. 'Freedom is fostered when the means of communication are dispersed, decentralized, and easily available ... Central control is more likely when the means of communication are concentrated, monopolized, and scarce, as are great networks' (de Sola Pool 1983: 5).

Ending with the failure of queer community, I hope that I have begun to mark the places where YouTube misses out. Namely, as YouTube explodes numbers, it minimizes elsewhere: a theory or theories; a politics; a sense of history; and a community. What YouTube achieves through open admission, it loses in focused vision. When I search for a queer documentary media praxis on YouTube, the tradition that undergirds contemporary queer realist images proves to be there, absolutely. On YouTube is available much I would have never had access to without it: short videos by undistributed queer artists, scenes from lectures, parades, protests, and bedrooms. However, these images, although exceedingly diverse, are undifferentiated and poorly categorized. They stand in sorry isolation from the time, place, community, aims, contexts, and theories from whence they were produced, each vying, and linking with other undifferentiated videos in a sea of queer documentary images that is removed from the specificity and motivating clarity of causes and communities. Now, certainly, each of these videos, re-contextualized on a queer page, or even more specifically, an AIDS page, or a page on lesbian sexuality or identity, would function more in the vein of media praxis. But this is not the language of YouTube: fragments, clutter, information, commerce, and slogans.

Eisenstein and others anticipated a slogan that would counter capitalist yearning with life-affirming knowing. This is what they hoped for in Latin America in the 1960s: 'The result – and motivation – of social documentary and realist cinema? Knowledge and consciousness; we repeat: the awakening of the consciousness of reality. The posing of problems. Change: from subject to life' (Birri 1997: 4). And we continue to want this via today's technologies:

> Such a cinema would tap into the potential of new video (and digital) technology, draw its resources from while serving communities that struggle against oppression and, most importantly, engage with and resist the decentered and dispersed forms of late capitalist domination that operate transnationally and across different identity formations'.
>
> (Leung 2004: 158)

I have seen slogans work in just this way. SILENCE EQUALS DEATH appeared on posters, buttons, and leaflets. It was chanted ad infinitum in meeting rooms, on city streets, and at government capitals. However, we used this slogan, in these varied spaces, to fire us up (We Can't Take it Anymore!), and then, to continue into conversation, interaction, and better yet, action, towards change, together, in the name of what we knew was right and what we communally and defiantly expressed could be better. Because I have yet to find this communal energy, or action, or interaction, on YouTube, and more critically, because I think it is not possible on its pages, I will continue to seek theories and practices of radical media elsewhere.

Acknowledgements

This chapter was workshopped in the LA Women's Group for the Collaborative Study of Race and Gender in Culture. The group, whose members include Gabrielle Foreman, Alexandra Juhasz, Laura Hyun Yi Kang, Rachel Lee, and Eve Oishi, theorizes, writes and produces new scholarship within a progressive, collective, feminist framework. I would like to express my thanks to the members of the group, as well as to my mother, Suzanne Juhasz, who also read a final draft. I encourage other scholars to create collaborative and supportive networks such as these.

Notes

1 I have written, taught about and produced activist video within the AIDS, feminist, and queer media movements of the 1980s, 1990s, and 2000s.
2 See http://mediacommons.futureofthebook.org.

3   I credit Rachel Lee with this observation.
4   See Juhasz (1995).
5   See Gray (2007).

Bibliography

Aaronovitch, D. (2003) Why we love *Wife Swap*, *Observer*, 5 October. www.guardian. co.uk/Columnists/Column/0,5673,1056306,00 (accessed 16 Jul. 2006).

Abel, R. (ed) (1988) *French Film Theory and Criticism, I, 1907–1939*, Princeton, NJ: Princeton University Press.

Adorno, T. (1978) *Minima Moralia: Reflections from Damaged Life*, trans. E.F.N. Jephcott. London: Verso.

Adorno, T. and Horkheimer, M. (1977) The culture industry: enlightenment as mass deception, in J. Curran, M. Gurevitch and J. Woolacott (eds) *Mass Communications and Society*. London: Open University Press.

Alea, T.G. (1997) The viewer's dialectic, in M. Martin (ed) *New Latin American Cinema*. Detroit: Wayne State University Press.

Andrejevic, M. (2004) *Reality TV: The Work of Being Watched*. Lanham. MD: Rowman and Littlefield.

Appadurai, A. (2006) *Fear of Small Numbers: An Essay on the Geography of Anger*. Durham, NC: Duke University Press.

Arthur, P. (1997) On the virtues and limitations of collage, *Documentary Box*, 11: 3.

Arthur, P. (2005) Extreme makeover: the changing face of documentary, *Cineaste*, 30(3): 18–23.

Arts and Humanities Research Council www.ahrc.ac.uk (accessed Aug. 2006).

Aufderheide, P. (2005) The changing documentary marketplace, *Cineaste*, 30(3): 25–8.

Austin, T. (2005) Seeing, feeling and knowing: a case study of audience perspectives on screen documentary, *Participations*, 2(1). Available at: www.participations.org

Austin, T. (2007) *Watching the World: Screen Documentary and Audiences*. Manchester: Manchester University Press.

Bachmann, G. (1977) The man on the volcano: a portrait of Werner Herzog, *Film Quarterly*, 31: 2–10.

Baker, M. (2006) *Documentary in the Digital Age*. London: Focal Press.

Bal, M. (2007) Exhibition as film, in S. Macdonald and P. Basu (eds) *Exhibition Experiments*. Oxford: Blackwell.

Banks, M. (1992) Which films are the ethnographic films? in P.I. Crawford and D. Turton (eds) *Film as Ethnography*. Manchester: Manchester University Press.

Banks, M. (1994) Television and anthropology: an unhappy marriage? *Visual Anthropology*, 7: 21–45.

Banks, M. (1998) Visual anthropology: image, object and interpretation, in J. Prosser (ed) *Image-based Research: A Sourcebook for Qualitative Researchers*. London: Falmer Press.

Banks, M. and Morphy, H. (eds) (1997) *Rethinking Visual Anthropology*. New Haven, CT: Yale University Press.

Barnouw, E. (1974) *Documentary: A History of the Non-Fiction Film*. Oxford: Oxford University Press.

Barsam, R.M. (1974) *Nonfiction Film: A Critical History*. London: George Allen and Unwin.

Barthes, R. (1974) *S/Z*. New York: Hill and Wang.

Barthes, R. (1977) The rhetoric of the image, trans. Stephen Heath, in *Image-Music-Text*. New York: Hill and Wang.

Barthes, R. (1980, 1984) *Camera Lucida: Reflections on Photography, trans.* Richard Howard. London: Flamingo.

Barthes, R. (1993) *Mythologies*. London: Vintage.

Baudrillard, J. (1994) *Simulacra and Simulation*, trans. S. Faria Glaser. Ann Arbor, MI: University of Michigan Press.

Bautista, A.M. (2006) Desperation and domesticity: reconfiguring the 'happy housewife' in *Desperate Housewives*, in J. McCabe and K. Akass (eds) *Reading* Desperate Housewives: *Beyond the White Picket Fence*. London: I.B. Tauris.

Bazin, A. ([1967] 2005) Cinema and exploration, in *What is Cinema?* Vol.1, ed and trans. Hugh Gray. Berkeley and Los Angeles: University of California Press.

BBC, Sir Alan Sugar confirmed for BBC Two's *The Apprentice*, press release, 18 May, www.bbc.co.uk/print/pressoffice/pressreleases/

Beacham, J. (1999) The value of theory/practice degrees, *Journal of Media Practice*, 1(2): 85–97.

Beck, U. (2000) *The Brave New World of Work*. Cambridge: Polity.

Becker, A. (1999) Ostdeutsche Truman Show. Für immer und ewig die Golzower Lebenswege: Brigitte und Marcel, *Die Tageszeitung*, 20 February.

Benjamin, W. (1973) *Charles Baudelaire: A Lyric Poet in the Era of High Capitalism*. London: New Left Books.

Benjamin,W. (1979) A small history of photography, in W. Benjamin, *One-Way Street*. London: Verso.

Benthall, J. (1986) The pale of anthropology, *Anthropology Today*, 2(3): 1–2.

Berger, J. (1980, 1991) *About Looking*. New York: Vintage International.

Berkhofer, Jr., R. (1995) *Beyond the Great Story: History as Text and Discourse*. Cambridge, MA: Harvard University Press.

Berrettini, M.L. (2005) Danger! Danger! Danger! or When animals might attack: adventure activism and wildlife film and television, *Scope*, (NS) 1, Spring. Available at: http://www.scope.nottingham.ac.uk/ article.php?issue=1&id=5&section=article &q=danger

Bill Viola. www.billviola.com (accessed Aug. 2006).

Biltereyst, D. (2004) *Big Brother* and its moral guardians, in E. Mathijs and J. Jones (eds) *Big Brother International*. London: Wallflower Press.

Birri, F. (1997) Cinema and underdevelopment, in M. Martin (ed) *New Latin American Cinema*, vol. 1. Detroit, MI: Wayne State University Press.

Bishop, C. (2004) Antagonism and relational aesthetics, *October*, 110, Fall: 51–79.

Blackburn, R. (2006) Finance and the fourth dimension, *New Left Review*, 39: 39–70.

Blair, H. (2001) You are only as good as your last job: the labour process and the labour market in the British film industry, *Work, Employment and Society*, 17(1): 149–69.

Bollas, C. (1993) *Being a Character*. London: Routledge.

Boltanski, L. and Chiapello, E. (2005) *The New Spirit of Capitalism*. London: Verso.

Bondebjerg, I. (1996) Public discourse, private fascination: hybridization in 'true-life-story' genres, *Media, Culture & Society*, 18: 27–45.

Bondebjerg, I. (2002) The mediation of everyday life: genre discourse and spectacle in reality TV, in A. Jerslev (ed) *Realism and Reality in Film and Media: Northern Lights Year Book*. Copenhagen: University of Copenhagen Press.

Boorstin, D. (1963) *The Image*. Harmondsworth: Penguin.

Bordwell, D. (1985) *Narration in the Fiction Film*. Madison, WI: University of Wisconsin Press.

Bourdieu, P. (1993) *The Field of Cultural Production*. Cambridge: Polity Press.

Bourdieu, P. (1998) *Acts of Resistance: Against the Tyranny of the Market*. New York: The New Press.

Bourriaud, N. (2000) *Postproduction. Culture as Screenplay: How Art Reprograms the World*. New York: Lucas & Sternberg.

Bousé, D. (2000) *Wildlife Films*. Philadelphia, PA: University of Pennsylvania Press.

Bowen, P. (2007) Reality check, Screendaily.com, 6 July.

Brecht, B. (1964) Alienation effects in Chinese acting, in J. Willett (ed) *Brecht on Theatre: The Development of an Aesthetic*. London: Methuen Drama.

Brecht, B. (2000) 'The threepenny lawsuit', in M. Silberman (ed) *Brecht on Film and Radio*. London: Methuen.

Brecht, B. (2001) The *Verfremdungseffekt* in the other arts, in M. Silberman (ed), *Brecht on Film and Radio*. London: Methuen.

Brenner, R. (2006) *The Economics of Global Turbulence*. London: Verso.

Bresson, R. (1977) *Notes on Cinematography*, trans. J. Griffin. New York: Urizon.

Brooker, W. and Jermyn, D. (eds) (2003) *The Audience Studies Reader*. London: Routledge.

Bruner, J. (1993) The autobiographical process, in R. Folkenflik (ed) *The Culture of Autobiography: Constructions of Self-Representation*. Stanford, CA: Stanford University Press.

Bruzzi, S. ([2000] 2006) *New Documentary: A Critical Introduction*. London: Routledge.

Bruzzi, S. (2007) *Seven Up*. London: British Film Insitute.

Buck-Morss, S. (1991) *The Dialectics of Seeing*. Boston: MIT Press.

Bunting, M. (2004) *Willing Slaves: How the Overwork Culture is Ruling our Lives*. London: HarperCollins.

Burnshaw, S. (1970) *The Seamless Web*. New York: George Braziller.

Burt, J. (2002) *Animals in Film*. London: Reaktion Books.

Burton, J. (1986) *Cinema and Social Change in Latin America: Conversations with Filmmakers*. Austin, TX: University of Texas Press.

Byg, B. (2001) GDR-up: The ideology of universality in long term documentary, *New German Critique*, 82, Winter.

Caillois, R. (1979) *Man Play and Games*. New York: Schocken Books.

Caplan, P. (2005) In search of the exotic: a discussion of the BBC2 series *Tribe*, *Anthropology Today*, 21(2): 3–7.

Carlsson, M. (1990) *Bad Attitude: The Processed World Anthology*. London: Verso.

Carolin, C. and Haynes, C. (2007) The politics of display: Ann-Sofi Sidén's *Warte Mal!*, art history and social documentary, in S. Macdonald and P. Basu (eds) *Exhibition Experiments*. Oxford: Blackwell.

Carroll, N. (2003) *Engaging the Moving Image*. New Haven, CT: Yale University Press.

Castonguay, J. (2004) The political economy of the indie blockbuster: fandom, intermediality and *The Blair Witch Project*, in S.L. Higley and J.A. Weinstock (eds) *Nothing That Is: Millennial Cinema and the Blair Witch Controversies*. Detroit: Wayne State University Press.

Chakrabarty, D. (2000) *Provincializing Europe: Postcolonial Thought and Historical Difference*. Princeton, NJ: Princeton University Press.

Chalfen, R. (1998) Interpreting family photography as pictorial communication, in J. Prosser (ed) *Image-based Research: A Sourcebook for Qualitative Researchers*. London: Falmer Press.

Chanan, M. (n.d.) On documentary: the Zapruder quotient, *Filmwaves,* 4. Available at: mchanan.dial.pipex.com/zapruder.htm

Chanan, M. (2007) *The Politics of Documentary*. London: British Film Institute.

Chatterjee, P. (2000) The nation and its peasants, in V. Chaturvedi (ed) *Mapping Subaltern Studies and the Postcolonial*. London: Verso.

Chun, W. (2006) *Control and Freedom: Power and Paranoia in the Age of Fiber Optics*. Cambridge, MA: The MIT Press.

Clifford, J. and Marcus, G.E. (eds) (1986) *Writing Culture: The Poetics and Politics of Ethnography*. Berkeley, CA: University of California Press.

Collingwood, R.G. (1946) *The Idea of History*. Oxford: Oxford University Press.

Connor, S. (2000) *Dumbstruck: A Cultural History of Ventriloquism*. Oxford: Oxford University Press.

Corner, J. (1996) *The Art of Record*. Manchester: Manchester University Press.

Corner, J. (1999) *Critical Ideas in Television Studies*. Oxford: Oxford University Press.

Corner, J. (2000) What can we say about 'documentary'? *Media, Culture & Society,* 22(5): 681–8.

Corner, J. (2001) Documentary in a post-documentary culture?: A note on forms and their functions. Available at: http://www.1boro.ac.uk/research/changing.media/John%20Corner%20paper.htm (accessed 14 Jan. 2002).

Corner, J. (2002) Performing the real: documentary diversions, *Television and New Media,* 3(3): 255–69.

Corner, J. (2004) Afterword: framing the new, in S. Holmes and D. Jermyn (eds) *Understanding Reality Television*. London: Routledge.

Corner J. (2005) Television documentary and the category of the aesthetic, in P. Rosenthal and J. Corner (eds) *New Challenges for Documentary*, 2nd edn. Manchester: Manchester University Press.

Corner, J. (2006) A fiction (un)like any other? *Critical Studies in Television,* 1(1): 89–96.

Corrigan, T. (1991) The commerce of auteurism, in *A Cinema Without Walls: Movies and Culture After Vietnam*. New Brunswick, NJ: Rutgers University Press.

Cottle, S. (2003) *Media Organization and Production*. London: Sage.

Cottle, S. (2004) Producing nature(s): on the changing production ecology of natural history TV, *Media, Culture & Society*, 26(1): 81–101.

Couldry, N. (2002) Playing for celebrity: *Big Brother* as ritual event, *Television and New Media*, 3(3): 283–94.

Couldry, N. (2003) *Media Rituals: A Critical Approach*. London: Routledge.

Couldry, N. (2006) Media and the ethics of 'reality' construction, *Southern Review*, 39(1): 42–54.

Cowie, E. (1999) The spectacle of actuality, in J. Gaines and M. Renov (eds) *Collecting Visible Evidence*. Minneapolis, MN: University of Minnesota Press.

Creeber, G. (ed) (2006) *Tele-visions: An Introduction to the Study of Television*. London: BFI.

Cronin, P. (ed) (2002) *Herzog on Herzog*. London: Faber and Faber.

Crowther, B. (1995) Towards a feminist critique of natural history programmes, in P. Florence and D. Reynolds (eds) *Feminist Subjects, Multimedia: Cultural Methodologies*. Manchester: Manchester University Press.

Cummings, N. and Lewandowska, M. (2007) From capital to enthusiasm: an exhibitionary practice, in S. Macdonald and P. Basu (eds) *Exhibition Experiments*. Oxford: Blackwell.

Dean, M. (1993) *Governmentality: Power and Rule in Modern Society*. London: Sage.

Deleuze, G. and Guattari, F. (2000) *Anti-Oedipus: Capitalism and Schizophrenia*. London: The Athlone Press.

Denhart, A. (2003) Reality Blurred Website. Available at: (http://www.realityblurred com/realitytv/archives/international_big_brothers/2003_Oct_06_columbias_big_ brother) posted 6 Oct 2003. (accessed 3 April 2007).

de Sola Pool, I. (1983) *Technologies of Freedom: On Free Speech in an Electronic Age*. Cambridge, MA: Harvard University Press.

Domanska, E. (ed) (1998) *Encounters: Philosophy of History after Postmodernism*. Charlottesville, VA: University of Virginia Press.

Dornfeld, B. (1998) *Producing Public Television, Producing Public Culture*. Princeton, NJ: Princeton University Press.

Dover, C. and Barnett, S. (2004) The world on the box: international issues in news and factual programmes on UK television, 1975–2003. *Report*, 3WE.

Dovey, J. (2000) *Freakshow: First Person Media and Factual TV*. London: Pluto Press.

Easthope, A. and McGowan, K. (2004) *A Critical and Cultural Theory Reader*. Maidenhead: Open University Press.

Eisenstein, S. (1988) *Our October*: Beyond the played and the non-played, in R. Taylor (ed) *The Eisenstein Reader*. London: BFI.

Eliot, T.S. (1944) *Four Quartets*. London: Faber and Faber.

Ellingson, T. (2001) *The Myth of the Noble Savage*. Berkeley, CA: University of California Press.

Ellis, J. (2000) *Seeing Things: Television in the Age of Uncertainty*. London: I.B. Tauris.

Espinosa, J.G. (1997) For an imperfect cinema, in M. Martin (ed) *New Latin American Cinema*. Detroit: Wayne State University Press.

Etzioni, A. (2004) Are virtual and democratic communities feasible? in H. Jenkins and D. Thorburn (eds) *Democracy and New Media*. Cambridge, MA: MIT Press.

Faulkner, L. and Anderson, A. (1987) Short term projects and emergent careers; evidence from Hollywood, *American Journal of Sociology*, 92(4): 479–509.

Feldman, C. and Kornfield, J. (eds) (1991) *Stories of the Spirit, Stories of the Heart*. London: HarperCollins.

Fetveit, A. (1999) Reality TV in the digital era: a paradox in visual culture? *Media, Culture & Society*, 21(6):

Firouazabadi, I. (2004) Would you like to be on TV? http/www.bcf.org.uk/national/2004/wife-swap.htm (accessed 11 Sept. 2006).

Fleck, R. (2002) Warte mal! (Hey wait!), in A.-S. Sidén, *Warte Mal! Prostitution After the Velvet Revolution*. London: Hayward Gallery.

Flynn, B. (2002) Factual hybridity: games documentary and simulated spaces, *Media International Australia*, 104: 42–54.

Flynn, B. (2005) Docobricolage in the age of simulation, in G. King (ed) *The Spectacle of the Real*. Bristol: Intellect.

Forrest, N. (2003) review of *Wife Swap*, www.thefword.org.uk/reviews/2003/02/wife-swap (accessed 11 Sept. 2006).

Foucault, M. (1982) The subject and power, in H.L. Dreyfus and P. Rabinow (eds) *Michel Foucault: Beyond Structuralism and Hermeneutics*. Chicago: The University of Chicago Press.

Foucault, M. (1984) The subject and power, in B. Wallis (ed) *Art After Modernism: Rethinking Representation*. New York: New Museum of Contemporary Art.

Fraser, N. (2007) Real appeal, *Sight and Sound* (NS) 17: 38.

Friedman, T. (2002) Civilisation and its discontents: simulation, subjectivity, and space, in G. Smith (ed) *On a Silver Platter: CD-ROMs and the Promises of a New Technology*. New York: New York University Press.

Gaines, J. (1999) Political mimesis, in J. Gaines and M. Renov (eds) *Collecting Visible Evidence*. Minneapolis, MN: University of Minnesota Press.

Galloway, A. (2004) *Protocol*. Cambridge, MA: The MIT Press.

Gant, C. (2007) What's up doc? *Sight and Sound* (NS) 17:9 (September).

Garcia Espinosa, J. (2005) Cuban cinema: a long journey towards the light, lecture at UCL, London, 16 February.

Geertz, C. (1973) Thick description: toward an interpretative theory of culture, in *The Interpretation of Cultures*. New York: Basic Books.

Geertz, C. (1988) *Works and Lives: The Anthropologist as Author*. Stanford, CA: Stanford University Press.

Geraghty, C. (1991) *Women and Soap Opera: A Study of Prime-time Soaps*. Oxford: Polity.

Geritz, K. (2006) Brave outsiders: the films of Kim Longinotto, www.bampfa.berkeley.edu/filmseries/braveout. (accessed 22 Nov. 2006).

Gibson, O. (2005) *Big Brother* and beyond: landmarks in reality format, *The Guardian*, 21 April.

Giddens, A. and Pierson, C. (1998) *Conversations with Anthony Giddens: Making Sense of Modernity*. Cambridge: Polity.

Gies, L. (forthcoming) Reality TV and the jurisprudence of *Wife Swap*, in L. Gies, *Law and the Media: The Future of an Uneasy Relationship*. London: Glasshouse Press.

Gilbert, N. and Conte, R. (eds) (1995) *Artificial Societies*: *The Computer Simulation of Social Life*. London: UCL Press.

Gilbert, N. and Doran, J. (eds) (1994) *Simulating Societies: The Computer Simulation of Social Phenomena*. London: UCL Press.

Gilroy, P. (2005) *After Empire*. London: Routledge.

Goffman, E. (1971) *The Presentation of Self in Everyday Life*. Harmondsworth: Penguin Books.

Graham, D. Associates Ltd (2006) Digital Platforms; Risks and opportunities for European Film-makers. Culture & Education Policy Department European Parliament http:/www.europarl.europa.eu/EST/download.do?file=13150.

Grant, B. and Sloniowksi, J. (eds) (1998) *Documenting the Documentary: Close Readings of Documentary Film and Video*. Detroit, MI: Wayne State University Press.

Grant, C. (2000) www.auteur.com? *Screen*, 41(1): 101–8.

Gray, M. L. (2007) Discovering self on the Discovery Channel: trans youth, paper presented at International Communications Associations Annual Conference.

Grierson, J. (1946) *Grierson on Documentary*, (ed) Forsyth Hardy, London: Collins.

Grimshaw, A. (2001) T*he Ethnographer's Eye*: *Ways of Seeing in Modern Anthropology*. Cambridge: Cambridge University Press.

Guha, R. (2002) *History at the Limit of World-History*. New York: Columbia University Press.

Hall, S. (2003) New Labour's double-shuffle, *Soundings*, 24: 10–25.

Hammersley, M. (1995) *The Politics of Social Research*. London: Sage.

Hardt, M. and Negri, N. (2004) *Empire*. Cambridge, MA: Harvard University Press.

Hardt, M. and Negri, A. (2005) *Multitude*. London: Penguin.

Hardy, F. (ed) (1979) *Grierson on Documentary*. London: Faber.

Harries, D. (2000) *Film Parody*. London: British Film Institute.

Hartley, J. (1999) *Uses of Television*. London: Routledge.

Harvey, D. (2003) *The New Imperialism*. Oxford: Oxford University Press.

Hastrup, K. (1992) Anthropological visions: some notes on visual and textual authority, in P.I. Crawford and D. Turton (eds) *Film as Ethnography*. Manchester: Manchester University Press.

Hastrup, K. and Elsass, P. (1990) Anthropological advocacy: a contradiction in terms? *Current Anthropology*, 31(3): 301–11.

Heider, K.G. (1976) *Ethnographic Film*. Austin, TX: University of Texas Press.

Henley, P. (2006) Anthropologists in television: a disappearing world? in S. Pink (ed) *Applications of Anthropology: Professional Anthropology in the Twenty-First Century*. Oxford: Berghahn Books.

Hesmondhalgh, D. (2002) *The Cultural Industries*. London: Sage.

Hesmondhalgh, D. (2006) *Media Production*. Maidenhead: Open University Press.

Hight, C. (2001) Webcam sites: the documentary genre moves online? *Media International Australia Incorporating Culture and Policy*, 100: 81–93.

Hight, C. (forthcoming) *Television Mockumentary: Documentary and Satire in the Televisual Space*. Manchester: Manchester University Press.

Hight, C. and Roscoe, J. (2006) Forgotten silver: a New Zealand television hoax and its audience, in A. Juhasz and J. Lerner (eds) *F Is for Phony. Fake Documentary and Truth's Undoing*. Minneapolis: Minnesota University Press.

Higley, S.L. and Weinstock, J.A. (eds) (2004) *Nothing That Is: Millennial Cinema and the Blair Witch Controversies*. Detroit, MI: Wayne State University Press.

Hill, A. (2002) *Big Brother*: the real audience, *Television and New Media*, 3(3).

Hill, A. (2005) *Reality TV: Audiences and Popular Factual Television*. London: Routledge.

Hill, A. (2007) *Restyling Factual Television*. London: Routledge.

Hillier, J. and Lovell, A. (1972) *Studies in Documentary*. New York: Viking.

Hockings, P. (ed) (1975) *Principles of Visual Anthropology*. The Hague: Mouton Publishers.

Hoggard, L. (2003) Thinking outside the box, *Observer*, 29 June: 23.

Höijer, B. (1998) Social psychological perspectives in reception analysis, in R. Dickinson, R. Harindranath and O. Linné (eds) *Approaches to Audiences: A Reader*. London: Arnold.

Holmes, S. and Jermyn, D. (eds) (2004) *Understanding Reality TV*. London: Routledge.

Honneth, A. (2004) Organized self-realization: some paradoxes of individualization, *European Journal of Social Theory*, 7(4): 463–78.

Horkheimer, M. (1989) Notes on science and the crisis, in S.E. Bronner and D. MacKay Kellner (eds) *Critical Theory and Society: A Reader*. London: Routledge.

Hughes-Freeland, F. (2006) Tribes and tribulations: a response to Pat Caplan, *Anthropology Today*, 22(2): 22–3.

Huizinga, J. (1949) *Homo Ludens: A Study of the Play-Element Culture*, London: Routledge.

Huizinga, J. (1955) *Homo Ludens*. London: Beacon Press.

Hutcheon, L. (2000) *A Theory of Parody: The Teachings of Twentieth-Century Art Forms*. Chicago: University of Illinois Press.

International Movie Database (IMDB) Workingman's Death Awards. Availiable at: www.imdb.com/title/tt0478331/awards (accessed 30 June 2007).

Ivens, J. (1969) *The Camera and I*. New York: International Publishers.

Ivens, J. (1955) Der Mensch im Dokumentarfilm, *Deutsche Filmkunst*, 6.

Jacobs, L. (ed) (1971) *The Documentary Tradition: From Nanook to Woodstock*. New York: Hopkinson and Blake.

Jacobsen, U. (2007) Potential source of income? *Dox* 68, January. EDN.

James, N. (2006) The greatest show on earth, *Sight and Sound*, 16(2): 22–6.

Jameson, F. (1998) *Brecht and Method*. London: Verso.

Jay, M. (1993) *Downcast Eyes: The Denigration of Vision in Twentieth-Century French Thought*. Berkeley, CA: University of California Press.

Jenkins, H. and Thorbun, D. (2004) Introduction, in H. Jenkins and D. Thorbun (eds) *Democracy and New Media*. Cambridge, MA: The MIT Press.

Jenkins, R. (2002) *Pierre Bourdieu*. London: Routledge.

Jerslev, A. (2005) Performativity and documentary, in R. Gade and A. Jerslev (eds) *Performative Realism*. Copenhagen: Museum Tusculanum Press.

Johnson, S. (2005) *Everything Bad Is Good For You: How Today's Popular Culture Is Actually Making Us Smarter*. New York: Riverhead Books.

Juhasz, A. (1994) "They said we were trying to show reality – all I want is to show my video": The politics of the realist feminist documentary, *Screen*, 35(2): 171–90.

Juhasz, A. (1995) *AIDS TV: Identity, Community and Alternative Video*. Durham, NC: Duke University Press.

Juhasz, A. and Lerner, J. (eds) (2006) *F Is for Phony: Fake Documentary and Truth's Undoing*. Minneapolis: Minnesota University Press.

Julien, I. and Mercer, K. (1988) Introduction: De Margin and De Centre, *Screen* 29.

Jung, C. G. (1961) *Modern Man in Search of a Soul*. London: Routledge.

Junge, W. (1995) Ästhetik des Vertrauens, in P. Zimmermann (ed) *Deutschlandbilder Ost. Dokumentarfilm der DEFA von der Nachkriegszeit bis zur Wiedervereinigung*. Konstanz: UVK-Medien/Ölschläger.

Kandinsky, W. (2006) *Concerning the Spiritual in Art*. London: Tate Publishing.

Kapsis, R.E. (1992) *Hitchcock: The Making of a Reputation*. Chicago: The University of Chicago Press.

Kellner, D. (2002) The Frankfurt School and British cultural studies: the missed articulation, in J.T. Nealon & C. Irr (eds) *Rethinking the Frankfurt School: Alternative Legacies of Cultural Critique*. New York: SUNY Press.

Kent, R. (2005) 'Reality at the service of fiction': the film art of Kutlug Ataman, in *Kutlug Ataman: Perfect Strangers*. Sydney: Museum of Contemporary Art.

Kilborn, R. (2003) *Staging the Real: Factual TV Programming in the Age of Big Brother*. Manchester: Manchester University Press.

Kilborn, R. and Izod, J. (1997) *An Introduction to Television Documentary: Confronting Reality*. Manchester: Manchester University Press.

Kilicbay, B. and Binark, M. (2004) Media monkeys: intertextuality, fandom and *Big Brother Turkey*, in E. Mathijs and J. Jones (eds) *Big Brother International*. London: Wallflower Press.

Klein, N (2007) *The Shock Doctrine: The Rise of Disaster Capitalism*. London: Allen Lane.

Klite, P., Bardwell, R. and Salzman, J. (1997) Local TV news: getting away with murder, *Press/Politics*, 2(2): 102–12.

Koestler, A. (1967) *The Ghost in the Machine*. London: Hutchinson.

Koestler, A. (1969) *The Act of Creation*. London: Hutchinson.

Krauss, R. (1986) Video: the aesthetics of narcissism, *October* 1 (1976); reprinted in J. Hanhardt (ed) *Video Culture*. Rochester, NY: Visual Studies Workshop and Peregrine Smith Books.

Lawson, N. (2006) A shameful report card, *Guardian*, 14 February.

Leadbeater, C. and Oakley, K. (1999) *The Independents: Britain's New Cultural Entrepreneurs*. London: Demos.

Léon, M. (1979) in *L'Humanité*, reprinted in Rosalind Delmar, *Joris Ivens: 50 Years of Film-making*. London: British Film Instititute.

Lessig, L. (2004) *Free Culture: How Big Media Uses Technology and the Law to Lock Down Culture and Control Creativity*. New York: Penguin.

Leung, H. (2004) New Queer Cinema and Third Cinema, in M. Aaron (ed) *New Queer Cinema*. New Brunswick, NJ: Rutgers University Press.

Levi-Faur, D. and Jordana, J. (2005) Preface: the making of a new regulatory order, *The Annals of the American Academy of Political and Social Science*, 598: 6–9.

Levin, R. (1971) *Documentary Explorations: 15 Interviews with Film-Makers*. New York: Anchor Doubleday.

Levitas, R. (2005) *The Inclusive Society? Social Exclusion and New Labour*, 2nd edn. Houndsmill: Palgrave Macmillan.

Lewis, J. (2004) The meaning of real life, in S. Murray and L. Ouellette (eds) *Reality TV: Remaking Television Culture*. New York: New York University Press.

Leyda, J. (1964) *Films Beget Films: A Study of the Compilation Film*. New York: Hill and Wang.

Lichtenstein, J. (1993) *The Eloquence of Color: Rhetoric and Painting in the French Classical Age*. Berkeley, CA: University of California Press.

Lima, W.J. (2002) 'Ônibus 174', the trajectory of a tragedy, *O Estado de S. Paulo*, 19 Nov. Available at: http://bus174.com.br/articles.htm#titulo06.

Lin Xu-dong (2005) Documentary in Mainland China, trans. C. Carter, *Documentary Box* 26, YIDFF. Available at: http://www.yidff.jp/docbox/26/box26–3-e.html.

Lipkin, S. N. (2002). *Real Emotional Logic: Film and Television Docudrama as Persuasive Practice*. Carbondale, IL: Southern Illinois University Press.

Lippit, A. (2000) *Electric Animal: Toward a Rhetoric of Wildlife*. Minneapolis: University of Minnesota Press.

Lister, M., Dovey, J., Giddings, S., Grant, I. and Kelly, K. (2003) *New Media: A Critical Introduction*. London: Routledge.

Littler, J. (2007) Celebrity CEOS and the cultural economy of tabloid intimacy, in S. Holmes and S. Redmond (eds) *A Reader in Stardom and Celebrity*. London: Sage.

Loizos, P. (1980) Granada Television's *Disappearing World* series: an appraisal, *American Anthropologist*, n.s., 82(3): 573–94.

Loizos, P. (1993) *Innovation in Ethnographic Film: From Innocence to Self-Consciousness, 1955–1985*. Manchester: Manchester University Press.

Lovell, T. (1980) *Pictures of Reality: Aesthetics, Politics and Pleasure*. London: British Film Institute.

Lukács, G. (1949) Der höchste Grad des Realismus, in E. Schubbe (ed) (1972) *Dokumente zur Kunst-, Literatur- und Kulturpolitik der SED*. Stuttgart: Seewald Verlag.

MacClancy, J. (ed) (2002) *Exotic No More: Anthropology on the Front Lines*. Chicago: The University of Chicago Press.

Macdonald, K. and Cousins, M. (1996) *Imagining Reality: The Faber Book of Documentary*. London: Faber.

Macdonald, M. (1998) Publicizing the personal: women's voices in British television documentaries, in C. Carter, G. Branston and S. Allan (eds) *News, Gender and Power*. London: Routledge.

MacDonald, M. (2006) Performing memory on television: documentary and the 1960s, *Screen*, 47(3): 327–45.

MacDougall, D. (1998) *Transcultural Cinema*. Princeton, NJ: Princeton University Press.

MacDougall, D. (2006) *The Corporeal Image: Film, Ethnography, and the Senses*. Princeton, NJ: Princeton University Press.

MacFarquhar, L. (2004) The populist: Michael Moore can make you cry, *The New Yorker*, 16 February.

Macnab, G. (2007) Wild Bunch has wunderbar EFM, *Screen Daily*, 13 February.

Maher, J. (2004) What do women watch? Tuning in to the compulsory heterosexuality channel, in S. Murray and L. Ouellette (eds) *Reality TV: Remaking Television Culture*. New York: New York University Press.

Maltby, R. (1995) *Hollywood Cinema*. London: Blackwell Publishing.

Marcus, G.E. and Fischer, M. (1986) *Anthropology as Cultural Critique*. Chicago: The University of Chicago Press.

Marcuse, H. (1989) Philosophy and critical theory, in S.E. Bronner and D. MacKay Kellner (eds) *Critical Theory and Society: A Reader*. London: Routledge.

Martineau, B.H. (1984) Talking about our lives and experiences: some thoughts about feminism, documentary and 'Talking Heads,' in T. Waugh (ed), *"Show Us Life": Toward a History and Aesthetics of the Committed Documentary*. Metuchen, NJ: Scarecrow Press.

Marx, K. (1973) Letter to Ferdinand Lasalle, April 19, 1859, in L. Baxandall and S. Morawski (eds) *Marx and Engels on Literature and Art*. St Louis, MO: Telos Press.

Massumi, B. (2002) Navigating movements, in M. Zournazi (ed) *Hope*. New York: Routledge.

McDowell, S. D. (2001) Method filmmaking: an interview with Daniel Myrick, co-director of *The Blair Witch Project*, *Journal of Film and Video* 53(2/3): 140–7.

McGuigan, J. (1996) The politics of cultural studies and cool capitalism, *Cultural Politics*, 2(2): 137–58.

McKee, R. (1999) *Story: Substance, Structure, Style and the Principles of Screen Writing*. London: Methuen.

McLeod, K. (2005) *Freedom of Expression: Overzealous Copyright Bozos and Other Enemies of Creativity*. New York: Doubleday.

Mekas, J. (1978) Notes on the New American Cinema, in P.A. Sitney (ed) *The Avant-Garde Film: A Reader of Theory and Criticism*. New York: New York University Press.

Mitchell, W. (2007) Lionsgate strikes US, UK and Australia deal for BBC's *Earth*, *Screen Daily*, 13 Feburary.

Mittell, J. (2004) *Genre and Television: From Cop Shows to Cartoons in American Culture*. London and New York: Routledge.

Monbiot, G. (2000) *The Captive State: The Corporate Takeover of Britain*. Bassingstoke: Macmillan.

Montaigne, M. de (1948) *The Complete Works of Montaigne*, trans. D. M. Frame. Stanford, CA: Stanford University Press.

Moorti, S. and Ross, K. (2004) Reality television: fairy tale or feminist nightmare? *Feminist Media Studies*, 4(2): 205–8.

Morris, M. and de Bary, B. (eds) (2001) *"Race" Panic and the Memory of Migration*. Hong Kong: Hong Kong University Press.

Murdock, G. (1997) Thin descriptions: questions of method in cultural analysis, in J. McGuigan (ed) *Cultural Methodologies*. London: Sage.

Murray, J. (2000) *Hamlet on the Holodeck: The Future of Narrative in Cyberspace*. Cambridge, MA: The MIT Press.

Murray, S. and Ouellette, L. (eds) (2004) *Reality TV: Remaking Television Culture*. New York: New York University Press.

Naficy, H. (1981) 'Iranian Documentary', *Jump Cut*, 26, December. Available at: http://www.ejumpcut.org/archive/onlinessays/JC26folder/IranDocy.html

Nash, M. (2005) Kutlug Ataman's experiments with truth, in *Kutlug Ataman: Perfect Strangers*. Sydney: Museum of Contemporary Art.

Nathan, S. (2004) Wife strop, *Sun*, Friday June 18. Available at: www.thesun.co.uk/article/0,,2001320029-2004281037,,00 (accessed 11 Sept. 2006).

National Association of Media Arts and Culture (2004) *Deep Focus: A Report on the Future of Independent Media*. San Francisco: National Association of Media Arts and Culture.

Nichols, B. (1976) Documentary theory and practice, *Screen*, 71(4): 34–48.

Nichols, B. (1983) The voice of documentary, *Film Quarterly*, 36(3): 17–30.

Nichols, B. (1991) *Representing Reality: Issues and Concepts in Documentary*. Bloomington, IN: Indiana University Press.

Nichols, B. (1994) *Blurred Boundaries: Questions of Meaning in Contemporary Culture*. Bloomington, IN: Indiana University Press.

Nichols, B. (1997) Documentary and the coming of sound, *Documentary Box*, originally published in Spanish in M. Palaci (ed) *Historia general del cine*, Madrid: Catedra Publishers.

Nichols, B. (2001) *Introduction to Documentary*. Bloomington, IN: Indiana University Press.

Noh, J. (2007) Fortissimo enjoys documentary sales, *Screen Daily*, 15 February.

Nomadsland (2007) Stats www.nomadsland.com (accessed 25 March).

Nunn, H. (2004) Errol Morris: documentary as psychic drama, *Screen*, 45(4): 413–22.

Ofcom (2006) *The Communications Market 2006*. London: Office of Communications.

One Day Films Limited www.onedayfiles.com/films (accessed Aug. 2006).

O'Neill, O. (2002) *A Question of Trust*. Cambridge: Cambridge University Press.

Online Film.Org (2007) Project ONLINEFILM.org. Available at: www.onlinefilm.org (accessed 10 April 2007).

Opel, A. and Smith, J. (2004) Zootycoon™: capitalism, nature, and the pursuit of happiness, *Ethics & the Environment*, 9(2): 103–20.

O'Riordan, K. and Phillips, D. (2007) Introduction, in *Queer Online: Media, Technology and Sexuality*. New York: Peter Lang.

Orr, J. (2006) *Panic Diaries: A Genealogy of Panic Disorder*. Durham, NC: Duke University Press.

Ouellette, L. and Hay, J. (forthcoming) *Better Living Through Television*. Oxford: Blackwell.

Paget, D. (1998) *No Other Way to Tell it: Dramadoc/Docudrama on Television*. Manchester: Manchester University Press.

Paget, D. and Roscoe, J. (2006) Giving voice: performance and authenticity in the documentary musical, *Jump Cut*, 48. Available at: http://www.ejumpcut.org/currentissue/MusicalDocy/index.html (accessed March 2007).

Palmer, G. (2002) *Big Brother*: an experiment in governance, *Television and New Media*, 3(3): 295–310.

Panse, S. (2003) unpublished interview with Winfried and Barbara Junge, London: Goethe Institute, 12 December.

Parmar, P. (1993) That moment of emergence, in M. Gever, J. Greyson and P. Parmar (eds) *Queer Looks: Perspectives on Lesbian and Gay Film and Video*. New York: Routledge.

Pasolini, P.P. (1980) 'Observations on the long take', *October*, No. 134.

Pearl, M. (2004) New Queer Cinema is AIDS cinema, in M. Aaron (ed) *New Queer Cinema*. Brunswick, NJ: Rutgers University Press.

Petric, V. (1987) *Constructivism in Film:* The Man with the Movie Camera – *A Cinematic Analysis*. Cambridge: Cambridge University Press.

Philo, G. and Miller, D. (2001) *Market Killing, What The Free Market Does and What Social Scientists Can Do About It*. Harlow: Longman.

Pick, A. (2004) New Queer Cinema and lesbian films, in M. Aaron (ed) *New Queer Cinema*. Brunswick, NJ: Rutgers University Press.

Pidduck, J. (2004) New Queer Cinema and experimental video, in M. Aaron (ed) *New Queer Cinema*. Brunswick NJ: Rutgers University Press.

Pinney, C. (1992) The lexical spaces of eye-spy, in P.I. Crawford and D. Turton (eds) *Film as Ethnography*. Manchester: Manchester University Press.

Piper, H. (2004) Reality TV, *Wife Swap* and the drama of banality, *Screen*, 45(4): 273–86.

Pitout, M. (2004) *Big Brother South Africa*: a popular form of cultural expression, in E. Mathijs and J. Jones (eds) *Big Brother International*. London: Wallflower Press.

Plantinga, C. (1998) Gender, power and a cucumber: satirizing masculinity in *This is Spinal Tap*, in B.K. Grant and J. Sloniowski (eds) *Documenting the Documentary: Close Readings of Documentary Film and Video*. Detroit, MI: Wayne State University Press.

Poole, S. (2000) *Trigger Happy: The Inner Life of Videogames*. London: Fourth Estate Limited.

Poster, M. (2006) *Information Please: Culture and Politics in the Age of Digital Machines*. Durham, NC: Duke University Press.

Prensky, M. (2001) *Digital Game Based Learning*. New York: McGraw-Hill.

Prose, F. (2004) Voting democracy off the island: reality TV and the republican ethos, *Harpers Magazine*, March: 58–64.

Prosser, J. (1998) The status of image-based research, in J. Prosser (ed) *Image-based Research: A Sourcebook for Qualitative Researchers*. London: Falmer Press.

Rabiger, M. (2004) *Directing the Documentary*. Amsterdam: Focal Press.

Rapfogel, J. (2001) A mirror facing a mirror, *Senses of Cinema*, 17. Available at: http://www.sensesofcinema.com/contents/01/17/close_up.html (accessed March 2007).

Raud, R. (2002) 'Objects and events: linguistic and philosophical notions of "thing-ness"', *Asian Philosophy*, 12(2).

Read, A. (1993) *Theatre and the Everyday: An Ethics of Performance*. London: Routledge.

Renoir, J. (1974) *My Life and My Films*. New York: Da Capo Press.

Renov, M. (ed) (1993) *Theorising Documentary*. London and New York: Routledge.

Renov, M. (1999) New subjectivities: documentary and self-representation in the post-verité age, in D. Waldman and J. Walter (eds) *Feminism and Documentary*: *Visible Evidence*. Vol. 5. Minneapolis: University of Minnesota Press.

Renov, M. (2004) *The Subject of Documentary*. Minneapolis: University of Minnesota Press.

Rhoads, K. (2004) Propaganda tactics and *Fahrenheit 9/11*. Available at: http://workingpsychology.com/fahrenheit.html

Rich, B.R. (2004) New Queer Cinema, in M. Aaron (ed) *New Queer Cinema*. Brunswick, NJ: Rutgers University Press.

Richardson, K. and Corner, J. (1986) Reading reception: mediation and transparency in viewers' accounts of a TV programme, *Media, Culture & Society*, 8(4): 485–508.

Richter, E. (2003) Gespräch mit Barbara und Winfried Junge, in *33. Internationales Forum des jungen Films*, Berlin: Berlinale.

Rickard, B. (1999) Season of the witch: the truth behind the year's scariest movie, *Fortean Times: The Journal of Strange Phenomena*, 128: 34–40.

Rifkin, J. (2000) *The Age of Access*. Harmondsworth: Penguin.

Robinson, J. (2004) Pap – or porn with a purpose? *Observer*, 18 July, p. 18.

Rony, F.T. (1992) Those who squat and those who sit: the iconography of race in the 1895 films of Félix-Louis Regnault, *Camera Obscura*, 28: 263–89.

Roscoe, J. (2000) *The Blair Witch Project*: mock-documentary goes mainstream, *Jump Cut: A Review of Contemporary Media*, 43: 3–8.

Roscoe, J. (2001) Real entertainment: new factual hybrid television, *Media International Australia*, 100: 9–20.

Roscoe, J. and Hight, C. (2001) *Faking It: Mock-documentary and the Subversion of Factuality*. Manchester: Manchester University Press.

Rose, N. (1996) Governing "advanced" liberal democracies, in A. Barry, T. Osborne and N. Rose (eds) *Foucault and Political Reason*. London: UCL Press.

Rose, N. (1999) *Governing the Soul: The Shaping of the Private Self*. London: Free Association Books.

Rosen, P. (2001) *Change Mummified: Cinema, Historicity, Theory*. Minneapolis: University of Minnesota Press.

Rosenthal, A. (1972) *The New Documentary in Action*. Berkeley, CA: University of California Press.

Rotha, P. (1952) *The Documentary Film*, 2nd edn. London: Faber and Faber.

Rouch, J. ([1975] 2003) The camera and the man, in P. Hockings (ed) *Principles of Visual Anthropology*. Chicago: Mouton de Gruyter.

Rouch, J. (2003) *Ciné-Ethnography*. Minneapolis: University of Minnesota Press.

Rubin, H.J. and Rubin, I.S. (1995) *Qualitative Interviewing: The Art of Hearing Data*. London: Sage.

Ruby, J. (1975) Is an ethnographic film a filmic ethnography? *Studies in the Anthropology of Visual Communication*, 2(2): 104–11.

Ruby, J. (1977) The image mirrored: reflexivity and the documentary film, in A. Rosenthal and J. Corner (eds) (2005) *New Challenges for Documentary*. Manchester: Manchester University Press.

Ruby, J. (2000) *Picturing Culture: Explorations of Film and Anthropology*. Chicago: The University of Chicago Press.

Russell, C. (1999) *Experimental Ethnography*. Durham, NC: Duke University Press.

Sarantakos, S. (1998) *Social Research*. Basingstoke: Macmillan.

Schenk, R. (2004) Lebensläufe – Ein Lebens- und Werkstattbericht: Ralf Schenk im Gespräch mit Winfried Junge, in W. Junge and B. Junge with D. Wolff (eds) *Lebensläufe – Die Kinder von Golzow. Bilder – Dokumente – Erinnerungen zur ältesten Lanzeitbeobachtung der Filmgeschichte*, Marburg: Schüren Presseverlag.

Schor, J. (1992) *The Overworked American*. New York: Basic Books.

Schrader, P. (1972) *Transcendental Style in Film*. Los Angeles: University of California Press.

Schreier, M. (2004) "Please help me; all I want to know is: is it real or not?" How recipients view the reality status of *The Blair Witch Project, Poetics Today*, 25(2): 305–34.

Schuler, D. (2004) Reports of the close relationship between democracy and the internet may have been exaggerated, in H. Jenkins and D. Thorbun (eds) *Democracy and New Media*. Cambridge, MA: The MIT Press.

Schwarz, B. (2004) Media times/historical times, *Screen*, 45(2): 93–105.

Scoble, R. and Israel, S. (2006) *Naked Conversations: How Blogs are Changing the Way Businesses Talk with Customers*. Hoboken, NJ: John Wiley & Sons, Ltd.

Screen International reporters (2007) Solid sales business boosts growing EFM, *Screen Dail*, 15 February.

Sennett (1999) *The Corrosion of Character: Personal Consequences of Work the New Captilalism*, New York: WW Norton & Co Ltd.

Sennett, R. (2006) *The Culture of the New Capitalism*. New Haven, CT: Yale University Press.

Shakespeare, W. (1970) *Hamlet*. London: Penguin.

Sharp, S. (2006) Disciplining the housewife in *Desperate Housewives* and domestic reality television, in J. McCabe and K. Akass (eds) *Reading* Desperate Housewives: *Beyond the White Picket Fence. London: I.B. Tauris*.

Sholle, D. (2004) What is information? in H. Jenkins and D. Thorbun (eds) *Democracy and New Media*. Cambridge, MA: The MIT Press.

Silverstone, R. (1985) *Framing Science: The Making of a BBC Documentary*. London: BFI.

Singer, A. (2006) Tribes and tribulations: a response to Hughes-Freeland, *Anthropology Today*, 22(3): 24–5.

Sitney, P. A. (1978) Autobiography in avant-garde film, in P. A. Sitney (ed) *The Avant-Garde Film: A Reader of Theory and Criticism*. New York: New York University Press.

Smeaton, D. (2003) Self-employed workers or hesitant independents? A consideration of a trend, *Work, Employment and Society*, 17(2): 379–91.

Sobchack, V. (1992) *The Address of the Eye: A Phenomenology of Film Experience*. Princeton, NJ: Princeton University Press.

Sobchack, V. (2004) *Carnal Thoughts: Embodiment and Moving Image Culture*. Berkeley, CA: University of California Press.

Solanas, F. and Getino, O. (1997) Towards a Third Cinema, in M. Martin (ed) *New Latin American Cinema*. Detroit, MI: Wayne State University Press.

Springer, K. (2004) *Wife Swap*: property rites, *Popmatters*. Available at: http://www.popmatters.com/tv/reviews/w/wife-swap.shtml (accessed 16 Sept. 2006).

Stahl, M. (2006) Reinventing certainties: popular music and American social structure, unpublished DPhil thesis, University of California.

Stam, R. (1998) Hybridity and the aesthetics of garbage: the case of Brazilian cinema. *Estudios Interdisciplinarios de América Latina y el Caribe (E.I.A.L.)* 9(1).

Stein, E. (2002) World citizen – cinema without borders: the films of Joris Ivens. *Village Voice*, March 20–26. Avaliable at: http://www.villagevoice.com/film/0212,stein,33220,20.html

Stephens, R. (2004) Socially soothing stories? Gender, race and class in TLC's *A Wedding Story* and *A Baby Story*, in S. Holmes and D. Jermyn (eds) *Understanding Reality Television*. London: Routledge.

Stocking, G.W. (1987) *Victorian Anthropology*. New York: Free Press.

Stone, R.A. (2000) Will the real body please stand up? in D. Bell (ed) *Cybercultures Reader*. New York: Routledge.

Stratton, J. and Ang, I. (1994) *Sylvania Waters* and the spectacular exploding family, *Screen*, 35(1): 1–21.

Sugar, A. (2005) *The Apprentice: How to Get Hired Not Fired*. London: BBC Books.

Suzuki, D. T. (1996) *Zen Buddhism: Selected Writings*. New York: Image.

Tarkovsky, A. (1994) *Time Within Time*, trans. K Hunter-Blair. London: Faber and Faber.

Tartaglione Vialette, N. (2007) TWC, SPC join wild bunch sales spree, *Screen International*, 14 Febuary.

Tate Modern: www.tate.org.uk/onlineevents/webcasts/bill_viola/default.jsp. (accessed Aug. 2006).

Taylor, L. (ed) (1994) *Visualizing Theory: Selected Essays from V.A.R., 1990–1994*. New York: Routledge.

Taylor, R. (ed) *The Eisenstein Reader*. London: BFI.

Telotte, J.P. (2004) *The Blair Witch Project* project: film and the internet, in S.L. Higley and J.A. Weinstock (eds) *Nothing That Is: Millennial Cinema and the Blair Witch Controversies*. Detroit, MI: Wayne State University Press.

Therborn, G. (1980) *The Ideology of Power and the Power of Ideology*. London: Verso.

Thompson, N. (2004) Trespassing relevance, in *The Interventionist: Users' Manual for the Creative Disruption of Everyday Life*. Cambridge, MA: The MIT Press.

Thrift, N. (2006) Re-inventing invention: new tendencies in capitalist commodification, *Economy and Society*, 35(2): 279–306.

Thumim, J. (2002) Women at work: popular drama on British television c1955–60, in J. Thumim (ed) *Small Screen, Big Ideas: Television in the 1950s*. London: I. B. Tauris.

Todorov, T. (2001) The uses and abuses of memory, in H. Marchitello (ed) *What Happens to History: The Renewal of Ethics in Contemporary Thought*. New York: Routledge.

Triangle, G. (2006) Click here for conspiracy, *Vanity Fair* (August).

Trinh, T.M. (1992) *Framer Framed*. New York: Routledge.

Tunstall, J. (1994) *The Media are American: Anglo-American Media in the World*. London: Constable.

Turner, G. (1996) *British Cultural Studies: An Introduction*. London: Routledge.

Tuters, M. and Varnelis, K. (n.d.) Beyond locative media. Available at: http://netpublics.annenberg.edu/locative_media/beyond_locative_media (accessed 2007).

Tyler, S.A. (1986) Post-modern ethnography: from document of the occult to occult document, in *Writing Culture: The Poetics and Politics of Ethnography*. Berkeley, CA: University of California Press.

Ugwumba, C. (2001) Behind the scenes: Uganda negotiates with WB & IMF, *Economic Justice News Online* 4(3). Available at: http://www.50years.org/cms/ejn/story/114

UK Film Council (2004) *Annual Review 2003/4*. London: UK Film Council.

van Zoonen, L. (1991) A tyranny of intimacy? Women, femininity and television news, in P. Dahlgren and C. Sparks (eds) *Communication and Citizenship*. London: Routledge.

van Zoonen, L. (2001) Desire and resistance: *Big Brother* and the recognition of everyday life, *Media, Culture & Society*, 23(5): 699–77.

Vaughan, D. (1976) *Television Documentary Usage*. London: British Film Institute.

Vaughan, D. (1981) Let there be Lumière, *Sight and Sound*, Spring, republished in T. Elsaesser with A. Barker (eds) (1990) *Early Cinema: Space, Frame, Narrative*. London: British Film Institute.

Vaughan, D. (1999) *For Documentary: Twelve Essays*. Berkeley, CA: University of California Press.

Vertov, D. (1984) The birth of Kino Eye, in *Kino Eye; The Writings of Dziga Vertov* trans. K. O'Brien. London: Pluto Press.

Waldman, D. and Walker, J. (eds)(1999) *Feminism and Documentary*. Minneapolis: University of Minnesota Press.

Walker, J.S. (2004) Mom and the Blair Witch: narrative, form, and the feminine, in S.L. Higley and J.A. Weinstock (eds) *Nothing That Is: Millennial Cinema and the Blair Witch Controversies*. Detroit, MI: Wayne State University Press.

Walsh, P. (2004) That withered paradigm: the web, the expert, and the information hegemony, in H. Jenkins and D. Thorbun (eds) *Democracy and New Media*. Cambridge, MA: The MIT Press.

Ward, P. (2005) *Documentary: The Margins of Reality*. London: Wallflower Press.

Ward, P. (2006) The future of documentary? 'Conditional tense' documentary and the historical record, in G. Rhodes and J. P. Springer (eds) *Docufictions: Essays on the Intersection of Documentary and Fictional Filmmaking*. Jefferson, NC: McFarland and Company, Inc.

Ward, P. (2007) The documentary form, in J. Nelmes (ed) *An Introduction to Film Studies*. 4th edn. London: Routledge.

Watson, M.A. (1989) Adventures in Reporting: John Kennedy and the Cinema Verité television documentaries of Drew Associates, *Film and History*, 19(2).

Waugh, T. (ed) (1984) *'Show Us Life': Toward a History and Aesthetics of the Committed Documentary*. Metuchen, NJ: The Scarecrow Press, Inc.

Wayne, M. (2003) *Marxism and Media Studies: Key Concepts and Contemporary Trends*. London: Pluto.

Weber, M. (1991) The sociology of charismatic authority, in H. Gerth and C. Wright Mills (eds) *From Max Weber*, new edn. London: Routledge.

Weinberger, E. (1992) The camera people, *Transition*, 55: 24–54.

Weiss, A. (2005) Transgressive cinema: lesbian independent film, in H. Benshoff and S. Griffin (eds) *Queer Cinema: The Film Reader*. New York: Routledge.

Wenger, E. (1999) *Communities of Practice: Learning, Meaning and Identity*. Cambridge: Cambridge University Press.

White, H. (1987) *The Content of the Form; Narrative Discourse and Historical Presentation*. Baltimore, MD: Johns Hopkins University Press.

Whitfield, D. (2001) *Public Service or Corporate Welfare?* London: Pluto Press.

Wice, H. (2006) The real-life business apprentices, *Independent*, Education Supplement, 6 April, pp. 4–5.

Williams, L. (1989) *Hard Core: Power, Pleasure and the 'Frenzy of the Visible'*. Berkeley, CA: University of California Press.

Williams, R. (1983) *Keywords: A Vocabulary of Culture and Society*. London: Flamingo.

Winston, B. (1995) *Claiming the Real: The Documentary Film Revisited*. London: British Film Institute.

Winston, B. (2000) *Lies, Damn Lies and Documentaries*. London: British Film Institute.

Yingchi Chu (2007) *Chinese Documentaries: From Dogma to Polyphony*. London: Routledge.

Yingjin Zhang (2007) Thinking outside the box: mediation of imaging and information in contemporary Chinese independent documentary, *Screen*, 48(2): 179–92.

Zalewski, D. (2006) The ecstatic truth, *New Yorker*, 24 April, 124–39.

Zimmermann, P. R. (2005) Public domains for public media. Available at: www.media-channel.org (accessed May 2005).

Žižek, S. (2004) *Organs Without Bodies: On Deleuze and the Consequences*. New York and London: Routledge.

Index

FEMINIST TELEVISION CRITICISM

A Reader

Charlotte Brunsdon and Lynn Spigel (eds)

The first edition of this book immediately became a defining text for feminist television criticism, with an influence extending across television, media and screen studies – and the second edition will be similarly agenda-setting. Completely revised and updated throughout, it takes into account the changes in the television industry, the academic field of television studies and the culture and politics of feminist movements.

With fifteen of the eighteen extracts being new to the second edition, the readings offer a detailed analysis of a wide range of case studies, topics and approaches, including genres, audiences, performers and programmes such as 'Sex and the City', 'Prime Suspect', Oprah and Buffy.

With a new introduction to the volume tracing developments in the field and introductions to each thematic section, the editors engage in a series of debates surrounding the main issues of feminist television scholarship. They explore how television represents feminism and consider how critics themselves have created feminism and post-feminism as historical categories and political identities. Readings consider women who are engaged in various aspects of television production on both sides of the camera and examine how television targets and imagines its female audience, as well as how women respond to and use television in their everyday lives.

Feminist Television Criticism is inspiring reading for film, media, cultural and gender studies students.

Contributors: *Ien Ang, Jane Arthurs , Sarah Banet-Weiser ,Karen Boyle, Marsha F. Cassidy, Geok-lian Chua ,Bonnie J. Dow, Joanne Hollows, Deborah Jermyn , Annette Kuhn, Elizabeth MacLachlan, Purnima Mankekar, Tania Modleski, Laurie Ouellette, Yeidy M. Rivero, Lee Ann Roripaugh, Beretta E. Smith-Shomade, Kimberly Springer, Ksenija Vidmar-Horvat, Susan J. Wolfe.*

2007 384pp

978-0-335-22545-3 (Paperback) 978-0-335-22544-6 (Hardback)

THE CULT FILM READER

Ernest Mathijs and Xavier Mendik (eds)

'*A really impressive and comprehensive collection of the key writings in the field. The editors have done a terrific job in drawing together the various traditions and providing a clear sense of this rich and rewarding scholarly terrain. This collection is as wild and diverse as the films that it covers. Fascinating.*'

Mark Jancovich, Professor of Film and Television Studies, University of East Anglia, UK

'*It's about time the lunatic fans and loyal theorists of cult movies were treated to a book they can call their own. The effort and knowledge contained in The Cult Film Reader will satisfy even the most ravenous zombie's desire for detail and insight. This book will gnaw, scratch and infect you just like the cult films themselves.*'

Brett Sullivan, Director of Ginger Snaps Unleashed and The Chair

'*The Cult Film Reader is a great film text book and a fun read.*'

John Landis, Director of The Blues Brothers, An American Werewolf in London and Michael Jackson's Thriller

Whether defined by horror, kung-fu, sci-fi, sexploitation, kitsch musical or 'weird world cinema', cult movies and their global followings are emerging as a distinct subject of film and media theory, dedicated to dissecting the world's unruliest images.

This book is the world's first reader on cult film. It brings together key works in the field on the structure, form, status, and reception of cult cinema traditions. Including work from key established scholars in the field such as Umberto Eco, Janet Staiger, Jeffrey Sconce, Henry Jenkins, and Barry Keith Grant, as well as new perspectives on the gradually developing canon of cult cinema, the book not only presents an overview of ways in which cult cinema can be approached, it also re-assesses the methods used to study the cult text and its audiences.

With editors' introductions to the volume and to each section, the book is divided into four clear thematic areas of study – The Conceptions of Cult; Cult Case Studies; National and International Cults; and Cult Consumption – to provide an accessible overview of the topic. It also contains an extensive bibliography for further related readings.

Written in a lively and accessible style, *The Cult Film Reader* dissects some of biggest trends, icons, auteurs and periods of global cult film production. Films discussed include *Casablanca*, *The Rocky Horror Picture Show*, *Eraserhead*, *The Texas Chainsaw Massacre*, *Showgirls* and *Ginger Snaps*.

Essays by: *Jinsoo An; Jane Arthurs; Bruce Austin; Martin Barker; Walter Benjamin; Harry Benshoff; Pierre Bourdieu; Noel Carroll; Steve Chibnall; Umberto Eco; Nezih Erdogan; Welch Everman; John Fiske; Barry Keith Grant ; Joan Hawkins; Gary Hentzi; Matt Hills; Ramaswami Harindranath; J.Hoberman; Leon Hunt; I.Q. Hunter; Mark Jancovich; Henry Jenkins; Anne Jerslev; Siegfried Kracauer; Gina Marchetti; Tom Mes; Gary Needham; Sheila J. Nayar; Annalee Newitz; Lawrence O'Toole; Harry Allan Potamkin; Jonathan Rosenbaum; Andrew Ross; David Sanjek; Eric Schaefer; Steven Jay Schneider; Jeffrey Sconce; Janet Staiger; J.P. Telotte; Parker Tyler; Jean Vigo; Harmony Wu*

Contents: *Section One: The Concepts of Cult – Section Two: Cult Case Studies – Section Three: National and International Cults – Bibliography of Cult Film Resources – Index.*

2007 576pp

978-0-335-21923-0 (Paperback) 978-0-335-21924-7 (Hardback)

CONTEMPORARY AMERICAN CINEMA

Linda Ruth Williams and Michael Hammond (eds)

"One of the rare collections I would recommend for use in undergraduate teaching – the chapters are lucid without being oversimplified and the contributors are adept at analyzing the key industrial, technological and ideological features of contemporary U.S. cinema."

Diane Negra, University of East Anglia, UK.

"Contemporary American Cinema is the book on the subject that undergraduate classes have been waiting for ... Comprehensive, detailed, and intelligently organized [and] written in accessible and compelling prose ... Contemporary American Cinema will be embraced by instructors and students alike."

Charlie Keil, Director, Cinema Studies Program, University of Toronto, Canada.

Contemporary American Cinema is the first comprehensive introduction to American cinema since 1960. The book is unique in its treatment of both Hollywood, alternative and non-mainstream cinema. Critical essays from leading film scholars are supplemented by boxed profiles of key directors, producers and actors; key films and key genres; and statistics from the cinema industry.

Illustrated in colour and black and white with film stills, posters and production images, the book has two tables of contents allowing students to use the book chronologically, decade-by-decade, or thematically by subject. Designed especially for courses in cinema studies and film studies, cultural studies and American studies, *Contemporary American Cinema* features a glossary of key terms, fully referenced resources and suggestions for further reading, questions for class discussion, and a comprehensive filmography.

Individual chapters include:
* The decline of the studio system
* The rise of American new wave cinema
* The history of the blockbuster
* The parallel histories of independent and underground film
* Black cinema from blaxploitation to the 1990s
* Changing audiences
* The effects of new technology
* Comprehensive overview of US documentary from 1960 to the present

Contributors include: Stephen Prince, Steve Neale, Susan Jeffords, Yvonne Tasker, Barbara Klinger, Jim Hillier, Peter Kramer, Mark Shiel, Sheldon Hall, Eithne Quinn, Michele Aaron, Jonathan Munby.

Contents: ***Introduction:*** *the whats, hows and whys of this book – **The 1960s** – Introduction – The American New Wave, Part 1: 1967–1970 – Debts Disasters and Mega-movies: the studios in the 1960s – Other Americas: The underground, exploitation and the avant garde – U.S Documentary Cinema in the 1960s – 'The Last Good Time We Ever Had'?: Revising the Hollywood Renaissance – Suggested Further Reading – Essay Questions – **The 1970s** – Introduction – The American New Wave, Part 2: 1970–1975 – New Hollywood and the Rise of the Blockbuster – Blaxploitation – U.S. Documentary in the 1970s – Suggested Further Reading – Essay Questions – **The 1980s** – Introduction – Film in the age of Reagan: action cinema and reactionary politics – Independent Cinema since the 1980s – Disney and the Family Adventure movie since the 1970s – The Vietnam War in American Cinema – U.S. Documentary in the 1980s Suggested Further Reading Essay Questions – **The 1990s and beyond** – Introduction – Big Budget Spectacles – What is Cinema Today? Home Viewing and New Technologies – U.S. Documentary in the 1970s – New Queer Cinema – Fantasising Gender and Race: Women in Contemporary U.S. Action Cinema – Smart Cinema – Suggested Further Reading – Essay Questions – Glossary – Bibliography – Filmography – Index.*

2006 584pp

978-0-335-21831-8 (Paperback) 978-0-335-21832-5 (Hardback)